EYEWITNESS ◉ HANDBOOKS
BUTTERFLIES
AND
MOTHS

EYEWITNESS ◉ HANDBOOKS

BUTTERFLIES
— AND —
MOTHS

DAVID CARTER

Photography by
FRANK GREENAWAY

DORLING KINDERSLEY, INC.
NEW YORK

A DORLING KINDERSLEY BOOK

Editors Alison Edmonds, Heather Dewhurst
Art Editor Elaine Hewson
Consultant Editor Dr John D. Bradley
Production Caroline Webber
U.S. Consultant Dr Paul A. Opler
U.S. Editor Charles A. Wills

Caterpillar illustrations by John Still

First American Edition, 1992
10 9 8 7 6 5 4 3 2 1

Dorling Kindersley, Inc.,
232 Madison Avenue, New York, NY 10016

Copyright © 1992
Dorling Kindersley Limited, London
Text copyright © 1992 David J. Carter

Published in the United States by Dorling Kindersley Inc., New York, NY.
Distributed by Houghton Mifflin Company, Boston, Massachusetts.
Published in Great Britain by Dorling Kindersley Limited, London.

Library of Congress Cataloguing-in-Publication Data:
Carter, David J. (David James), 1943-
The eyewitness handbook of butterflies & moths / by David Carter.
–1st American ed.
p.   cm.– (The Eyewitness handbooks)
Includes Index.
Summary: A field guide to butterflies and moths around the world, each depicted by a full-color photograph
with a caption that describes key features and points of differentiation.
ISBN 1-56458-034-2 [HC]
ISBN 1-56458-062-8 [flexibound]
1. Butterflies–Identification–Juvenile literature. 2. Moths–Identification--Juvenile literature.
[1 Butterflies–Identification. 2.Moths–Identification.] I. Title. II. Series.
QL544.2.C37 1992
595.78–dc20   91-58221
                                                                                                           CIP
                                                                                                            AC

Computer page make-up by
The Cooling Brown Partnership, Great Britain
Text film output by The Right Type, Great Britain
Reproduced by Colourscan, Singapore
Printed and bound by Kyodo Printing Co., Singapore

CONTENTS

AUTHOR'S INTRODUCTION

Of all the insects, butterflies and moths are the most celebrated. Butterflies are probably the most popular because they are active by day and are renowned for their beautiful colors and graceful flight. Moths are often regarded as less engaging but, with their diversity of shapes, sizes, and colors, they are as fascinating as butterflies.

BUTTERFLIES AND MOTHS are known scientifically as Lepidoptera (meaning scaly wings), because their wings are covered with thousands of tiny, overlapping scales. These scales are often quite brilliantly colored and account for the distinctive patterns that can be found on both butterflies and moths.

There are approximately 170,000 known species of Lepidoptera: about one-tenth of these are butterflies, and the rest are moths. Butterflies and moths are amazing in their variety of size, shape, and color. Their immense diversity, and ability to adapt to virtually any climate, has made them some of the most

THE SMALLEST
*With a tiny wingspan of around ⅗ in (1.5 cm), the western pygmy blue (*Brephidium exilis, *see p.97) is one of the smallest butterflies in the world. These specimens are shown in proportion to one another.*

THE LARGEST
*The atlas moth (*Attacus atlas *see p.221) is the world's largest moth in overall size, with a wingspan of up to 12 in (30 cm).*

successful creatures on earth, with habitats ranging from Arctic tundra to Alpine mountain summits, as well as the warmer tropical rain forests and coastal mangrove swamps.

FLOWER ASSOCIATION

As adult butterflies are only able to feed on fluids, flower nectar is the major source of sustenance for most species. (Other butterfly foods range from fermenting sap, to liquids from dung and decaying carrion.) Plants benefit from these associations because, while feeding, the insects transfer pollen from one plant to another. Butterflies and moths feed by means of a long, hollow feeding tube, or proboscis. This remains coiled up beneath the head when not in use, but when extended it can probe the depths of a flower in search of nectar. Different species have different lengths of tongue, a feature that is influenced by the particular flowers on which they feed.

SELECTION

The 500 or more species described and illustrated in this book have been selected to represent as wide a range of different types of butterflies and moths as possible. Emphasis has been placed on common species, or those with interesting features. It would have been impossible to include all the interesting and common examples of butterflies and moths when the range is so enormous, so I have chosen a selection that I hope will stimulate your interest.

HABITATS

Watching butterflies and moths in their natural habitats is always rewarding for the interested amateur. Learn to recognize the species in your area, and you will build up an understanding of their flight times, habits, and foodplants.

HOUSE MOTH

With a wingspan of about ¾ in (2 cm), the common brown house moth or false clothes moth *(Hofmannophila pseudospretella)*, is one representative of many thousands of small moth species, including the notorious clothes moths, that belong to Microlepidoptera. The smallest Microlepidoptera have a wingspan of just a few millimeters.

Despite their small size, many Microlepidoptera are significant pests. Two of the most common are the codling moth, or apple maggot *(Cydia pomonella)*, and the diamondback moth *(Plutella xylostella)* which attacks cole crops. I have not been able cover Microlepidoptera in this book, but a vast number of small species exist, often with colors and shapes that are as beautiful as their larger cousins.

Lepidoptera Evolution

The earliest moth fossils are estimated to be between 100 and 140 million years old; butterflies have a fossil record that goes back 40 million years. Lepidoptera originated when flowering plants were beginning to proliferate, and have developed in close association with them. Caddis flies (Trichoptera), the most closely related group of insects to butterflies and moths, are believed to have originated about 250 million years ago, but transitional forms have yet to be identified.

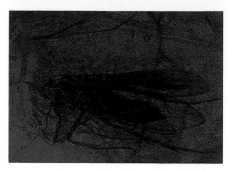

Fossilized Moth
This early example of a moth has been preserved in amber (the fossilized resin of an ancient plant).

HEDYLID MOTH

Butterfly or Moth?

Until very recently, South American *hedylid* "moths" were believed to belong to the moth family Geometridae, but detailed study has revealed that they are more closely related to butterflies. Superficially they resemble moths, but many of their internal and external body features are like those of butterflies.

The Naming System

Common names vary from country to country. Thus, scientists usually use the system established in the eighteenth century by the Swedish naturalist, Carl von Linné (his name is commonly latinized as Linnaeus). The generic name, which always appears first, groups the species with others sharing similar features. The second, or specific name, differentiates the species from other members of the genus. About 170,000 described species of butterflies and moths exist, but there are at least as many species yet to be described.

When a new species is named, it should be described from a number of specimens. A single specimen, the type, is then selected as the one upon which the identity of the species is judged for all time.

TAGORA PALLIDA

HYLES LINEATA

Named Specimen
Type specimens are often labeled with a red dot.

Linnaeus
One of many species named by Linnaeus.

HOW THIS BOOK WORKS

THIS BOOK is arranged to include all five butterfly families, followed by twenty-two of the major moth families. Each separate family has a short introduction describing its general characteristics. The entries that follow give detailed information, in words and pictures, about selected species found in that group. This annotated example shows how a typical entry is organized.

name of the family to which the butterfly or moth belongs •

name of genus and species of butterfly •

• name of original describer

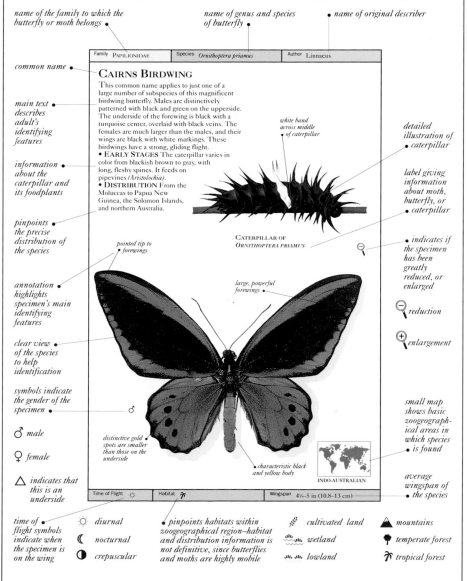

| Family PAPILIONIDAE | Species *Ornithoptera priamus* | Author Linnaeus |

common name •

CAIRNS BIRDWING

main text describes adult's identifying features

This common name applies to just one of a large number of subspecies of this magnificent birdwing butterfly. Males are distinctively patterned with black and green on the upperside. The underside of the forewing is black with a turquoise center, overlaid with black veins. The females are much larger than the males, and their wings are black with white markings. These birdwings have a strong, gliding flight.

information about the caterpillar and its foodplants

• **EARLY STAGES** The caterpillar varies in color from blackish brown to gray, with long, fleshy spines. It feeds on pipevines (*Aristolochia*).
• **DISTRIBUTION** From the Moluccas to Papua New Guinea, the Solomon Islands, and northern Australia.

pinpoints the precise distribution of the species

white band across middle of caterpillar

detailed illustration of caterpillar

label giving information about moth, butterfly, or caterpillar

CATERPILLAR OF
ORNITHOPTERA PRIAMUS

• indicates if the specimen has been greatly reduced, or enlarged

pointed tip to forewings

annotation highlights specimen's main identifying features

large, powerful forewings

⊖ *reduction*

⊕ *enlargement*

clear view of the species to help identification

symbols indicate the gender of the specimen •

♂

small map shows basic zoogeographical areas in which species • is found

♂ *male*

♀ *female*

△ *indicates that this is an underside*

distinctive gold spots are smaller than those on the underside

characteristic black and yellow body

INDO-AUSTRALIAN

average wingspan of • the species

| Time of Flight ☼ | Habitat 🌴 | Wingspan 4¼–5 in (10.8–13 cm) |

time of • flight symbols indicate when the specimen is on the wing

☼ *diurnal*

☾ *nocturnal*

◑ *crepuscular*

• pinpoints habitats within zoogeographical region–habitat and distribution information is not definitive, since butterflies and moths are highly mobile

🌾 *cultivated land*

🌊 *wetland*

🌿 *lowland*

⛰ *mountains*

🌳 *temperate forest*

🌴 *tropical forest*

BUTTERFLY OR MOTH?

BUTTERFLY CHARACTERISTICS

Butterflies are a group of specialized, day-flying Lepidoptera. Generally, they can be recognized by their bright colors and clubbed antennae, but also by the way they rest, with the wings held together over the back. In butterflies, the base of the hindwing is expanded and strengthened, supporting and coupling with the forewing when in flight.

typical scale-covered wings of butterfly •

ORANGE TIP

WING SHAPE
Butterflies have a wide variety of wing shapes, as shown by these two specimens.

COMMON IMPERIAL BLUE

antennae thickened at the tips •

bright colors of typical dayflying • butterfly

BUTTERFLY ANATOMY
Orange-barred giant sulphur (Phoebis philea, *see right), has all the features common to a typical butterfly.*

• characteristic large and rounded wings

ORANGE-BARRED SULPHUR

RESTING BUTTERFLY
This butterfly from the family Nymphalid is seen here resting in the typical butterfly posture, with its wings held together above its back (see left).

HINDWING COUPLING
A close look at the underside of a common blue butterfly (Polyommatus icarus) *shows the expanded hindwing base typical of butterflies (see right).*

MOTH CHARACTERISTICS

Moths are so diverse that it is difficult to give a general description. There are even many dayflying species. Moths can be distinguished by their antennae, which lack clubbed tips and are filamentous or feathered. Most moths have a wing-coupling device consisting of bristles on the base of the hindwing that engage with a flap or "catch" on the forewing. Males have single stout bristles, whereas females have a number of slender bristles.

FIERY CAMPYLOTES

• elongated wings typical of moths

OWL MOTH

WING SHAPE
Moth wings vary in size, shape, and color.

most moths have feathered antennae •

A TYPICAL MOTH
The acacia carpenter moth (Xyleutes eucalypti) is a fairly typical moth with dull camouflage colors and a robust body.

• *characteristically robust moth body*

ACACIA CARPENTER MOTH

• *hook and bristle wing-coupling device hidden behind wings*

RESTING MOTH
The white ermine moth (Spilosoma lubricipeda), resting in a characteristic moth posture with its wings folded, rooflike, over the back (see left).

WING-COUPLING
A closer look at the underside of the wings of the Jersey tiger (Euplagia quadripunctaria) reveals the typical moth wing-coupling device (see right).

LIFE CYCLE

BUTTERFLIES AND MOTHS have a complex life cycle consisting of four phases: egg, caterpillar (larva), pupa, and adult. In the egg stage, a caterpillar develops within a protective envelope. The caterpillar stage is the main feeding period. In order to grow, the caterpillar must shed its skin several times. During the pupa phase, the body components are broken down and reformed into an adult butterfly or moth. This life cycle is called a complete metamorphosis.

1 EGG The egg darkens, and you can see the young caterpillar moving about inside, shortly before its emergence. It first cuts a circular "lid" in the tough eggshell *(A)*, and then pulls its body free of the egg with wriggling movements *(B and C)*. This is one of the most vulnerable stages. Once it has emerged *(D)*, the caterpillar usually eats its empty eggshell *(E)*. This provides the nutrients that help it to survive until it can locate its foodplant.

caterpillar enjoying its important first meal

E

a fully emerged caterpillar moves toward its egg to eat it

D

SOUTH AMERICAN OWL BUTTERFLY

• the caterpillar finally breaks free of its egg

C

B

A

CHECKERED SWALLOWTAIL

4 ADULT Some choose the upper surface of leaves *(O)* on which to lay their eggs, while others choose the undersides, where the eggs may be better protected. Certain species lay their eggs in crevices or inside plant tissues. Females avoid plants that already have eggs laid on them. This ensures that food is there for her eggs only. The female usually glues the eggs to the surface of a leaf or to a similar support, with a viscous secretion from her body. Some butterflies lay their eggs singly, while others lay them in large batches. Butterflies and moths whose caterpillars feed on a wide range of plants often scatter eggs in flight.

butterflies select the right plant to lay eggs on by sight, smell, taste, and touch

O

N

eggs on underside of leaf

2 CATERPILLAR In the case of the citrus swallowtail, the caterpillar selects a suitable stem and spins a silken pad to which it attaches its tail *(F)*. The caterpillar next spins a loop or "girdle" of silk that passes around the middle of the body and is attached to the plant stem as a support *(G)*. The caterpillar's skin splits along the back, and the pupa begins to emerge *(H)*. A series of wriggling movements forces the old caterpillar skin toward the tail *(I)*. The old skin is released and a series of hooks on the tail are engaged into the silken support pad. The pupa now takes on its final shape.

caterpillar spinning its girdle for support

fine, silken girdle

the caterpillar is protected by its effective camouflage

discarded skin of caterpillar

CITRUS SWALLOWTAIL

at the final stage the pupa hardens

3 PUPA Shortly before emergence, the color of the butterfly becomes faintly visible *(J)*. The pupa case splits and the butterfly starts to struggle out *(K)*. When completely free *(L)*, the butterfly releases a fluid called meconium from the tip of its abdomen. This contains the waste materials accumulated during the pupa phase. After emergence, the butterfly rests with its crumpled wings hanging down and expands them by pumping blood into the wing veins *(M)*. It is important that the wings expand fairly rapidly before they harden, or they will be permanently deformed.

wings of butterfly still folded

proboscis of butterfly folded under head

the butterfly holds onto the empty case with claws at the tip of its legs

butterfly allowing its wings to form correctly

EARLY STAGES

ᴇACH STAGE of the development of a butterfly or moth is specially adapted to enable it to carry out particular functions. As many species of butterflies and moths spend most of their lives as soft-bodied caterpillars, they have developed a wide range of devices to protect themselves from predators. The pupa stage is immobile and therefore even more vulnerable to attack.

CATERPILLARS

Caterpillars often blend into the background or mimic an object such as a dead leaf to conceal themselves. Looper caterpillars of the moth family Geometridae mimic twigs so that they are safe when at rest. Other caterpillars are covered with hairs or spines that make an unpleasant mouthful for a bird or small mammal. (Cuckoos are one of the few birds that will eat hairy caterpillars.) The hairs of some species are poisonous and can cause a rash if handled. Those caterpillars that are poisonous or distasteful advertise the fact with bright and distinctive wing patterns.

TWIG MIMIC
The purple thorn (Selenia tetralunaria) caterpillar has a highly developed camouflage that is hard to distinguish it from the twig on which it rests.

• *even bark blemishes are accurately reproduced*

SPINY CATERPILLAR
The bright pattern on this saddle (Sibine sp.) caterpillar warns that it has stinging spines.

POISONOUS MOUTHFUL
Most predators will avoid the pine lappet (Dendrolimus pini) *caterpillar as its hairs have irritant properties.*

LEAF MIMIC
This green Lycaenid caterpillar (Castalius rosimon), *blends with a leaf of its foodplant.*

WARNING PATTERN
This strongly patterned magpie moth (Abraxas grossulariata) *caterpillar, is distasteful to birds.*

FRIGHT TACTIC
The lobster moth (Stauropus fagi) *caterpillar raises its head and scorpion-like tail when alarmed.*

• *this caterpillar needs no camouflage, since it is such a fearsome sight*

PUPA

The pupa of a butterfly is commonly called a chrysalis, a term derived from the Greek word for gold, since a number of butterfly pupae have metallic markings. Although pupae have hard, protective, outer shells, they are still vulnerable to birds, mice, and other creatures that regard them as tasty morsels. Like caterpillars, many gain protection by merging into the background some are even able to change their color to match the surface on which they are resting. Others resemble dead leaves or pieces of twig, while poisonous pupae are usually quite conspicuous and brightly colored. Moth pupae are often formed in a protective silken case called a cocoon.

LEAF MIMIC
The chrysalis of the owl butterfly (Caligo beltrao) resembles a dead leaf.

vivid yellow markings • *on pupa*

FRUIT MIMIC
A berrylike chrysalis of a blue morpho (Morpho sp.) butterfly.

DISTASTEFUL SPECIES
The pupae of the queen butterfly (Danaus gilippus) are poisonous to predators.

• *the poison of this pupa comes from the plant on which it feeds*

WING VEINS
The chrysalis of the cloudless sulphur (Phoebis sennae) shows the developing wing veins.

the head is at this end of the pupa •

butterfly's • *developing wing veins*

SILKEN SUPPORT
The giant swallowtail (Papilio cresphontes) chrysalis is supported by a silken girdle, which was spun by the caterpillar at an earlier stage.

BRIGHT GREEN
The chrysalis of the common bluebottle (Graphium sarpedon), varies in color from green to brown.

SURVIVAL

BUTTERFLIES AND MOTHS have always been depicted as fragile creatures, and as objects of great beauty; as such, they have to survive in a hostile world. They have no offensive weapons such as stingers or biting jaws to defend themselves, unlike so many other insects. To protect themselves from birds and other predators they have had to adopt defensive strategies.

CAMOUFLAGE

The most universal defense tactic among adult butterflies and moths is to blend into the background, a feat achieved in various ways. When resting, butterflies hold their wings together so that only the dull underside shows. Thus, a brightly colored butterfly seems to disappear as it lands in a hedge and closes its wings. Many moths avoid birds by flying at night, but they are then in danger from bats. However, many species are able to hear the cries of bats and therefore avoid them. Most night-flying moths have dull-colored wings that provide good camouflage when they rest on tree trunks. Other species have elaborate patterns that break up the wing and body shape, making it difficult to recognize. Moths, in particular, are good mimics of a wide range of objects from dead twigs and leaves to wasps and spiders.

BARK MIMIC

Like many moths, this carpenter moth (Cossidae) has wings that blend with the bark on which it rests.

LEAF BUTTERFLY

So called because of its remarkable camouflage, even the leaf veins and blemishes are accurately reproduced by the Indian leaf butterfly (Kallima inachus).

wing underside resembles dead leaf

hindwing tip of the butterfly is just visible

WARNING COLORS

Most butterflies and moths defend themselves by camouflage, but those species that are poisonous advertise their defense mechanism with bright colors. Inexperienced predators, such as young birds, soon learn to leave insects with warning colors alone. Some moths have dull forewing colors that provide good camouflage when the moth is resting. If the moth is threatened, it reveals brightly colored hindwings in a startling flash. In addition, some species have false eyespots, which create a face to startle the attacker.

forewing dull in comparison to • hindwing

FLASH COLORATION
The ilia underwing (Catocala ilia), scares would-be attackers with the flash of bright color.

ILIA UNDERWING

yellow of hindwing presents flash of color

EYESPOTS
The twin-spotted sphinx (Smerinthus jamaicensis) displays large eyespots on its brightly colored hindwings to warn off predators.

double, black- • ringed, metallic- blue hindwing eyespots

unusual jagged shape of forewing margins

TWIN-SPOTTED SPHINX

MIMICRY

vivid red of inner margins is a deterrent to would-be • predators

Poisonous butterflies of the same species often fly together so that their warning colors are more easily recognized. A number of poisonous species even share a similar warning pattern. In this way, birds have only to learn that one species is poisonous to avoid all the rest. Some nonpoisonous species mimic poisonous species, so that they too are left alone. In the past, these mimicry associations have confused entomologists, who have only recognized one species where several in fact existed.

SMALL POSTMAN BUTTERFLY

MIMICRY ASSOCIATIONS
These two species of distasteful butterfly are difficult to tell apart. By sharing the same pattern, they help protect each other.

these butterflies are very difficult to tell apart, and would fool most hungry birds

POSTMAN BUTTERFLY

CONSERVATION

IN MANY PARTS of the world, butterfly and moth numbers have decreased alarmingly in recent times, and many species have become extinct. It is essential that we take steps to find out what is going wrong before it is too late to save these fascinating creatures for future generations. In the Victorian era, when collectors had their heyday, their activities had little effect on butterfly and moth populations. This is hardly surprising since each insect lays many, and often hundreds, of eggs in the expectation that only one or two will survive to maturity. Today, however with the numbers of some species now dangerously low, even collecting a few specimens of a rare species may be enough to tip the balance against survival. Some conservation organisations are recommending that certain species should be protected from collection. There is little that can be done to save our butterflies and moths if their habitats are destroyed, so it is important that we manage our environment, and avoid further damaging the already fragile balance of nature.

APOLLO BUTTERFLY

LARGE COPPER

EXTINCTION
These two butterflies are at risk from changes in their habitats; the large copper due to drainage of wetlands for farming, and the apollo because of tourism in mountainous areas.

BUTTERFLIES, MOTHS, AND HUMANS

Butterflies and moths can be both allies and enemies of man. When we grow vast areas of the same type of plants, for example fields of wheat and rice or plantations of conifers, we create the ideal conditions for certain species to build up huge populations and become pests. In some cases, an insect may be accidentally introduced to another country and become a pest because its natural predators and competition are absent. Butterflies are valuable pollinators when they move from plant to plant gathering nectar. Some caterpillars feed on weeds and are agents of control. Other species have been cultivated for centuries for their silk.

PEACOCK

GYPSY MOTH

FRIEND OR FOE?
The peacock (Inachis io), *pollinates plants, thus indirectly helping man. The gypsy moth* (Lymantria dispar), *is a common pest in fruit orchards.*

MARSH FRITILLARY

The countryside is now an environment controlled by humans. Many butterfly and moth habitats have been destroyed by clearing and draining of land to cultivate crops. The marsh fritillary (above) is at risk from land-drainage.

INSECTICIDES
The use of sprays and herbicides has become a great threat to the habitats of butterflies and moths. Not only insects, but other animals too, are killed, which interferes with the balance of nature.

FARMING
Threatened species of birdwing butterfly are being farmed in an effort to ensure their survival.

QUEEN ALEXANDRA'S BIRDWING

The world's tropical rain forests, with their huge variety of plants, and wonderful fauna, are the richest habitats for butterflies, providing homes for some of the most beautiful and spectacular species known to man. Their continued destruction by both farming and the logging industry threaten these species. Much has yet to be learned about the complex communities of insects that live in tropical forests. Butterflies and moths are now an integral part of this research, because they are relatively easy to recognize, and are already well-documented.

OBSERVATION

THE STUDY of butterflies and moths in their natural environment is always rewarding. The first closeup view of a live butterfly through a magnifying glass is an amazing experience that can never be matched by looking at preserved specimens.

As butterflies and day-flying moths are such active creatures, it is best to observe them when they are feeding or drinking. The flower garden is one of the easiest places to start butterfly watching. Patience is essential. Stand close to a group of nectar-bearing flowers and wait for a butterfly to visit. When it is well settled, it is possible to approach without disturbing it. Remember that butterflies are very sensitive to

even the slightest movement, and take care not to cast your shadow over them.

With experience, you soon learn to recognize a good butterfly site. Hedgerows, forest margins, and any sheltered, sunny spot will usually

WHERE TO LOOK
Butterflies often gather to drink from puddles on muddy ground, providing an ideal opportunity to study these beautiful creatures.

• *these leaves conceal several species from the Papilionidae family, but at this early stage they are hard to identify*

• *by looking like bird droppings these caterpillars are not attracting the attention of birds, or other predators*

these caterpillars are all tropical
• *species*

FINDING SPECIMENS
When looking for caterpillars remember the effectiveness of their camouflage. These swallowtail caterpillars disguise themselves by resembling bird droppings.

prove fruitful. Damp areas by streams and puddles can be popular drinking places for butterflies, particularly in tropical environments.

Many butterflies and moths are attracted to fermenting fruit or to sap oozing from wounds in tree trunks. Moth hunters have taken advantage of this to attract moths for study. They smear a bait of sugar, molasses, rum, and beer onto tree trunks or fenceposts at dusk and then visit at hourly intervals throughout the night. By flashlight they can watch moths gorging themselves on the sweet alcoholic mixture.

Moths are dazzled and disorientated by lights (not attracted to them, as many people think) so they often tend

NIGHT LIGHT
Any ordinary lamp will attract moths at night, but mercury vapor lamps are by far the most efficient.

this kerosene lamp is easily portable

flat-bottom gives lamp stability, and prevents it becoming a fire-risk

BUTTERFLY FEEDING
This cracker butterfly (Hamadryas feronia) *is feeding on the juices from a piece of fruit. Both butterflies and moths enjoy feeding on fruits.*

to fly toward them. Using this principle, many different forms of light traps have been devised, and these are used to enable scientists both to collect moths, and to monitor numbers and species, in biological surveys. However, a simple lantern or light bulb in front of a white sheet will attract many different species.

EQUIPMENT FOR THE FIELD

One of the best ways to keep a record of butterflies and moths you have seen is to take photographs of them. You can equip most modern single-lens reflex cameras with a macro lens for butterfly close-ups, and achieve excellent results with practice and patience. A simple snapshot camera is useful for recording butterfly habitats. Write down times of appearance, distribution, mating behavior, and foodplants, to build up a picture of the various species' habits. Many students have made important discoveries in this way.

tape recorder

notebook and field guides

short-focus telescope

camera

REARING

ONE OF THE BEST ways to learn more about butterflies and moths is to rear them from eggs. There are a number of large and spectacular exotic species, including silkmoths and moonmoths, that are relatively easily reared in captivity, as well as the more common and native species.

Keep eggs in small transparent plastic boxes until they hatch. If left in too large a container, they may dry up and die. As soon as the tiny caterpillars hatch, transfer them into a container that holds some of their foodplant. While small, you can keep most caterpillars in plastic boxes lined with absorbent paper. Provide them with a regular supply of fresh foliage. At this stage, there is no need to punch holes in the lid for ventilation, as this causes the food to dry up too rapidly. Condensation can endanger small caterpillars, but the paper lining should prevent this from happening. As caterpillars grow, it will be necessary to transfer them to larger containers or

twigs of oak are used to rear the oak (Antheraea harti) *silkmoth*

silkmoth caterpillar

foodplant must be changed regularly to ensure fresh food for the caterpillar

twigs reach down to ground, so that caterpillars can climb back on plant if they fall off

KEEPING CATERPILLARS
When rearing caterpillars on cut food, it is essential to plug the neck of the water jar. Otherwise the caterpillars will crawl in and drown.

cages. Some caterpillars require a growing plant. Place a potted plant in the cage or make a cage by tying a sleeve of netting over the branch of a shrub.

Pupa Stage

Many butterfly species will simply attach their pupae to the foodplant, but some moths form their pupae below ground or under bark. To provide a pupation site, place a thick layer of slightly damp sphagnum on the floor of the cage. Some pupae overwinter with the adults emerging in the following year. In the spring

you should transfer them to a spacious emergence cage, and spray them from time to time with a fine mist of water. The balance of moisture is critical at all stages of development, as too much will encourage mold. Cages should be cleaned regularly. It is essential to provide twigs for the newly emerged butterflies and moths to cling to while they are expanding their wings. Not all adults will feed, but those that do will take nectar from cut flowers provided, or substitute nectar that can be made quite easily from a diluted honey or sugar solution.

Range Of Cages
Commercially made cages are available for rearing caterpillars; alternatively, improvise with a cardboard box covered with mesh on one side.

a zip-fastener allows easy access to the cage

Cage Design
Where possible, cages should always provide the caterpillar with light and ventilation. They must also be easy to clean.

fresh or cut plants make suitable food for the caterpillars

mesh cage provides adequate ventilation

Handling Caterpillars

Try to avoid handling caterpillars but, if it is necessary, move smaller ones with a fine paintbrush. Many caterpillar species have stinging hairs- these should be handled with caution. When caterpillars are about to molt, they usually look dull and shrunken. They must not be moved at this stage as any disturbance is likely to prevent molting.

BUTTERFLY GARDEN

ONE WAY IN WHICH you can contribute towards conservation is to make your garden as attractive as possible to butterflies and moths. In doing this, you will encourage a range of other wildlife so that your garden will be an even more enjoyable place.

The first step is to grow flowers that provide a rich source of nectar. Night-scented flowers, such as honeysuckle, are usually attractive to moths. Make sure that you grow plants that flower at different times of year to provide a continuous food supply throughout the seasons.

It is also desirable to grow caterpillar foodplants, as these will encourage female butterflies to lay their eggs in your garden. With a little research you can find out which butterfly and moth species inhabit your area so that you can provide them with a range of suitable plants. If space permits, you could develop an area of wild garden for native plants to flourish.

If you plan to attract butterflies and moths to your garden, you should avoid using insecticides if possible. Those that kill aphids are said to be harmless to caterpillars, but all garden chemicals should be used with care.

PIPEVINE SWALLOWTAIL

BUDDLEIA
Also called the butterfly bush, the flowers of this shrub attract many butterfly and moth species, including the pipevine swallowtail.

honey-scented buddleia bush flowers in summer •

ICEPLANT
Small tortoiseshells (Aglais urticae) *enjoying the iceplant's nectar (see left).*

HONEYSUCKLE
This attracts long-tongued moths, like this hawkmoth (Macroglossum stellatarum).

APPLE
Moth caterpillars like the foliage of this tree; the fallen fruit attracts butterflies like the Mourning Cloak (Nymphalis antiopa).

HUMMINGBIRD HAWKMOTH

MOURNING CLOAK

MARJORAM
This herb is attractive to butterflies such as the meadow brown (Maniola jurtina).

MEADOW BROWN

HEBE
This is a useful plant for attracting such butterflies as the peacock (Inachis io).

PEACOCK

WILD FLOWERS
A small area devoted to wild flowers and grasses will also attract butterflies and moths.

this plant attracts a wide variety of insects

PALEARCTIC REGION

THE PALEARCTIC REGION is the largest of the zoogeographic regions, extending across the northern hemisphere from Europe to China and Japan, and extending southward to North Africa, including the Sahara. The climate of this region is mainly temperate but ranges from arctic to subtropical. As temperature and climate are distinctly seasonal, butterflies and moths usually have a constant number of generations each year, and

ZOOGEOGRAPHICAL PALEARCTIC REGION

their flight periods can be predicted with some accuracy. Butterflies and moths of the Palearctic region are better known than those in any other part of the world because the study of these insects first began in Europe. The fauna in parts of this region, for instance central Asia, is still very poorly known.

AGRICULTURE
Many areas of the Palearctic region have been subjected to intense agricultural activity for some centuries, and this has had a profound effect on the fauna.

Maniola jurtina
(Nymphalidae)

Sphinx ligustri
(Sphingidae)

Cerura vinula
(Notodontidae)

Orgyia antiqua
(Lymantriidae)

Arctia caja
(Arctiidae)

Parnassius apollo
(Papilionidae)

Argynnis lathonia
(Nymphalidae)

Ochlodes venatus
(Hesperiidae)

Inachis io
(Nymphalidae)

Polyommatus icarus
(Lycaenidae)

Pieris brassicae
(Pieridae)

Boarmia roboraria
(Geometridae)

Zygaena filipendulae
(Zygaenidae)

Papilio machaon
(Papilionidae)

Bombyx mori
(Bombycidae)

Saturnia pyri
(Saturniidae)

Noctua pronuba
(Noctuidae)

Lycaena dispar
(Lycaenidae)

*Anthocharis
cardamines*
(Pieridae)

*Lasiocampa
quercus*
(Lasiocampidae)

AFROTROPICAL REGION

THE AFROTROPICAL REGION includes the whole of Africa south of the Sahara. Madagascar is normally placed in a zoogeographic region of its own because so many of its species occur nowhere else in the world. However, for the purposes of this book, it is included with the Afrotropical region. This region boasts more than 2,500 described species of butterflies and many more species of moths, although little is known about the smaller

ZOOGEOGRAPHICAL AFROTROPICAL REGION

moths. The richest parts of the region are the lowland tropical rain forests, with those in West Africa having the most species. The other major habitat for Lepidoptera is grassland and savanna, which has a smaller but characteristic butterfly and moth fauna of its own.

SAVANNA
Grassland with trees and scrub is just one of the many habitats of the African continent.

Lampides boeticus
(Lycaenidae)

Papilio demodocus
(Papilionidae)

Colotis danae
(Pieridae)

Anaphe panda
(Notodontidae)

Dactylocerus swanzii
(Brahmaeidae

Poecilmitis thysbe
(Lycaenidae)

Dasychira pyrosoma
(Lymantridae)

Bunaea alcinoe
(Saturniidae)

Eurytela dryope
(Nymphalidae)

*Grammodora
nigrolineata*
(Lasiocampidae)

Coeliades forestan
(Hesperiidae)

Anaphe panda
(Notodontidae)

Omphax plantaria
(Geometridae)

Catopsilia florella
(Pieridae)

Chrysiridia rhiphearia
(Uraniidae)

Danaus chrysippus
(Nymphalidae)

Acherontia atropos
(Sphingidae)

INDO-AUSTRALIAN REGION

THE INDO-AUSTRALIAN region encompasses two zoogeographical areas known as the Oriental and Australian regions. It stretches from Pakistan and India to Australia and New Zealand. There are profound differences in the fauna of the two regions, but many butterfly species extend from the Oriental to the Australian region, and I have found it practical to consider them together. This is one of the richest parts of the world for butterflies and moths.

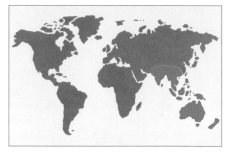

ZOOGEOGRAPHICAL INDO-AUSTRALIAN REGION

Virtually the whole of this region lies within the tropics, except parts of Australia and New Zealand. However, many habitats are represented, from tropical forests to plains, swamps, and mountains.

PADDY FIELDS
This is a typical man-made landscape in the Oriental region.

Danis danis
(Lycaenidae)

Papilio paris
(Papilionidae)

Cethosia biblis
(Nymphalidae)

Danima banksiae
(Notodontidae)

Crypsiphona ocultaria
(Geometridae)

Ogyris genoveva
(Lycaenidae)

Gangara thyrsis
(Hesperiidae)

Teia anartoides
(Lymantridae)

Tisiphone abeone
(Nymphalidae)

Actias selene
(Saturniidae)

Utetheisa species
(Arctiidae)

Appias nero
(Pieridae)

Digglesia australasiae
(Lasiocampidae)

Achaea janata
(Noctuidae)

Coequosa triangularis
(Sphingidae)

Delias mysis
(Pieridae)

NEARCTIC REGION

THE NEARCTIC REGION is largely temperate in climate but extends from arctic Canada and Alaska to subtropical Florida and southern California. It bears many resemblances in climate and fauna to the Palearctic region, and a number of species are common to both regions. Insects occurring in both the Nearctic and Palearctic regions (of which there are many), are said to have a Holarctic distribution. About 700 species of butterfly occur in the

ZOOGEOGRAPHICAL NEARCTIC REGION

Nearctic region, but the moth fauna is very much more extensive than this. Probably the best known of all the butterflies occurring in this region is the monarch, famed for its annual migration from the USA to Mexico.

FOREST
Many species in this region inhabit temperate forests, or areas bordering agricultural land.

Schizura ipomoeae
(Notodontidae)

Prochoerodes transversata
(Geometridae)

Danaus plexippus
(Nymphalidae)

Cercyonis pegala
(Nymphalidae)

Apantesis virgo
(Arctiidae)

Hemiargus isola
(Lycaenidae)

Prionoxystus robiniae
(Cossidae)

Zerene eurydice
(Pieridae)

Epargyreus clarus
(Hesperiidae)

Peridroma saucia
(Noctuidae)

Atlides halesus
(Lycaenidae)

Megathymus yuccae
(Hesperiidae)

Eurytides marcellus
(Papilionidae)

Malacosoma americanum
(Lasiocampidae)

Agrius cingulata
(Sphingidae)

Lymantria dispar
(Lymantriidae)

Hyalophora cecropia
(Saturniidae)

Sibine stimulea
(Limacodidae)

Junonia coenia
(Nymphalidae)

*Neophasia
menapia*
(Pieridae)

NEOTROPICAL REGION

THE NEOTROPICAL REGION extends from Mexico to Tierra del Fuego in South America. It covers a wide range of habitats and climates, but the tropical rain forests of South America have the greatest diversity of species.

The lycaenid butterflies, represented on p.35 by *Thecla coronata*, include some of the most beautiful and jewel-like species, yet they are so little studied that there is no reliable guide for their identification. The moths include

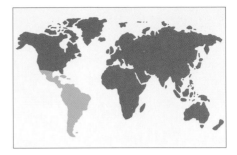

ZOOGEOGRAPHICAL NEOTROPICAL REGION

some distinctive species such as the giant agrippa *(Thysania agrippina)*, and the giant gray sphinx *(Pseudosphinx tetrio)*, but many of the smaller moth species have yet to be identified.

RAIN FOREST
This area contains the richest butterfly and moth populations in the world.

Premolis semirufa
(Arctiidae)

Eupackardia calleta
(Saturniidae)

Battus philenor
(Papilionidae)

Heliconius charitonius
(Nymphalidae)

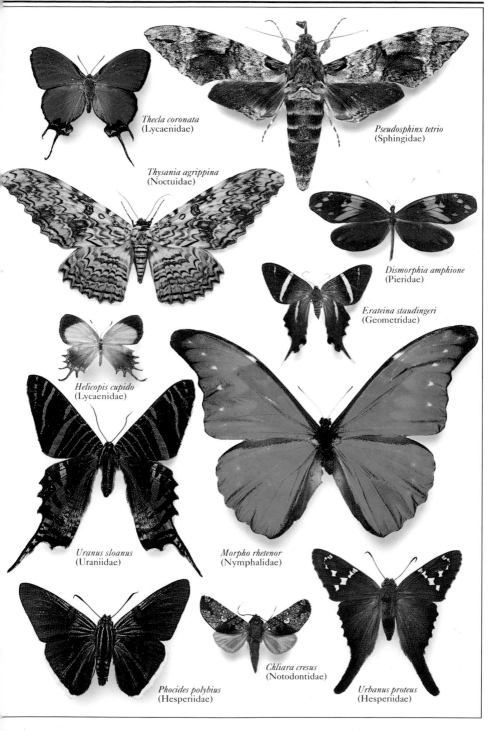

Thecla coronata
(Lycaenidae)

Pseudosphinx tetrio
(Sphingidae)

Thysania agrippina
(Noctuidae)

Dismorphia amphione
(Pieridae)

Erateina staudingeri
(Geometridae)

Helicopis cupido
(Lycaenidae)

Uranus sloanus
(Uraniidae)

Morpho rhetenor
(Nymphalidae)

Phocides polybius
(Hesperiidae)

Chliara cresus
(Notodontidae)

Urbanus proteus
(Hesperiidae)

BUTTERFLIES

HESPERIIDAE

T HE FAMILY Hesperiidae, more familiarly referred to as skippers, is a large, primitive group of some 3,000 species occurring throughout the world. Although generally considered to be butterflies, they frequently lack butterfly-style clubs to the antennae. They can be recognized by their large heads, stout bodies, and short, triangular-shaped forewings. They are mostly small to medium-sized insects with drab colors, although a few of the larger species are quite brightly colored, and attractively patterned.

•

Skippers earned their common name from the characteristic way they dart from flower to flower.

Family HESPERIIDAE	Species *Urbanus proteus*	Author Linnaeus

LONG-TAILED SKIPPER

This is one of the most recognizable skippers, and can be distinguished from other North American longtails by the iridescent green on the upperside of the wings and body. It is an erratic flier.
• **EARLY STAGES** The caterpillar is olive-green with brown lines and yellow and black spotting. The head is brown with two yellow spots. It often feeds on varieties of cultivated bean *(Phaseolus)*.
• **DISTRIBUTION** Widespread in South America, from Argentina, extending northward into the USA as far north as Connecticut.

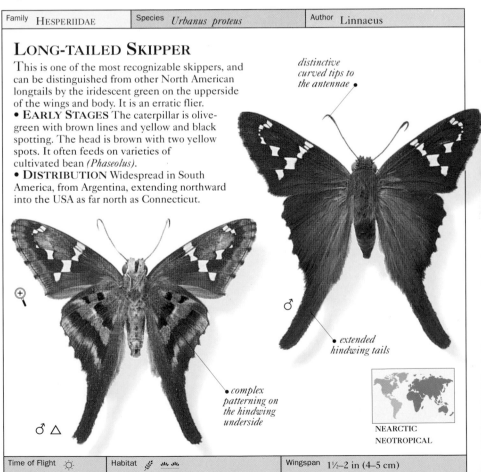

distinctive curved tips to the antennae

♂

extended hindwing tails

complex patterning on the hindwing underside

♂ △

NEARCTIC
NEOTROPICAL

Time of Flight ☀	Habitat	Wingspan 1½–2 in (4–5 cm)

Family HESPERIIDAE	Species *Zophopetes dysmephila*	Author Trimen

PALM SKIPPER

The robust, chocolate-brown palm skipper is one of several similar species found in Africa. The underside of the hindwing is brown with scattered black dots and a purplish tinge. The adult palm skippers are active at dusk.
• **EARLY STAGES** The caterpillar is apparently undescribed, but feeds on date palm *(Phoenix dactylifera)* and other palms.
• **DISTRIBUTION** Widespread at low altitudes in grasslands, riversides, and forests, from South Africa to Eritrea and Senegal, south of the Sahara.

AFROTROPICAL

white clubs on the antennae

triangular-shaped forewings

white margins on the forewings

♂

three white patches on the forewings

Time of Flight ◑	Habitat ⬞⬞	Wingspan 1½–1¾ in (4–4.5 cm)

Family HESPERIIDAE	Species *Epargyreus clarus*	Author Cramer

SILVER-SPOTTED SKIPPER

This large skipper is dark brown with orange markings on the forewings, and a small cluster of white eyespots at the forewing tip.
• **EARLY STAGES** The caterpillar is yellow green with darker markings and has a reddish brown head. There is one generation a year in the temperate north, and two or three in warmer, southern regions.
• **DISTRIBUTION** Found in North America.

curved tip to antennae

♂

both sexes have small, blunt, curved lobes

♂ △

silvery white patch on the hindwing underside

NEARCTIC
NEOTROPICAL

Time of Flight ☼	Habitat 🌳	Wingspan 1¾–2½ in (4.5–6 cm)

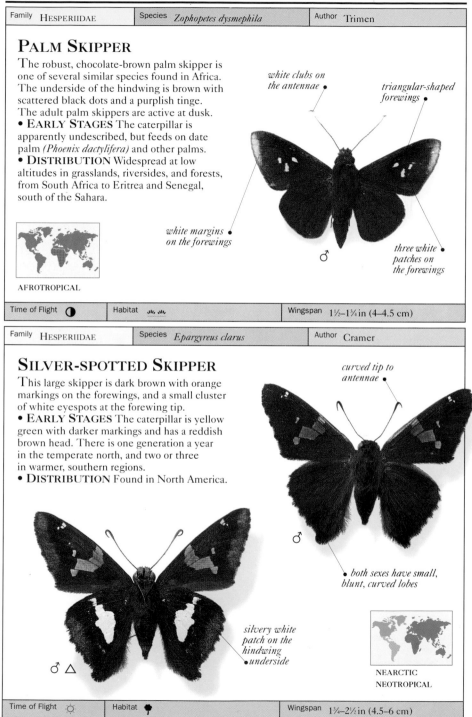

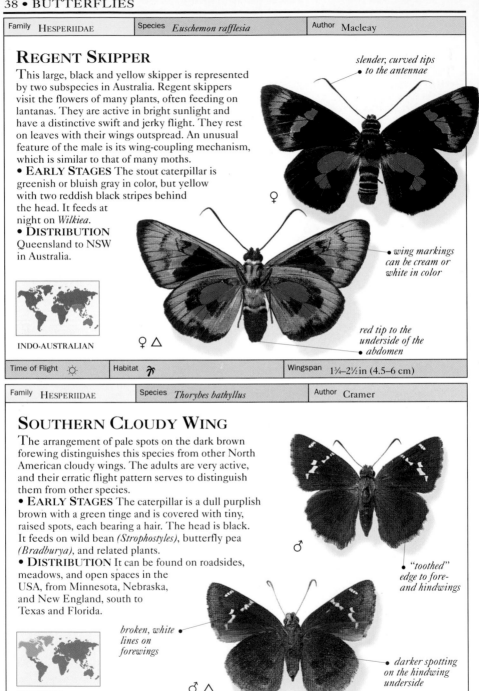

| Family | HESPERIIDAE | Species | *Euschemon rafflesia* | Author | Macleay |

REGENT SKIPPER

This large, black and yellow skipper is represented
by two subspecies in Australia. Regent skippers
visit the flowers of many plants, often feeding on
lantanas. They are active in bright sunlight and
have a distinctive swift and jerky flight. They rest
on leaves with their wings outspread. An unusual
feature of the male is its wing-coupling mechanism,
which is similar to that of many moths.
• **EARLY STAGES** The stout caterpillar is
greenish or bluish gray in color, but yellow
with two reddish black stripes behind
the head. It feeds at
night on *Wilkiea*.
• **DISTRIBUTION**
Queensland to NSW
in Australia.

slender, curved tips
to the antennae

wing markings
can be cream or
white in color

red tip to the
underside of the
abdomen

INDO-AUSTRALIAN

| Time of Flight ☼ | Habitat | Wingspan 1¼–2½ in (4.5–6 cm) |

| Family | HESPERIIDAE | Species | *Thorybes bathyllus* | Author | Cramer |

SOUTHERN CLOUDY WING

The arrangement of pale spots on the dark brown
forewing distinguishes this species from other North
American cloudy wings. The adults are very active,
and their erratic flight pattern serves to distinguish
them from other species.
• **EARLY STAGES** The caterpillar is a dull purplish
brown with a green tinge and is covered with tiny,
raised spots, each bearing a hair. The head is black.
It feeds on wild bean *(Strophostyles)*, butterfly pea
(Bradburya), and related plants.
• **DISTRIBUTION** It can be found on roadsides,
meadows, and open spaces in the
USA, from Minnesota, Nebraska,
and New England, south to
Texas and Florida.

"toothed"
edge to fore-
and hindwings

broken, white
lines on
forewings

darker spotting
on the hindwing
underside

NEARCTIC

| Time of Flight ☼ | Habitat | Wingspan 1¼–1¾ in (3–4.5 cm) |

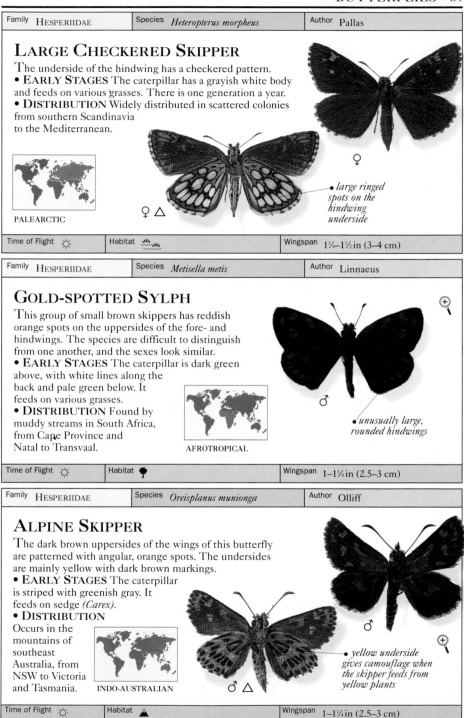

| Family | HESPERIIDAE | Species | *Heteropterus morpheus* | Author | Pallas |

LARGE CHECKERED SKIPPER

The underside of the hindwing has a checkered pattern.
• **EARLY STAGES** The caterpillar has a grayish white body
and feeds on various grasses. There is one generation a year.
• **DISTRIBUTION** Widely distributed in scattered colonies
from southern Scandinavia
to the Mediterranean.

PALEARCTIC

♀ △

♀

*large ringed
spots on the
hindwing
underside*

| Time of Flight ☼ | Habitat 〰 | Wingspan 1¼–1½ in (3–4 cm) |

| Family | HESPERIIDAE | Species | *Metisella metis* | Author | Linnaeus |

GOLD-SPOTTED SYLPH

This group of small brown skippers has reddish
orange spots on the uppersides of the fore- and
hindwings. The species are difficult to distinguish
from one another, and the sexes look similar.
• **EARLY STAGES** The caterpillar is dark green
above, with white lines along the
back and pale green below. It
feeds on various grasses.
• **DISTRIBUTION** Found by
muddy streams in South Africa,
from Cape Province and
Natal to Transvaal.

AFROTROPICAL

⊕

♂

*unusually large,
rounded hindwings*

| Time of Flight ☼ | Habitat ♣ | Wingspan 1–1¼ in (2.5–3 cm) |

| Family | HESPERIIDAE | Species | *Oreisplanus munionga* | Author | Olliff |

ALPINE SKIPPER

The dark brown uppersides of the wings of this butterfly
are patterned with angular, orange spots. The undersides
are mainly yellow with dark brown markings.
• **EARLY STAGES** The caterpillar
is striped with greenish gray. It
feeds on sedge *(Carex).*
• **DISTRIBUTION**
Occurs in the
mountains of
southeast
Australia, from
NSW to Victoria
and Tasmania.

INDO-AUSTRALIAN

♂ △

♂

⊕

*yellow underside
gives camouflage when
the skipper feeds from
yellow plants*

| Time of Flight ☼ | Habitat ▲ | Wingspan 1–1¼ in (2.5–3 cm) |

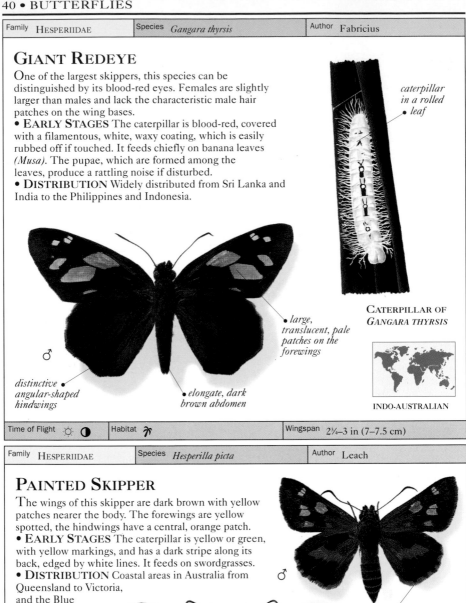

Family HESPERIIDAE	Species *Gangara thyrsis*	Author Fabricius

GIANT REDEYE

One of the largest skippers, this species can be distinguished by its blood-red eyes. Females are slightly larger than males and lack the characteristic male hair patches on the wing bases.
• **EARLY STAGES** The caterpillar is blood-red, covered with a filamentous, white, waxy coating, which is easily rubbed off if touched. It feeds chiefly on banana leaves *(Musa)*. The pupae, which are formed among the leaves, produce a rattling noise if disturbed.
• **DISTRIBUTION** Widely distributed from Sri Lanka and India to the Philippines and Indonesia.

caterpillar in a rolled leaf

large, translucent, pale patches on the forewings

**CATERPILLAR OF
GANGARA THYRSIS**

♂

distinctive angular-shaped hindwings

elongate, dark brown abdomen

INDO-AUSTRALIAN

Time of Flight ☼ ◐	Habitat 🌴	Wingspan 2¾–3 in (7–7.5 cm)

Family HESPERIIDAE	Species *Hesperilla picta*	Author Leach

PAINTED SKIPPER

The wings of this skipper are dark brown with yellow patches nearer the body. The forewings are yellow spotted, the hindwings have a central, orange patch.
• **EARLY STAGES** The caterpillar is yellow or green, with yellow markings, and has a dark stripe along its back, edged by white lines. It feeds on swordgrasses.
• **DISTRIBUTION** Coastal areas in Australia from Queensland to Victoria, and the Blue Mountains in NSW.

♂

checkered fringe on the hindwings

white patterning on the hindwing underside

INDO-AUSTRALIAN

♀ △

Time of Flight ☼	Habitat 〰️	Wingspan 1¼–1½ in (3–4 cm)

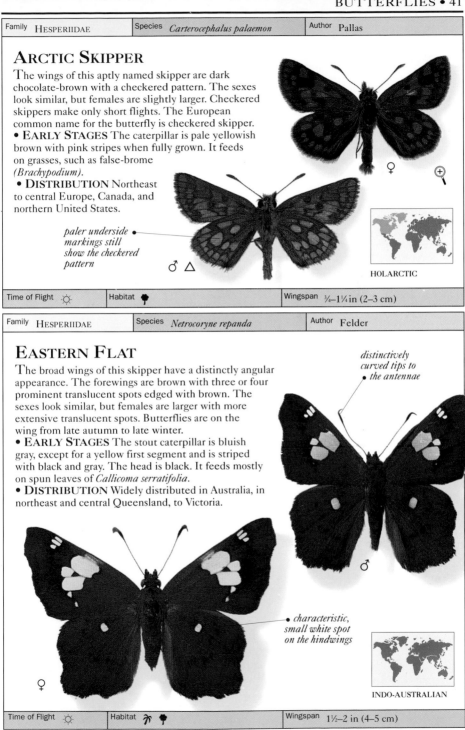

Family	HESPERIIDAE	Species	*Carterocephalus palaemon*	Author	Pallas

ARCTIC SKIPPER

The wings of this aptly named skipper are dark
chocolate-brown with a checkered pattern. The sexes
look similar, but females are slightly larger. Checkered
skippers make only short flights. The European
common name for the butterfly is checkered skipper.
• **EARLY STAGES** The caterpillar is pale yellowish
brown with pink stripes when fully grown. It feeds
on grasses, such as false-brome
(Brachypodium).
• **DISTRIBUTION** Northeast
to central Europe, Canada, and
northern United States.

*paler underside
markings still
show the checkered
pattern*

♂ △

♀

HOLARCTIC

Time of Flight ☼	Habitat ♣	Wingspan ¾–1¼ in (2–3 cm)

Family	HESPERIIDAE	Species	*Netrocoryne repanda*	Author	Felder

EASTERN FLAT

The broad wings of this skipper have a distinctly angular
appearance. The forewings are brown with three or four
prominent translucent spots edged with brown. The
sexes look similar, but females are larger with more
extensive translucent spots. Butterflies are on the
wing from late autumn to late winter.
• **EARLY STAGES** The stout caterpillar is bluish
gray, except for a yellow first segment and is striped
with black and gray. The head is black. It feeds mostly
on spun leaves of *Callicoma serratifolia*.
• **DISTRIBUTION** Widely distributed in Australia, in
northeast and central Queensland, to Victoria.

*distinctively
curved tips to
the antennae*

♂

*characteristic,
small white spot
on the hindwings*

♀

INDO-AUSTRALIAN

Time of Flight ☼	Habitat 🌴 ♣	Wingspan 1½–2 in (4–5 cm)

Family HESPERIIDAE	Species *Phocides polybius*	Author Fabricius

GUAVA SKIPPER

A striking skipper, this species has sharply angled fore- and hindwings which are black with metallic-greenish blue streaks. Each forewing has two vermilion spots, which distinguish this skipper from similar species. The upperside of the body is black with metallic-blue, the underside is black.
• **EARLY STAGES** The young caterpillar is red with yellow rings, becoming white with a brown and yellow head as it develops. It feeds on guava *(Psidium guajava)* and related species.
• **DISTRIBUTION** South and Central America extending to Argentina.

narrow, scarlet collar behind head

white fringe to hindwings

♂

NEOTROPICAL

Time of Flight ☼	Habitat 🌴	Wingspan 2–2½ in (5–6 cm)

Family HESPERIIDAE	Species *Coeliades forestan*	Author Stoll

STRIPED POLICEMAN

This robust species has grayish brown, triangular forewings, which are centrally suffused with white on the undersides. The rounded hindwings with their broad, short tails are characteristic of this mainly African genus of skippers. Striped policemen have a rapid flight, and their habit of patrolling their territory from dawn to dusk gives rise to their common name. They are attracted to the flowers of various low-growing plants.
• **EARLY STAGES** The caterpillar is pale yellow with purplish red bands. Its head is red or yellow, with black spots. It feeds on geranium.
• **DISTRIBUTION** Found in Africa south of the Sahara, including Madagascar and the Seychelles.

♂

chrome-yellow scaling of the tail fringes

large, white stripes on the hindwing undersides

♂ △

AFROTROPICAL

Time of Flight ☼	Habitat 🌴	Wingspan 1¾–2 in (4.5–5 cm)

Family HESPERIIDAE	Species *Pyrrhochalcia iphis*	Author Drury

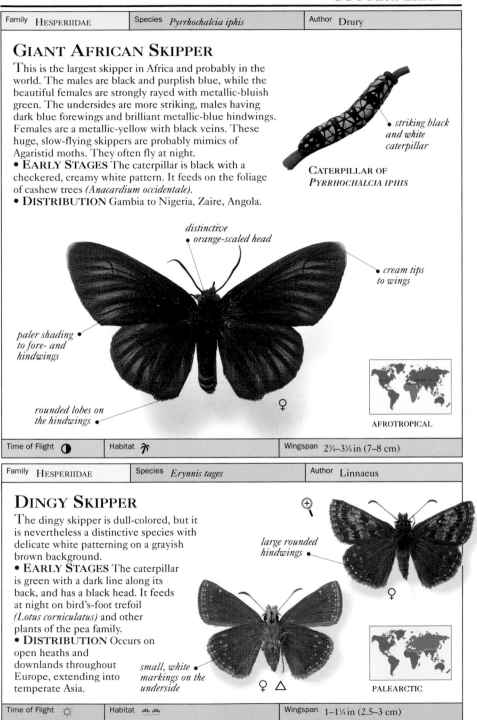

GIANT AFRICAN SKIPPER

This is the largest skipper in Africa and probably in the world. The males are black and purplish blue, while the beautiful females are strongly rayed with metallic-bluish green. The undersides are more striking, males having dark blue forewings and brilliant metallic-blue hindwings. Females are a metallic-yellow with black veins. These huge, slow-flying skippers are probably mimics of Agaristid moths. They often fly at night.

• **EARLY STAGES** The caterpillar is black with a checkered, creamy white pattern. It feeds on the foliage of cashew trees *(Anacardium occidentale)*.

• **DISTRIBUTION** Gambia to Nigeria, Zaire, Angola.

• *striking black and white caterpillar*

CATERPILLAR OF PYRRHOCHALCIA IPHIS

distinctive
• *orange-scaled head*

• *cream tips to wings*

paler shading to fore- and hindwings •

rounded lobes on the hindwings •

♀

AFROTROPICAL

Time of Flight ◑	Habitat 🌴	Wingspan 2¾–3¼ in (7–8 cm)

Family HESPERIIDAE	Species *Erynnis tages*	Author Linnaeus

DINGY SKIPPER

The dingy skipper is dull-colored, but it is nevertheless a distinctive species with delicate white patterning on a grayish brown background.

• **EARLY STAGES** The caterpillar is green with a dark line along its back, and has a black head. It feeds at night on bird's-foot trefoil *(Lotus corniculatus)* and other plants of the pea family.

• **DISTRIBUTION** Occurs on open heaths and downlands throughout Europe, extending into temperate Asia.

⊕

large rounded hindwings •

♀

small, white markings on the underside

♀ △

PALEARCTIC

Time of Flight ☼	Habitat 🌿 🌿	Wingspan 1–1¼ in (2.5–3 cm)

Family HESPERIIDAE	Species *Calpodes ethlius*	Author Stoll

BRAZILIAN SKIPPER

This skipper has dark brown wings, spotted with silvery white. The forewings are narrow and pointed in contrast with the broad, lobed hindwings. It can fly over large distances.

• **EARLY STAGES** The caterpillar is grayish green with a white line down the back and brown spots along the sides. The head is orange and black. It feeds on canna leaves *(Canna flaccida)*, and sometimes damages cultivated forms of this plant. It is known as the canna leaf roller. The pale green pupa is camouflaged in a leaf roll.

• **DISTRIBUTION** Widely distributed in South America, and the West Indies. Occurs in southern parts of the USA.

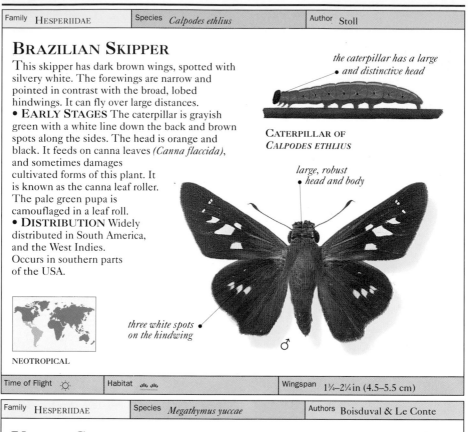

the caterpillar has a large and distinctive head

CATERPILLAR OF CALPODES ETHLIUS

large, robust head and body

three white spots on the hindwing

♂

NEOTROPICAL

Time of Flight ☼	Habitat ⠆⠆	Wingspan 1¾–2¼ in (4.5–5.5 cm)

Family HESPERIIDAE	Species *Megathymus yuccae*	Authors Boisduval & Le Conte

YUCCA SKIPPER

Large-bodied and hairy, this skipper has blackish wings, which are distinctively patterned with yellow and white. Males are much smaller than females. They can be seen from spring to early summer. These skippers do not feed as adults, although related species have been observed drinking on moist ground.

• **EARLY STAGES** The caterpillar is large and grublike with a small head. It feeds on yucca.

• **DISTRIBUTION** This is the most widespread of the North American giant skippers. It lives in various habitats, including forest margins where the foodplants grow. Its range extends from Utah and Nebraska, south to Florida and Mexico.

distinctive clubs to the antennae

♀

yellow shading to hindwing edge

NEARCTIC

Time of Flight ☼	Habitat	Wingspan 1¾–3¼ in (4.5–8 cm)

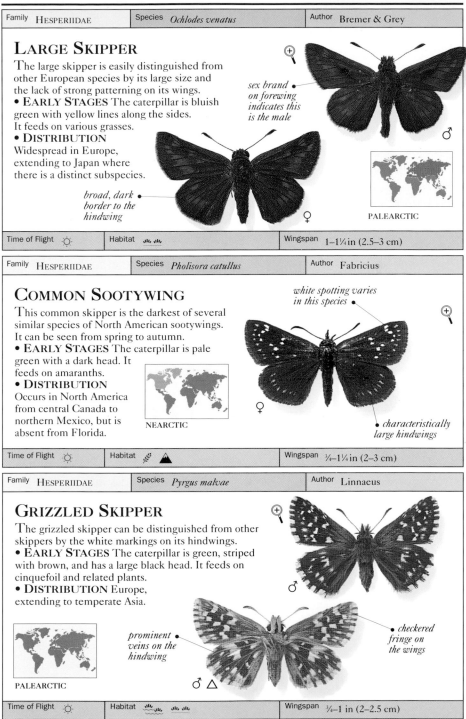

Family HESPERIIDAE	Species *Ochlodes venatus*	Author Bremer & Grey

LARGE SKIPPER

The large skipper is easily distinguished from other European species by its large size and the lack of strong patterning on its wings.
• **EARLY STAGES** The caterpillar is bluish green with yellow lines along the sides. It feeds on various grasses.
• **DISTRIBUTION** Widespread in Europe, extending to Japan where there is a distinct subspecies.

sex brand • on forewing indicates this is the male

♂

broad, dark • border to the hindwing

♀

PALEARCTIC

Time of Flight ☼	Habitat ⚊ ⚊	Wingspan 1–1¼ in (2.5–3 cm)

Family HESPERIIDAE	Species *Pholisora catullus*	Author Fabricius

COMMON SOOTYWING

This common skipper is the darkest of several similar species of North American sootywings. It can be seen from spring to autumn.
• **EARLY STAGES** The caterpillar is pale green with a dark head. It feeds on amaranths.
• **DISTRIBUTION** Occurs in North America from central Canada to northern Mexico, but is absent from Florida.

white spotting varies in this species •

♀

NEARCTIC

• characteristically large hindwings

Time of Flight ☼	Habitat 🌿 ▲	Wingspan ¾–1¼ in (2–3 cm)

Family HESPERIIDAE	Species *Pyrgus malvae*	Author Linnaeus

GRIZZLED SKIPPER

The grizzled skipper can be distinguished from other skippers by the white markings on its hindwings.
• **EARLY STAGES** The caterpillar is green, striped with brown, and has a large black head. It feeds on cinquefoil and related plants.
• **DISTRIBUTION** Europe, extending to temperate Asia.

♂

prominent • veins on the hindwing

• checkered fringe on the wings

PALEARCTIC

♂ △

Time of Flight ☼	Habitat ⚊⚊ ⚊ ⚊	Wingspan ¾–1 in (2–2.5 cm)

PAPILIONIDAE

T HIS LARGE family of butterflies contains some of the biggest and most beautiful species in the world. It is also the most widely studied and well-known of all the butterfly groups.

•

Most species occur in the tropics, but some are also found in temperate climates. Because many Papilionidae species have tailed hindwings, their popular name is swallowtail. However, not all Papilionids have tailed wings, for example, the birdwings of tropical Australasia. Swallowtail butterflies can be recognized by their large, striking wings and by the fact that they have three fully developed pairs of legs. They are usually strong fliers.

Family PAPILIONIDAE	Species *Papilio aegeus*	Author Donovan

ORCHARD SWALLOWTAIL

Male orchard swallowtails are distinguished by the small, oblique band of white spots on the black forewings, and the single red spot on the inner margin of each hindwing. There are several female forms, but all of them have forewings marked with white, and hindwings patterned with a band of red spots along the outer margin. They have a strong, uneven flight pattern.
• **EARLY STAGES** When first hatched, the caterpillar is brownish with white markings and resembles a bird's dropping. When grown, it is green with short, fleshy spines along the back. The caterpillar feeds on cultivated *Citrus* and *Microcitrus* plants.
• **DISTRIBUTION** Australia from Queensland to Victoria, and also in Papua New Guinea and adjacent islands.

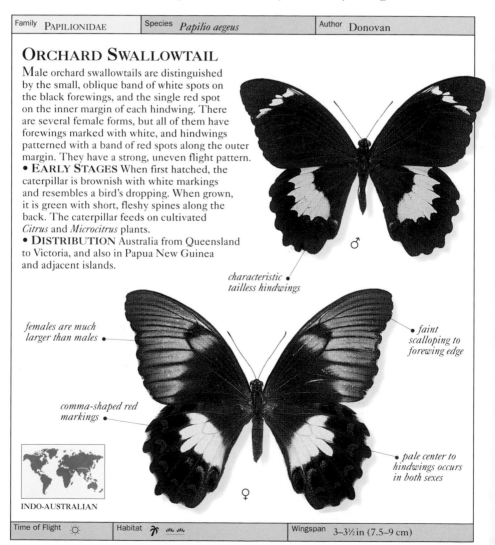

♂

characteristic tailless hindwings

females are much larger than males

faint scalloping to forewing edge

comma-shaped red markings

pale center to hindwings occurs in both sexes

♀

INDO-AUSTRALIAN

Time of Flight ☼	Habitat 🌴 🌾 🌾	Wingspan 3–3½ in (7.5–9 cm)

Family PAPILIONIDAE	Species *Papilio paris*	Author Linnaeus

PARIS PEACOCK

The striking patches of metallic color found on the hindwings place this butterfly in a group called the gloss papilios. Female Paris peacocks are usually yellower than the males.
• **EARLY STAGES** The caterpillar is green with white or yellow markings and yellow scent horns. It feeds on a wide range of plants, including *Citrus*.
• **DISTRIBUTION** Mainly at low altitudes in India, Thailand, Sumatra, and Java, although absent from the Malay Peninsula. It occurs at higher altitudes in southwest China.

INDO-AUSTRALIAN

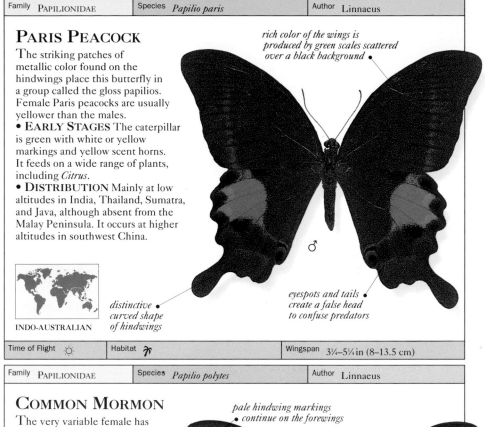

rich color of the wings is produced by green scales scattered over a black background

♂

distinctive curved shape of hindwings

eyespots and tails create a false head to confuse predators

Time of Flight ☼	Habitat 🌱	Wingspan 3¼–5¼ in (8–13.5 cm)

Family PAPILIONIDAE	Species *Papilio polytes*	Author Linnaeus

COMMON MORMON

The very variable female has three different color forms. One form resembles the male, the others mimic different species of swallowtail. Males have a swifter flight than females.
• **EARLY STAGES** The caterpillar is green with brown markings, very similar to that of the checkered swallowtail (*P. demoleus*, see p.48). It feeds on cultivated *Citrus*, especially orange *(C. sinensis)*, and lime *(C. aurantifolia)*, as well as on related native plants such as *Murraya* and *Triplasia*.
• **DISTRIBUTION** Widespread throughout India and Sri Lanka to China, Japan, Malaysia, the Philippines, and the Moluccas.

pale hindwing markings continue on the forewings

♂

INDO-AUSTRALIAN

band of cream spots on the hindwings

Time of Flight ☼	Habitat 🌿	Wingspan 3½–4 in (9–10 cm)

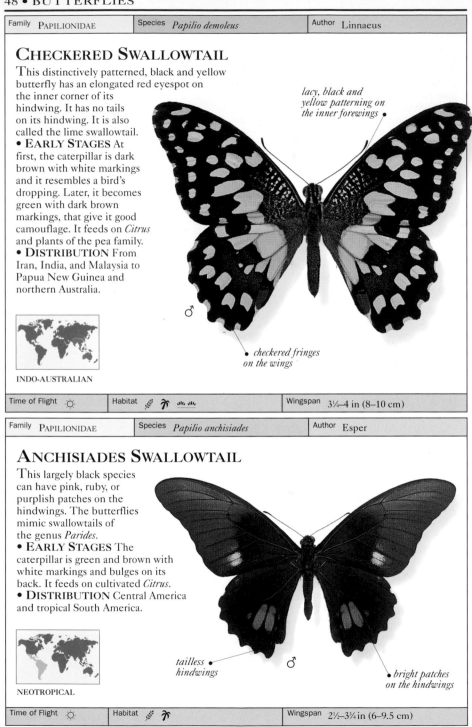

Family PAPILIONIDAE	Species *Papilio demoleus*	Author Linnaeus

CHECKERED SWALLOWTAIL

This distinctively patterned, black and yellow butterfly has an elongated red eyespot on the inner corner of its hindwing. It has no tails on its hindwing. It is also called the lime swallowtail.

• **EARLY STAGES** At first, the caterpillar is dark brown with white markings and it resembles a bird's dropping. Later, it becomes green with dark brown markings, that give it good camouflage. It feeds on *Citrus* and plants of the pea family.

• **DISTRIBUTION** From Iran, India, and Malaysia to Papua New Guinea and northern Australia.

INDO-AUSTRALIAN

lacy, black and yellow patterning on the inner forewings

♂

checkered fringes on the wings

Time of Flight ☼	Habitat	Wingspan 3¼–4 in (8–10 cm)

Family PAPILIONIDAE	Species *Papilio anchisiades*	Author Esper

ANCHISIADES SWALLOWTAIL

This largely black species can have pink, ruby, or purplish patches on the hindwings. The butterflies mimic swallowtails of the genus *Parides*.

• **EARLY STAGES** The caterpillar is green and brown with white markings and bulges on its back. It feeds on cultivated *Citrus*.

• **DISTRIBUTION** Central America and tropical South America.

NEOTROPICAL

tailless hindwings

♂

bright patches on the hindwings

Time of Flight ☼	Habitat	Wingspan 2½–3¾ in (6–9.5 cm)

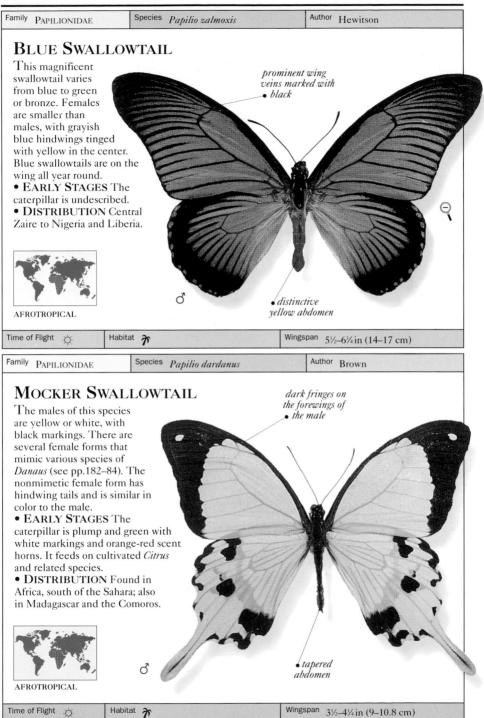

| Family | PAPILIONIDAE | Species | *Papilio zalmoxis* | Author | Hewitson |

BLUE SWALLOWTAIL

This magnificent swallowtail varies from blue to green or bronze. Females are smaller than males, with grayish blue hindwings tinged with yellow in the center. Blue swallowtails are on the wing all year round.
• **EARLY STAGES** The caterpillar is undescribed.
• **DISTRIBUTION** Central Zaire to Nigeria and Liberia.

AFROTROPICAL

prominent wing
veins marked with
• *black*

♂

• *distinctive
yellow abdomen*

| Time of Flight | ☼ | Habitat | 🦋 | Wingspan | 5½–6¾ in (14–17 cm) |

| Family | PAPILIONIDAE | Species | *Papilio dardanus* | Author | Brown |

MOCKER SWALLOWTAIL

The males of this species are yellow or white, with black markings. There are several female forms that mimic various species of *Danaus* (see pp.182–84). The nonmimetic female form has hindwing tails and is similar in color to the male.
• **EARLY STAGES** The caterpillar is plump and green with white markings and orange-red scent horns. It feeds on cultivated *Citrus* and related species.
• **DISTRIBUTION** Found in Africa, south of the Sahara; also in Madagascar and the Comoros.

AFROTROPICAL

*dark fringes on
the forewings of
• the male*

♂

• *tapered
abdomen*

| Time of Flight | ☼ | Habitat | 🦋 | Wingspan | 3½–4¼ in (9–10.8 cm) |

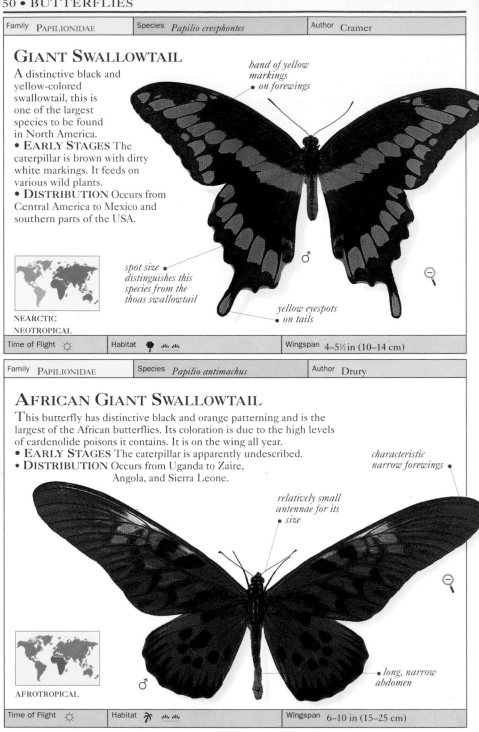

| Family PAPILIONIDAE | Species *Papilio cresphontes* | Author Cramer |

GIANT SWALLOWTAIL

A distinctive black and yellow-colored swallowtail, this is one of the largest species to be found in North America.
• **EARLY STAGES** The caterpillar is brown with dirty white markings. It feeds on various wild plants.
• **DISTRIBUTION** Occurs from Central America to Mexico and southern parts of the USA.

band of yellow markings on forewings

♂

spot size distinguishes this species from the thoas swallowtail

yellow eyespots on tails

NEARCTIC
NEOTROPICAL

| Time of Flight ☼ | Habitat 🌳 ⚕ ⚕ | Wingspan 4–5½ in (10–14 cm) |

| Family PAPILIONIDAE | Species *Papilio antimachus* | Author Drury |

AFRICAN GIANT SWALLOWTAIL

This butterfly has distinctive black and orange patterning and is the largest of the African butterflies. Its coloration is due to the high levels of cardenolide poisons it contains. It is on the wing all year.
• **EARLY STAGES** The caterpillar is apparently undescribed.
• **DISTRIBUTION** Occurs from Uganda to Zaire, Angola, and Sierra Leone.

characteristic narrow forewings

relatively small antennae for its size

♂

long, narrow abdomen

AFROTROPICAL

| Time of Flight ☼ | Habitat 🌴 ⚕ ⚕ | Wingspan 6–10 in (15–25 cm) |

Family PAPILIONIDAE	Species *Papilio demodocus*	Author Esper

CITRUS SWALLOWTAIL

This black and yellow
butterfly is tailless. It is the
African counterpart of *Papilio
demoleus* (see p.48), but it is
generally larger with a band of
black on the hindwing. It is also
called the Christmas butterfly.
• **EARLY STAGES** The
caterpillar feeds on cultivated
Citrus and legumes.
• **DISTRIBUTION** Occurs in
tropical Africa and is a pest
in South Africa. Also found
in Madagascar.

*bold yellow
spotting*

*characteristic
"toothed" edge
to the hindwing*

♂

AFROTROPICAL

Time of Flight ☼	Habitat	Wingspan 3½–4¼ in (9–12 cm)

Family PAPILIONIDAE	Species *Papilio machaon*	Author Linnaeus

OLD WORLD SWALLOWTAIL

This butterfly has a singular
bold patterning of black on
yellow. The hindwings have
fairly short tails and are variably
marked with orange patches. In
Britain this species is known as
the swallowtail.
• **EARLY STAGES** The
caterpillar has bright green and
black bands, spotted with red. It
feeds on milk parsley *(Peucedanum
palustre)* and other related plants.
• **DISTRIBUTION** Found in fen
and meadowland in Europe, across
temperate Asia to Japan. Also occurs
in subarctic and Arctic regions of
Canada and in Alaska.

*thin, pale leading
edge to forewings*

*broad, black
band is dusted
with blue*

♀

*red eyespot in
the corner of each
hindwing*

HOLARCTIC

Time of Flight ☼	Habitat	Wingspan 2¾–4 in (7–10 cm)

| Family PAPILIONIDAE | Species *Papilio glaucus* | Author Linnaeus |

TIGER SWALLOWTAIL

Males and some females of this species are yellow
with tiger stripes. A female form occurs in which
the ground color is dark brown or black. This form
is found most frequently in the southern parts of
the species' range, and is known to be a mimic of the
poisonous pipevine swallowtail (*Battus philenor,* see
p.55). Tiger swallowtails have a strong, sailing flight.
• **EARLY STAGES** The plump caterpillar is green
with bright yellow and black eyespots. The caterpillars
when they are young, resemble bird droppings. They feed
on tulip-tree (*Liriodendron tulipifera*), wild cherry *(Prunus)*
and cottonwoods *(Populus).* There are one to three broods
a year depending on location.
• **DISTRIBUTION** This butterfly species
can be found widely throughout Canada and
the USA, to the Gulf of Mexico.

• *well-camouflaged caterpillar with startling eyespots*

CATERPILLAR OF *PAPILIO GLAUCUS*

striking tiger striping on forewings

forewing eyespots fade at base of margin

• *unusual V-shaped marking on inner margin of hindwings*

black stripe along length of body matches wings

• *hooked hindwing tails*

yellow spotting along wing margins

NEARCTIC

| Time of Flight ☼ | Habitat 🌳 | Wingspan 3½–6½ in (9–16.5 cm) |

Family PAPILIONIDAE	Species *Eurytides marcellus*	Author Cramer

ZEBRA SWALLOWTAIL

With its distinctive black zebra
stripes and long, swordlike tails, this
butterfly cannot be confused with
other North American swallowtails.
It may be the commonest of the kite
swallowtails – so named because of their
triangular wings and pointed tails. Early
spring specimens are paler, smaller, and
have shorter tails than those appearing
in the summer.
• **EARLY STAGES** The caterpillar is
yellowish green with fine yellow and black
cross-bands. It feeds on pawpaw *(Carica)*.
• **DISTRIBUTION** Eastern Canada to
Florida, and the Gulf of Mexico.

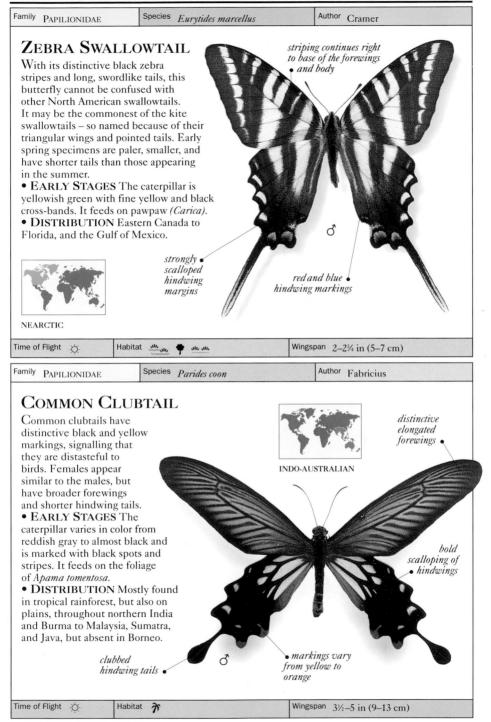

striping continues right
to base of the forewings
and body

♂

strongly
scalloped
hindwing
margins

red and blue
hindwing markings

NEARCTIC

Time of Flight ☼	Habitat 〰〰 🌳 〰〰	Wingspan 2–2¾ in (5–7 cm)

Family PAPILIONIDAE	Species *Parides coon*	Author Fabricius

COMMON CLUBTAIL

Common clubtails have
distinctive black and yellow
markings, signalling that
they are distasteful to
birds. Females appear
similar to the males, but
have broader forewings
and shorter hindwing tails.
• **EARLY STAGES** The
caterpillar varies in color from
reddish gray to almost black and
is marked with black spots and
stripes. It feeds on the foliage
of *Apama tomentosa*.
• **DISTRIBUTION** Mostly found
in tropical rainforest, but also on
plains, throughout northern India
and Burma to Malaysia, Sumatra,
and Java, but absent in Borneo.

INDO-AUSTRALIAN

distinctive
elongated
forewings

bold
scalloping of
hindwings

clubbed
hindwing tails

♂

markings vary
from yellow to
orange

Time of Flight ☼	Habitat 🌴	Wingspan 3½–5 in (9–13 cm)

Family PAPILIONIDAE	Species *Pachliopta aristolochiae*	Author Fabricius

COMMON ROSE SWALLOWTAIL

The markings of this butterfly vary and may even be absent. The forewings can be rayed with white markings. The wings are rounded in the female form. The female *Papilio polytes* (see p.47), mimics this species.

• **EARLY STAGES** The caterpillar varies from pinkish gray to black. It feeds on pipevines *(Aristolochia)*, extracting poisons from them which make it distasteful to birds.

• **DISTRIBUTION** From India and Sri Lanka through southern China and Malaysia, to the Lesser Sunda Islands.

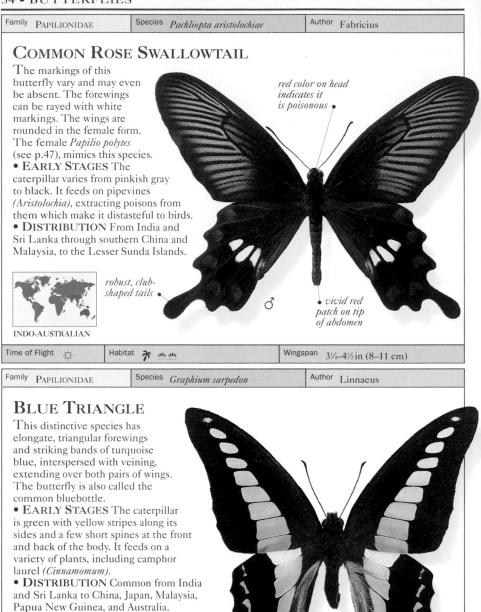

red color on head indicates it is poisonous

robust, club-shaped tails

♂

• vivid red patch on tip of abdomen

INDO-AUSTRALIAN

Time of Flight ☼	Habitat 🌴 ⃰ ⃰	Wingspan 3¼–4½ in (8–11 cm)

Family PAPILIONIDAE	Species *Graphium sarpedon*	Author Linnaeus

BLUE TRIANGLE

This distinctive species has elongate, triangular forewings and striking bands of turquoise blue, interspersed with veining, extending over both pairs of wings. The butterfly is also called the common bluebottle.

• **EARLY STAGES** The caterpillar is green with yellow stripes along its sides and a few short spines at the front and back of the body. It feeds on a variety of plants, including camphor laurel *(Cinnamomum)*.

• **DISTRIBUTION** Common from India and Sri Lanka to China, Japan, Malaysia, Papua New Guinea, and Australia.

unusual • hindwing shape

• distinctive pocket of pale scent scales distinguishes the male

♂

INDO-AUSTRALIAN

Time of Flight ☼	Habitat 🌴 ⃰ ⃰	Wingspan 3¼–3½ in (8–9 cm)

Family PAPILIONIDAE	Species *Battus philenor*	Author Linnaeus

PIPEVINE SWALLOWTAIL

The male butterfly has a metallic-blue sheen on the hindwings. This swallowtail is mimicked by several other butterfly species. It is also called the blue swallowtail.
• **EARLY STAGES** The caterpillar is reddish brown, with rows of red fleshy tentacles on its back. It feeds on the foliage of pipevines *(Aristolochia)* and other plants.
• **DISTRIBUTION** From southern Canada to Mexico.

forewings much duller than hindwings

pale, arrow-shaped markings on hindwings

♂

NEARCTIC
NEOTROPICAL

Time of Flight ☼	Habitat 🌳 ⸛ ⸛	Wingspan 3–4½ in (7.5–11 cm)

Family PAPILIONIDAE	Species *Battus polydamas*	Author Linnaeus

POLYDAMAS SWALLOWTAIL

This golden-yellow fringed butterfly has no tails. It is dark, and the hindwings usually have a green luster. The underside is patterned with red. These swallowtails are distasteful to birds.
• **EARLY STAGES** The caterpillar is black, and feeds on pipevines *(Aristolochia)*.
• **DISTRIBUTION** From northern Argentina to the West Indies, Central America, and southern parts of the USA.

distinctive yellow band on both wings

♀

strongly scalloped hindwings

NEARCTIC
NEOTROPICAL

Time of Flight ☼	Habitat 🌴 ⸛ ⸛	Wingspan 2¾–3½ in (7–9 cm)

Family PAPILIONIDAE	Species *Iphiclides podalirius*	Author Scopoli

SCARCE SWALLOWTAIL

This pale yellow species has slender, transverse stripes and long tails. In some forms, the background color is almost white and the black stripes are much heavier.
• **EARLY STAGES** The caterpillar is sluglike. Its body is green with yellow lines often spotted with red. It feeds on blackthorn *(Prunus spinosa)*.
• **DISTRIBUTION** Despite its common name, this species is widespread in Europe. Its range extends to North Africa and across temperate Asia to China.

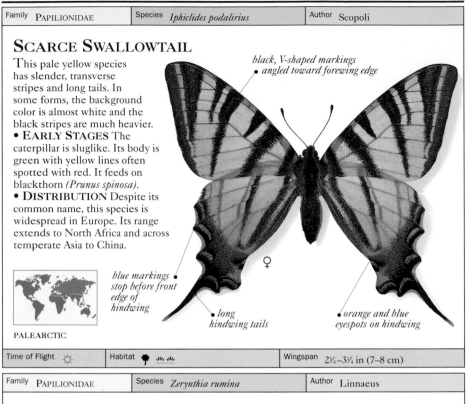

black, V-shaped markings angled toward forewing edge

♀

blue markings stop before front edge of hindwing

long hindwing tails

orange and blue eyespots on hindwing

PALEARCTIC

Time of Flight ☼	Habitat 🌳 ⚘ ⚘	Wingspan 2¾–3¼ in (7–8 cm)

Family PAPILIONIDAE	Species *Zerynthia rumina*	Author Linnaeus

SPANISH FESTOON

A very distinctive black and yellow butterfly with an intricate, lace-like and delicate pattern, the Spanish festoon belongs to an easily recognizable group of tailless swallowtails. It can be distinguished from other closely related festoons by the vivid, and conspicuous red markings on the forewing. Spanish festoons can be seen on the wing from late winter to late spring. Females are usually larger than the male, and are a darker shade of yellow.
• **EARLY STAGES** The caterpillar is pale brown with rows of blunt, red spines along its body. It feeds on birthwort *(Aristolochia)*.
• **DISTRIBUTION** This butterfly species can be found among the rough, stony hillsides of southeastern France, Spain, and Portugal. It is particularly common around coastal regions within its habitat.

short, robust antennae

♀

fine black scale tufts on hindwing margins

characteristic zigzag pattern to wing margins

PALEARCTIC

Time of Flight ☼	Habitat ⚘ ⚘	Wingspan 1¾–2 in (4.5–5 cm)

Family PAPILIONIDAE	Species *Lamproptera meges*	Author Zincken

GREEN DRAGONTAIL

This butterfly is easily recognized by its translucent
forewings and drooping tail. The only other species in
this genus *(Lamproptera curius)* can be distinguished
by the presence of a transverse white band on the wings.
Green dragontails resemble dragonflies in flight and
have a very rapid wingbeat. Even when resting, they
vibrate their wings. Unlike the majority of butterflies,
they hover over flowers while feeding.
• **EARLY STAGES** Although the caterpillar does not
appear to be known, the related *Lamproptera curius*
has a dark apple-green caterpillar that feeds on
Illigera cordata foliage.
• **DISTRIBUTION** Usually found in
sunlit forest clearings from India to
southern China, Malaysia, the
Philippines, and Sulawesi.

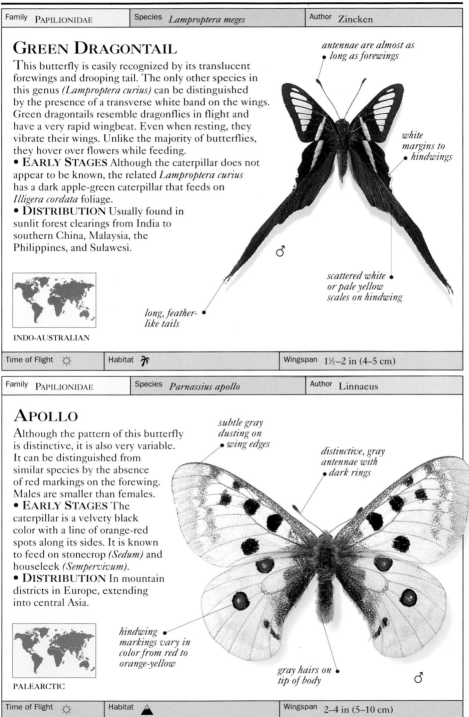

antennae are almost as long as forewings

white margins to hindwings

♂

scattered white or pale yellow scales on hindwing

long, feather-like tails

INDO-AUSTRALIAN

Time of Flight ☼	Habitat 🦋	Wingspan 1½–2 in (4–5 cm)

Family PAPILIONIDAE	Species *Parnassius apollo*	Author Linnaeus

APOLLO

Although the pattern of this butterfly
is distinctive, it is also very variable.
It can be distinguished from
similar species by the absence
of red markings on the forewing.
Males are smaller than females.
• **EARLY STAGES** The
caterpillar is a velvety black
color with a line of orange-red
spots along its sides. It is known
to feed on stonecrop *(Sedum)* and
houseleek *(Sempervivum)*.
• **DISTRIBUTION** In mountain
districts in Europe, extending
into central Asia.

subtle gray dusting on wing edges

distinctive, gray antennae with dark rings

hindwing markings vary in color from red to orange-yellow

gray hairs on tip of body

♂

PALEARCTIC

Time of Flight ☼	Habitat ⛰	Wingspan 2–4 in (5–10 cm)

Family PAPILIONIDAE	Species *Cressida cressida*	Author Fabricius

BIG GREASY BUTTERFLY

The male butterfly has transparent forewings with two large black spots on each. Freshly emerged females are dark gray with a distinctive pattern, but most of the wing scales are soon shed and the wings take on a paler, greasy appearance.
• **EARLY STAGES** The caterpillar is dark brown (often mottled with creamy white) but is variable in color and pattern. It feeds on pipevines *(Aristolochia)*.
• **DISTRIBUTION** There are two subspecies of this butterfly found in Australia. A third subspecies occurs in Papua New Guinea.

distinctive brown and cream caterpillar

red spots on cream bands

CATERPILLAR OF
CRESSIDA CRESSIDA

the male has narrower forewings than the female

red spots on hindwings

♂

dull appearance due to loss of scales

black and red body indicates that this is a poisonous species

♀

INDO-AUSTRALIAN

Time of Flight ☀	Habitat 🌴	Wingspan 2¼–3 in (7–7.5 cm)

| Family PAPILIONIDAE | Species *Ornithoptera alexandrae* | Author Rothschild |

QUEEN ALEXANDRA'S BIRDWING

This is the largest known butterfly in the world. The males are considerably smaller than the females and are distinguishable from related species by their striking wing pattern and color. The underside of the male hindwing is golden-yellow with black veining and is shaded with green.

• **EARLY STAGES** The caterpillar is reddish black with bright red, fleshy, pointed tentacles and a cream-colored saddle marking in the middle of its body. It feeds on *Aristolochia schlecteri*.

• **DISTRIBUTION** Confined to southeast Papua New Guinea east of the Owen Stanley Mountains. On US Endangered Species List.

caterpillar has brightly colored tentacles

CATERPILLAR OF
ORNITHOPTERA ALEXANDRAE

metallic-blue, black, and greenish yellow coloring on wings

♂

bright color of body indicates that it may be distasteful

small white spot on hindwings distinguish this from other species

strong black veining on hindwings

pale body color

♀

INDO-AUSTRALIAN

| Time of Flight ☼ | Habitat 🌴 | Wingspan 6¾–11 in (17–28 cm) |

| Family PAPILIONIDAE | Species *Ornithoptera priamus* | Author Linnaeus |

CAIRNS BIRDWING

This common name applies to just one of a
large number of subspecies of this magnificent
birdwing butterfly. Males are distinctively
patterned with black and green on the upperside.
The underside of the forewing is black with a
turquoise center, overlaid with black veins. The
females are much larger than the males, and their
wings are black with white markings. These
birdwings have a strong, gliding flight.

• **EARLY STAGES** The caterpillar varies in
color from blackish brown to gray, with
long, fleshy spines. It feeds on
pipevines *(Aristolochia)*.

• **DISTRIBUTION** From the
Moluccas to Papua New
Guinea, the Solomon Islands,
and northern Australia.

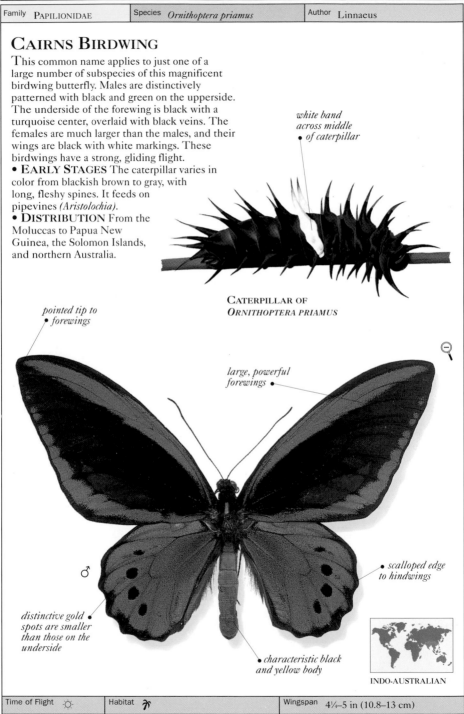

white band
across middle
• of caterpillar

**CATERPILLAR OF
*ORNITHOPTERA PRIAMUS***

pointed tip to
• forewings

large, powerful
forewings •

♂

distinctive gold •
spots are smaller
than those on the
underside

• scalloped edge
to hindwings

• characteristic black
and yellow body

INDO-AUSTRALIAN

| Time of Flight ☼ | Habitat 🌴 | Wingspan 4¼–5 in (10.8–13 cm) |

Family PAPILIONIDAE	Species *Troides brookiana*	Author Wallace

RAJAH BROOKE'S BIRDWING

Although there are several named subspecies, all
males are similar in appearance with a distinctive
green pattern on a black background. Females vary
in color from olive-green with white or green
markings to black with coppery green markings.
The hindwings of the females are often flushed
with metallic-blue at the base. These birdwings
have a powerful, soaring flight. Males can often
be found drinking from wet mud; both sexes
are attracted to flowers.

PUPA OF
TROIDES BROOKIANA

• **EARLY STAGES** The caterpillar is dark
brown to gray with a lighter saddle marking
in the middle of the body. It has long,
tentaclelike projections, which are a pale
yellowish brown. The shorter "tentacles"
are the same color as the body. The head
is large, black, and shiny. The caterpillar
eats pipevines *(Aristolochia)*.

• **DISTRIBUTION** Occurs from
Malaysia to Sumatra and Borneo.

*• the pupa
resembles a
dead leaf*

*typical elongated
forewing shape of
• birdwing butterflies*

*striking contrast
of green on solid
black base •*

• red collar

*• characteristic
wing pattern is
also present in
some females*

♂

• jet-black body

INDO-AUSTRALIAN

Time of Flight ☼	Habitat 🕷	Wingspan 4¾–7 in (12–17.8 cm)

PIERIDAE

T HIS IS A LARGE family of more than 1,000 species of butterfly. Most of the species are predominantly white, yellow, or orange in color and are often referred to collectively as whites, yellows, or sulphurs. Pigments that are derived from the body's waste products explain the distinct coloring, which is a feature peculiar to this family of butterflies. It is believed that the name "butterfly" originates from a member of the Pieridae – the bright yellow brimstone *(Gonepteryx rhamni)* that was known to the early British naturalists as the butter-colored fly.

This family includes the cabbage white butterflies *(Pieris brassicae* and *Pieris rapae)*, which are commonly seen in gardens, and are notorious pests.

Family PIERIDAE	Species *Appias nero*	Author Fabricius

ORANGE ALBATROSS

This striking butterfly is probably the only species in the world that is entirely orange in color. Females look similar to males but have a black border around the wings and a black band on the hindwing. Males are often seen drinking from the moist sand of riverbanks. Females are much less bold and tend to keep high in the tree canopy. They are known to feed from the flowers of a variety of trees.
• **EARLY STAGES** Little seems to be known about the early stages of this species except that the caterpillar feeds on plants of the family Capparidaceae.
• **DISTRIBUTION** Widely distributed from northern India to Burma, Malaysia, the Philippines, and Sulawesi.

INDO-AUSTRALIAN

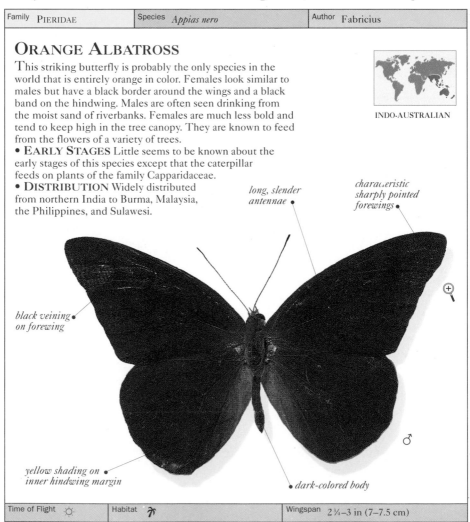

long, slender antennae

characteristic sharply pointed forewings

black veining on forewing

yellow shading on inner hindwing margin

dark-colored body

♂

Time of Flight ☼	Habitat 🌴	Wingspan 2¼–3 in (7–7.5 cm)

Family PIERIDAE	Species *Mylothris chloris*	Author Fabricius

COMMON DOTTED BORDER

This species of butterfly has two distinct geographical forms (the race shown here is from western Africa). The upperside of the female's forewing is similar to the underside but the hindwing upperside is a pale salmon-pink. Males of the east and the South African races differ. The base of the forewings is flushed with pink and black colored markings on the hindwings reduced to black dots.

• **EARLY STAGES** The caterpillar is black with transverse reddish bands. It feeds on the foliage of various mistletoes (Loranthaceae).

• **DISTRIBUTION** Very common in woodland, savanna, parks, and gardens throughout Africa south of the Sahara.

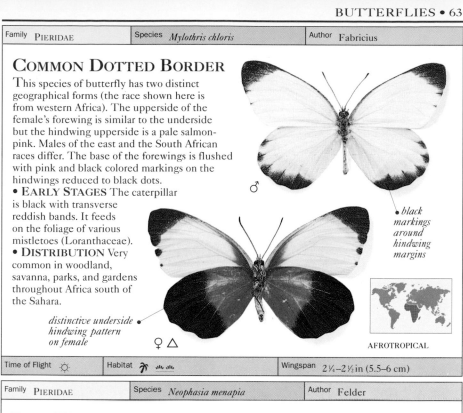

• *black markings around hindwing margins*

distinctive underside hindwing pattern on female

♂

♀ △

AFROTROPICAL

Time of Flight ☼	Habitat 🌿 ⚘ ⚘	Wingspan 2¼–2½ in (5.5–6 cm)

Family PIERIDAE	Species *Neophasia menapia*	Author Felder

PINE WHITE

The leading edge and apex of the forewing of this distinctive white butterly are strongly marked with black. The hindwing is covered with a fine network of black veins. In the female these veins are more strongly marked towards the wing margins. On the underside of the hindwing, the veins are strongly outlined with black in both sexes. Pine whites are on the wing from midsummer to early autumn but are most commonly seen in late summer.

• **EARLY STAGES** The caterpillar is dark green with white stripes along the back and sides, giving it effective camouflage when it feeds on pine needles.

• **DISTRIBUTION** Found in coniferous woodland from southern Canada to southern California in the USA, and Mexico.

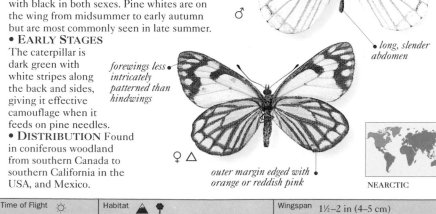

♂

• *long, slender abdomen*

forewings less intricately patterned than hindwings

♀ △

outer margin edged with orange or reddish pink

NEARCTIC

Time of Flight ☼	Habitat ⛰ 🌳	Wingspan 1½–2 in (4–5 cm)

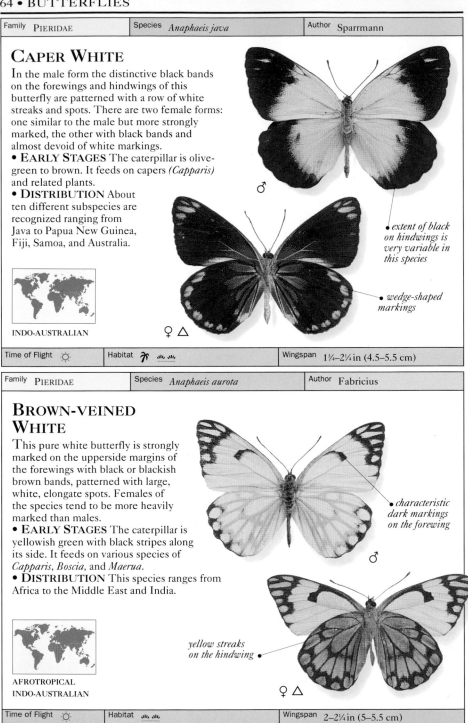

Family PIERIDAE	Species *Anaphaeis java*	Author Sparrmann

CAPER WHITE

In the male form the distinctive black bands on the forewings and hindwings of this butterfly are patterned with a row of white streaks and spots. There are two female forms: one similar to the male but more strongly marked, the other with black bands and almost devoid of white markings.
• **EARLY STAGES** The caterpillar is olive-green to brown. It feeds on capers *(Capparis)* and related plants.
• **DISTRIBUTION** About ten different subspecies are recognized ranging from Java to Papua New Guinea, Fiji, Samoa, and Australia.

INDO-AUSTRALIAN

• *extent of black on hindwings is very variable in this species*

• *wedge-shaped markings*

♀ △

Time of Flight ☼	Habitat 🦋 ⚘ ⚘	Wingspan 1¾–2¼ in (4.5–5.5 cm)

Family PIERIDAE	Species *Anaphaeis aurota*	Author Fabricius

BROWN-VEINED WHITE

This pure white butterfly is strongly marked on the upperside margins of the forewings with black or blackish brown bands, patterned with large, white, elongate spots. Females of the species tend to be more heavily marked than males.
• **EARLY STAGES** The caterpillar is yellowish green with black stripes along its side. It feeds on various species of *Capparis*, *Boscia*, and *Maerua*.
• **DISTRIBUTION** This species ranges from Africa to the Middle East and India.

AFROTROPICAL
INDO-AUSTRALIAN

• *characteristic dark markings on the forewing*

♂

yellow streaks on the hindwing •

♀ △

Time of Flight ☼	Habitat ⚘ ⚘	Wingspan 2–2¼ in (5–5.5 cm)

Family PIERIDAE	Species *Delias mysis*	Author Fabricius

UNION JACK

The Union Jack has distinctive black tips on the forewings, marked with four white spots. The hindwing is marked with black along the margins.
• **EARLY STAGES** The caterpillar is yellowish green with long, white hairs. Its head is black. The caterpillar feeds on mistletoe *(Viscum).*
• **DISTRIBUTION** Found in rain forests of northern Australia, Papua New Guinea, and adjacent islands.

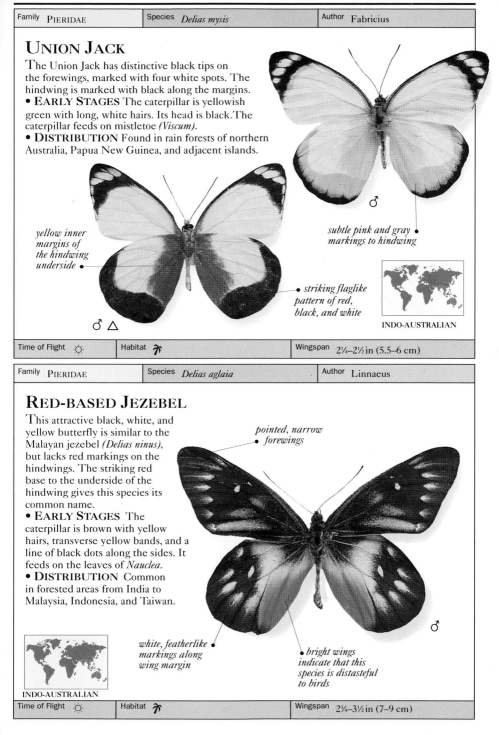

yellow inner margins of the hindwing underside •

♂ △

♂

• *subtle pink and gray markings to hindwing*

• *striking flaglike pattern of red, black, and white*

INDO-AUSTRALIAN

Time of Flight ☼	Habitat 🌴	Wingspan 2¼–2½ in (5.5–6 cm)

Family PIERIDAE	Species *Delias aglaia*	Author Linnaeus

RED-BASED JEZEBEL

This attractive black, white, and yellow butterfly is similar to the Malayan jezebel *(Delias ninus),* but lacks red markings on the hindwings. The striking red base to the underside of the hindwing gives this species its common name.
• **EARLY STAGES** The caterpillar is brown with yellow hairs, transverse yellow bands, and a line of black dots along the sides. It feeds on the leaves of *Nauclea.*
• **DISTRIBUTION** Common in forested areas from India to Malaysia, Indonesia, and Taiwan.

pointed, narrow • forewings

♂

white, featherlike markings along wing margin •

• *bright wings indicate that this species is distasteful to birds*

INDO-AUSTRALIAN

Time of Flight ☼	Habitat 🌴	Wingspan 2¼–3½ in (7–9 cm)

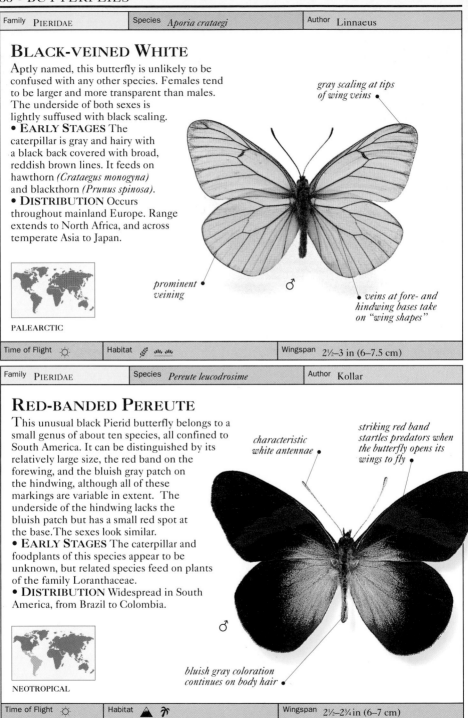

Family PIERIDAE	Species *Aporia crataegi*	Author Linnaeus

BLACK-VEINED WHITE

Aptly named, this butterfly is unlikely to be confused with any other species. Females tend to be larger and more transparent than males. The underside of both sexes is lightly suffused with black scaling.
• **EARLY STAGES** The caterpillar is gray and hairy with a black back covered with broad, reddish brown lines. It feeds on hawthorn *(Crataegus monogyna)* and blackthorn *(Prunus spinosa)*.
• **DISTRIBUTION** Occurs throughout mainland Europe. Range extends to North Africa, and across temperate Asia to Japan.

PALEARCTIC

gray scaling at tips of wing veins

prominent veining

♂

veins at fore- and hindwing bases take on "wing shapes"

Time of Flight ☼	Habitat	Wingspan 2½–3 in (6–7.5 cm)

Family PIERIDAE	Species *Pereute leucodrosime*	Author Kollar

RED-BANDED PEREUTE

This unusual black Pierid butterfly belongs to a small genus of about ten species, all confined to South America. It can be distinguished by its relatively large size, the red band on the forewing, and the bluish gray patch on the hindwing, although all of these markings are variable in extent. The underside of the hindwing lacks the bluish patch but has a small red spot at the base. The sexes look similar.
• **EARLY STAGES** The caterpillar and foodplants of this species appear to be unknown, but related species feed on plants of the family Loranthaceae.
• **DISTRIBUTION** Widespread in South America, from Brazil to Colombia.

NEOTROPICAL

characteristic white antennae

striking red band startles predators when the butterfly opens its wings to fly

♂

bluish gray coloration continues on body hair

Time of Flight ☼	Habitat	Wingspan 2½–2¾ in (6–7 cm)

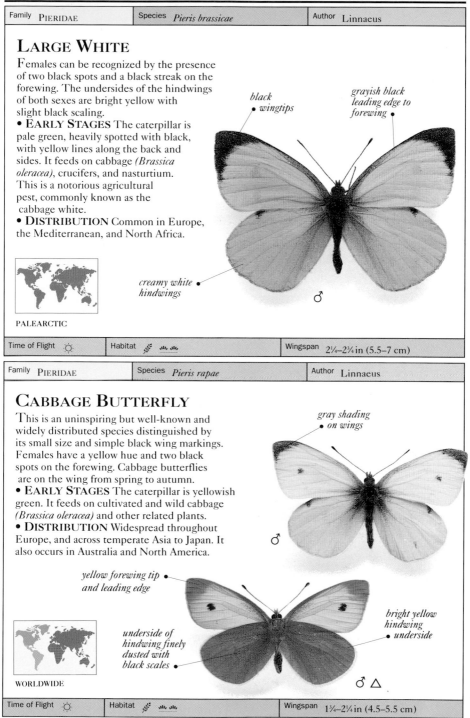

| Family PIERIDAE | Species *Pieris brassicae* | Author Linnaeus |

LARGE WHITE

Females can be recognized by the presence of two black spots and a black streak on the forewing. The undersides of the hindwings of both sexes are bright yellow with slight black scaling.
• **EARLY STAGES** The caterpillar is pale green, heavily spotted with black, with yellow lines along the back and sides. It feeds on cabbage *(Brassica oleracea)*, crucifers, and nasturtium. This is a notorious agricultural pest, commonly known as the cabbage white.
• **DISTRIBUTION** Common in Europe, the Mediterranean, and North Africa.

black
• wingtips

grayish black
leading edge to
forewing •

creamy white •
hindwings

♂

PALEARCTIC

| Time of Flight ☼ | Habitat | Wingspan 2¼–2¾ in (5.5–7 cm) |

| Family PIERIDAE | Species *Pieris rapae* | Author Linnaeus |

CABBAGE BUTTERFLY

This is an uninspiring but well-known and widely distributed species distinguished by its small size and simple black wing markings. Females have a yellow hue and two black spots on the forewing. Cabbage butterflies are on the wing from spring to autumn.
• **EARLY STAGES** The caterpillar is yellowish green. It feeds on cultivated and wild cabbage *(Brassica oleracea)* and other related plants.
• **DISTRIBUTION** Widespread throughout Europe, and across temperate Asia to Japan. It also occurs in Australia and North America.

gray shading
• on wings

♂

yellow forewing tip •
and leading edge

bright yellow
hindwing
• underside

underside of
hindwing finely
dusted with
black scales •

WORLDWIDE

♂ △

| Time of Flight ☼ | Habitat | Wingspan 1¾–2¼ in (4.5–5.5 cm) |

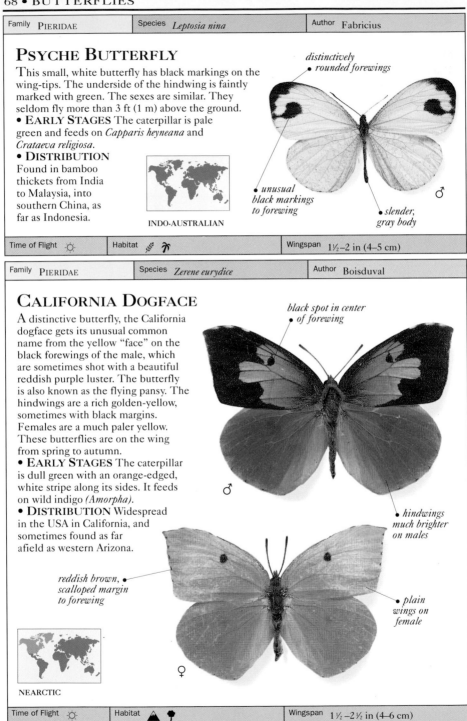

Family PIERIDAE	Species *Leptosia nina*	Author Fabricius

PSYCHE BUTTERFLY

This small, white butterfly has black markings on the wing-tips. The underside of the hindwing is faintly marked with green. The sexes are similar. They seldom fly more than 3 ft (1 m) above the ground.
• **EARLY STAGES** The caterpillar is pale green and feeds on *Capparis heyneana* and *Crataeva religiosa*.
• **DISTRIBUTION** Found in bamboo thickets from India to Malaysia, into southern China, as far as Indonesia.

INDO-AUSTRALIAN

distinctively • rounded forewings

• unusual black markings to forewing

♂

• slender, gray body

Time of Flight ☼	Habitat 🌿 🌴	Wingspan 1½–2 in (4–5 cm)

Family PIERIDAE	Species *Zerene eurydice*	Author Boisduval

CALIFORNIA DOGFACE

A distinctive butterfly, the California dogface gets its unusual common name from the yellow "face" on the black forewings of the male, which are sometimes shot with a beautiful reddish purple luster. The butterfly is also known as the flying pansy. The hindwings are a rich golden-yellow, sometimes with black margins. Females are a much paler yellow. These butterflies are on the wing from spring to autumn.
• **EARLY STAGES** The caterpillar is dull green with an orange-edged, white stripe along its sides. It feeds on wild indigo *(Amorpha)*.
• **DISTRIBUTION** Widespread in the USA in California, and sometimes found as far afield as western Arizona.

black spot in center • of forewing

♂

hindwings • much brighter on males

reddish brown, • scalloped margin to forewing

• plain wings on female

♀

NEARCTIC

Time of Flight ☼	Habitat ⛰ 🌷	Wingspan 1½–2½ in (4–6 cm)

Family PIERIDAE	Species *Catopsilia florella*	Author Fabricius

AFRICAN MIGRANT

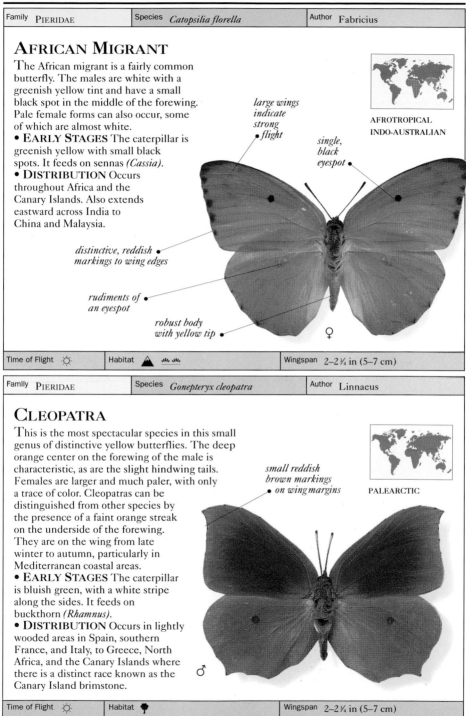

The African migrant is a fairly common butterfly. The males are white with a greenish yellow tint and have a small black spot in the middle of the forewing. Pale female forms can also occur, some of which are almost white.
• **EARLY STAGES** The caterpillar is greenish yellow with small black spots. It feeds on sennas *(Cassia)*.
• **DISTRIBUTION** Occurs throughout Africa and the Canary Islands. Also extends eastward across India to China and Malaysia.

large wings indicate strong flight

single, black eyespot

AFROTROPICAL
INDO-AUSTRALIAN

distinctive, reddish markings to wing edges

rudiments of an eyespot

robust body with yellow tip

♀

Time of Flight ☼	Habitat ▲ ⬚ ⬚	Wingspan 2–2 ¾ in (5–7 cm)

Family PIERIDAE	Species *Gonepteryx cleopatra*	Author Linnaeus

CLEOPATRA

This is the most spectacular species in this small genus of distinctive yellow butterflies. The deep orange center on the forewing of the male is characteristic, as are the slight hindwing tails. Females are larger and much paler, with only a trace of color. Cleopatras can be distinguished from other species by the presence of a faint orange streak on the underside of the forewing. They are on the wing from late winter to autumn, particularly in Mediterranean coastal areas.
• **EARLY STAGES** The caterpillar is bluish green, with a white stripe along the sides. It feeds on buckthorn *(Rhamnus)*.
• **DISTRIBUTION** Occurs in lightly wooded areas in Spain, southern France, and Italy, to Greece, North Africa, and the Canary Islands where there is a distinct race known as the Canary Island brimstone.

small reddish brown markings on wing margins

PALEARCTIC

♂

Time of Flight ☼	Habitat ♠	Wingspan 2–2 ¾ in (5–7 cm)

Family	PIERIDAE	Species	*Phoebis philea*	Author	Johansson

ORANGE-BARRED SULPHUR

Males of this species have a broad orange bar on the
forewing, giving rise to the common name. Females are
yellow or white with brown or black markings on both the
fore- and hindwing borders. The underside is variably
colored with salmon-pink and purplish hues. The
butterfly is also commonly known as the yellow apricot.

• **EARLY STAGES** The caterpillar is yellowish green
with transverse wrinkles and a brownish black band along
the sides. It feeds on sennas *(Cassia)*.

• **DISTRIBUTION** Widespread from southern Brazil
to Central America
and southern
Florida, in the
USA, where it
often occurs in
parks and
gardens. It also
strays as far north
as New York.

NEOTROPICAL

*traces of dark markings
on forewing tips
of male*

*V-shaped
marking
to forewing*

*dark shading
to hindwing
margin*

♂

*central
spot in
forewing
of female*

*slight
scalloping to
hindwings*

*smoky-red
hindwing
borders*

♀

Time of Flight	☼	Habitat	🌴	Wingspan	2¾–3¼ in (7–8 cm)

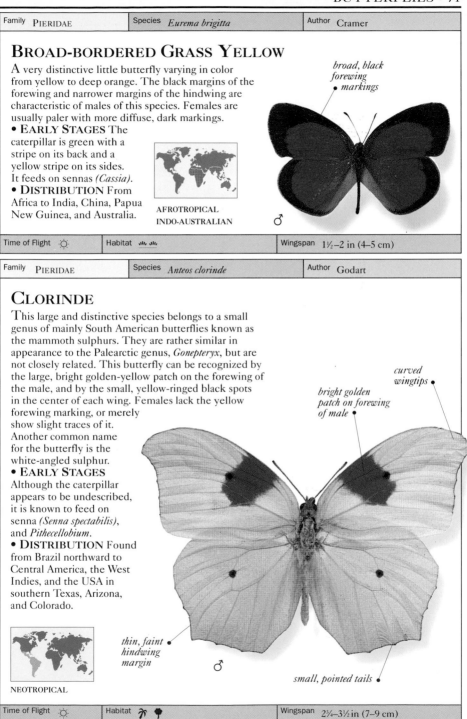

| Family | PIERIDAE | Species | *Eurema brigitta* | Author | Cramer |

BROAD-BORDERED GRASS YELLOW

A very distinctive little butterfly varying in color
from yellow to deep orange. The black margins of the
forewing and narrower margins of the hindwing are
characteristic of males of this species. Females are
usually paler with more diffuse, dark markings.
• **EARLY STAGES** The
caterpillar is green with a
stripe on its back and a
yellow stripe on its sides.
It feeds on sennas *(Cassia)*.
• **DISTRIBUTION** From
Africa to India, China, Papua
New Guinea, and Australia.

*broad, black
forewing
markings*

AFROTROPICAL
INDO-AUSTRALIAN

♂

| Time of Flight ☼ | Habitat ⏜ ⏜ | Wingspan 1½–2 in (4–5 cm) |

| Family | PIERIDAE | Species | *Anteos clorinde* | Author | Godart |

CLORINDE

This large and distinctive species belongs to a small
genus of mainly South American butterflies known as
the mammoth sulphurs. They are rather similar in
appearance to the Palearctic genus, *Gonepteryx*, but are
not closely related. This butterfly can be recognized by
the large, bright golden-yellow patch on the forewing of
the male, and by the small, yellow-ringed black spots
in the center of each wing. Females lack the yellow
forewing marking, or merely
show slight traces of it.
Another common name
for the butterfly is the
white-angled sulphur.
• **EARLY STAGES**
Although the caterpillar
appears to be undescribed,
it is known to feed on
senna *(Senna spectabilis)*,
and *Pithecellobium*.
• **DISTRIBUTION** Found
from Brazil northward to
Central America, the West
Indies, and the USA in
southern Texas, Arizona,
and Colorado.

*curved
wingtips •*

*bright golden
patch on forewing
of male •*

*thin, faint •
hindwing
margin*

♂

small, pointed tails •

NEOTROPICAL

| Time of Flight ☼ | Habitat ⏜ ♣ | Wingspan 2¾–3½ in (7–9 cm) |

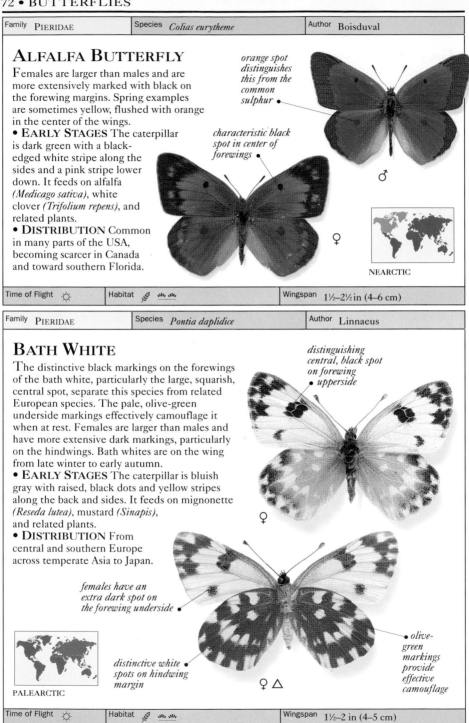

| Family PIERIDAE | Species *Colias eurytheme* | Author Boisduval |

ALFALFA BUTTERFLY

Females are larger than males and are
more extensively marked with black on
the forewing margins. Spring examples
are sometimes yellow, flushed with orange
in the center of the wings.
• **EARLY STAGES** The caterpillar
is dark green with a black-
edged white stripe along the
sides and a pink stripe lower
down. It feeds on alfalfa
(Medicago sativa), white
clover *(Trifolium repens)*, and
related plants.
• **DISTRIBUTION** Common
in many parts of the USA,
becoming scarcer in Canada
and toward southern Florida.

orange spot
distinguishes
this from the
common
sulphur

characteristic black
spot in center of
forewings

♂

♀

NEARCTIC

| Time of Flight ☼ | Habitat | Wingspan 1½–2½ in (4–6 cm) |

| Family PIERIDAE | Species *Pontia daplidice* | Author Linnaeus |

BATH WHITE

The distinctive black markings on the forewings
of the bath white, particularly the large, squarish,
central spot, separate this species from related
European species. The pale, olive-green
underside markings effectively camouflage it
when at rest. Females are larger than males and
have more extensive dark markings, particularly
on the hindwings. Bath whites are on the wing
from late winter to early autumn.
• **EARLY STAGES** The caterpillar is bluish
gray with raised, black dots and yellow stripes
along the back and sides. It feeds on mignonette
(Reseda lutea), mustard *(Sinapis)*,
and related plants.
• **DISTRIBUTION** From
central and southern Europe
across temperate Asia to Japan.

distinguishing
central, black spot
on forewing
upperside

♀

females have an
extra dark spot on
the forewing underside

distinctive white
spots on hindwing
margin

olive-
green
markings
provide
effective
camouflage

♀ △

PALEARCTIC

| Time of Flight ☼ | Habitat | Wingspan 1½–2 in (4–5 cm) |

Family PIERIDAE	Species *Anthocharis cardamines*	Author Linnaeus

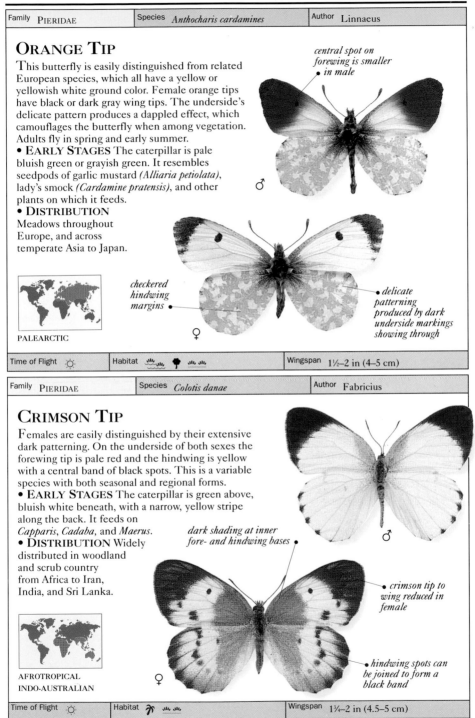

ORANGE TIP

This butterfly is easily distinguished from related European species, which all have a yellow or yellowish white ground color. Female orange tips have black or dark gray wing tips. The underside's delicate pattern produces a dappled effect, which camouflages the butterfly when among vegetation. Adults fly in spring and early summer.

• **EARLY STAGES** The caterpillar is pale bluish green or grayish green. It resembles seedpods of garlic mustard *(Alliaria petiolata)*, lady's smock *(Cardamine pratensis)*, and other plants on which it feeds.

• **DISTRIBUTION** Meadows throughout Europe, and across temperate Asia to Japan.

central spot on forewing is smaller in male

checkered hindwing margins

delicate patterning produced by dark underside markings showing through

PALEARCTIC

Time of Flight ☼	Habitat 〰🌳	Wingspan 1½–2 in (4–5 cm)

Family PIERIDAE	Species *Colotis danae*	Author Fabricius

CRIMSON TIP

Females are easily distinguished by their extensive dark patterning. On the underside of both sexes the forewing tip is pale red and the hindwing is yellow with a central band of black spots. This is a variable species with both seasonal and regional forms.

• **EARLY STAGES** The caterpillar is green above, bluish white beneath, with a narrow, yellow stripe along the back. It feeds on *Capparis*, *Cadaba*, and *Maerus*.

• **DISTRIBUTION** Widely distributed in woodland and scrub country from Africa to Iran, India, and Sri Lanka.

dark shading at inner fore- and hindwing bases

crimson tip to wing reduced in female

hindwing spots can be joined to form a black band

AFROTROPICAL
INDO-AUSTRALIAN

Time of Flight ☼	Habitat 🌴	Wingspan 1¾–2 in (4.5–5 cm)

Family PIERIDAE	Species *Dismorphia amphione*	Author Cramer

TIGER PIERID

This unusual Pierid butterfly belongs to a large genus of about 40 species of South American butterfly that are remarkable mimics of various distasteful butterflies. The striking black, orange, and yellow patterning of both sexes, which has earned them their common name, is very variable. There are many named forms and subspecies. They are mostly seen flying along forest edges from sea level to about 3,300 ft (1,000 m).

• **EARLY STAGES** The caterpillar is a dark, translucent green. It feeds on *Inga sapindoides*, *Inga densiflora*, and related species.

• **DISTRIBUTION** Common in South and Central America and also in the West Indies, and Mexico.

unusual wing shape for this family

large translucent white patch on male hindwing

bands of yellow spots on each forewing

long, slender body

NEOTROPICAL

Time of Flight ☼	Habitat 🦋	Wingspan 1½–1¾ in (4–4.5 cm)

Family PIERIDAE	Species *Leptidea sinapis*	Author Linnaeus

WOOD WHITE

A delicate white butterfly, the wood white belongs to a small group of European species with long, slender abdomens. It is distinguished by its relatively small size and pure white wings with gray markings. Males have a distinctive gray spot at the tip of the forewing, while females simply have a few pale gray streaks. The underside is tinted with yellow, and the hindwings are patterned with gray along the veins. The butterflies have a weak, fluttering flight close to the ground.

• **EARLY STAGES** The caterpillar is yellowish green with a dark line along the back, and yellow lines along the sides. It feeds on the foliage of various wild plants of the pea family, particularly *Lathyrus*.

• **DISTRIBUTION** Occurs locally in wooded country in many areas of Europe, including the British Isles.

pale yellow tips to underside of forewings

slender body is typical of this group

PALEARCTIC

Time of Flight ☼	Habitat 🌳	Wingspan 1½–2 in (4–5 cm)

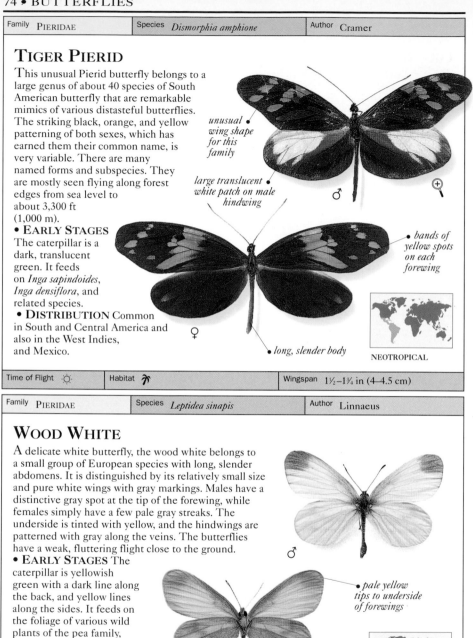

Family PIERIDAE	Species *Hebomoia glaucippe*	Author Linnaeus

GREAT ORANGE TIP

This handsome species is the largest Pierid
butterfly in Asia. Females are much darker than
males and have an extensive pattern of dark spots
on the hindwings. The undersides of both sexes are
similar, but strikingly different from the uppersides.
The entire hindwing and the outer half of the
forewing are delicately patterned with shades of
brown and buff, creating the appearance of a dead
leaf when the butterfly rests on the ground with
its wings closed. Great orange tips have a fast
and powerful flight. Males are often seen
congregating on moist
ground by streams,
but females seldom
leave the shelter of
the forest.
• **EARLY STAGES**
The caterpillar is green
with a pale stripe along
each side. It feeds on
Crataeva religiosa and
Capparis moonii.
• **DISTRIBUTION** Occurs
from India to Malaysia,
China, and Japan.

INDO-AUSTRALIAN
PALEARCTIC

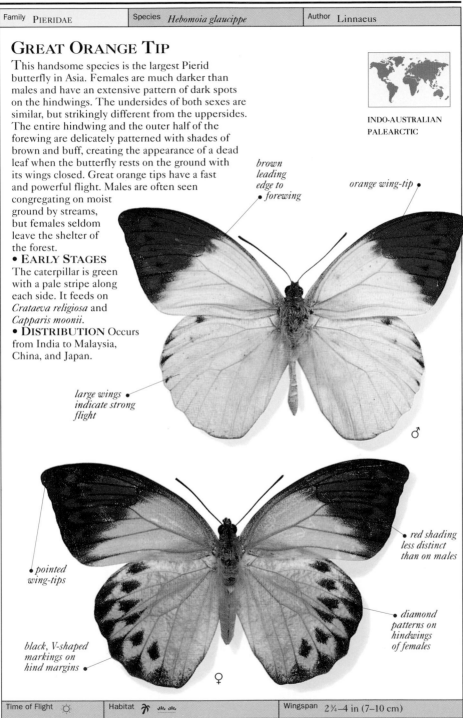

brown
leading
edge to
• forewing

orange wing-tip •

large wings •
indicate strong
flight

♂

• pointed
wing-tips

• red shading
less distinct
than on males

• diamond
patterns on
hindwings
of females

black, V-shaped
markings on
hind margins •

♀

Time of Flight ☼	Habitat 🌴 ⚘ ⚘	Wingspan 2¾–4 in (7–10 cm)

LYCAENIDAE

THIS is a large family of more than 5,000 small, brightly-colored butterflies occurring throughout the world, but mostly in tropical and subtropical regions. The sexes often differ in coloration, and the undersides usually differ from the upper surfaces. There are several distinct groups of Lycaenidae. One large group, the hairstreaks, have tails and bright eyespot markings on their hindwings, which create a false "head" at the rear, thus diverting attackers from this area.

———— • ————

The caterpillars are often described as "sluglike." Many draw their head back into the body when threatened or resting. Some of them secrete a sweetish substance, which is very attractive to various species of ants.

Family LYCAENIDAE	Species *Liphyra brassolis*	Author Westwood

MOTH BUTTERFLY

This very large orange and black butterfly has an almost mothlike appearance and behavior, hence its common name. The males are much more extensively marked with black than the females.
• **EARLY STAGES** The caterpillar is smooth, elliptical in shape, and very flattened. It lives in the nests of tree ants, and feeds on the larvae. When the butterfly emerges from the pupa, the wings and body are covered with highly adhesive scales, which will stick to any ants that may attack it.
• **DISTRIBUTION** From India, across Southeast Asia to northern Australia.

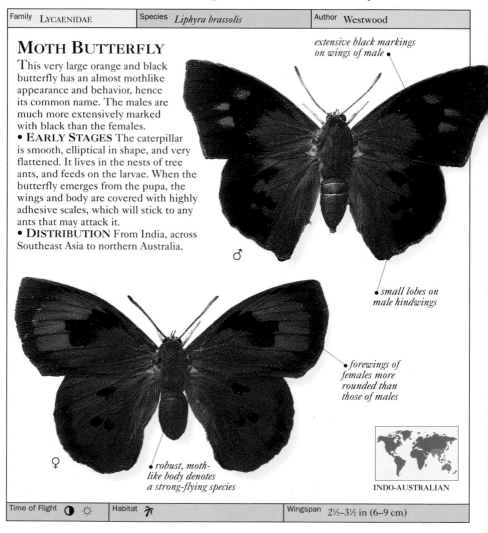

extensive black markings on wings of male •

♂

• small lobes on male hindwings

• forewings of females more rounded than those of males

♀

• robust, moth-like body denotes a strong-flying species

INDO-AUSTRALIAN

Time of Flight ◑ ☼	Habitat 🎋	Wingspan 2½–3½ in (6–9 cm)

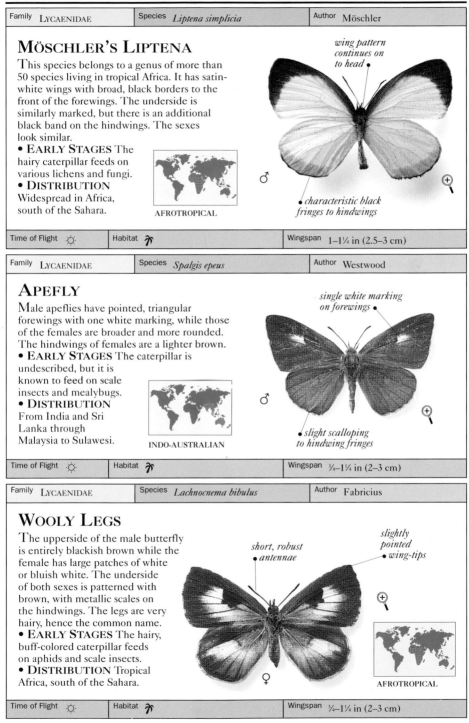

| Family | LYCAENIDAE | Species | *Liptena simplicia* | Author | Möschler |

MÖSCHLER'S LIPTENA

This species belongs to a genus of more than 50 species living in tropical Africa. It has satin-white wings with broad, black borders to the front of the forewings. The underside is similarly marked, but there is an additional black band on the hindwings. The sexes look similar.
• **EARLY STAGES** The hairy caterpillar feeds on various lichens and fungi.
• **DISTRIBUTION** Widespread in Africa, south of the Sahara.

wing pattern continues on to head

♂

AFROTROPICAL

characteristic black fringes to hindwings

| Time of Flight ☼ | Habitat 🜸 | | Wingspan 1–1¼ in (2.5–3 cm) |

| Family | LYCAENIDAE | Species | *Spalgis epeus* | Author | Westwood |

APEFLY

Male apeflies have pointed, triangular forewings with one white marking, while those of the females are broader and more rounded. The hindwings of females are a lighter brown.
• **EARLY STAGES** The caterpillar is undescribed, but it is known to feed on scale insects and mealybugs.
• **DISTRIBUTION** From India and Sri Lanka through Malaysia to Sulawesi.

single white marking on forewings

♂

INDO-AUSTRALIAN

slight scalloping to hindwing fringes

| Time of Flight ☼ | Habitat 🜸 | | Wingspan ¾–1¼ in (2–3 cm) |

| Family | LYCAENIDAE | Species | *Lachnocnema bibulus* | Author | Fabricius |

WOOLY LEGS

The upperside of the male butterfly is entirely blackish brown while the female has large patches of white or bluish white. The underside of both sexes is patterned with brown, with metallic scales on the hindwings. The legs are very hairy, hence the common name.
• **EARLY STAGES** The hairy, buff-colored caterpillar feeds on aphids and scale insects.
• **DISTRIBUTION** Tropical Africa, south of the Sahara.

short, robust antennae

slightly pointed wing-tips

♀

AFROTROPICAL

| Time of Flight ☼ | Habitat 🜸 | | Wingspan ¾–1¼ in (2–3 cm) |

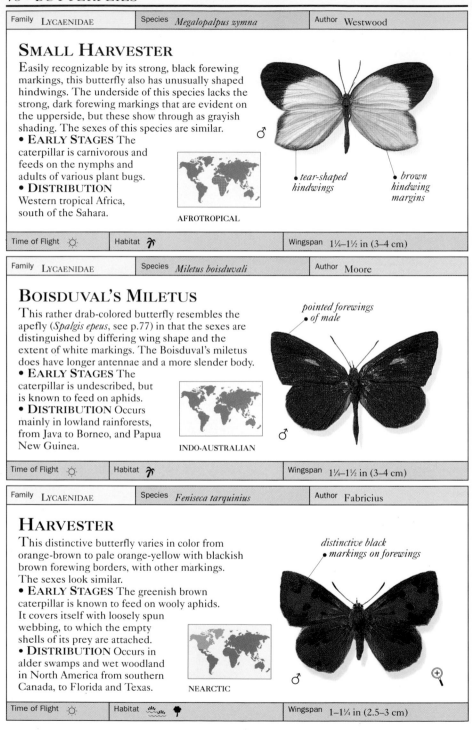

| Family LYCAENIDAE | Species *Megalopalpus zymna* | Author Westwood |

SMALL HARVESTER

Easily recognizable by its strong, black forewing markings, this butterfly also has unusually shaped hindwings. The underside of this species lacks the strong, dark forewing markings that are evident on the upperside, but these show through as grayish shading. The sexes of this species are similar.
• **EARLY STAGES** The caterpillar is carnivorous and feeds on the nymphs and adults of various plant bugs.
• **DISTRIBUTION** Western tropical Africa, south of the Sahara.

AFROTROPICAL

♂

• *tear-shaped hindwings*

• *brown hindwing margins*

| Time of Flight ☼ | Habitat 🌱 | Wingspan 1¼–1½ in (3–4 cm) |

| Family LYCAENIDAE | Species *Miletus boisduvali* | Author Moore |

BOISDUVAL'S MILETUS

This rather drab-colored butterfly resembles the apefly (*Spalgis epeus*, see p.77) in that the sexes are distinguished by differing wing shape and the extent of white markings. The Boisduval's miletus does have longer antennae and a more slender body.
• **EARLY STAGES** The caterpillar is undescribed, but is known to feed on aphids.
• **DISTRIBUTION** Occurs mainly in lowland rainforests, from Java to Borneo, and Papua New Guinea.

pointed forewings of male

♂

INDO-AUSTRALIAN

| Time of Flight ☼ | Habitat 🌱 | Wingspan 1¼–1½ in (3–4 cm) |

| Family LYCAENIDAE | Species *Feniseca tarquinius* | Author Fabricius |

HARVESTER

This distinctive butterfly varies in color from orange-brown to pale orange-yellow with blackish brown forewing borders, with other markings. The sexes look similar.
• **EARLY STAGES** The greenish brown caterpillar is known to feed on wooly aphids. It covers itself with loosely spun webbing, to which the empty shells of its prey are attached.
• **DISTRIBUTION** Occurs in alder swamps and wet woodland in North America from southern Canada, to Florida and Texas.

distinctive black markings on forewings

♂

NEARCTIC

| Time of Flight ☼ | Habitat 〰🌳 | Wingspan 1–1¼ in (2.5–3 cm) |

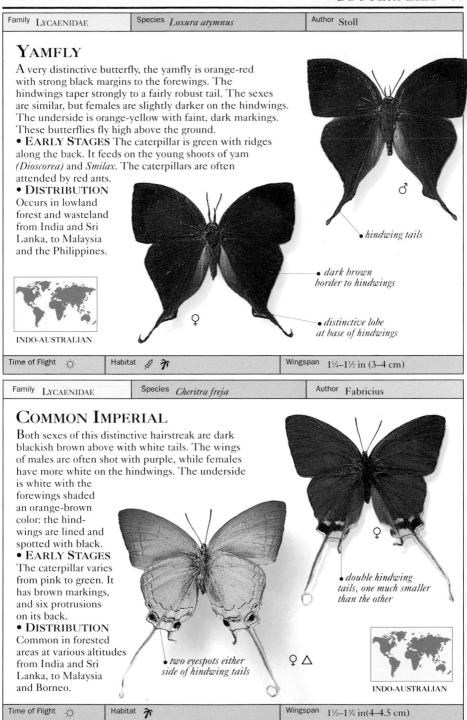

| Family | LYCAENIDAE | Species *Loxura atymnus* | Author Stoll |

YAMFLY

A very distinctive butterfly, the yamfly is orange-red with strong black margins to the forewings. The hindwings taper strongly to a fairly robust tail. The sexes are similar, but females are slightly darker on the hindwings. The underside is orange-yellow with faint, dark markings. These butterflies fly high above the ground.

• **EARLY STAGES** The caterpillar is green with ridges along the back. It feeds on the young shoots of yam *(Dioscorea)* and *Smilax*. The caterpillars are often attended by red ants.

• **DISTRIBUTION** Occurs in lowland forest and wasteland from India and Sri Lanka, to Malaysia and the Philippines.

INDO-AUSTRALIAN

• *hindwing tails*

• *dark brown border to hindwings*

• *distinctive lobe at base of hindwings*

| Time of Flight ☼ | Habitat | Wingspan 1¼–1½ in (3–4 cm) |

| Family | LYCAENIDAE | Species *Cheritra freja* | Author Fabricius |

COMMON IMPERIAL

Both sexes of this distinctive hairstreak are dark blackish brown above with white tails. The wings of males are often shot with purple, while females have more white on the hindwings. The underside is white with the forewings shaded an orange-brown color: the hindwings are lined and spotted with black.

• **EARLY STAGES** The caterpillar varies from pink to green. It has brown markings, and six protrusions on its back.

• **DISTRIBUTION** Common in forested areas at various altitudes from India and Sri Lanka, to Malaysia and Borneo.

• *double hindwing tails, one much smaller than the other*

• *two eyespots either side of hindwing tails*

♀ △

INDO-AUSTRALIAN

| Time of Flight ☼ | Habitat | Wingspan 1½–1¾ in (4–4.5 cm) |

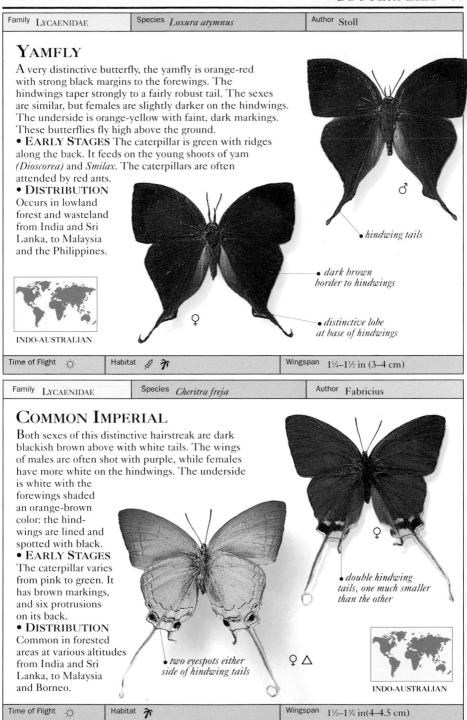

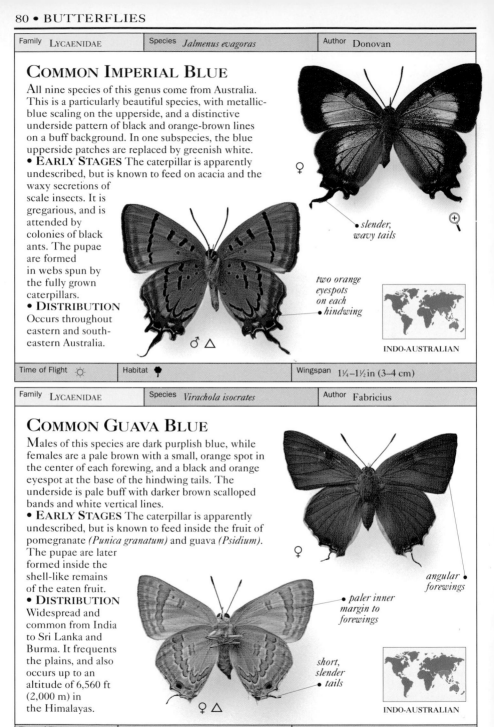

Family LYCAENIDAE	Species *Jalmenus evagoras*	Author Donovan

COMMON IMPERIAL BLUE

All nine species of this genus come from Australia. This is a particularly beautiful species, with metallic-blue scaling on the upperside, and a distinctive underside pattern of black and orange-brown lines on a buff background. In one subspecies, the blue upperside patches are replaced by greenish white.

• **EARLY STAGES** The caterpillar is apparently undescribed, but is known to feed on acacia and the waxy secretions of scale insects. It is gregarious, and is attended by colonies of black ants. The pupae are formed in webs spun by the fully grown caterpillars.

• **DISTRIBUTION** Occurs throughout eastern and south-eastern Australia.

♀

slender, wavy tails

two orange eyespots on each hindwing

♂ △

INDO-AUSTRALIAN

Time of Flight ☼	Habitat ❦	Wingspan 1¼–1½ in (3–4 cm)

Family LYCAENIDAE	Species *Virachola isocrates*	Author Fabricius

COMMON GUAVA BLUE

Males of this species are dark purplish blue, while females are a pale brown with a small, orange spot in the center of each forewing, and a black and orange eyespot at the base of the hindwing tails. The underside is pale buff with darker brown scalloped bands and white vertical lines.

• **EARLY STAGES** The caterpillar is apparently undescribed, but is known to feed inside the fruit of pomegranate *(Punica granatum)* and guava *(Psidium)*. The pupae are later formed inside the shell-like remains of the eaten fruit.

• **DISTRIBUTION** Widespread and common from India to Sri Lanka and Burma. It frequents the plains, and also occurs up to an altitude of 6,560 ft (2,000 m) in the Himalayas.

♀

angular forewings

paler inner margin to forewings

short, slender tails

♀ △

INDO-AUSTRALIAN

Time of Flight ☼	Habitat	Wingspan 1¼–2 in (3–5 cm)

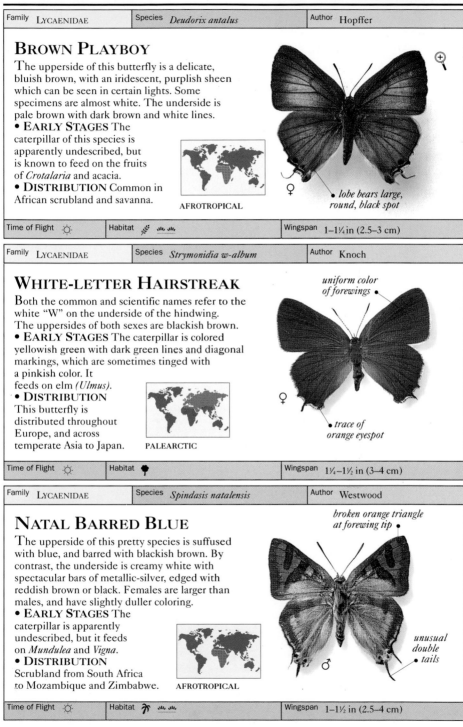

| Family LYCAENIDAE | Species *Deudorix antalus* | Author Hopffer |

BROWN PLAYBOY

The upperside of this butterfly is a delicate, bluish brown, with an iridescent, purplish sheen which can be seen in certain lights. Some specimens are almost white. The underside is pale brown with dark brown and white lines.
• **EARLY STAGES** The caterpillar of this species is apparently undescribed, but is known to feed on the fruits of *Crotalaria* and acacia.
• **DISTRIBUTION** Common in African scrubland and savanna.

AFROTROPICAL

♀
• *lobe bears large, round, black spot*

| Time of Flight ☀ | Habitat | Wingspan 1–1¼ in (2.5–3 cm) |

| Family LYCAENIDAE | Species *Strymonidia w-album* | Author Knoch |

WHITE-LETTER HAIRSTREAK

uniform color of forewings •

Both the common and scientific names refer to the white "W" on the underside of the hindwing. The uppersides of both sexes are blackish brown.
• **EARLY STAGES** The caterpillar is colored yellowish green with dark green lines and diagonal markings, which are sometimes tinged with a pinkish color. It feeds on elm *(Ulmus)*.
• **DISTRIBUTION** This butterfly is distributed throughout Europe, and across temperate Asia to Japan.

PALEARCTIC

♀
• *trace of orange eyespot*

| Time of Flight ☀ | Habitat | Wingspan 1¼–1½ in (3–4 cm) |

| Family LYCAENIDAE | Species *Spindasis natalensis* | Author Westwood |

NATAL BARRED BLUE

broken orange triangle at forewing tip •

The upperside of this pretty species is suffused with blue, and barred with blackish brown. By contrast, the underside is creamy white with spectacular bars of metallic-silver, edged with reddish brown or black. Females are larger than males, and have slightly duller coloring.
• **EARLY STAGES** The caterpillar is apparently undescribed, but it feeds on *Mundulea* and *Vigna*.
• **DISTRIBUTION** Scrubland from South Africa to Mozambique and Zimbabwe.

AFROTROPICAL

♂
unusual double • *tails*

| Time of Flight ☀ | Habitat | Wingspan 1–1½ in (2.5–4 cm) |

Family LYCAENIDAE	Species *Ogyris genoveva*	Author Hewitson

GENOVEVA AZURE

Males vary from dull violet-brown to deep
purplish blue, while the much larger females
are blackish brown with metallic-blue patches.
• **EARLY STAGES** The caterpillar is yellowish
brown with darker markings and has a flattened
appearance. It feeds on mistletoe *(Amyema)*.
• **DISTRIBUTION** Widespread in eastern,
northern, and southeastern regions of Australia.

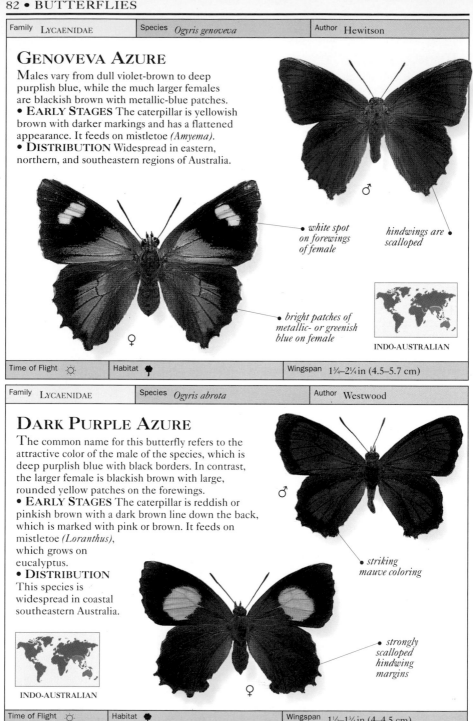

• *white spot
on forewings
of female*

*hindwings are
scalloped* •

♂

• *bright patches of
metallic- or greenish
blue on female*

♀

INDO-AUSTRALIAN

Time of Flight ☼	Habitat 🌳	Wingspan 1¾–2¼ in (4.5–5.7 cm)

Family LYCAENIDAE	Species *Ogyris abrota*	Author Westwood

DARK PURPLE AZURE

The common name for this butterfly refers to the
attractive color of the male of the species, which is
deep purplish blue with black borders. In contrast,
the larger female is blackish brown with large,
rounded yellow patches on the forewings.
• **EARLY STAGES** The caterpillar is reddish or
pinkish brown with a dark brown line down the back,
which is marked with pink or brown. It feeds on
mistletoe *(Loranthus)*,
which grows on
eucalyptus.
• **DISTRIBUTION**
This species is
widespread in coastal
southeastern Australia.

♂

• *striking
mauve coloring*

• *strongly
scalloped
hindwing
margins*

♀

INDO-AUSTRALIAN

Time of Flight ☼	Habitat 🌳	Wingspan 1½–1¾ in (4–4.5 cm)

| Family | LYCAENIDAE | Species | *Hypochrysops ignita* | Author | Leach |

FIERY JEWEL

The upper surfaces of all wings have broad borders. The centers of the forewings are azure and those of the hindwings are violet. The fiery red and blue underside gives rise to its name.
• EARLY STAGES The caterpillar feeds on acacia, camellia, and various other plants.
• DISTRIBUTION Widespread throughout Australia and Papua New Guinea.

silvery white underside of body

black and white fringes

♀

♀ △   INDO-AUSTRALIAN

| Time of Flight ☀ | Habitat 🌿 | | Wingspan 1–1¼ in (2.5–3 cm) |

| Family | LYCAENIDAE | Species | *Scoptes alphaeus* | Author | Cramer |

ORANGE-BANDED PROTEA

The upperside is marked with red bands on all the wings. On the underside the red color is restricted to a triangle on the forewings. Both the fore- and hindwings are slightly scalloped.
• EARLY STAGES The caterpillar is a pale gray color with bluish spots. It can be found feeding inside the flower heads of sugarbushes *(Protea)*.
• DISTRIBUTION Widespread throughout hilly and mountainous country in South Africa.

AFROTROPICAL

♂

checkered wing fringes

characteristic small tails

| Time of Flight ☀ | Habitat ▲ ⸱⸱⸱ | | Wingspan 1¼–1½ in (3–4 cm) |

| Family | LYCAENIDAE | Species | *Tajuria cippus* | Author | Fabricius |

PEACOCK ROYAL

The color of the male gives this species its name. Females are paler and have more rounded wings. The underside is gray with black lines, with an orange and black eyespot on the hindwings.
• EARLY STAGES The caterpillar is brown with pinkish markings. It feeds on mistletoes *(Dendrophthoe, Loranthus)*.
• DISTRIBUTION This species of butterfly is found in India, Sri Lanka, across to southern China, Malaysia, as far as the island of Borneo.

INDO-AUSTRALIAN

long narrow hindwings of male

♂

slender tails on both sexes

| Time of Flight ☀ | Habitat 🌿 | | Wingspan 1¼–1¾ in (3–4.5 cm) |

Family LYCAENIDAE	Species *Chrysozephyrus syla*	Author Kollar

SILVER HAIRSTREAK

Males are metallic golden-green with narrow, brown borders. Females have purplish blue forewings with broad, black margins. The hindwings are dark brown with greenish blue rays towards the margins. The common name derives from the silvery underside of both sexes, which has brown markings and orange and black eyespots at the tail bases.
• **EARLY STAGES** The caterpillar is apparently undescribed, but is known to feed on oak *(Quercus).*
• **DISTRIBUTION** Between 5,900 and 1,1480 ft (1,800–3,500 m) in the Himalayas.

PALEARCTIC
INDO-AUSTRALIAN

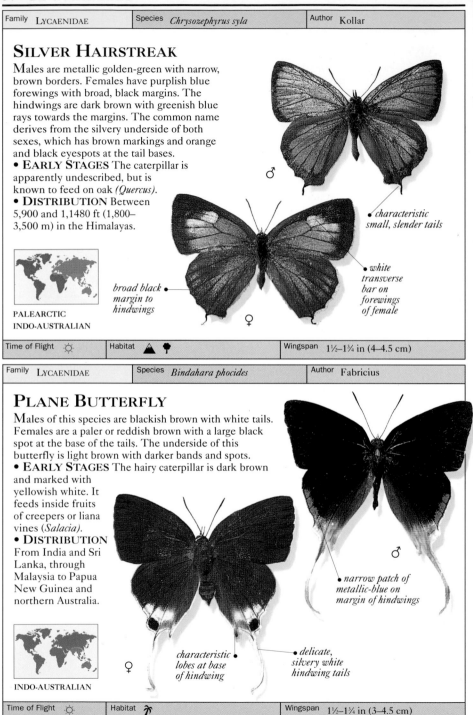

characteristic small, slender tails

white transverse bar on forewings of female

broad black margin to hindwings

Time of Flight ☼	Habitat ▲ 🌳	Wingspan 1½–1¾ in (4–4.5 cm)

Family LYCAENIDAE	Species *Bindahara phocides*	Author Fabricius

PLANE BUTTERFLY

Males of this species are blackish brown with white tails. Females are a paler or reddish brown with a large black spot at the base of the tails. The underside of this butterfly is light brown with darker bands and spots.
• **EARLY STAGES** The hairy caterpillar is dark brown and marked with yellowish white. It feeds inside fruits of creepers or liana vines *(Salacia).*
• **DISTRIBUTION** From India and Sri Lanka, through Malaysia to Papua New Guinea and northern Australia.

INDO-AUSTRALIAN

narrow patch of metallic-blue on margin of hindwings

characteristic lobes at base of hindwing

delicate, silvery white hindwing tails

Time of Flight ☼	Habitat 🌿	Wingspan 1½–1¾ in (3–4.5 cm)

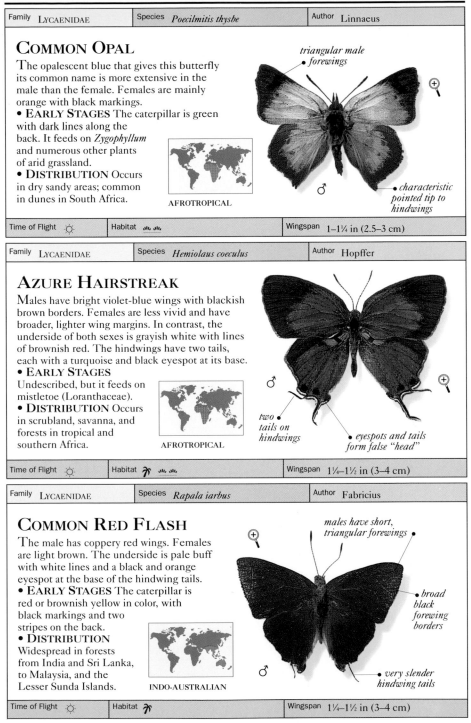

| Family LYCAENIDAE | Species *Poecilmitis thysbe* | Author Linnaeus |

COMMON OPAL

The opalescent blue that gives this butterfly its common name is more extensive in the male than the female. Females are mainly orange with black markings.
• **EARLY STAGES** The caterpillar is green with dark lines along the back. It feeds on *Zygophyllum* and numerous other plants of arid grassland.
• **DISTRIBUTION** Occurs in dry sandy areas; common in dunes in South Africa.

triangular male forewings

♂

characteristic pointed tip to hindwings

AFROTROPICAL

| Time of Flight | Habitat | Wingspan 1–1¼ in (2.5–3 cm) |

| Family LYCAENIDAE | Species *Hemiolaus coeculus* | Author Hopffer |

AZURE HAIRSTREAK

Males have bright violet-blue wings with blackish brown borders. Females are less vivid and have broader, lighter wing margins. In contrast, the underside of both sexes is grayish white with lines of brownish red. The hindwings have two tails, each with a turquoise and black eyespot at its base.
• **EARLY STAGES** Undescribed, but it feeds on mistletoe (Loranthaceae).
• **DISTRIBUTION** Occurs in scrubland, savanna, and forests in tropical and southern Africa.

♂

two tails on hindwings

eyespots and tails form false "head"

AFROTROPICAL

| Time of Flight | Habitat | Wingspan 1¼–1½ in (3–4 cm) |

| Family LYCAENIDAE | Species *Rapala iarbus* | Author Fabricius |

COMMON RED FLASH

The male has coppery red wings. Females are light brown. The underside is pale buff with white lines and a black and orange eyespot at the base of the hindwing tails.
• **EARLY STAGES** The caterpillar is red or brownish yellow in color, with black markings and two stripes on the back.
• **DISTRIBUTION** Widespread in forests from India and Sri Lanka, to Malaysia, and the Lesser Sunda Islands.

males have short, triangular forewings

broad black forewing borders

♂

very slender hindwing tails

INDO-AUSTRALIAN

| Time of Flight | Habitat | Wingspan 1¼–1½ in (3–4 cm) |

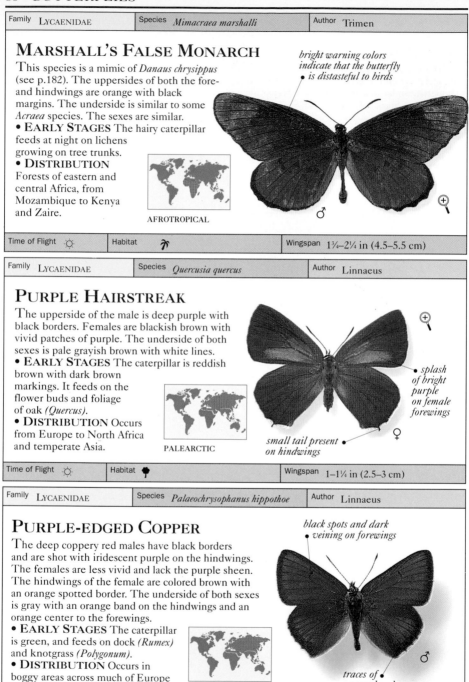

| Family LYCAENIDAE | Species *Mimacraea marshalli* | Author Trimen |

MARSHALL'S FALSE MONARCH

This species is a mimic of *Danaus chrysippus* (see p.182). The uppersides of both the fore- and hindwings are orange with black margins. The underside is similar to some *Acraea* species. The sexes are similar.

• **EARLY STAGES** The hairy caterpillar feeds at night on lichens growing on tree trunks.

• **DISTRIBUTION** Forests of eastern and central Africa, from Mozambique to Kenya and Zaire.

AFROTROPICAL

bright warning colors indicate that the butterfly is distasteful to birds

♂

| Time of Flight ☼ | Habitat 🌴 | Wingspan 1¾–2¼ in (4.5–5.5 cm) |

| Family LYCAENIDAE | Species *Quercusia quercus* | Author Linnaeus |

PURPLE HAIRSTREAK

The upperside of the male is deep purple with black borders. Females are blackish brown with vivid patches of purple. The underside of both sexes is pale grayish brown with white lines.

• **EARLY STAGES** The caterpillar is reddish brown with dark brown markings. It feeds on the flower buds and foliage of oak *(Quercus)*.

• **DISTRIBUTION** Occurs from Europe to North Africa and temperate Asia.

PALEARCTIC

splash of bright purple on female forewings

small tail present on hindwings

♀

| Time of Flight ☼ | Habitat ♣ | Wingspan 1–1¼ in (2.5–3 cm) |

| Family LYCAENIDAE | Species *Palaeochrysophanus hippothoe* | Author Linnaeus |

PURPLE-EDGED COPPER

The deep coppery red males have black borders and are shot with iridescent purple on the hindwings. The females are less vivid and lack the purple sheen. The hindwings of the female are colored brown with an orange spotted border. The underside of both sexes is gray with an orange band on the hindwings and an orange center to the forewings.

• **EARLY STAGES** The caterpillar is green, and feeds on dock *(Rumex)* and knotgrass *(Polygonum)*.

• **DISTRIBUTION** Occurs in boggy areas across much of Europe and temperate Asia, to Siberia.

PALEARCTIC

black spots and dark veining on forewings

traces of orange band

♂

| Time of Flight ☼ | Habitat 〰️ | Wingspan 1¼–1½ in (3–4 cm) |

Family LYCAENIDAE	Species *Amblypodia anita*	Author Hewitson

LEAF BLUE

Males are a dull purplish blue with a black border.
Females are either blackish brown over the entire
upperside or have large patches of brilliant metallic-blue
on the forewings and smaller patches on the hindwings.
The underside is patterned with brown and resembles
a dead leaf when the butterfly is at rest.

• **EARLY STAGES** The caterpillar is undescribed, but
is known to feed
on young shoots of
a climbing shrub
(Olax scandens).

• **DISTRIBUTION**
Occurs from India
and Sri Lanka, to
Malaysia and Java.

INDO-AUSTRALIAN

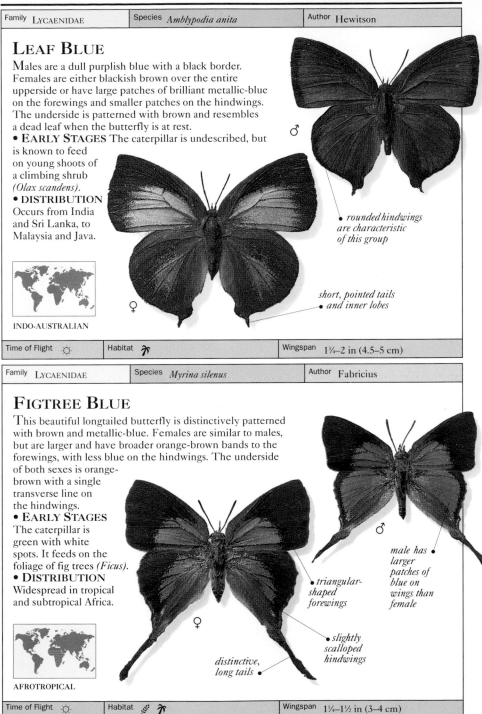

♂

• *rounded hindwings
are characteristic
of this group*

♀

*short, pointed tails
• and inner lobes*

Time of Flight ☀	Habitat 🌿	Wingspan 1¼–2 in (4.5–5 cm)

Family LYCAENIDAE	Species *Myrina silenus*	Author Fabricius

FIGTREE BLUE

This beautiful longtailed butterfly is distinctively patterned
with brown and metallic-blue. Females are similar to males,
but are larger and have broader orange-brown bands to the
forewings, with less blue on the hindwings. The underside
of both sexes is orange-
brown with a single
transverse line on
the hindwings.

• **EARLY STAGES**
The caterpillar is
green with white
spots. It feeds on the
foliage of fig trees *(Ficus).*

• **DISTRIBUTION**
Widespread in tropical
and subtropical Africa.

AFROTROPICAL

♂

*male has
larger
patches of
blue on
wings than
female*

*• triangular-
shaped
forewings*

♀

*• slightly
scalloped
hindwings*

*distinctive,
long tails •*

Time of Flight ☀	Habitat 🌿	Wingspan 1¼–1½ in (3–4 cm)

Family LYCAENIDAE	Species *Thecla coronata*	Author Hewitson

HEWITSON'S BLUE HAIRSTREAK

Females differ from the males by the broader, black borders to the wings and a large, brick-red patch at the base of the hindwing tails. The underside is dark green with a black line extending over fore- and hindwings. This species is one of many South American lycaenid butterflies incorrectly placed in the genus *Thecla* that still need to be more accurately classified.
• **EARLY STAGES** Nothing is known of the caterpillar or its foodplants.
• **DISTRIBUTION** Occurs from tropical South America north to Mexico.

♂

• *strongly indented inner edge of hindwings*

• *narrow black borders are characteristic of males of this species*

♀

• *dark patch at base of hindwing tails*

NEOTROPICAL

Time of Flight ☼	Habitat 🌿	Wingspan 1¾–2½ in (4.5–6 cm)

Family LYCAENIDAE	Species *Thecla betulae*	Author Linnaeus

BROWN HAIRSTREAK

Males lack the strong, orange markings on the forewing, although traces of orange may still remain.
• **EARLY STAGES** The caterpillar is green with yellowish lines.
• **DISTRIBUTION** Europe to temperate Asia.

PALEARCTIC

♀ △

♀

• *orange markings on tails are variable in extent*

Time of Flight ☼	Habitat 🌶	Wingspan 1¼–1½ in (3–4 cm)

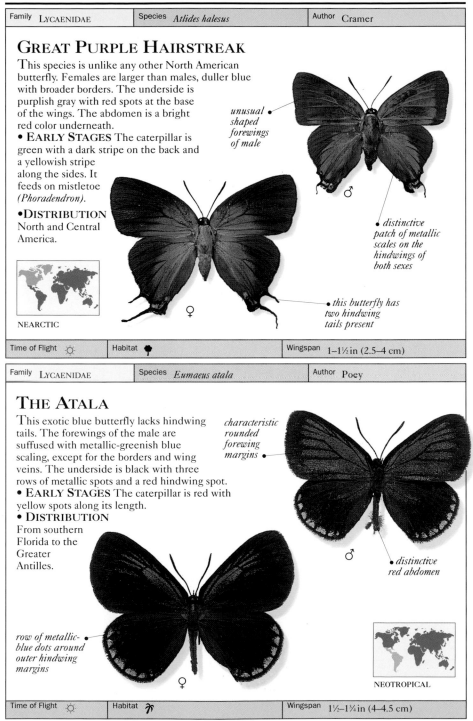

| Family LYCAENIDAE | Species *Atlides halesus* | Author Cramer |

GREAT PURPLE HAIRSTREAK

This species is unlike any other North American butterfly. Females are larger than males, duller blue with broader borders. The underside is purplish gray with red spots at the base of the wings. The abdomen is a bright red color underneath.

• **EARLY STAGES** The caterpillar is green with a dark stripe on the back and a yellowish stripe along the sides. It feeds on mistletoe *(Phoradendron)*.

• **DISTRIBUTION** North and Central America.

NEARCTIC

unusual shaped forewings of male

♂

distinctive patch of metallic scales on the hindwings of both sexes

♀

this butterfly has two hindwing tails present

| Time of Flight ☼ | Habitat 🌿 | Wingspan 1–1½ in (2.5–4 cm) |

| Family LYCAENIDAE | Species *Eumaeus atala* | Author Poey |

THE ATALA

This exotic blue butterfly lacks hindwing tails. The forewings of the male are suffused with metallic-greenish blue scaling, except for the borders and wing veins. The underside is black with three rows of metallic spots and a red hindwing spot.

• **EARLY STAGES** The caterpillar is red with yellow spots along its length.

• **DISTRIBUTION** From southern Florida to the Greater Antilles.

characteristic rounded forewing margins

♂

distinctive red abdomen

row of metallic-blue dots around outer hindwing margins

♀

NEOTROPICAL

| Time of Flight ☼ | Habitat 🌴 | Wingspan 1½–1¾ in (4–4.5 cm) |

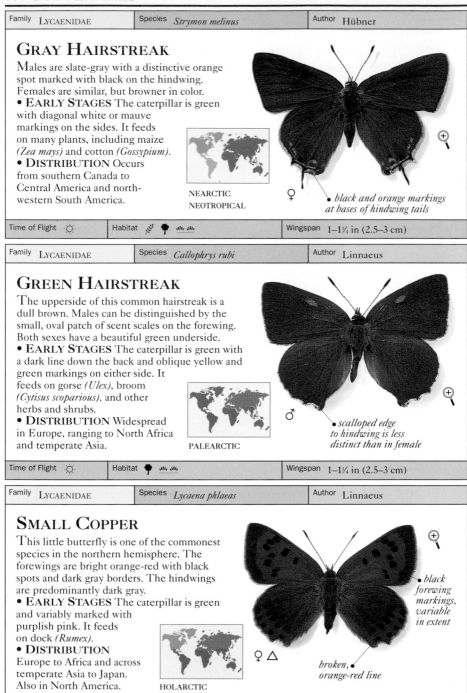

Family	LYCAENIDAE	Species	*Strymon melinus*	Author	Hübner

GRAY HAIRSTREAK

Males are slate-gray with a distinctive orange
spot marked with black on the hindwing.
Females are similar, but browner in color.
• EARLY STAGES The caterpillar is green
with diagonal white or mauve
markings on the sides. It feeds
on many plants, including maize
(Zea mays) and cotton *(Gossypium)*.
• DISTRIBUTION Occurs
from southern Canada to
Central America and northwestern South America.

NEARCTIC
NEOTROPICAL

♀ • *black and orange markings
at bases of hindwing tails*

Time of Flight ☼	Habitat 🌿 🌳	Wingspan 1–1¼ in (2.5–3 cm)

Family	LYCAENIDAE	Species	*Callophrys rubi*	Author	Linnaeus

GREEN HAIRSTREAK

The upperside of this common hairstreak is a
dull brown. Males can be distinguished by the
small, oval patch of scent scales on the forewing.
Both sexes have a beautiful green underside.
• EARLY STAGES The caterpillar is green with
a dark line down the back and oblique yellow and
green markings on either side. It
feeds on gorse *(Ulex)*, broom
(Cytisus scoparious), and other
herbs and shrubs.
• DISTRIBUTION Widespread
in Europe, ranging to North Africa
and temperate Asia.

PALEARCTIC

♂ • *scalloped edge
to hindwing is less
distinct than in female*

Time of Flight ☼	Habitat 🌿	Wingspan 1–1¼ in (2.5–3 cm)

Family	LYCAENIDAE	Species	*Lycaena phlaeas*	Author	Linnaeus

SMALL COPPER

This little butterfly is one of the commonest
species in the northern hemisphere. The
forewings are bright orange-red with black
spots and dark gray borders. The hindwings
are predominantly dark gray.
• EARLY STAGES The caterpillar is green
and variably marked with
purplish pink. It feeds
on dock *(Rumex)*.
• DISTRIBUTION
Europe to Africa and across
temperate Asia to Japan.
Also in North America.

HOLARCTIC

• *black
forewing
markings,
variable
in extent*

♀ △ *broken, •
orange-red line*

Time of Flight ☼	Habitat	Wingspan 1–1¼ in (2.5–3 cm)

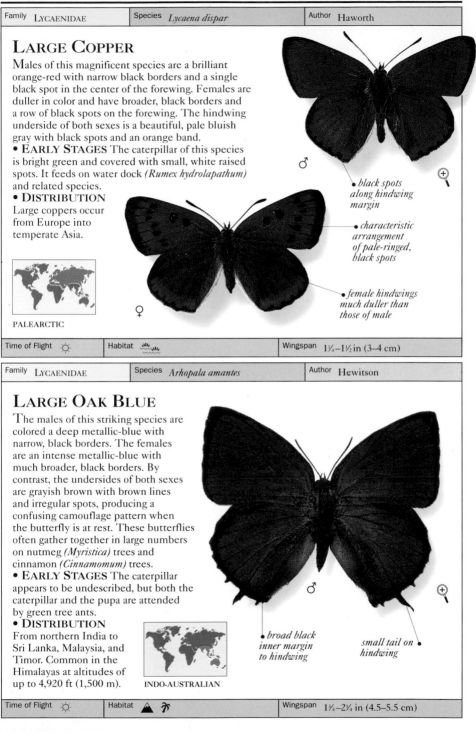

| Family | LYCAENIDAE | Species | *Lycaena dispar* | Author | Haworth |

LARGE COPPER

Males of this magnificent species are a brilliant orange-red with narrow black borders and a single black spot in the center of the forewing. Females are duller in color and have broader, black borders and a row of black spots on the forewing. The hindwing underside of both sexes is a beautiful, pale bluish gray with black spots and an orange band.

• **EARLY STAGES** The caterpillar of this species is bright green and covered with small, white raised spots. It feeds on water dock *(Rumex hydrolapathum)* and related species.

• **DISTRIBUTION** Large coppers occur from Europe into temperate Asia.

PALEARCTIC

♂

♀

• *black spots along hindwing margin*

• *characteristic arrangement of pale-ringed, black spots*

• *female hindwings much duller than those of male*

| Time of Flight ☀ | Habitat | Wingspan 1¼–1½ in (3–4 cm) |

| Family | LYCAENIDAE | Species | *Arhopala amantes* | Author | Hewitson |

LARGE OAK BLUE

The males of this striking species are colored a deep metallic-blue with narrow, black borders. The females are an intense metallic-blue with much broader, black borders. By contrast, the undersides of both sexes are grayish brown with brown lines and irregular spots, producing a confusing camouflage pattern when the butterfly is at rest. These butterflies often gather together in large numbers on nutmeg *(Myristica)* trees and cinnamon *(Cinnamomum)* trees.

• **EARLY STAGES** The caterpillar appears to be undescribed, but both the caterpillar and the pupa are attended by green tree ants.

• **DISTRIBUTION** From northern India to Sri Lanka, Malaysia, and Timor. Common in the Himalayas at altitudes of up to 4,920 ft (1,500 m).

INDO-AUSTRALIAN

♂

• *broad black inner margin to hindwing*

• *small tail on hindwing*

| Time of Flight ☀ | Habitat | Wingspan 1¾–2¼ in (4.5–5.5 cm) |

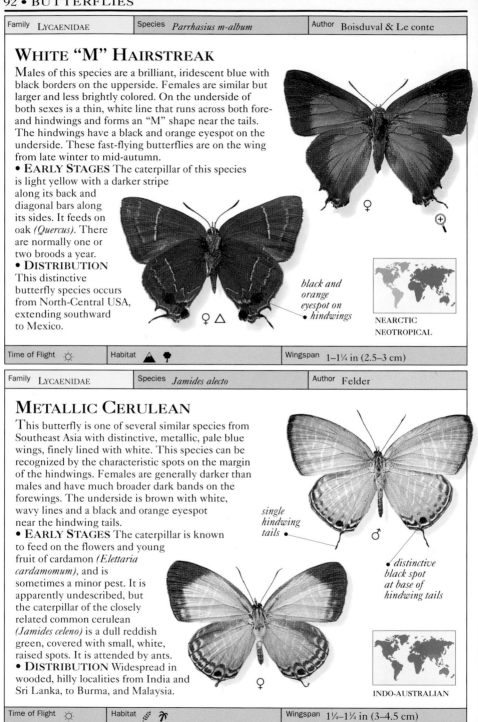

Family LYCAENIDAE	Species *Parrhasius m-album*	Author Boisduval & Le conte

WHITE "M" HAIRSTREAK

Males of this species are a brilliant, iridescent blue with
black borders on the upperside. Females are similar but
larger and less brightly colored. On the underside of
both sexes is a thin, white line that runs across both fore-
and hindwings and forms an "M" shape near the tails.
The hindwings have a black and orange eyespot on the
underside. These fast-flying butterflies are on the wing
from late winter to mid-autumn.

• **EARLY STAGES** The caterpillar of this species
is light yellow with a darker stripe
along its back and
diagonal bars along
its sides. It feeds on
oak *(Quercus)*. There
are normally one or
two broods a year.

• **DISTRIBUTION**
This distinctive
butterfly species occurs
from North-Central USA,
extending southward
to Mexico.

♀

black and
orange
eyespot on
• hindwings

♀ △

NEARCTIC
NEOTROPICAL

Time of Flight ☼	Habitat ▲ 🌳	Wingspan 1–1¼ in (2.5–3 cm)

Family LYCAENIDAE	Species *Jamides alecto*	Author Felder

METALLIC CERULEAN

This butterfly is one of several similar species from
Southeast Asia with distinctive, metallic, pale blue
wings, finely lined with white. This species can be
recognized by the characteristic spots on the margin
of the hindwings. Females are generally darker than
males and have much broader dark bands on the
forewings. The underside is brown with white,
wavy lines and a black and orange eyespot
near the hindwing tails.

• **EARLY STAGES** The caterpillar is known
to feed on the flowers and young
fruit of cardamon *(Elettaria
cardamomum)*, and is
sometimes a minor pest. It is
apparently undescribed, but
the caterpillar of the closely
related common cerulean
(Jamides celeno) is a dull reddish
green, covered with small, white,
raised spots. It is attended by ants.

• **DISTRIBUTION** Widespread in
wooded, hilly localities from India and
Sri Lanka, to Burma, and Malaysia.

single
hindwing
tails •

♂

• distinctive
black spot
at base of
hindwing tails

♀

INDO-AUSTRALIAN

Time of Flight ☼	Habitat 🌾 🌴	Wingspan 1¼–1¾ in (3–4.5 cm)

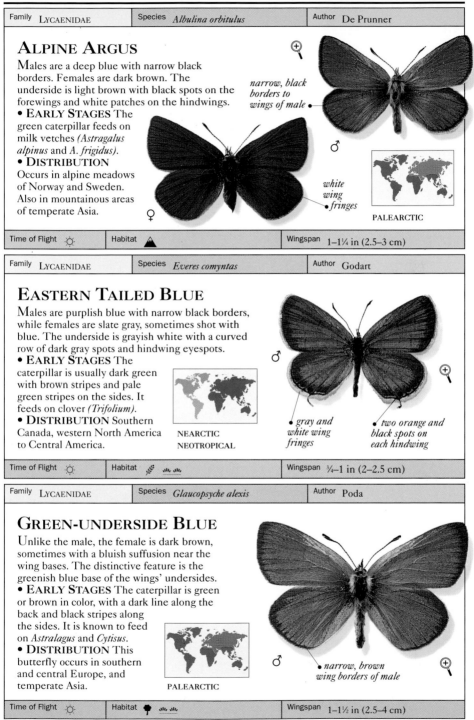

Family	LYCAENIDAE	Species	Albulina orbitulus	Author	De Prunner

ALPINE ARGUS

Males are a deep blue with narrow black borders. Females are dark brown. The underside is light brown with black spots on the forewings and white patches on the hindwings.
• **EARLY STAGES** The green caterpillar feeds on milk vetches *(Astragalus alpinus* and *A. frigidus).*
• **DISTRIBUTION** Occurs in alpine meadows of Norway and Sweden. Also in mountainous areas of temperate Asia.

narrow, black borders to wings of male

♂

white wing fringes

PALEARCTIC

♀

Time of Flight	☼	Habitat	▲	Wingspan	1–1¼ in (2.5–3 cm)

Family	LYCAENIDAE	Species	Everes comyntas	Author	Godart

EASTERN TAILED BLUE

Males are purplish blue with narrow black borders, while females are slate gray, sometimes shot with blue. The underside is grayish white with a curved row of dark gray spots and hindwing eyespots.
• **EARLY STAGES** The caterpillar is usually dark green with brown stripes and pale green stripes on the sides. It feeds on clover *(Trifolium).*
• **DISTRIBUTION** Southern Canada, western North America to Central America.

♂

NEARCTIC
NEOTROPICAL

gray and white wing fringes

two orange and black spots on each hindwing

Time of Flight	☼	Habitat	🌾 ⚘ ⚘	Wingspan	¾–1 in (2–2.5 cm)

Family	LYCAENIDAE	Species	Glaucopsyche alexis	Author	Poda

GREEN-UNDERSIDE BLUE

Unlike the male, the female is dark brown, sometimes with a bluish suffusion near the wing bases. The distinctive feature is the greenish blue base of the wings' undersides.
• **EARLY STAGES** The caterpillar is green or brown in color, with a dark line along the back and black stripes along the sides. It is known to feed on *Astralagus* and *Cytisus.*
• **DISTRIBUTION** This butterfly occurs in southern and central Europe, and temperate Asia.

♂

narrow, brown wing borders of male

PALEARCTIC

Time of Flight	☼	Habitat	🌳 ⚘ ⚘	Wingspan	1–1½ in (2.5–4 cm)

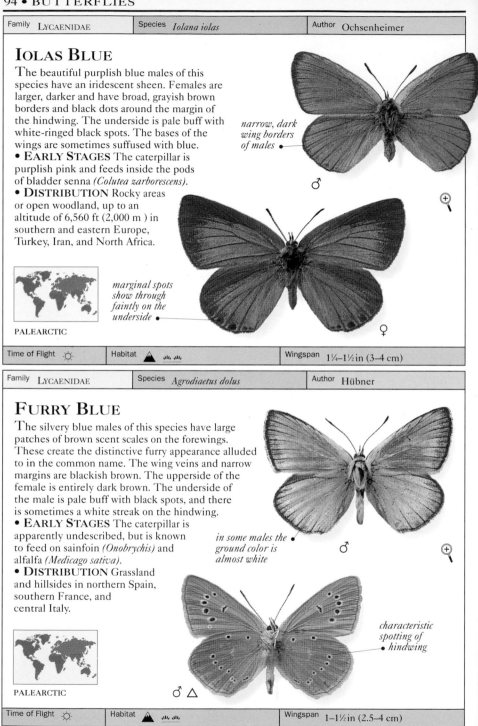

| Family LYCAENIDAE | Species *Iolana iolas* | Author Ochsenheimer |

IOLAS BLUE

The beautiful purplish blue males of this
species have an iridescent sheen. Females are
larger, darker and have broad, grayish brown
borders and black dots around the margin of
the hindwing. The underside is pale buff with
white-ringed black spots. The bases of the
wings are sometimes suffused with blue.
• **EARLY STAGES** The caterpillar is
purplish pink and feeds inside the pods
of bladder senna *(Colutea zarborescens)*.
• **DISTRIBUTION** Rocky areas
or open woodland, up to an
altitude of 6,560 ft (2,000 m) in
southern and eastern Europe,
Turkey, Iran, and North Africa.

narrow, dark wing borders of males

♂

marginal spots show through faintly on the underside

♀

PALEARCTIC

| Time of Flight | Habitat | Wingspan 1¼–1½ in (3–4 cm) |

| Family LYCAENIDAE | Species *Agrodiaetus dolus* | Author Hübner |

FURRY BLUE

The silvery blue males of this species have large
patches of brown scent scales on the forewings.
These create the distinctive furry appearance alluded
to in the common name. The wing veins and narrow
margins are blackish brown. The upperside of the
female is entirely dark brown. The underside of
the male is pale buff with black spots, and there
is sometimes a white streak on the hindwing.
• **EARLY STAGES** The caterpillar is
apparently undescribed, but is known
to feed on sainfoin *(Onobrychis)* and
alfalfa *(Medicago sativa)*.
• **DISTRIBUTION** Grassland
and hillsides in northern Spain,
southern France, and
central Italy.

in some males the ground color is almost white

♂

characteristic spotting of hindwing

♂ △

PALEARCTIC

| Time of Flight | Habitat | Wingspan 1–1½ in (2.5–4 cm) |

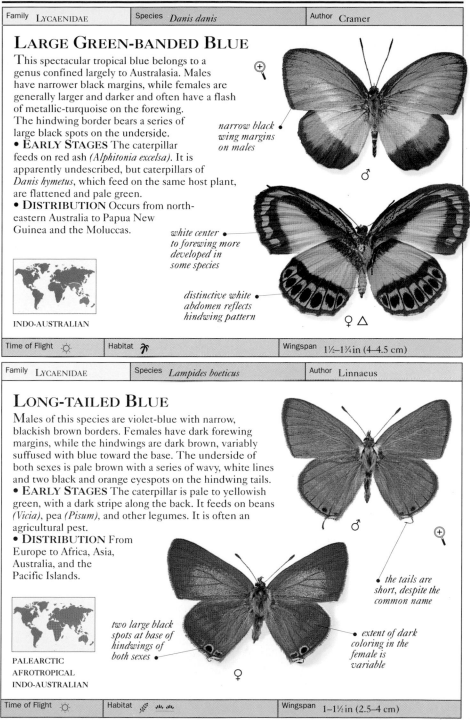

Family LYCAENIDAE	Species *Danis danis*	Author Cramer

LARGE GREEN-BANDED BLUE

This spectacular tropical blue belongs to a genus confined largely to Australasia. Males have narrower black margins, while females are generally larger and darker and often have a flash of metallic-turquoise on the forewing. The hindwing border bears a series of large black spots on the underside.
• **EARLY STAGES** The caterpillar feeds on red ash *(Alphitonia excelsa)*. It is apparently undescribed, but caterpillars of *Danis hymetus*, which feed on the same host plant, are flattened and pale green.
• **DISTRIBUTION** Occurs from north-eastern Australia to Papua New Guinea and the Moluccas.

INDO-AUSTRALIAN

narrow black • wing margins on males

♂

white center • to forewing more developed in some species

distinctive white • abdomen reflects hindwing pattern

♀ △

Time of Flight ☀	Habitat 🌿	Wingspan 1½–1¾ in (4–4.5 cm)

Family LYCAENIDAE	Species *Lampides boeticus*	Author Linnaeus

LONG-TAILED BLUE

Males of this species are violet-blue with narrow, blackish brown borders. Females have dark forewing margins, while the hindwings are dark brown, variably suffused with blue toward the base. The underside of both sexes is pale brown with a series of wavy, white lines and two black and orange eyespots on the hindwing tails.
• **EARLY STAGES** The caterpillar is pale to yellowish green, with a dark stripe along the back. It feeds on beans *(Vicia)*, pea *(Pisum)*, and other legumes. It is often an agricultural pest.
• **DISTRIBUTION** From Europe to Africa, Asia, Australia, and the Pacific Islands.

PALEARCTIC
AFROTROPICAL
INDO-AUSTRALIAN

♂

• the tails are short, despite the common name

two large black spots at base of hindwings of both sexes •

• extent of dark coloring in the female is variable

♀

Time of Flight ☀	Habitat 🌿	Wingspan 1–1½ in (2.5–4 cm)

| Family LYCAENIDAE | Species *Candalides xanthospilos* | Author Hübner |

YELLOW-SPOT BLUE

The males of this species are black with a slight purplish blue suffusion in the center of each wing. Females are similar, but they lack the purplish blue suffusion. The undersides of the wings of both sexes are bluish white with pure white centers and small black dots along the outer margins.

• **EARLY STAGES** The caterpillar is green to bluish green with oblique, dark green markings and a yellow line along its sides. It feeds at night on the foliage of *Pimelea*.

• **DISTRIBUTION** Found in wooded country in Australia.

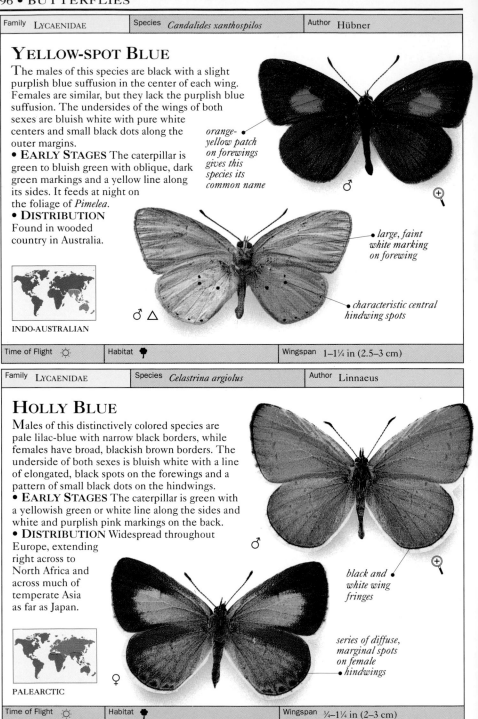

orange-yellow patch on forewings gives this species its common name

♂

large, faint white marking on forewing

characteristic central hindwing spots

♂ △

INDO-AUSTRALIAN

| Time of Flight ☼ | Habitat ♣ | Wingspan 1–1¼ in (2.5–3 cm) |

| Family LYCAENIDAE | Species *Celastrina argiolus* | Author Linnaeus |

HOLLY BLUE

Males of this distinctively colored species are pale lilac-blue with narrow black borders, while females have broad, blackish brown borders. The underside of both sexes is bluish white with a line of elongated, black spots on the forewings and a pattern of small black dots on the hindwings.

• **EARLY STAGES** The caterpillar is green with a yellowish green or white line along the sides and white and purplish pink markings on the back.

• **DISTRIBUTION** Widespread throughout Europe, extending right across to North Africa and across much of temperate Asia as far as Japan.

♂

black and white wing fringes

series of diffuse, marginal spots on female hindwings

♀

PALEARCTIC

| Time of Flight ☼ | Habitat ♣ | Wingspan ¼–1¼ in (2–3 cm) |

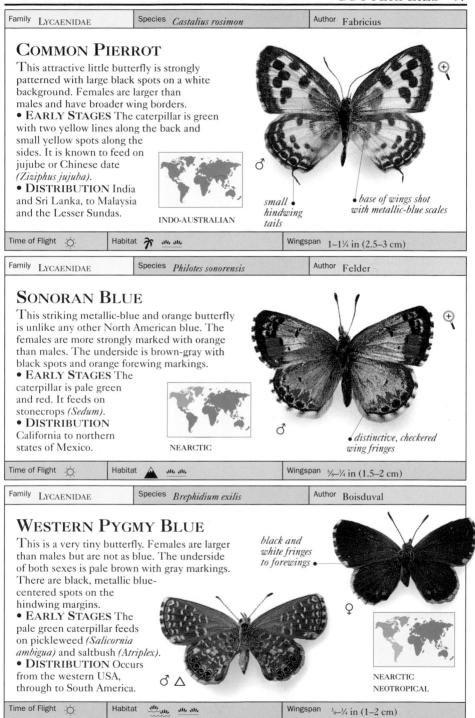

Family LYCAENIDAE	Species *Castalius rosimon*	Author Fabricius

COMMON PIERROT

This attractive little butterfly is strongly patterned with large black spots on a white background. Females are larger than males and have broader wing borders.
• **EARLY STAGES** The caterpillar is green with two yellow lines along the back and small yellow spots along the sides. It is known to feed on jujube or Chinese date *(Ziziphus jujuba)*.
• **DISTRIBUTION** India and Sri Lanka, to Malaysia and the Lesser Sundas.

INDO-AUSTRALIAN

♂

small hindwing tails

base of wings shot with metallic-blue scales

Time of Flight	Habitat	Wingspan 1–1¼ in (2.5–3 cm)

Family LYCAENIDAE	Species *Philotes sonorensis*	Author Felder

SONORAN BLUE

This striking metallic-blue and orange butterfly is unlike any other North American blue. The females are more strongly marked with orange than males. The underside is brown-gray with black spots and orange forewing markings.
• **EARLY STAGES** The caterpillar is pale green and red. It feeds on stonecrops *(Sedum)*.
• **DISTRIBUTION** California to northern states of Mexico.

NEARCTIC

♂

distinctive, checkered wing fringes

Time of Flight	Habitat	Wingspan ⅝–¾ in (1.5–2 cm)

Family LYCAENIDAE	Species *Brephidium exilis*	Author Boisduval

WESTERN PYGMY BLUE

This is a very tiny butterfly. Females are larger than males but are not as blue. The underside of both sexes is pale brown with gray markings. There are black, metallic blue-centered spots on the hindwing margins.
• **EARLY STAGES** The pale green caterpillar feeds on pickleweed *(Salicornia ambigua)* and saltbush *(Atriplex)*.
• **DISTRIBUTION** Occurs from the western USA, through to South America.

black and white fringes to forewings

♀

♂ △

NEARCTIC
NEOTROPICAL

Time of Flight	Habitat	Wingspan ⅛–¾ in (1–2 cm)

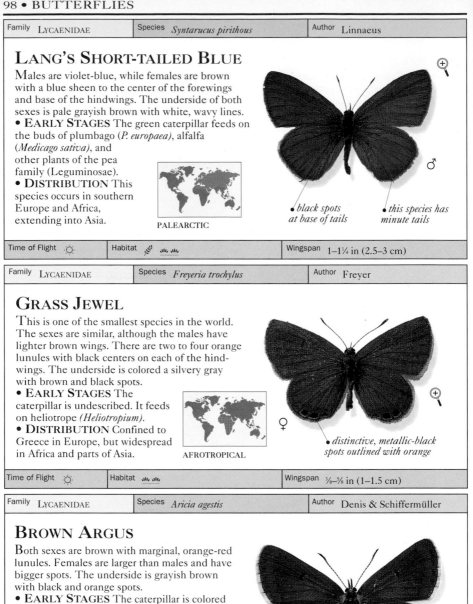

| Family | LYCAENIDAE | Species | *Syntarucus pirithous* | Author | Linnaeus |

LANG'S SHORT-TAILED BLUE

Males are violet-blue, while females are brown
with a blue sheen to the center of the forewings
and base of the hindwings. The underside of both
sexes is pale grayish brown with white, wavy lines.
• **EARLY STAGES** The green caterpillar feeds on
the buds of plumbago (*P. europaea*), alfalfa
(*Medicago sativa*), and
other plants of the pea
family (Leguminosae).
• **DISTRIBUTION** This
species occurs in southern
Europe and Africa,
extending into Asia.

PALEARCTIC

• *black spots
at base of tails*

♂

• *this species has
minute tails*

| Time of Flight | ☼ | Habitat | | Wingspan | 1–1¼ in (2.5–3 cm) |

| Family | LYCAENIDAE | Species | *Freyeria trochylus* | Author | Freyer |

GRASS JEWEL

This is one of the smallest species in the world.
The sexes are similar, although the males have
lighter brown wings. There are two to four orange
lunules with black centers on each of the hindwings. The underside is colored a silvery gray
with brown and black spots.
• **EARLY STAGES** The
caterpillar is undescribed. It feeds
on heliotrope (*Heliotropium*).
• **DISTRIBUTION** Confined to
Greece in Europe, but widespread
in Africa and parts of Asia.

AFROTROPICAL

♀

• *distinctive, metallic-black
spots outlined with orange*

| Time of Flight | ☼ | Habitat | | Wingspan | ⅛–⅝ in (1–1.5 cm) |

| Family | LYCAENIDAE | Species | *Aricia agestis* | Author | Denis & Schiffermüller |

BROWN ARGUS

Both sexes are brown with marginal, orange-red
lunules. Females are larger than males and have
bigger spots. The underside is grayish brown
with black and orange spots.
• **EARLY STAGES** The caterpillar is colored
green with purple stripes and oblique dark green
lines. It feeds on rock rose
(*Helianthemum*) and
cranesbill (*Geranium*).
• **DISTRIBUTION** Occurs
in heathland throughout
Europe, extending across
temperate Asia.

PALEARCTIC

♂

• *pale wing fringes*

| Time of Flight | ☼ | Habitat | | Wingspan | ¼–1¼ in (2–3cm) |

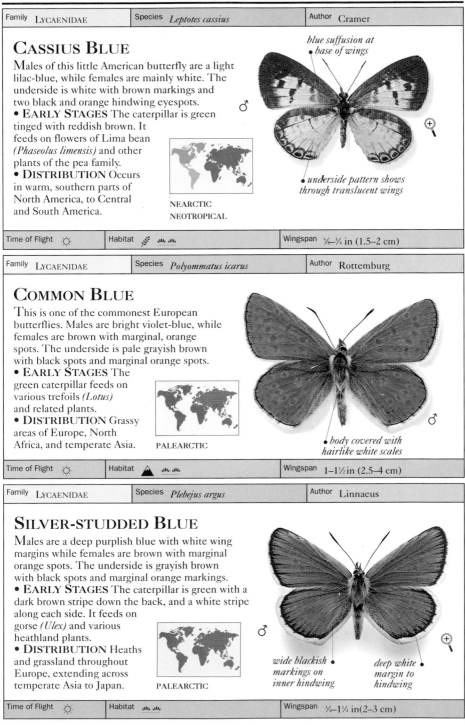

Family	LYCAENIDAE	Species	*Leptotes cassius*	Author	Cramer

CASSIUS BLUE

Males of this little American butterfly are a light lilac-blue, while females are mainly white. The underside is white with brown markings and two black and orange hindwing eyespots.
• **EARLY STAGES** The caterpillar is green tinged with reddish brown. It feeds on flowers of Lima bean *(Phaseolus limensis)* and other plants of the pea family.
• **DISTRIBUTION** Occurs in warm, southern parts of North America, to Central and South America.

♂

blue suffusion at base of wings

• underside pattern shows through translucent wings

NEARCTIC
NEOTROPICAL

Time of Flight	☼	Habitat		Wingspan	⅝–¾ in (1.5–2 cm)

Family	LYCAENIDAE	Species	*Polyommatus icarus*	Author	Rottemburg

COMMON BLUE

This is one of the commonest European butterflies. Males are bright violet-blue, while females are brown with marginal, orange spots. The underside is pale grayish brown with black spots and marginal orange spots.
• **EARLY STAGES** The green caterpillar feeds on various trefoils *(Lotus)* and related plants.
• **DISTRIBUTION** Grassy areas of Europe, North Africa, and temperate Asia.

♂

• body covered with hairlike white scales

PALEARCTIC

Time of Flight	☼	Habitat		Wingspan	1–1½ in (2.5–4 cm)

Family	LYCAENIDAE	Species	*Plebejus argus*	Author	Linnaeus

SILVER-STUDDED BLUE

Males are a deep purplish blue with white wing margins while females are brown with marginal orange spots. The underside is grayish brown with black spots and marginal orange markings.
• **EARLY STAGES** The caterpillar is green with a dark brown stripe down the back, and a white stripe along each side. It feeds on gorse *(Ulex)* and various heathland plants.
• **DISTRIBUTION** Heaths and grassland throughout Europe, extending across temperate Asia to Japan.

♂

wide blackish • markings on inner hindwing

deep white • margin to hindwing

PALEARCTIC

Time of Flight	☼	Habitat		Wingspan	¾–1¼ in (2–3 cm)

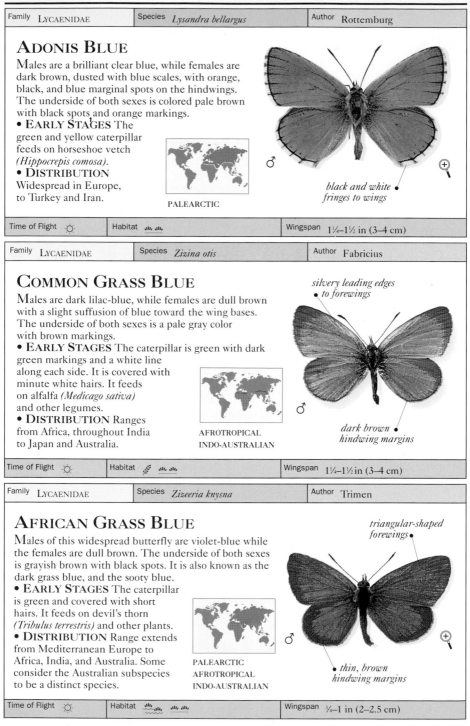

| Family LYCAENIDAE | Species *Lysandra bellargus* | Author Rottemburg |

ADONIS BLUE

Males are a brilliant clear blue, while females are
dark brown, dusted with blue scales, with orange,
black, and blue marginal spots on the hindwings.
The underside of both sexes is colored pale brown
with black spots and orange markings.
• **EARLY STAGES** The
green and yellow caterpillar
feeds on horseshoe vetch
(Hippocrepis comosa).
• **DISTRIBUTION**
Widespread in Europe,
to Turkey and Iran.

PALEARCTIC

♂

black and white fringes to wings

| Time of Flight ☼ | Habitat | Wingspan 1¼–1½ in (3–4 cm) |

| Family LYCAENIDAE | Species *Zizina otis* | Author Fabricius |

COMMON GRASS BLUE

silvery leading edges to forewings

Males are dark lilac-blue, while females are dull brown
with a slight suffusion of blue toward the wing bases.
The underside of both sexes is a pale gray color
with brown markings.
• **EARLY STAGES** The caterpillar is green with dark
green markings and a white line
along each side. It is covered with
minute white hairs. It feeds
on alfalfa *(Medicago sativa)*
and other legumes.
• **DISTRIBUTION** Ranges
from Africa, throughout India
to Japan and Australia.

AFROTROPICAL
INDO-AUSTRALIAN

♂

dark brown hindwing margins

| Time of Flight ☼ | Habitat | Wingspan 1¼–1½ in (3–4 cm) |

| Family LYCAENIDAE | Species *Zizeeria knysna* | Author Trimen |

AFRICAN GRASS BLUE

triangular-shaped forewings

Males of this widespread butterfly are violet-blue while
the females are dull brown. The underside of both sexes
is grayish brown with black spots. It is also known as the
dark grass blue, and the sooty blue.
• **EARLY STAGES** The caterpillar
is green and covered with short
hairs. It feeds on devil's thorn
(Tribulus terrestris) and other plants.
• **DISTRIBUTION** Range extends
from Mediterranean Europe to
Africa, India, and Australia. Some
consider the Australian subspecies
to be a distinct species.

PALEARCTIC
AFROTROPICAL
INDO-AUSTRALIAN

♂

thin, brown hindwing margins

| Time of Flight ☼ | Habitat | Wingspan ¼–1 in (2–2.5 cm) |

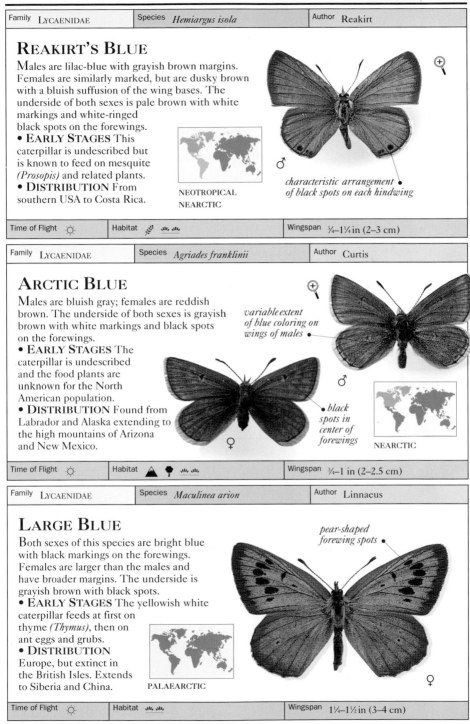

Family LYCAENIDAE	Species *Hemiargus isola*	Author Reakirt

REAKIRT'S BLUE

Males are lilac-blue with grayish brown margins. Females are similarly marked, but are dusky brown with a bluish suffusion of the wing bases. The underside of both sexes is pale brown with white markings and white-ringed black spots on the forewings.
• **EARLY STAGES** This caterpillar is undescribed but is known to feed on mesquite *(Prosopis)* and related plants.
• **DISTRIBUTION** From southern USA to Costa Rica.

NEOTROPICAL
NEARCTIC

♂

characteristic arrangement of black spots on each hindwing

Time of Flight ☼	Habitat	Wingspan ¾–1¼ in (2–3 cm)

Family LYCAENIDAE	Species *Agriades franklinii*	Author Curtis

ARCTIC BLUE

Males are bluish gray; females are reddish brown. The underside of both sexes is grayish brown with white markings and black spots on the forewings.
• **EARLY STAGES** The caterpillar is undescribed and the food plants are unknown for the North American population.
• **DISTRIBUTION** Found from Labrador and Alaska extending to the high mountains of Arizona and New Mexico.

variable extent of blue coloring on wings of males

♂

black spots in center of forewings

NEARCTIC

♀

Time of Flight ☼	Habitat	Wingspan ¾–1 in (2–2.5 cm)

Family LYCAENIDAE	Species *Maculinea arion*	Author Linnaeus

LARGE BLUE

Both sexes of this species are bright blue with black markings on the forewings. Females are larger than the males and have broader margins. The underside is grayish brown with black spots.
• **EARLY STAGES** The yellowish white caterpillar feeds at first on thyme *(Thymus)*, then on ant eggs and grubs.
• **DISTRIBUTION** Europe, but extinct in the British Isles. Extends to Siberia and China.

pear-shaped forewing spots

PALAEARCTIC

♀

Time of Flight ☼	Habitat	Wingspan 1¼–1½ in (3–4 cm)

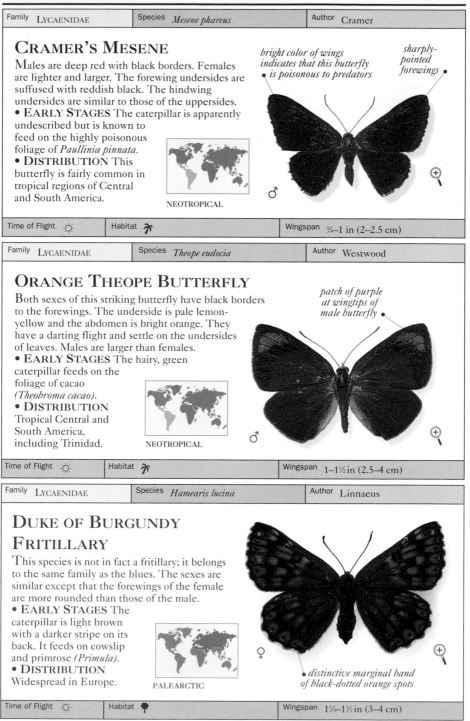

Family LYCAENIDAE	Species *Mesene phareus*	Author Cramer

CRAMER'S MESENE

Males are deep red with black borders. Females are lighter and larger. The forewing undersides are suffused with reddish black. The hindwing undersides are similar to those of the uppersides.

• **EARLY STAGES** The caterpillar is apparently undescribed but is known to feed on the highly poisonous foliage of *Paullinia pinnata*.

• **DISTRIBUTION** This butterfly is fairly common in tropical regions of Central and South America.

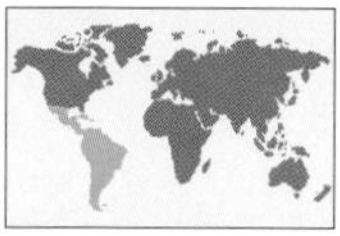

NEOTROPICAL

bright color of wings indicates that this butterfly is poisonous to predators
sharply-pointed forewings
♂

Time of Flight	Habitat	Wingspan ¾–1 in (2–2.5 cm)

Family LYCAENIDAE	Species *Theope eudocia*	Author Westwood

ORANGE THEOPE BUTTERFLY

Both sexes of this striking butterfly have black borders to the forewings. The underside is pale lemon-yellow and the abdomen is bright orange. They have a darting flight and settle on the undersides of leaves. Males are larger than females.

• **EARLY STAGES** The hairy, green caterpillar feeds on the foliage of cacao *(Theobroma cacao)*.

• **DISTRIBUTION** Tropical Central and South America, including Trinidad.

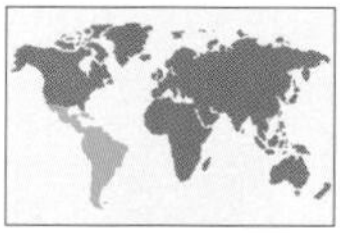

NEOTROPICAL

patch of purple at wingtips of male butterfly
♂

Time of Flight	Habitat	Wingspan 1–1½ in (2.5–4 cm)

Family LYCAENIDAE	Species *Hamearis lucina*	Author Linnaeus

DUKE OF BURGUNDY FRITILLARY

This species is not in fact a fritillary; it belongs to the same family as the blues. The sexes are similar except that the forewings of the female are more rounded than those of the male.

• **EARLY STAGES** The caterpillar is light brown with a darker stripe on its back. It feeds on cowslip and primrose *(Primula)*.

• **DISTRIBUTION** Widespread in Europe.

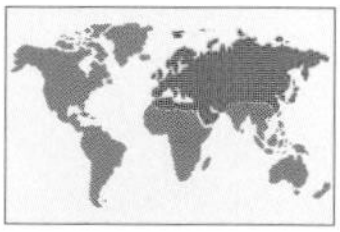

PALEARCTIC

♀
distinctive marginal band of black-dotted orange spots

Time of Flight	Habitat	Wingspan 1¼–1½ in (3–4 cm)

Family LYCAENIDAE	Species *Syrmatia dorilas*	Author Cramer

WHITE-SPOTTED TADPOLE BUTTERFLY

This is one of a genus of about five species confined to tropical Central and South America. They are slow-flying but their rapid wingbeat is like that of wasps. Females have broader forewings with orange spots.
• **EARLY STAGES** Undescribed.
• **DISTRIBUTION** Brazil and Venezuela.

NEOTROPICAL

distinctive white forewing spots

♂

dull wing color

characteristic shape of hindwings

Time of Flight ☼	Habitat 🌴	Wingspan ⅝–¾ in (1.5–2 cm)

Family LYCAENIDAE	Species *Menander menander*	Author Stoll

BLUE THAROPS

One of about ten species in a South and Central American genus of brightly colored, iridescent metalmark butterflies. Males are greenish blue with black streaks, while females are darker metallic-blue. The underside of both sexes is yellowish white with reddish brown spots forming broken lines across the fore- and hindwings. Blue tharops are fast-flying and feed at flowers of agrimony *(Eupatorium)*.
• **EARLY STAGES** Nothing appears to be known of the appearance of the caterpillar or its foodplants.
• **DISTRIBUTION** Occurs from Panama to the tropical regions of northern South America, and also in Trinidad.

blackish-brown forewing tips of male

males are a lighter color than females

black wing margins

♂

blue coloration ceases at wing-tips

vivid blue on leading edge

♀

wings have fringed appearance

broken black lines running across wings of female

NEOTROPICAL

Time of Flight ☼	Habitat 🌴	Wingspan 1¼–1½ in (3–4 cm)

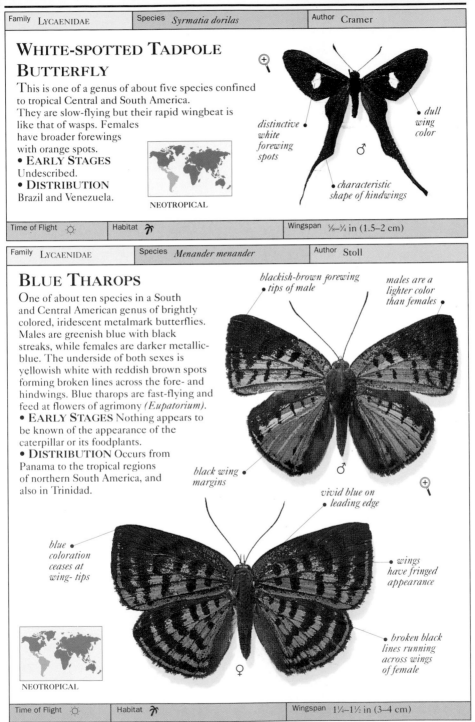

| Family LYCAENIDAE | Species *Apodemia nais* | Author Edwards |

NAIS METALMARK

The upperside of this species is mainly
brownish orange with a distinctive pattern of
brown spots and bars that form zigzag lines and
bands across both wings. Females are larger
and lighter than males and have slightly
rounded forewings. The underside of both
sexes is grayish white, strongly suffused with
orange over most of the forewings,
and with an orange band along the
hindwing margins. The wings are
patterned with black spots.
Adults are on the wing in
summer; they visit flowers
and settle on damp ground.
• **EARLY STAGES** The
caterpillar is pale green with
small tufts of bristles over the
upper surface. It feeds on
buckbrush *(Ceanothus fendleri)*.
• **DISTRIBUTION** Found in the
USA from Colorado extending
south to New Mexico, and Mexico.

checkered wing fringes

♂

• *white patch on front edge of forewings*

♂ △

NEARCTIC

| Time of Flight ☼ | Habitat | Wingspan 1¼–1½ in (3–4 cm) |

| Family LYCAENIDAE | Species *Helicopis cupido* | Author Linnaeus |

GOLD-DROP HELICOPIS

The forewings of the males are yellowish
white edged with brown, while the bases are
orange-yellow. The hindwings are dark brown
with an orange-yellow base. The females are
lighter and are marked with brown around the
hindwing margins. The undersides are similar
to the uppersides except for several metallic
spots on the inner hindwing, and margins.
• **EARLY STAGES** The caterpillar appears to
be undescribed, but is
known to feed on wild
tania *(Montrichardia)*.
• **DISTRIBUTION**
Found in tropical
South America, from
Venezuela to Trinidad
and Brazil.

♀

• *distinctive dark forewing borders*

striking pattern of "metalmarks" on hindwing underside is present in both sexes

♂ △

NEOTROPICAL

| Time of Flight ☼ | Habitat | Wingspan 1¼–1½ in (3–4 cm) |

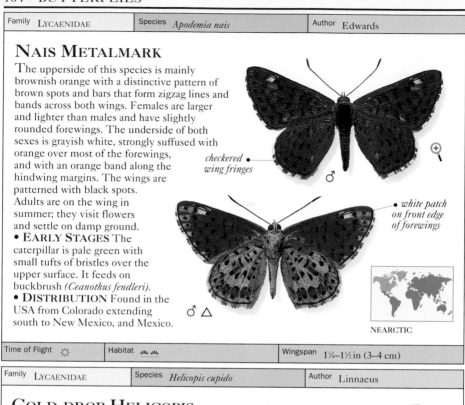

Family	LYCAENIDAE	Species	*Calephelis mutica*	Author	McAlpine

SWAMP METALMARK

This species is reddish brown with black lines and spots, and rows of silvery blue or bluish green-metallic markings. The underside varies from yellow to orange-brown, but has a similar pattern of black and metallic-blue markings. The sexes are similar.
• **EARLY STAGES** The hairy, pale green caterpillar feeds on swamp thistle *(Cirsium muticum)*.
• **DISTRIBUTION** Swamps from western Pennsylvania to southern Minnesota.

body matches color of • *wings*

♂

• *metallic markings on upper- and undersides*   NEARCTIC

♂ △

Time of Flight ☼	Habitat	Wingspan ¾–1 in (2–2.5 cm)

Family	LYCAENIDAE	Species	*Uraneis ucubis*	Author	Hewitson

HEWITSON'S URANEIS

This distinctive butterfly belongs to a genus of three South American species, all of them believed to be mimics of day-flying *Hypsid* moths. Males are smaller than females and have straighter outer margins to the wings. The underside is similar to the upperside. There are various forms of this butterfly.
• **EARLY STAGES** The caterpillar is undescribed and its foodplants are unknown.
• **DISTRIBUTION** Occurs throughout the tropical forests of Colombia.

♂

long, slender • *antennae*

• *white wing markings are smaller in males*

triangular, white markings •

• *females have more rounded wings*

pale • *wing fringes*

♀

• *distinctive blackish blue coloring*   NEOTROPICAL

Time of Flight ☼	Habitat	Wingspan 1¼–1½ in (3–4 cm)

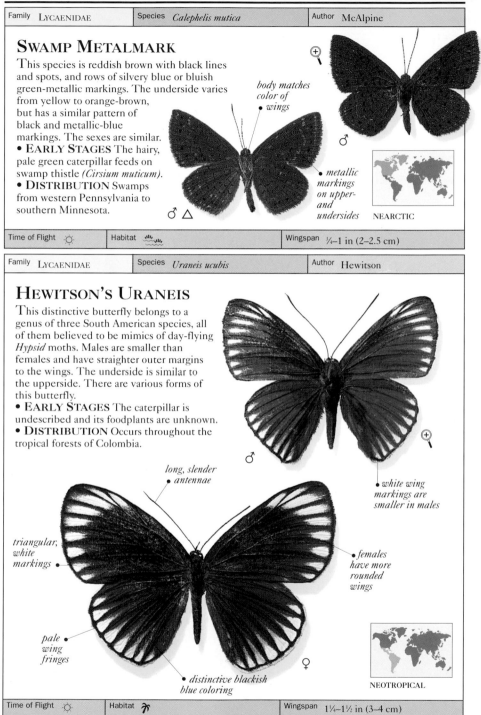

NYMPHALIDAE

A HUGE FAMILY composed of over 5,000 species, the Nymphalidae contains some of the world's most beautiful and spectacular butterflies, incorporating emperors, monarchs, fritillaries, admirals, and many others.

⸺ • ⸺

The most important characteristic separating this large group from other species of butterfly is the front pair of legs, which are usually undeveloped so they no longer have a walking function. In males they are often covered with dense tufts of scales, giving rise to the term "brush-footed butterflies" that is commonly applied to this family. The Nymphalidae are divided into numerous subfamilies, most of which, at one time, were regarded as distinct in their own right.

Family NYMPHALIDAE	Species *Cethosia biblis*	Author Drury

RED LACEWING

There are two female forms of this butterfly: one resembles the male, the other has a dull green ground color. The undersides of both sexes are orange-red with lacy patterns of white lines outlined in black. Several species in the genus are similar. These butterflies are on the wing throughout the year.
• **EARLY STAGES** The caterpillar is reputed to have poisonous, branched spines. It lives gregariously on passion flowers *(Passiflora)*.
• **DISTRIBUTION** Widespread from northern India to China, Malaysia, Indonesia, and the Philippines.

males of this species are rich reddish brown •

♂

• *V-shaped, white markings along margin*

♀

INDO–AUSTRALIAN

Time of Flight ☼	Habitat 🌴	Wingspan 3¼–3½ in (8–9 cm)

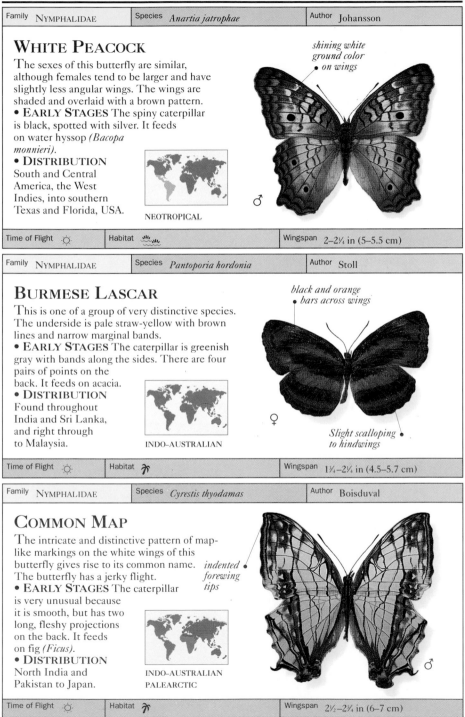

Family NYMPHALIDAE	Species *Anartia jatrophae*	Author Johansson

WHITE PEACOCK

The sexes of this butterfly are similar, although females tend to be larger and have slightly less angular wings. The wings are shaded and overlaid with a brown pattern.
• **EARLY STAGES** The spiny caterpillar is black, spotted with silver. It feeds on water hyssop *(Bacopa monnieri)*.
• **DISTRIBUTION** South and Central America, the West Indies, into southern Texas and Florida, USA.

shining white
ground color
on wings

NEOTROPICAL

♂

Time of Flight ☼	Habitat 〰	Wingspan 2–2¼ in (5–5.5 cm)

Family NYMPHALIDAE	Species *Pantoporia hordonia*	Author Stoll

BURMESE LASCAR

This is one of a group of very distinctive species. The underside is pale straw-yellow with brown lines and narrow marginal bands.
• **EARLY STAGES** The caterpillar is greenish gray with bands along the sides. There are four pairs of points on the back. It feeds on acacia.
• **DISTRIBUTION** Found throughout India and Sri Lanka, and right through to Malaysia.

black and orange
bars across wings

INDO–AUSTRALIAN

♀

Slight scalloping
to hindwings

Time of Flight ☼	Habitat 🌿	Wingspan 1¾–2¼ in (4.5–5.7 cm)

Family NYMPHALIDAE	Species *Cyrestis thyodamas*	Author Boisduval

COMMON MAP

The intricate and distinctive pattern of map-like markings on the white wings of this butterfly gives rise to its common name. The butterfly has a jerky flight.
• **EARLY STAGES** The caterpillar is very unusual because it is smooth, but has two long, fleshy projections on the back. It feeds on fig *(Ficus)*.
• **DISTRIBUTION** North India and Pakistan to Japan.

indented
forewing
tips

INDO–AUSTRALIAN
PALEARCTIC

♂

Time of Flight ☼	Habitat 🌿	Wingspan 2½–2¾ in (6–7 cm)

Family NYMPHALIDAE	Species *Araschnia levana*	Author Linnaeus

EUROPEAN MAP BUTTERFLY

This butterfly is remarkable for having quite distinct
spring and summer seasonal forms. Spring forms are orange
with dark brown markings, while summer forms are dark
chocolate-brown with white bands. There is a
characteristic, maplike pattern of yellowish white lines on
the dark underside that gives rise to the common name.
• **EARLY STAGES** The black, spiny caterpillar
feeds on stinging nettle *(Urtica dioica)*.
• **DISTRIBUTION**
Widespread in
Europe. Range
extends across
temperate Asia.

SPRING BROOD ♂

distinctively scalloped forewing

SUMMER BROOD

characteristic black and white wing fringes

PALEARCTIC

♂

Time of Flight ☼	Habitat	Wingspan 1¼–1½ in (3–4 cm)

Family NYMPHALIDAE	Species *Polyura delphis*	Author Doubleday

JEWELED NAWAB

The characteristic hindwing
tails of this butterfly are similar
to those of the closely related
Charaxes butterflies. The
upperside is pale, greenish
yellow to white, with a black,
triangular tip to the forewing.
The underside is pale blue
with brown, green, and darker
blue markings. This species
varies in pattern.
• **EARLY STAGES** The
caterpillar is undescribed; other
caterpillars of this group have
distinctive horned heads. The
foodplant is unknown.
• **DISTRIBUTION** Extends from
north India and Pakistan to Burma.

triangular, dark tip to forewing

marginal markings on hindwing are variable

robust body ♂

INDO-AUSTRALIAN

Time of Flight ☼	Habitat	Wingspan 3¾–4 in (9.5–10 cm)

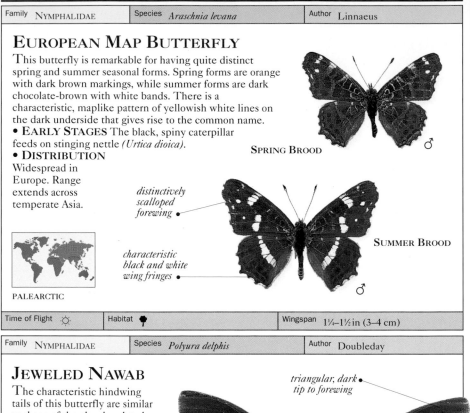

| Family NYMPHALIDAE | Species *Polyura pyrrhus* | Author Linnaeus |

TAILED EMPEROR

The extent of black on the upperside of this butterfly is very variable and some specimens are predominantly creamy yellow with narrow, black margins. There is always a marginal band of blue on the hindwing that runs into the distinctive paired tails. The underside is brown with a creamy white center, banded with black. The outer margin of the hindwing is orange with a black border on either side, and inside this is a series of striking, maroon-red spots. The sexes are similar. These butterflies have a powerful flight. They rest high up in treetops, descending to feed on rotting fruit. Some subspecies, including *Semproneus fabricius* from Australia, are now regarded as distinct species.
• **EARLY STAGES** The caterpillar is green and finely speckled with white spots. There is a yellow line along the sides and two or more striking yellow transverse bands on the back. It feeds on acacia.
• **DISTRIBUTION** Occurs from the Moluccas to Papua New Guinea and Australia.

the caterpillar is well camouflaged on its food plant •

CATERPILLAR OF POLYURA PYRRHUS

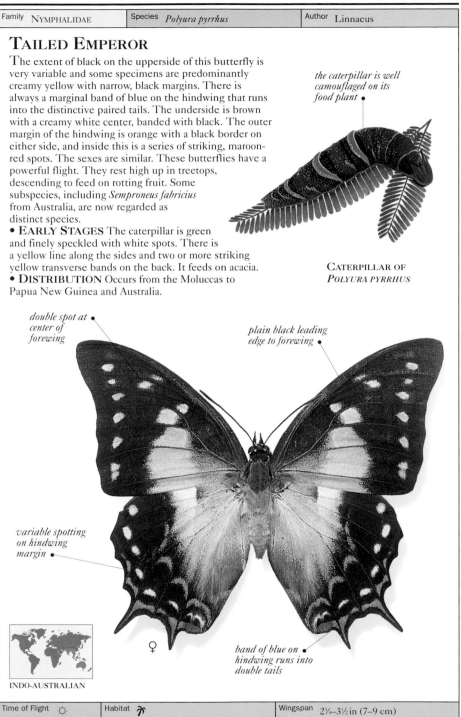

double spot at center of forewing

plain black leading edge to forewing •

variable spotting on hindwing margin •

♀

band of blue on • hindwing runs into double tails

INDO-AUSTRALIAN

| Time of Flight ☼ | Habitat | Wingspan 2¾–3½ in (7–9 cm) |

Family NYMPHALIDAE	Species *Aglais urticae*	Author Linnaeus

SMALL TORTOISESHELL

One of the most common European butterflies, this species is relatively small and bright. A distinctive marginal row of blue spots extends across the fore- and hindwing. The sexes are very similar. Butterflies are on the wing from spring to autumn. Those that emerge in late summer hibernate.
• **EARLY STAGES** The spiny caterpillar is black with broken, yellow bands. It feeds on stinging nettle *(Urtica dioica)*.
• **DISTRIBUTION** Widespread across Europe, extending through temperate Asia to Japan.

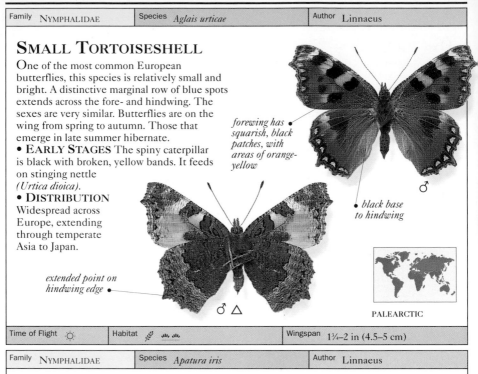

forewing has squarish, black patches, with areas of orange-yellow

♂

• black base to hindwing

extended point on hindwing edge •

♂ △

PALEARCTIC

Time of Flight ☀	Habitat 🌾 🌿 🌿	Wingspan 1¾–2 in (4.5–5 cm)

Family NYMPHALIDAE	Species *Apatura iris*	Author Linnaeus

PURPLE EMPEROR

Males of this beautiful species are suffused with iridescent purple. The underlying pattern is blackish brown with white markings. These butterflies fly around the treetops.
• **EARLY STAGES** The plump green caterpillar tapers at each end. It feeds on willow *(Salix)*.
• **DISTRIBUTION** Widespread in woodlands in Europe and across temperate Asia to Japan.

♂

• large orange, black, and purple eyespot on each hindwing

• the undersides of both sexes are shaded brown and marked with white

♂ △

PALEARCTIC

Time of Flight ☀	Habitat 🌳	Wingspan 2½–3 in (6–7.5 cm)

Family	NYMPHALIDAE	Species	Asterocampa celtis	Authors	Boisduval & Leconte

HACKBERRY BUTTERFLY

This brown butterfly is intricately and variably patterned with dark brown spots and bands. The tip of the forewing is characteristically spotted with white. Females are larger and paler than males, and their hindwings are more rounded. Butterflies are on the wing from spring to autumn, depending on the locality.
• **EARLY STAGES** The caterpillar is bright green with yellow stripes. The head has small branched horns. It feeds on hackberry *(Celtis)*.
• **DISTRIBUTION** Widespread in North America, from southern Ontario to Florida and Texas.

slight scalloping to wings

♂

distinctive angular hindwings

black and white eyespots on hindwing underside

NEARCTIC

♂ △

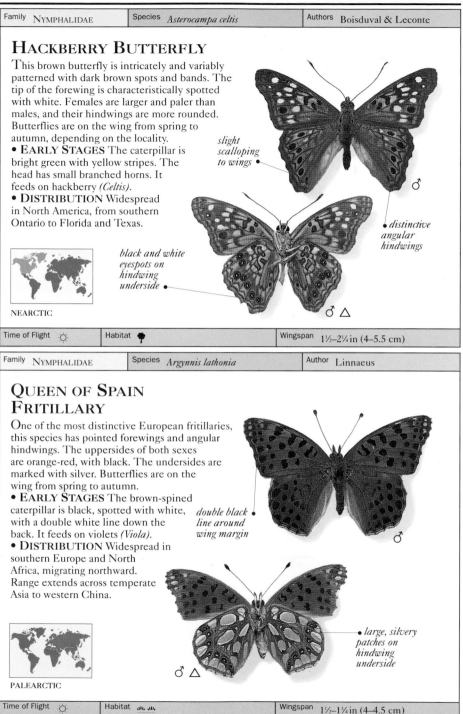

Time of Flight ☼	Habitat 🌳	Wingspan 1½–2¼ in (4–5.5 cm)

Family	NYMPHALIDAE	Species	Argynnis lathonia	Author	Linnaeus

QUEEN OF SPAIN FRITILLARY

One of the most distinctive European fritillaries, this species has pointed forewings and angular hindwings. The uppersides of both sexes are orange-red, with black. The undersides are marked with silver. Butterflies are on the wing from spring to autumn.
• **EARLY STAGES** The brown-spined caterpillar is black, spotted with white, with a double white line down the back. It feeds on violets *(Viola)*.
• **DISTRIBUTION** Widespread in southern Europe and North Africa, migrating northward. Range extends across temperate Asia to western China.

double black line around wing margin

♂

large, silvery patches on hindwing underside

♂ △

PALEARCTIC

Time of Flight ☼	Habitat ⸲⸲ ⸲⸲	Wingspan 1½–1¾ in (4–4.5 cm)

| Family NYMPHALIDAE | Species *Euthalia aconthea* | Author Cramer |

BARON

Males have dark brown wings with blackish brown markings, and a diffuse, whitish gray band on the forewing. Females are larger and paler, and are usually marked with varying degrees of white on both fore- and hindwings. The undersides of both sexes are pale brown with a band of blackish spots along the wing margins, and blackish rings at the wing bases.

• **EARLY STAGES** The caterpillar is green with a yellow stripe along the back. It feeds on mango *(Mangifera indica)* and cashew *(Anacardium).*

• **DISTRIBUTION** Found from India and Sri Lanka, to China, and through Malaysia to Indonesia.

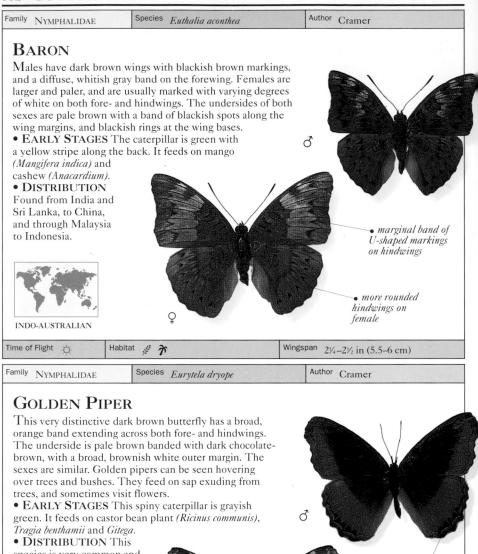

♂

♀

• *marginal band of U-shaped markings on hindwings*

• *more rounded hindwings on female*

INDO-AUSTRALIAN

| Time of Flight ☼ | Habitat 🌿 🌴 | Wingspan 2¼–2½ in (5.5–6 cm) |

| Family NYMPHALIDAE | Species *Eurytela dryope* | Author Cramer |

GOLDEN PIPER

This very distinctive dark brown butterfly has a broad, orange band extending across both fore- and hindwings. The underside is pale brown banded with dark chocolate-brown, with a broad, brownish white outer margin. The sexes are similar. Golden pipers can be seen hovering over trees and bushes. They feed on sap exuding from trees, and sometimes visit flowers.

• **EARLY STAGES** This spiny caterpillar is grayish green. It feeds on castor bean plant *(Ricinus communis)*, *Tragia benthamii* and *Gitega*.

• **DISTRIBUTION** This species is very common and widespread in tropical and southern Africa. It also occurs in Madagascar and the Middle East.

♂

dark brown • outer margin to upperside hindwing

• distinctive scalloped outline to wings

♂ △

AFROTROPICAL

| Time of Flight ☼ | Habitat 🌴 | Wingspan 2–2½ in (5–6 cm) |

Family NYMPHALIDAE	Species *Phyciodes tharos*	Author Drury

PEARL CRESCENT

This is a common North American butterfly. The upperside is orange with blackish brown borders and black markings at the wing bases. The forewing underside is pale orange with two black patches on the hind margin. It also has crescent-shaped markings on the hindwing. Another name for the butterfly is the pearly crescentspot.
• **EARLY STAGES** The caterpillar is black with white and black spines. Its food-plants are unknown.
• **DISTRIBUTION** From southern Canada, south to Mexico.

series of spots on hindwing

♂

white crescent on hindwing margin

NEARCTIC

♂ △

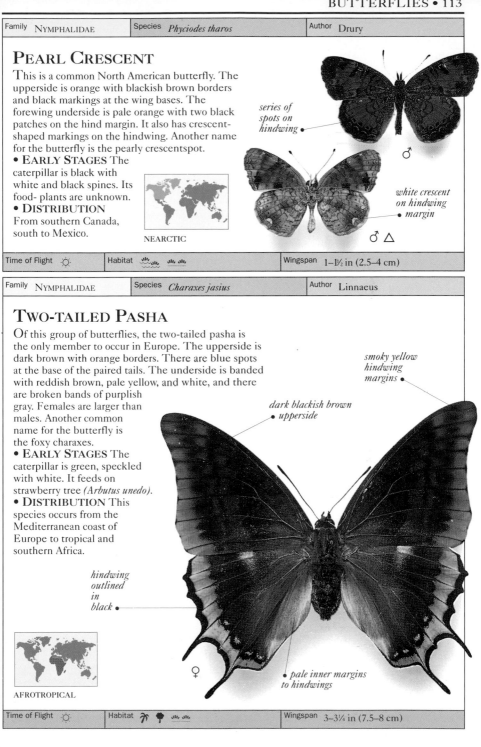

Time of Flight ☼	Habitat	Wingspan 1–1½ in (2.5–4 cm)

Family NYMPHALIDAE	Species *Charaxes jasius*	Author Linnaeus

TWO-TAILED PASHA

Of this group of butterflies, the two-tailed pasha is the only member to occur in Europe. The upperside is dark brown with orange borders. There are blue spots at the base of the paired tails. The underside is banded with reddish brown, pale yellow, and white, and there are broken bands of purplish gray. Females are larger than males. Another common name for the butterfly is the foxy charaxes.
• **EARLY STAGES** The caterpillar is green, speckled with white. It feeds on strawberry tree *(Arbutus unedo)*.
• **DISTRIBUTION** This species occurs from the Mediterranean coast of Europe to tropical and southern Africa.

smoky yellow hindwing margins

dark blackish brown upperside

hindwing outlined in black

pale inner margins to hindwings

♀

AFROTROPICAL

Time of Flight ☼	Habitat	Wingspan 3–3¼ in (7.5–8 cm)

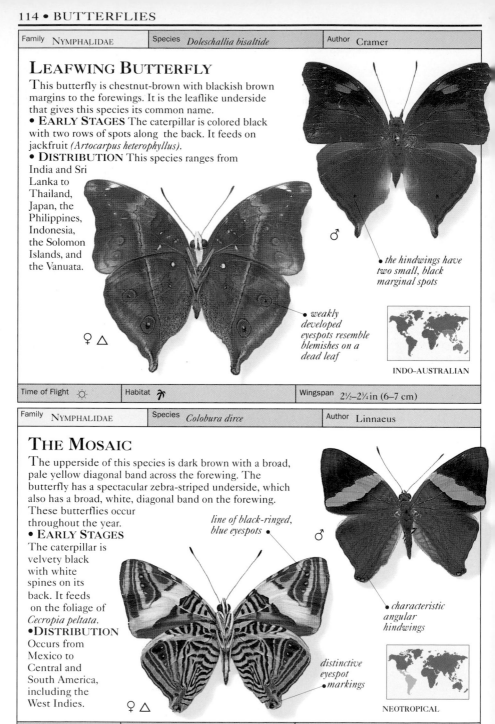

Family NYMPHALIDAE	Species *Doleschallia bisaltide*	Author Cramer

LEAFWING BUTTERFLY

This butterfly is chestnut-brown with blackish brown margins to the forewings. It is the leaflike underside that gives this species its common name.

• **EARLY STAGES** The caterpillar is colored black with two rows of spots along the back. It feeds on jackfruit *(Artocarpus heterophyllus)*.

• **DISTRIBUTION** This species ranges from India and Sri Lanka to Thailand, Japan, the Philippines, Indonesia, the Solomon Islands, and the Vanuata.

♂

• *the hindwings have two small, black marginal spots*

• *weakly developed eyespots resemble blemishes on a dead leaf*

♀ △

INDO–AUSTRALIAN

Time of Flight ☼	Habitat 🦋	Wingspan 2½–2¾ in (6–7 cm)

Family NYMPHALIDAE	Species *Colobura dirce*	Author Linnaeus

THE MOSAIC

The upperside of this species is dark brown with a broad, pale yellow diagonal band across the forewing. The butterfly has a spectacular zebra-striped underside, which also has a broad, white, diagonal band on the forewing. These butterflies occur throughout the year.

line of black-ringed, blue eyespots •

♂

• **EARLY STAGES** The caterpillar is velvety black with white spines on its back. It feeds on the foliage of *Cecropia peltata*.

• **DISTRIBUTION** Occurs from Mexico to Central and South America, including the West Indies.

• *characteristic angular hindwings*

distinctive eyespot • *markings*

♀ △

NEOTROPICAL

Time of Flight ☼	Habitat 🦋	Wingspan 2¼–3 in (5.5–7.5 cm)

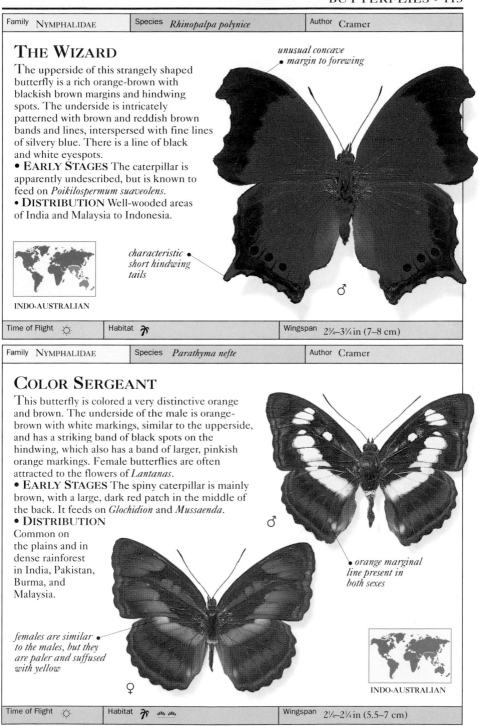

Family NYMPHALIDAE	Species *Rhinopalpa polynice*	Author Cramer

THE WIZARD

The upperside of this strangely shaped butterfly is a rich orange-brown with blackish brown margins and hindwing spots. The underside is intricately patterned with brown and reddish brown bands and lines, interspersed with fine lines of silvery blue. There is a line of black and white eyespots.

• **EARLY STAGES** The caterpillar is apparently undescribed, but is known to feed on *Poikilospermum suaveolens*.

• **DISTRIBUTION** Well-wooded areas of India and Malaysia to Indonesia.

unusual concave • margin to forewing

characteristic • short hindwing tails

INDO-AUSTRALIAN

♂

Time of Flight ☼	Habitat 🌴	Wingspan 2¾–3¼ in (7–8 cm)

Family NYMPHALIDAE	Species *Parathyma nefte*	Author Cramer

COLOR SERGEANT

This butterfly is colored a very distinctive orange and brown. The underside of the male is orange-brown with white markings, similar to the upperside, and has a striking band of black spots on the hindwing, which also has a band of larger, pinkish orange markings. Female butterflies are often attracted to the flowers of *Lantanas*.

• **EARLY STAGES** The spiny caterpillar is mainly brown, with a large, dark red patch in the middle of the back. It feeds on *Glochidion* and *Mussaenda*.

• **DISTRIBUTION** Common on the plains and in dense rainforest in India, Pakistan, Burma, and Malaysia.

♂

• orange marginal line present in both sexes

females are similar • to the males, but they are paler and suffused with yellow

♀

INDO-AUSTRALIAN

Time of Flight ☼	Habitat 🌴 〰 〰	Wingspan 2¼–2¾ in (5.5–7 cm)

Family NYMPHALIDAE	Species *Charaxes bernardus*	Author Fabricius

TAWNY RAJAH

This beautiful Asian *Charaxes* butterfly is orange with a broad, white, central band and a blackish brown border to the forewing. The underside is grayish brown with an irregular pattern of darker lines. Females are similarly patterned to males, but are larger and have more developed hindwing tails. These butterflies fly rapidly around the treetops.

• **EARLY STAGES** The caterpillar is dark green with red spots on the body, and four red horns on the head. It feeds on various tropical trees and shrubs, including red sandalwood (*Adenanthera pavonia)* and albizias (Leguminosae).

• **DISTRIBUTION** Occurs in the jungles of India, Pakistan, Sri Lanka, Burma, and Malaysia.

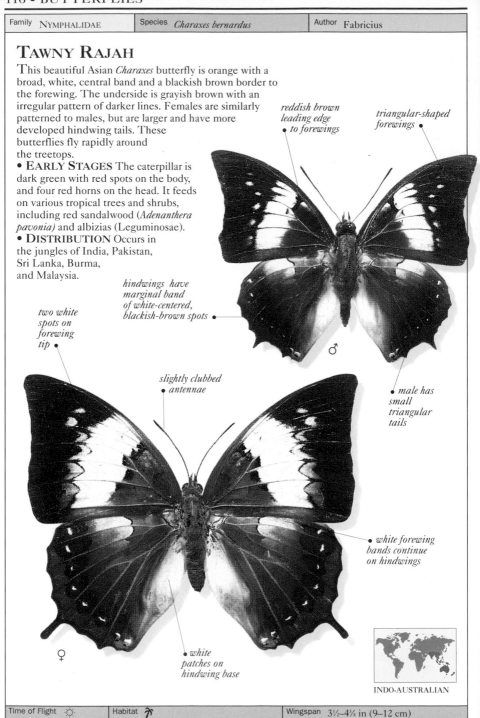

reddish brown leading edge to forewings

triangular-shaped forewings

hindwings have marginal band of white-centered, blackish-brown spots

two white spots on forewing tip

slightly clubbed antennae

male has small triangular tails

white forewing bands continue on hindwings

white patches on hindwing base

INDO-AUSTRALIAN

Time of Flight ☼	Habitat 🌿		Wingspan 3½–4¼ in (9–12 cm)

Family NYMPHALIDAE	Species *Brenthis ino*	Author Rottemburg

LESSER MARBLED FRITILLARY

This little butterfly has the typical fritillary markings: black spots on an orange ground. The undersides of the hindwings are yellow. Several geographical forms are known, but the species can usually be recognized by its small size and the solid black margins to the wings. The sexes are similar. These butterflies have a weak flight.
• **EARLY STAGES** The caterpillar is black with a double white stripe and orange-brown spines along its back. It feeds on great burnet *(Sanguisorba officinalis)*, meadowsweet *(Filipendula ulmaria)*, and raspberry *(Rubus idaea)*.
• **DISTRIBUTION** The lesser marbled fritillary is widespread across marshy areas of Europe, but not the British Isles. The range extends from temperate Asia to Japan.

clubbed antennae

black wing margins

♂

scalloped wing margins

black and cream wing margins

♂ △

characteristic brown-ringed spots on hindwings

PALEARCTIC

Time of Flight ☼	Habitat 〰	Wingspan 1¼–1½ in (3–4 cm)

Family NYMPHALIDAE	Species *Charaxes bohemani*	Author Felder

LARGE BLUE CHARAXES

The blue on the upperside of this beautiful *Charaxes* butterfly is slightly iridescent and is broadly bordered with black. Females are larger than males and have characteristic white diagonal forewing bands and longer hindwing tails. The underside of both sexes is dull purplish gray.
• **EARLY STAGES** The green caterpillar feeds on mahogany bean *(Afzelia quanzensis)* and related plants.
• **DISTRIBUTION** Occurs in open woodland and areas of scrub, throughout tropical Africa from Kenya to Malawi, Zambia, and Angola.

distinctive, white forewing spots

♂

two small, pointed tails

pale brown inner margin

AFROTROPICAL

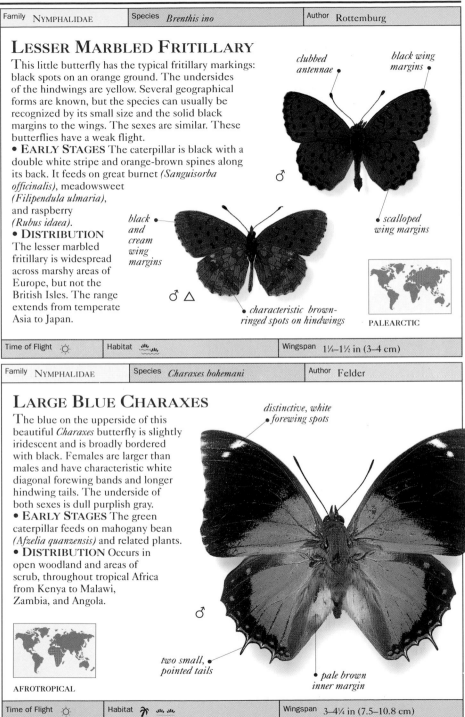

Time of Flight ☼	Habitat 🌴 〰 〰	Wingspan 3–4¼ in (7.5–10.8 cm)

Family NYMPHALIDAE	Species *Hypolimnas bolina*	Author Linnaeus

GREAT EGG-FLY

The males of this geographically variable butterfly are
generally velvety black with purple-edged white patches
in the middle of each wing. The larger females are blackish
brown with a much more complex pattern of white markings;
they have an orange-red patch on the forewing. In some
forms of this species, females lack the orange markings,
and the white markings are greatly reduced. The
undersides of both sexes are rather similar – they are
brown, with bands of white spots and patches. The
forewing is suffused toward the base with reddish
brown. These butterflies are attracted to *Lantanas*.
• **EARLY STAGES** The caterpillar is dark brown or black
with orange-yellow branched spines and a yellow line along
the side. It feeds on various tropical plants.
• **DISTRIBUTION** A very widespread species occurring
from India to Taiwan, Malaysia, Indonesia, and Australia.
There are many described subspecies.

*spiny, black
caterpillar*

CATERPILLAR OF
HYPOLIMNAS BOLINA

♂

*wavy black and
white fringes are
characteristic of
both sexes*

*the forewing is
suffused with
reddish brown
toward the base*

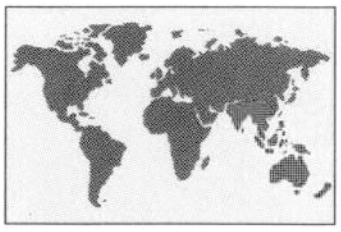

*concave
margin to
forewing*

♀

INDO-AUSTRALIAN

Time of Flight ☀	Habitat 🦋	Wingspan 2¾–4½ in (7–11 cm)

Family NYMPHALIDAE	Species *Hypolimnas salmacis*	Author Drury

BLUE DIADEM

Males of this appropriately named butterfly are rich blue with black wing margins and bases, and white dots. Females are often suffused with yellow. The underside is chocolate-brown with white bands and elongate, purple spots.
• **EARLY STAGES** The blue diadem caterpillar is dark brown with red spines. It feeds on *Urera hypselodendron* and *Fleurya*.
• **DISTRIBUTION** Lowland forests from tropical west to east Africa.

white spots at tip of forewing distinguish this butterfly from • *similar species*

wavy, black and white wing fringes •

AFROTROPICAL

♂

Time of Flight ☼	Habitat 🌴	Wingspan 3½–3¾ in (9–9.5 cm)

Family NYMPHALIDAE	Species *Prepona meander*	Author Cramer

BANDED KING SHOEMAKER

This beautiful butterfly belongs to a group of similar species. The pattern of metallic, greenish blue on black is very striking and quite variable, and many forms have been named. The underside by contrast is grayish brown, with a dark brown central band. The sexes are similar. When in flight these butterflies make a crackling sound.
• **EARLY STAGES** The caterpillar's head has two spiny horns. It feeds on plants of the family Annonaceae.
• **DISTRIBUTION** Widespread in Central and South America, including the West Indies.

blue band broken at top, leaving two floating spots of color •

slight scalloping to hindwing edge •

NEOTROPICAL

♀

• *robust body*

Time of Flight ☼	Habitat 🌴	Wingspan 3¼–4¼ in (8–10.8 cm)

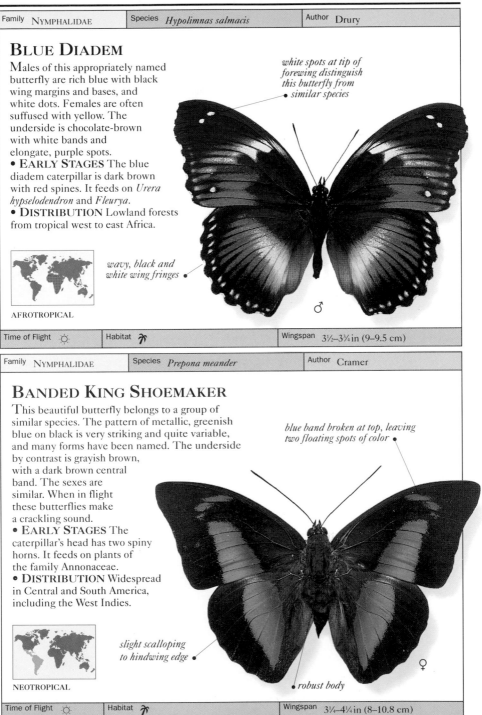

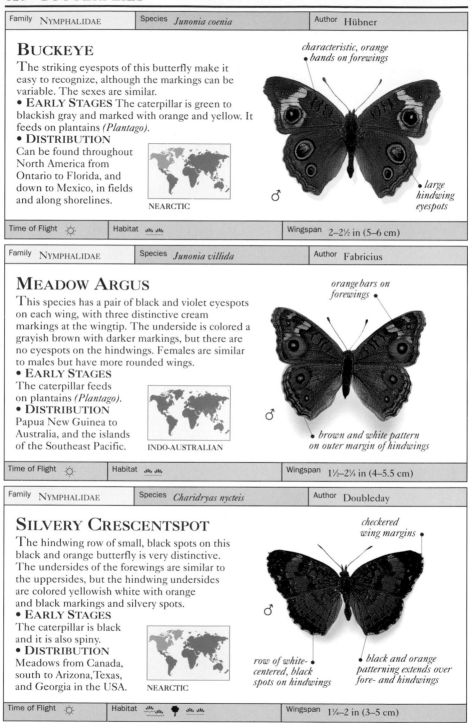

| Family NYMPHALIDAE | Species *Junonia coenia* | Author Hübner |

BUCKEYE

The striking eyespots of this butterfly make it easy to recognize, although the markings can be variable. The sexes are similar.
• **EARLY STAGES** The caterpillar is green to blackish gray and marked with orange and yellow. It feeds on plantains *(Plantago)*.
• **DISTRIBUTION**
Can be found throughout North America from Ontario to Florida, and down to Mexico, in fields and along shorelines.

NEARCTIC

characteristic, orange bands on forewings

♂

large hindwing eyespots

| Time of Flight ☀ | Habitat ⸌⸍ ⸌⸍ | Wingspan 2–2½ in (5–6 cm) |

| Family NYMPHALIDAE | Species *Junonia villida* | Author Fabricius |

MEADOW ARGUS

This species has a pair of black and violet eyespots on each wing, with three distinctive cream markings at the wingtip. The underside is colored a grayish brown with darker markings, but there are no eyespots on the hindwings. Females are similar to males but have more rounded wings.
• **EARLY STAGES**
The caterpillar feeds on plantains *(Plantago)*.
• **DISTRIBUTION**
Papua New Guinea to Australia, and the islands of the Southeast Pacific.

INDO-AUSTRALIAN

orange bars on forewings

♂

brown and white pattern on outer margin of hindwings

| Time of Flight ☀ | Habitat ⸌⸍ ⸌⸍ | Wingspan 1½–2¼ in (4–5.5 cm) |

| Family NYMPHALIDAE | Species *Charidryas nycteis* | Author Doubleday |

SILVERY CRESCENTSPOT

The hindwing row of small, black spots on this black and orange butterfly is very distinctive. The undersides of the forewings are similar to the uppersides, but the hindwing undersides are colored yellowish white with orange and black markings and silvery spots.
• **EARLY STAGES**
The caterpillar is black and it is also spiny.
• **DISTRIBUTION**
Meadows from Canada, south to Arizona, Texas, and Georgia in the USA.

NEARCTIC

checkered wing margins

♂

row of white-centered, black spots on hindwings

black and orange patterning extends over fore- and hindwings

| Time of Flight ☀ | Habitat ⸌⸍ 🌳 ⸌⸍ ⸌⸍ | Wingspan 1¼–2 in (3–5 cm) |

Family NYMPHALIDAE	Species *Salamis parhassus*	Author Drury

MOTHER-OF-PEARL BUTTERFLY

This beautifully patterned butterfly is a
translucent pale green, suffused with
iridescent purple. Both the fore- and
hindwings have dark eyespots, but
those near the hindwing tails are
brightly colored and prominent. The
underside is similar to the upperside but
lacks dark wing margins and has smaller
red eyespots. The sexes are alike.
• EARLY STAGES The spiny caterpillar
is dark brown with a band of orange-red
markings along its back.
• DISTRIBUTION Common in dense
woodland, particularly along forest rivers, in
tropical Africa, extending into South Africa.

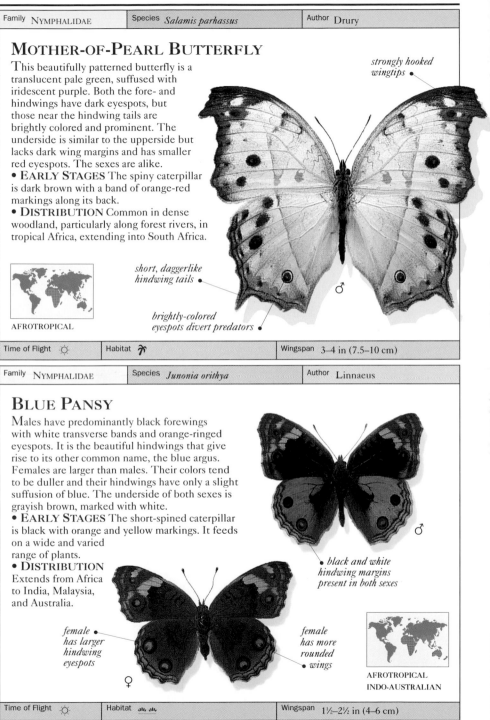

*strongly hooked
wingtips* •

AFROTROPICAL

*short, daggerlike
hindwing tails* •

♂

*brightly-colored
eyespots divert predators* •

Time of Flight ☼	Habitat 🌴	Wingspan 3–4 in (7.5–10 cm)

Family NYMPHALIDAE	Species *Junonia orithya*	Author Linnaeus

BLUE PANSY

Males have predominantly black forewings
with white transverse bands and orange-ringed
eyespots. It is the beautiful hindwings that give
rise to its other common name, the blue argus.
Females are larger than males. Their colors tend
to be duller and their hindwings have only a slight
suffusion of blue. The underside of both sexes is
grayish brown, marked with white.
• EARLY STAGES The short-spined caterpillar
is black with orange and yellow markings. It feeds
on a wide and varied
range of plants.
• DISTRIBUTION
Extends from Africa
to India, Malaysia,
and Australia.

♂

• *black and white
hindwing margins
present in both sexes*

*female •
has larger
hindwing
eyespots*

♀

*female
has more
rounded
• wings*

AFROTROPICAL
INDO-AUSTRALIAN

Time of Flight ☼	Habitat ⚘ ⚘	Wingspan 1½–2½ in (4–6 cm)

Family NYMPHALIDAE	Species *Poladryas minuta*	Author Edwards

DOTTED CHECKERSPOT

With its pretty, checkered pattern of black and orange, this is a typical fritillary. The underside is mainly pale orange with a series of large, white, marginal markings on both wings and distinctive black spots. Females are considerably larger than males.

• **EARLY STAGES** The caterpillar is orange with orange and black spines. It feeds on beardtongue *(Penstemon)*. There are several broods a year.

• **DISTRIBUTION** Found in limestone and chalk districts where the foodplant flourishes; from Colorado, Arizona, and Texas south to Mexico.

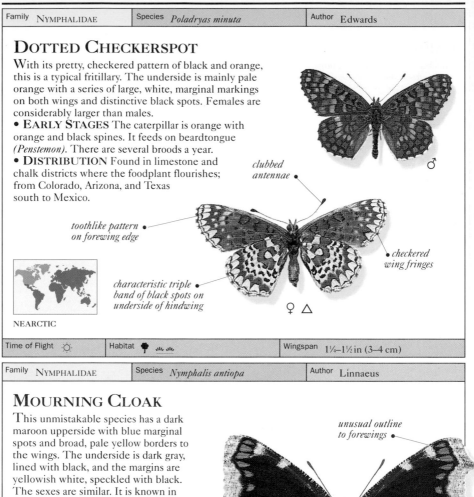

clubbed antennae •

♂

toothlike pattern • on forewing edge

• checkered wing fringes

characteristic triple • band of black spots on underside of hindwing

♀ △

NEARCTIC

Time of Flight ☀	Habitat 🦋 ⸜ ⸜	Wingspan 1¼–1½ in (3–4 cm)

Family NYMPHALIDAE	Species *Nymphalis antiopa*	Author Linnaeus

MOURNING CLOAK

This unmistakable species has a dark maroon upperside with blue marginal spots and broad, pale yellow borders to the wings. The underside is dark gray, lined with black, and the margins are yellowish white, speckled with black. The sexes are similar. It is known in Britain as the camberwell beauty.

• **EARLY STAGES** The spiny caterpillar is velvety black, finely spotted with white, with a row of reddish brown patches along the back. It feeds on various deciduous trees.

• **DISTRIBUTION** Found in Europe and temperate Asia. Also occurs from North America to central Mexico.

unusual outline to forewings •

♂

speckled effect • to yellow borders

distinctive row • of black-ringed blue spots

HOLARCTIC

Time of Flight ☀	Habitat 🌳 ⸜ ⸜ ⛰	Wingspan 2½–3¼ in (6–8 cm)

Family NYMPHALIDAE	Species *Nymphalis polychloros*	Author Linnaeus

LARGE TORTOISESHELL

This butterfly can be distinguished from the small tortoiseshell (*Aglais urticae*, see p.110) by its larger size, its hairy appearance, and the lack of white markings on the leading edge of its forewing. The underside is patterned with various shades of brown and has a distinctive marginal band of slate-gray.

• **EARLY STAGES** The caterpillar is black, speckled finely with white, and has orange-brown spines. Orange lines extend along the back and sides. It feeds on the foliage of various broadleaves.

• **DISTRIBUTION** Widespread in Europe, extending to North Africa and the Himalayas.

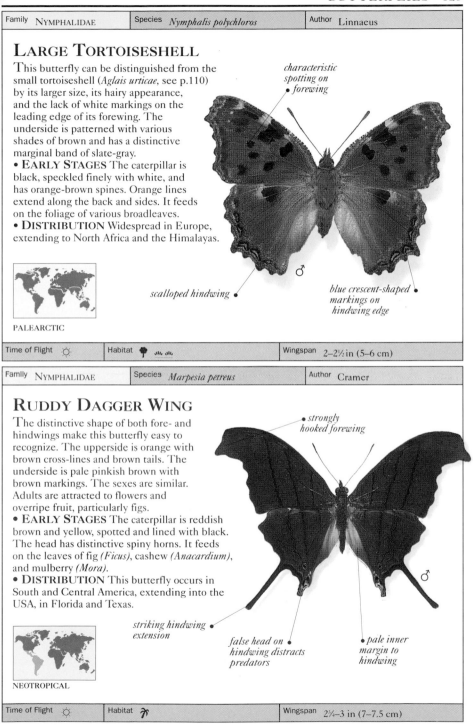

characteristic spotting on forewing

scalloped hindwing

♂

blue crescent-shaped markings on hindwing edge

PALEARCTIC

Time of Flight ☼	Habitat 🌳 🌿 🌿	Wingspan 2–2½ in (5–6 cm)

Family NYMPHALIDAE	Species *Marpesia petreus*	Author Cramer

RUDDY DAGGER WING

The distinctive shape of both fore- and hindwings make this butterfly easy to recognize. The upperside is orange with brown cross-lines and brown tails. The underside is pale pinkish brown with brown markings. The sexes are similar. Adults are attracted to flowers and overripe fruit, particularly figs.

• **EARLY STAGES** The caterpillar is reddish brown and yellow, spotted and lined with black. The head has distinctive spiny horns. It feeds on the leaves of fig *(Ficus)*, cashew *(Anacardium)*, and mulberry *(Mora)*.

• **DISTRIBUTION** This butterfly occurs in South and Central America, extending into the USA, in Florida and Texas.

strongly hooked forewing

striking hindwing extension

false head on hindwing distracts predators

♂

pale inner margin to hindwing

NEOTROPICAL

Time of Flight ☼	Habitat 🌴	Wingspan 2¾–3 in (7–7.5 cm)

Family NYMPHALIDAE	Species *Basilarchia archippus*	Author Cramer

THE VICEROY

The viceroy has a remarkable resemblance to the monarch butterfly (*Danaus plexippus*, see p.184), but it can be distinguished by the black line that crosses the wing veins. These butterflies are on the wing from spring to autumn. They are attracted to honeydew secreted by aphids.
• **EARLY STAGES** The humped caterpillar is mottled olive-green and brown, and has a pair of bristly tufts behind the head. It feeds on the foliage of willow *(Salix)*, and cottonwood *(Populus)*.
• **DISTRIBUTION** From Canada, right through the USA, down to Mexico.

NEARCTIC
NEOTROPICAL

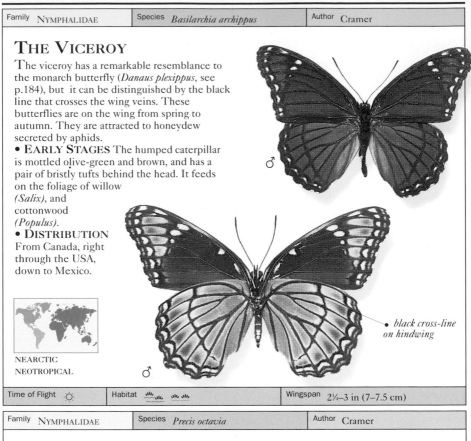

♂

• *black cross-line on hindwing*

♂

Time of Flight ☼	Habitat 〰〰 〰〰	Wingspan 2¾–3 in (7–7.5 cm)

Family NYMPHALIDAE	Species *Precis octavia*	Author Cramer

THE GAUDY COMMODORE

This beautiful butterfly occurs in two distinct seasonal forms. The dry season form (shown right) is dark brown, variably suffused with blue. The wet season form is orange-red with dark brown spotting and borders. There is geographic variation in this species.
• **EARLY STAGES** The spiny caterpillar is dark brown with a reddish brown head. It feeds on *Coleus* and Labiatae.
• **DISTRIBUTION** Wooded localities in tropical and southern Africa.

AFROTROPICAL

marginal band of red-ringed black spots

♂

distinctive scalloped outline to hindwing

Time of Flight ☼	Habitat 🌴	Wingspan 2–2½ in (5–6 cm)

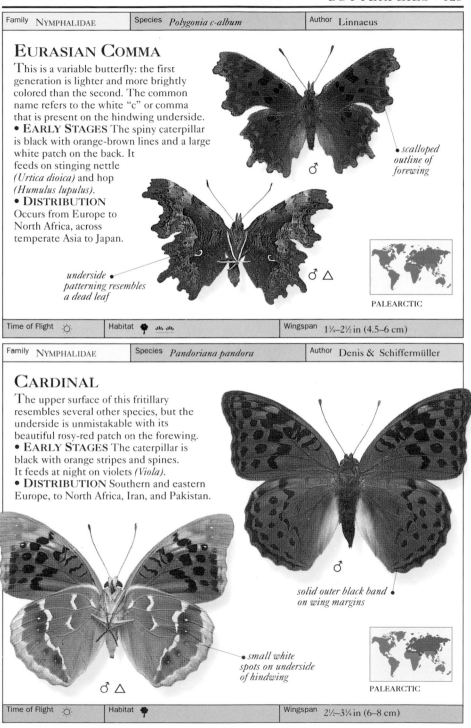

| Family NYMPHALIDAE | Species *Polygonia c-album* | Author Linnaeus |

EURASIAN COMMA

This is a variable butterfly: the first generation is lighter and more brightly colored than the second. The common name refers to the white "c" or comma that is present on the hindwing underside.
• **EARLY STAGES** The spiny caterpillar is black with orange-brown lines and a large white patch on the back. It feeds on stinging nettle *(Urtica dioica)* and hop *(Humulus lupulus)*.
• **DISTRIBUTION** Occurs from Europe to North Africa, across temperate Asia to Japan.

scalloped outline of forewing

♂

underside patterning resembles a dead leaf

♂ △

PALEARCTIC

| Time of Flight ☼ | Habitat | Wingspan 1¾–2½ in (4.5–6 cm) |

| Family NYMPHALIDAE | Species *Pandoriana pandora* | Author Denis & Schiffermüller |

CARDINAL

The upper surface of this fritillary resembles several other species, but the underside is unmistakable with its beautiful rosy-red patch on the forewing.
• **EARLY STAGES** The caterpillar is black with orange stripes and spines. It feeds at night on violets *(Viola).*
• **DISTRIBUTION** Southern and eastern Europe, to North Africa, Iran, and Pakistan.

♂

solid outer black band on wing margins

♂ △

small white spots on underside of hindwing

PALEARCTIC

| Time of Flight ☼ | Habitat | Wingspan 2½–3¼ in (6–8 cm) |

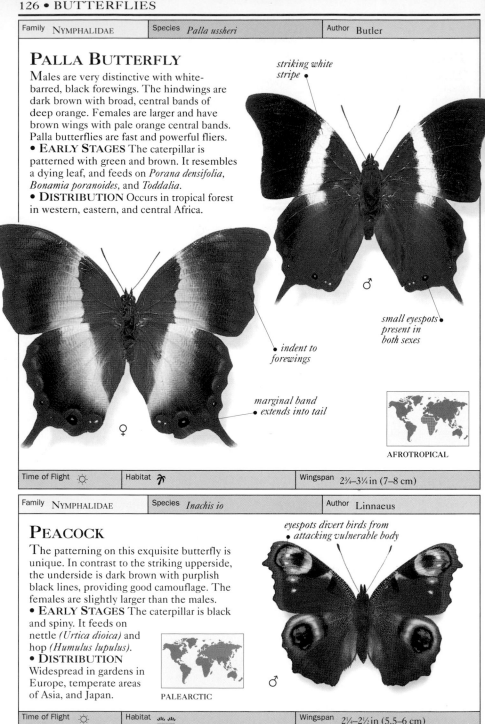

Family NYMPHALIDAE	Species *Palla ussheri*	Author Butler

PALLA BUTTERFLY

Males are very distinctive with white-barred, black forewings. The hindwings are dark brown with broad, central bands of deep orange. Females are larger and have brown wings with pale orange central bands. Palla butterflies are fast and powerful fliers.
• **EARLY STAGES** The caterpillar is patterned with green and brown. It resembles a dying leaf, and feeds on *Porana densifolia*, *Bonamia poranoides*, and *Toddalia*.
• **DISTRIBUTION** Occurs in tropical forest in western, eastern, and central Africa.

striking white stripe •

♂

small eyespots • present in both sexes

• *indent to forewings*

marginal band • extends into tail

♀

AFROTROPICAL

Time of Flight ☼	Habitat 🌴	Wingspan 2¾–3¼ in (7–8 cm)

Family NYMPHALIDAE	Species *Inachis io*	Author Linnaeus

PEACOCK

The patterning on this exquisite butterfly is unique. In contrast to the striking upperside, the underside is dark brown with purplish black lines, providing good camouflage. The females are slightly larger than the males.
• **EARLY STAGES** The caterpillar is black and spiny. It feeds on nettle *(Urtica dioica)* and hop *(Humulus lupulus)*.
• **DISTRIBUTION** Widespread in gardens in Europe, temperate areas of Asia, and Japan.

eyespots divert birds from • attacking vulnerable body

♂

PALEARCTIC

Time of Flight ☼	Habitat	Wingspan 2¼–2½ in (5.5–6 cm)

Family NYMPHALIDAE	Species *Kallima inachus*	Author Boisduval

INDIAN LEAF BUTTERFLY

The uppersides of both the male and the female butterfly are brightly and attractively colored with orange and purplish blue. However, the brown patterning of the underside, coupled with the unusual wing shape, makes this one of the most remarkable leaf mimics of all. This facility for camouflage has given the Indian leaf butterfly its very apt common name.

• **EARLY STAGES** The caterpillar is velvety black with red spines and long yellow hairs. It feeds on *Girardinia* and *Strobilanthes*, as well as other plants.

• **DISTRIBUTION** This species is widespread from India and Pakistan, to southern China and Taiwan.

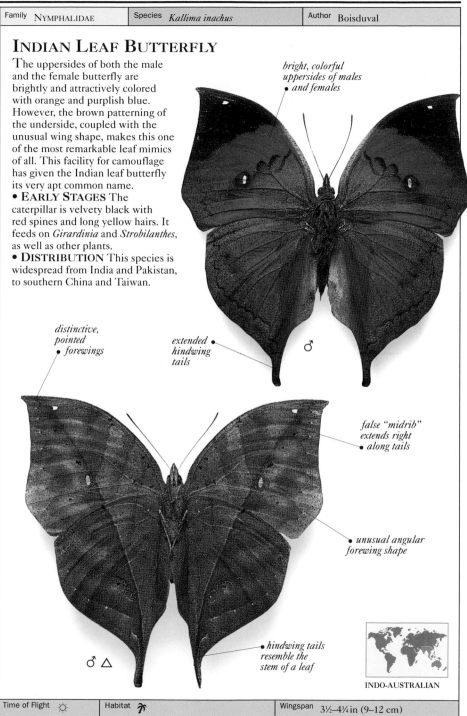

bright, colorful uppersides of males and females

distinctive, pointed forewings

extended hindwing tails

♂

false "midrib" extends right along tails

unusual angular forewing shape

♂ △

hindwing tails resemble the stem of a leaf

INDO-AUSTRALIAN

Time of Flight ☼	Habitat 🌿	Wingspan 3½–4¾ in (9–12 cm)

Family NYMPHALIDAE	Species *Vindula erota*	Author Fabricius

CRUISER BUTTERFLY

Males are orange-brown with a paler,
central band. The underside is similar
but with reddish brown lines. Females are
grayish brown with orange on the hindwing
and a central white band. The underside has
red lines and pale patches.
• EARLY STAGES The caterpillar is pale
yellow with brown markings and feeds on
Adenia and passion flower *(Passiflora)*.
• DISTRIBUTION Occurs in forests,
from India and Pakistan, to Malaysia
and Indonesia.

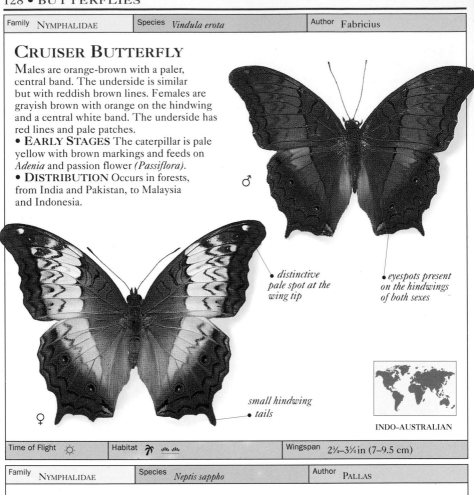

♂

• *distinctive
pale spot at the
wing tip*

• *eyespots present
on the hindwings
of both sexes*

♀

*small hindwing
• tails*

INDO–AUSTRALIAN

Time of Flight ☼	Habitat 🌴 ⸙ ⸙	Wingspan 2¾–3¾ in (7–9.5 cm)

Family NYMPHALIDAE	Species *Neptis sappho*	Author PALLAS

COMMON GLIDER

This distinctive European species belongs to
a genus of butterflies occurring throughout
Africa and Southeast Asia. Its wing pattern of
black and white bands distinguishes it from
other European butterflies. The underside of
the common glider is a rusty, reddish brown.
• EARLY STAGES The caterpillar is smooth
with four pairs of spiny projections on the back.
It feeds on spring
pea *(Lathyrus)*.
• DISTRIBUTION
Found in woodland
and on scrub-covered
hillsides in central
and eastern Europe.

*central forewing
streak* •

♂

*characteristic
double, white
hindwing band*

PALEARCTIC

Time of Flight ☼	Habitat 🌳	Wingspan 1¾–2 in (4.5–5 cm)

Family NYMPHALIDAE	Species *Sasakia charonda*	Author Hewitson

JAPANESE EMPEROR

This beautiful species is the national butterfly of Japan.
Male Japanese emperors have distinctive, dark brown
wings with a bronze-green sheen, richly suffused with
iridescent purple. The females are brown, but without
the purple iridescence. In both sexes the underside of
the forewing is blackish brown with white spots and
pale grayish green tips. The underside of the hindwing
is pale grayish green with paler spots and a pink spot
on the base of the hindwing. This is a very variable
butterfly with several named subspecies. Japanese
emperors are powerful fliers and can be seen on
the wing in the summer.

• **EARLY STAGES** The caterpillar is colored
green and has several pairs of pointed, fleshy
protuberances along its back. The green head
has a pair of long horns. The caterpillar
feeds on *Celtis*.

• **DISTRIBUTION** Occurs in China and Japan.

CATERPILLAR OF
SASAKIA CHARONDA

• *caterpillar blends
with leaf on
which it feeds*

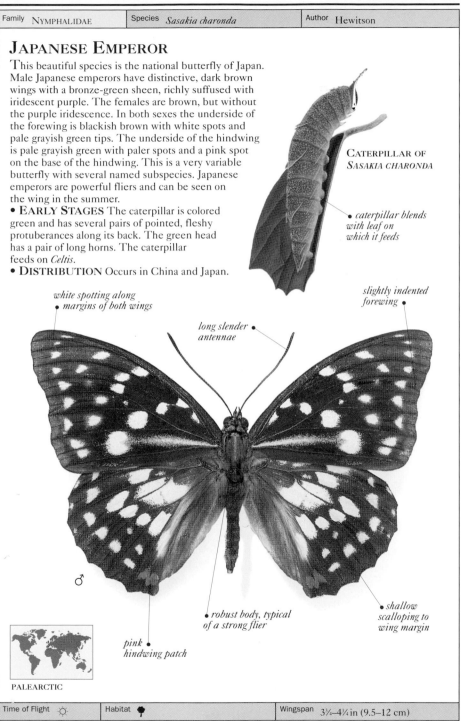

*white spotting along
• margins of both wings*

*long slender •
antennae*

*slightly indented
forewing •*

♂

*robust body, typical
of a strong flier*

*shallow
scalloping to
wing margin*

*pink •
hindwing patch*

PALEARCTIC

Time of Flight ☼	Habitat 🌳	Wingspan 3¾–4¾ in (9.5–12 cm)

| Family NYMPHALIDAE | Species *Kallimoides rumia* | Author Westwood |

AFRICAN LEAF BUTTERFLY

The males of the species are dark brown with purple and red markings on the forewings. The females are larger than the males and are marked with pale blue on the forewings and cream on the hindwings. The underside of this species has the typical leaflike brown pattern of this particular group. It is this distinctive underside that gives the African leaf butterfly its common name.
• **EARLY STAGES** The caterpillar is reddish gray with black lines. Its foodplant is apparently unknown.
• **DISTRIBUTION** This species is found in tropical eastern and western Africa

strongly angled leading edge to forewings

red, crescent-shaped flash across forewings

forewings are less pointed than those of most Kallima species

hindwings much plainer than forewings

small, white spots at forewing tips

♂

purple streak in hindwing tips

yellow-ringed black eyespots on hindwings

♂ △

central line down hindwings resembles leaf vein

AFROTROPICAL

| Time of Flight ☼ | Habitat 🌿 | Wingspan 2¼–3¼ in (7–8 cm) |

Family NYMPHALIDAE	Species *Eurodryas aurinia*	Author Rottemburg

MARSH FRITILLARY

The upperside of both sexes is orange, cream, and brown. The underside is paler with fewer black markings. Females are larger than males.
• **EARLY STAGES** The spiny caterpillar is black with white spots. It normally feeds on the leaves of devil's bit scabious *(Succisa pratensis)*.
• **DISTRIBUTION** Widespread in Europe, and extending to temperate Asia.

PALEARCTIC

intricate patterning varies within the species

♀

black spotting on hindwings

Time of Flight ☼	Habitat	Wingspan 1¼–1¾ in (3–4.5 cm)

Family NYMPHALIDAE	Species *Speyeria cybele*	Author Fabricius

GREAT SPANGLED FRITILLARY

Females of this large American fritillary can be identified by the strong, black suffusion of the basal half of both the fore- and hindwings. In males this suffusion is much less distinct. The underside of this fritillary can be distinguished by its pale orange color, with black markings on the forewings and silvery patches on the hindwings.
• **EARLY STAGES** The caterpillar is black with orange-based spines. It feeds on the leaves of violet *(Viola rotundifolia)*.
• **DISTRIBUTION** Occurs from southern Canada to Georgia, and west to California and Oregon.

NEARCTIC

characteristic fritillary wing spots

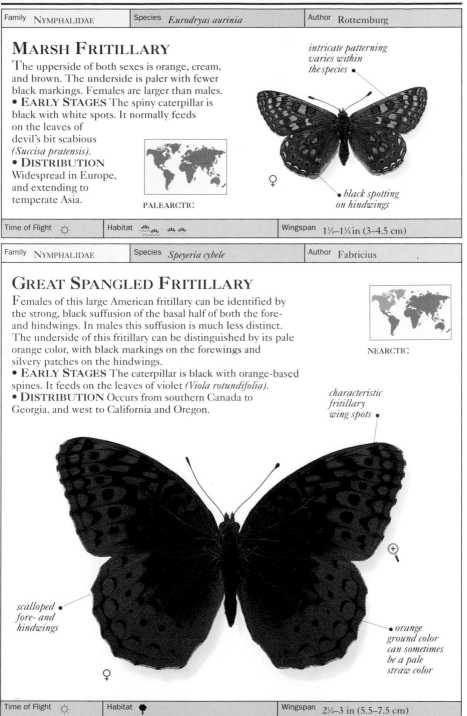

scalloped fore- and hindwings

orange ground color can sometimes be a pale straw color

♀

Time of Flight ☼	Habitat	Wingspan 2¼–3 in (5.5–7.5 cm)

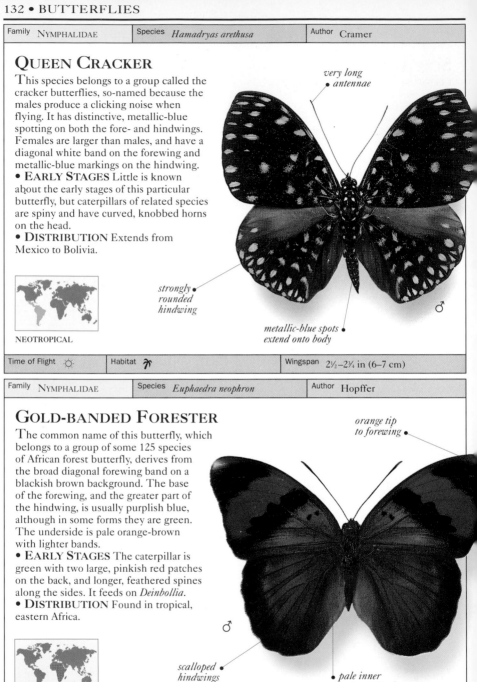

| Family NYMPHALIDAE | Species *Hamadryas arethusa* | Author Cramer |

QUEEN CRACKER

This species belongs to a group called the cracker butterflies, so-named because the males produce a clicking noise when flying. It has distinctive, metallic-blue spotting on both the fore- and hindwings. Females are larger than males, and have a diagonal white band on the forewing and metallic-blue markings on the hindwing.

• **EARLY STAGES** Little is known about the early stages of this particular butterfly, but caterpillars of related species are spiny and have curved, knobbed horns on the head.

• **DISTRIBUTION** Extends from Mexico to Bolivia.

NEOTROPICAL

very long antennae

strongly rounded hindwing

metallic-blue spots extend onto body

♂

| Time of Flight ☼ | Habitat 🦋 | Wingspan 2½–2¾ in (6–7 cm) |

| Family NYMPHALIDAE | Species *Euphaedra neophron* | Author Hopffer |

GOLD-BANDED FORESTER

The common name of this butterfly, which belongs to a group of some 125 species of African forest butterfly, derives from the broad diagonal forewing band on a blackish brown background. The base of the forewing, and the greater part of the hindwing, is usually purplish blue, although in some forms they are green. The underside is pale orange-brown with lighter bands.

• **EARLY STAGES** The caterpillar is green with two large, pinkish red patches on the back, and longer, feathered spines along the sides. It feeds on *Deinbollia*.

• **DISTRIBUTION** Found in tropical, eastern Africa.

AFROTROPICAL

orange tip to forewing

♂

scalloped hindwings

pale inner margins to hindwing

| Time of Flight ☼ | Habitat 🦋 | Wingspan 2½–3 in (6–7.5 cm) |

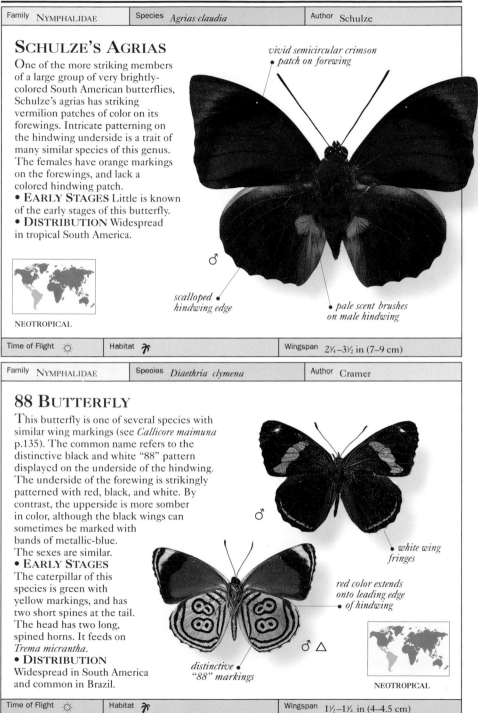

Family NYMPHALIDAE	Species *Agrias claudia*	Author Schulze

SCHULZE'S AGRIAS

One of the more striking members of a large group of very brightly-colored South American butterflies, Schulze's agrias has striking vermilion patches of color on its forewings. Intricate patterning on the hindwing underside is a trait of many similar species of this genus. The females have orange markings on the forewings, and lack a colored hindwing patch.

• **EARLY STAGES** Little is known of the early stages of this butterfly.

• **DISTRIBUTION** Widespread in tropical South America.

NEOTROPICAL

vivid semicircular crimson patch on forewing

♂

scalloped hindwing edge

pale scent brushes on male hindwing

Time of Flight ☼	Habitat 🌱	Wingspan 2¾–3½ in (7–9 cm)

Family NYMPHALIDAE	Species *Diaethria clymena*	Author Cramer

88 BUTTERFLY

This butterfly is one of several species with similar wing markings (see *Callicore maimuna* p.135). The common name refers to the distinctive black and white "88" pattern displayed on the underside of the hindwing. The underside of the forewing is strikingly patterned with red, black, and white. By contrast, the upperside is more somber in color, although the black wings can sometimes be marked with bands of metallic-blue. The sexes are similar.

• **EARLY STAGES** The caterpillar of this species is green with yellow markings, and has two short spines at the tail. The head has two long, spined horns. It feeds on *Trema micrantha*.

• **DISTRIBUTION** Widespread in South America and common in Brazil.

♂

♂ △

white wing fringes

red color extends onto leading edge of hindwing

distinctive "88" markings

NEOTROPICAL

Time of Flight ☼	Habitat 🌱	Wingspan 1½–1¾ in (4–4.5 cm)

Family NYMPHALIDAE	Species *Boloria selene*	Authors Denis & Schiffermüller

SILVER-BORDERED FRITILLARY

This fritillary has a distinctive upperside pattern of black spots on orange. Its colorful underside markings distinguish it from similar species. A common name for the butterfly in Britain is the small pearl-bordered fritillary.
• **EARLY STAGES** The caterpillar is brown, speckled with white, and with yellowish brown spines. It feeds on violets *(Viola)*.
• **DISTRIBUTION** This fritillary can be found in the northern United States, Canada, Alaska, and Eurasia.

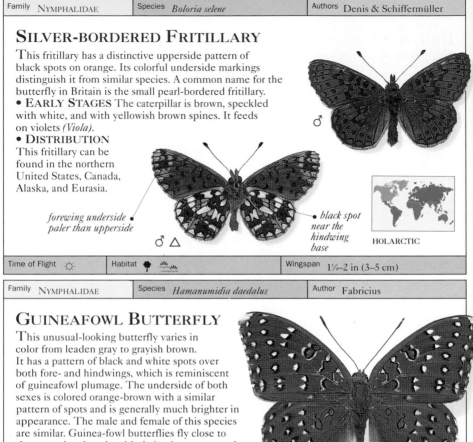

forewing underside paler than upperside

♂ △

black spot near the hindwing base

HOLARCTIC

Time of Flight ☼	Habitat 🌳	Wingspan 1¼–2 in (3–5 cm)

Family NYMPHALIDAE	Species *Hamanumidia daedalus*	Author Fabricius

GUINEAFOWL BUTTERFLY

This unusual-looking butterfly varies in color from leaden gray to grayish brown. It has a pattern of black and white spots over both fore- and hindwings, which is reminiscent of guineafowl plumage. The underside of both sexes is colored orange-brown with a similar pattern of spots and is generally much brighter in appearance. The male and female of this species are similar. Guinea-fowl butterflies fly close to the ground and settle with their wings outspread.
• **EARLY STAGES** The caterpillar is covered with long feathery spines and feeds on *Combretum*.
• **DISTRIBUTION** This species is common in semi-desert and open scrubland throughout Africa.

"toothed" edge to fore- and hindwings

distinctive black markings at base of hindwing

white-spotted wing fringes

AFROTROPICAL

♂ △

Time of Flight ☼	Habitat	Wingspan 2–2½ in (5–6 cm)

Family NYMPHALIDAE	Species *Callicore maimuna*	Author Hewitson

FIGURE-OF-EIGHT BUTTERFLY

This butterfly is one of forty species from Central and South America, which are distinguished by the striking "88" pattern on the underside of the hindwing. The upperside surface is black with diagonal, orange markings at the wingtips and a large basal patch of red on the forewing. The hindwing often has an iridescent purplish sheen in males.
• **EARLY STAGES** Little is known of the early stages of this butterfly, but other *Callicore* butterflies have long, slender caterpillars.
• **DISTRIBUTION** Throughout tropical South America from Brazil to Colombia, and up to the West Indies.

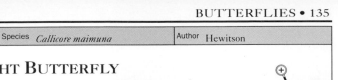

♂

• small white markings on hindwing margin

• "88" marking is bordered by a black and blue band

NEOTROPICAL ♂ △

Time of Flight ☼	Habitat 🌿	Wingspan 2–2¼in (5–5.5 cm)

Family NYMPHALIDAE	Species *Argynnis paphia*	Author Linnaeus

SILVER-WASHED FRITILLARY

Males of this butterfly have distinctive black forewing stripes that carry scent scales. Females are usually orange with black spotting. The hindwing underside, although mainly green, is "silver-washed," hence the common name.
• **EARLY STAGES** The caterpillar is dark brown with two orange-yellow stripes on the back, and reddish brown spines. It feeds on violets *(Viola)*.
• **DISTRIBUTION** Widespread in Europe extending to north Africa, and across temperate Asia to Japan.

male butterfly has rather angular forewings •

♂

PALEARCTIC

Time of Flight ☼	Habitat ♣	Wingspan 2¼–2¾in (5.5–7 cm)

| Family NYMPHALIDAE | Species *Catacroptera cloanthe* | Author Cramer |

PIRATE BUTTERFLY

This reddish brown butterfly has distinctive rows of black-ringed blue spots on both the fore- and hindwings. The leading edge of the forewing is speckled with black, and all wings have dark bases and outer margins. Males have a distinct, iridescent purple sheen, but this is absent from the larger females. The underside is variable in color. Adults drink from damp mud and are attracted to flowers.
• **EARLY STAGES** The caterpillar is grayish yellow with black spines. The head is brown with two bulbous horns. It feeds on *Gomphocarpus* and *Justicia*.
• **DISTRIBUTION** Common in grasslands and swampy areas in Africa.

leading edge of the forewing
• *speckled with black*

♂

• *scale tufts on wing fringes*

• *small hindwing tail*

AFROTROPICAL

| Time of Flight ☼ | Habitat 〰〰 〰〰 | Wingspan 2¼–2¾ in (5.5–7 cm) |

| Family NYMPHALIDAE | Species *Siproeta epaphus* | Author Latreille |

BROWN SIPROETA

This striking, blackish brown butterfly, with its bright orange-brown wingtips and white bands is easily recognizable. Females are similar to males but larger. The underside pattern is paler and duller than the upperside, and the white hindwing band is margined with orange-brown. Adults tend to fly close to the ground, where they feed from forest flowers.
• **EARLY STAGES** The caterpillar is very distinctive, and has a maroon-colored body with long, branched, bright yellow spines. Its head is shiny black. It feeds on *Ruellia*.
• **DISTRIBUTION** Occurs in tropical rain forest in Central and South America, where it flies at high altitudes.

dark wing veins and
• *forewing fringes*

♂

• *small but distinct hindwing tail*

NEOTROPICAL

| Time of Flight ☼ | Habitat 🌴 | Wingspan 2¾–3 in (7–7.5 cm) |

Family NYMPHALIDAE	Species *Melitaea didyma*	Author Esper

SPOTTED FRITILLARY

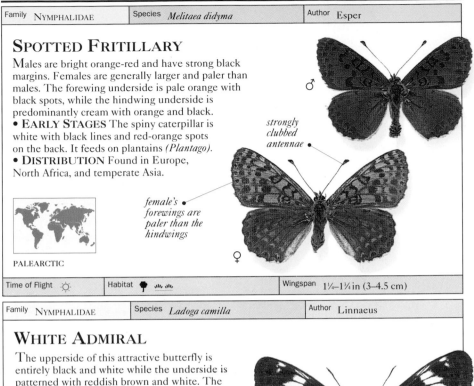

Males are bright orange-red and have strong black margins. Females are generally larger and paler than males. The forewing underside is pale orange with black spots, while the hindwing underside is predominantly cream with orange and black.
• **EARLY STAGES** The spiny caterpillar is white with black lines and red-orange spots on the back. It feeds on plantains *(Plantago)*.
• **DISTRIBUTION** Found in Europe, North Africa, and temperate Asia.

♂

strongly clubbed antennae •

female's • forewings are paler than the hindwings

♀

PALEARCTIC

Time of Flight ☼	Habitat 🌳 ⁂ ⁂	Wingspan 1¼–1¾ in (3–4.5 cm)

Family NYMPHALIDAE	Species *Ladoga camilla*	Author Linnaeus

WHITE ADMIRAL

The upperside of this attractive butterfly is entirely black and white while the underside is patterned with reddish brown and white. The inner margin of the hindwing is flushed with pale blue. Females are larger and slightly paler in color than males. Butterflies are on the wing in early and midsummer, and are attracted to flowers of bramble *(Rubus)*.
• **EARLY STAGES** The caterpillar is green above and brown beneath, with two rows of brown spines on the back, and a brown, spiny head. It feeds on honeysuckle *(Lonicera)*.
• **DISTRIBUTION** Widespread in Europe, extending across temperate Asia to Japan.

♀

distinctive row of black spots on hindwing margin •

inner margin of hindwing flushed with • pale blue

PALEARCTIC

♀ △

Time of Flight ☼	Habitat 🌳	Wingspan 2–2½ in (5–6 cm)

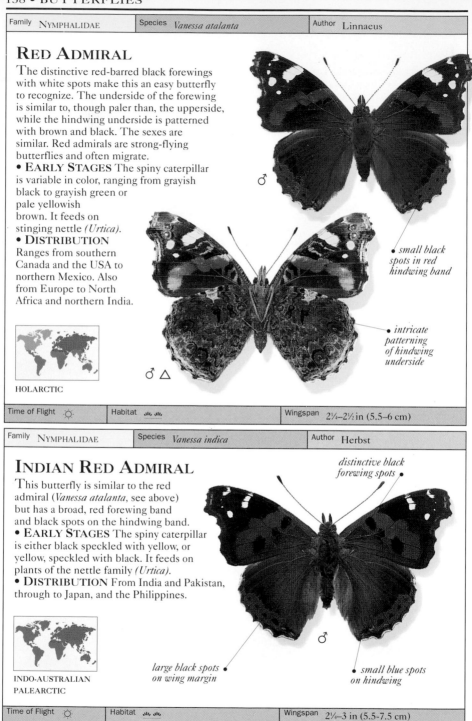

Family NYMPHALIDAE	Species *Vanessa atalanta*	Author Linnaeus

RED ADMIRAL

The distinctive red-barred black forewings
with white spots make this an easy butterfly
to recognize. The underside of the forewing
is similar to, though paler than, the upperside,
while the hindwing underside is patterned
with brown and black. The sexes are
similar. Red admirals are strong-flying
butterflies and often migrate.
• **EARLY STAGES** The spiny caterpillar
is variable in color, ranging from grayish
black to grayish green or
pale yellowish
brown. It feeds on
stinging nettle *(Urtica)*.
• **DISTRIBUTION**
Ranges from southern
Canada and the USA to
northern Mexico. Also
from Europe to North
Africa and northern India.

♂

small black
spots in red
hindwing band

intricate
patterning
of hindwing
underside

♂ △

HOLARCTIC

Time of Flight ☼	Habitat ⸲⸲⸲	Wingspan 2¼–2½ in (5.5–6 cm)

Family NYMPHALIDAE	Species *Vanessa indica*	Author Herbst

INDIAN RED ADMIRAL

This butterfly is similar to the red
admiral *(Vanessa atalanta*, see above)
but has a broad, red forewing band
and black spots on the hindwing band.
• **EARLY STAGES** The spiny caterpillar
is either black speckled with yellow, or
yellow, speckled with black. It feeds on
plants of the nettle family *(Urtica)*.
• **DISTRIBUTION** From India and Pakistan,
through to Japan, and the Philippines.

distinctive black
forewing spots

♂

large black spots
on wing margin

small blue spots
on hindwing

INDO-AUSTRALIAN
PALEARCTIC

Time of Flight ☼	Habitat ⸲⸲⸲	Wingspan 2¼–3 in (5.5-7.5 cm)

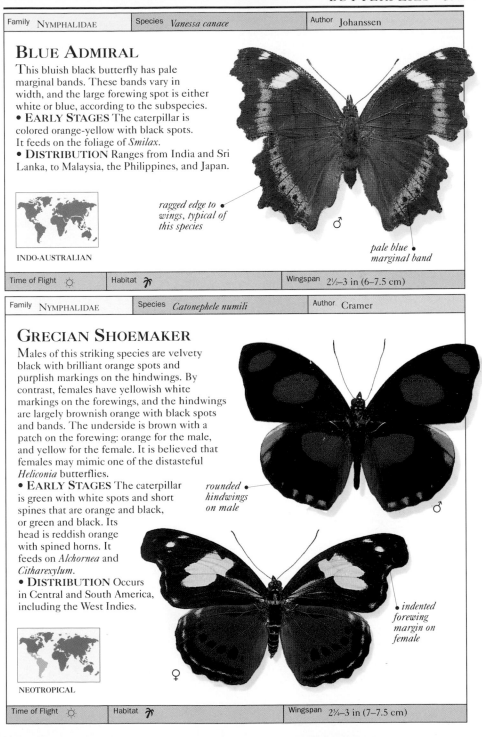

| Family NYMPHALIDAE | Species *Vanessa canace* | Author Johanssen |

BLUE ADMIRAL

This bluish black butterfly has pale
marginal bands. These bands vary in
width, and the large forewing spot is either
white or blue, according to the subspecies.
• **EARLY STAGES** The caterpillar is
colored orange-yellow with black spots.
It feeds on the foliage of *Smilax*.
• **DISTRIBUTION** Ranges from India and Sri
Lanka, to Malaysia, the Philippines, and Japan.

*ragged edge to
wings, typical of
this species*

♂

*pale blue
marginal band*

INDO-AUSTRALIAN

| Time of Flight ☼ | Habitat 🌿 | Wingspan 2½–3 in (6–7.5 cm) |

| Family NYMPHALIDAE | Species *Catonephele numili* | Author Cramer |

GRECIAN SHOEMAKER

Males of this striking species are velvety
black with brilliant orange spots and
purplish markings on the hindwings. By
contrast, females have yellowish white
markings on the forewings, and the hindwings
are largely brownish orange with black spots
and bands. The underside is brown with a
patch on the forewing: orange for the male,
and yellow for the female. It is believed that
females may mimic one of the distasteful
Heliconia butterflies.
• **EARLY STAGES** The caterpillar
is green with white spots and short
spines that are orange and black,
or green and black. Its
head is reddish orange
with spined horns. It
feeds on *Alchornea* and
Citharexylum.
• **DISTRIBUTION** Occurs
in Central and South America,
including the West Indies.

*rounded
hindwings
on male*

♂

*indented
forewing
margin on
female*

♀

NEOTROPICAL

| Time of Flight ☼ | Habitat 🌿 | Wingspan 2¾–3 in (7–7.5 cm) |

Family NYMPHALIDAE	Species *Pseudacraea boisduvali*	Author Doubleday

BOISDUVAL'S FALSE ACRAEA

The bright orange, red, and black colors of this butterfly are typical of a distasteful species, and closely mimic the pattern of the poisonous *Acraea* butterflies. The front part of the forewing is gray with striking, black wing veins. The hindwing is rich orange-red with black markings. The underside is paler than the upperside. Females are larger and paler, and have more rounded hindwings than males.

• **EARLY STAGES** The caterpillar is very unusual in appearance. It has a spiny head and large, fleshy, spiny projections along its dark brown body. It is difficult to distinguish the head from the tail. It feeds on *Chrysophyllum* and *Mimusops*.

• **DISTRIBUTION** Found in tropical rainforest, particularly in clearings and near streams, in tropical Africa, south to Natal.

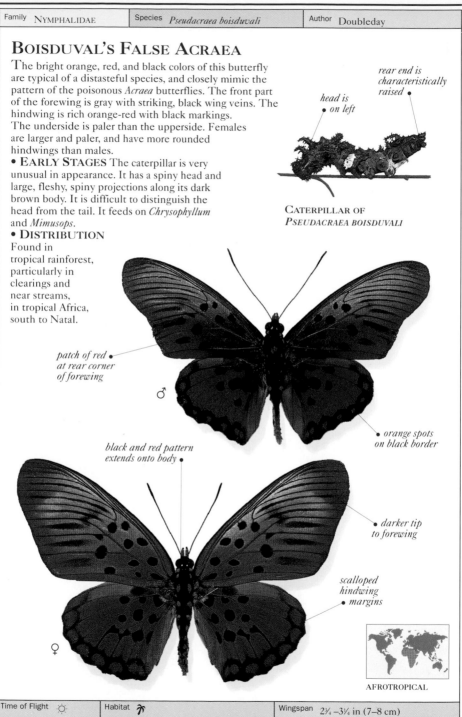

rear end is characteristically raised •

head is • on left

CATERPILLAR OF
PSEUDACRAEA BOISDUVALI

patch of red • at rear corner of forewing

♂

• orange spots on black border

black and red pattern extends onto body •

• darker tip to forewing

scalloped hindwing • margins

♀

AFROTROPICAL

Time of Flight ☼	Habitat 🎋	Wingspan 2¾–3¼ in (7–8 cm)

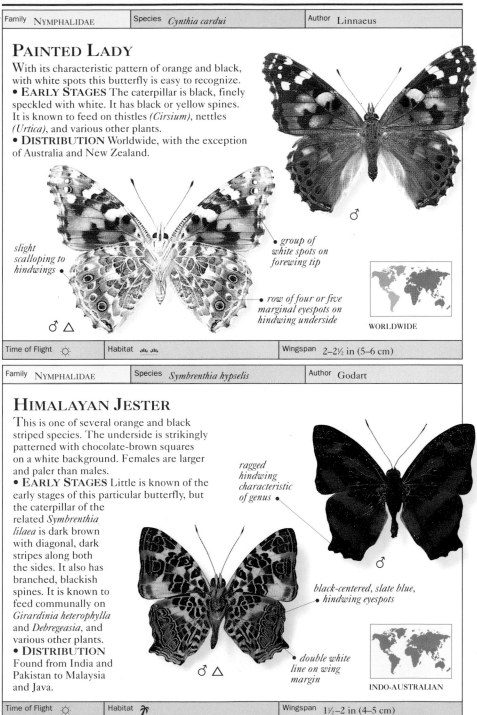

| Family NYMPHALIDAE | Species *Cynthia cardui* | Author Linnaeus |

PAINTED LADY

With its characteristic pattern of orange and black, with white spots this butterfly is easy to recognize.
• **EARLY STAGES** The caterpillar is black, finely speckled with white. It has black or yellow spines. It is known to feed on thistles *(Cirsium)*, nettles *(Urtica)*, and various other plants.
• **DISTRIBUTION** Worldwide, with the exception of Australia and New Zealand.

slight scalloping to hindwings •

♂

• group of white spots on forewing tip

• row of four or five marginal eyespots on hindwing underside

♂ △

WORLDWIDE

| Time of Flight ☼ | Habitat | Wingspan 2–2½ in (5–6 cm) |

| Family NYMPHALIDAE | Species *Symbrenthia hypselis* | Author Godart |

HIMALAYAN JESTER

This is one of several orange and black striped species. The underside is strikingly patterned with chocolate-brown squares on a white background. Females are larger and paler than males.
• **EARLY STAGES** Little is known of the early stages of this particular butterfly, but the caterpillar of the related *Symbrenthia lilaea* is dark brown with diagonal, dark stripes along both the sides. It also has branched, blackish spines. It is known to feed communally on *Girardinia heterophylla* and *Debregeasia*, and various other plants.
• **DISTRIBUTION** Found from India and Pakistan to Malaysia and Java.

ragged hindwing characteristic of genus •

♂

• black-centered, slate blue, hindwing eyespots

♂ △

• double white line on wing margin

INDO-AUSTRALIAN

| Time of Flight ☼ | Habitat | Wingspan 1½–2 in (4–5 cm) |

Family NYMPHALIDAE	Species *Terinos terpander*	Author Hewitson

ROYAL ASSYRIAN

The regal name of this butterfly derives from the purple iridescence of the male's blackish wings. Females have less purplish suffusion.
• **EARLY STAGES** The caterpillar is greenish with longitudinal lines, blackish spines and a yellow-colored head. It feeds on *Antidesma*.
• **DISTRIBUTION** Malaysia to Java and Borneo.

♂

two distinct triangular spots on hindwing

♂ △

row of dark brown marginal, hindwing spots

INDO-AUSTRALIAN

Time of Flight ☼	Habitat 🐾	Wingspan 2¾–3 in (7–7.5 cm)

Family NYMPHALIDAE	Species *Doxocopa cherubina*	Author Felder

BLUE-GREEN REFLECTOR

three white spots on forewing tip

This beautiful butterfly belongs to a group noted for their brilliant iridescent colors. The underside is pale brown with blackish markings.
• **EARLY STAGES** The caterpillar is apparently undescribed, but is known to feed on *Celtis*.
• **DISTRIBUTION** Widespread in Central and South America.

♂

small hindwing tail of male

♀ △

delicate, white and pale brown patterning

NEOTROPICAL

Time of Flight ☼	Habitat 🐾	Wingspan 2½–2¾ in (6–7 cm)

Family NYMPHALIDAE	Species *Euxanthe wakefieldii*	Author Ward

FOREST QUEEN

This species belongs to a group of African butterflies noted for their distinctively rounded wings. The white markings on the black wings of the male have a bluish green iridescence. The underside is similar, but the black coloring is largely replaced by brown. The butterflies tend to fly in dappled shade, where their black and white pattern blends into the background. Females are larger and paler, and lack the bluish tint of the males.

• **EARLY STAGES** The caterpillar is green with two black-ringed white spots on the back, each spot having two green markings within. The head is green and pale brown with four large curved horns. It feeds on *Deinbollia*.

• **DISTRIBUTION** Tropical East Africa to Mozambique and Natal Province in South Africa.

dramatically horned head

CATERPILLAR OF
EUXANTHE WAKEFIELDII

marginal row of rounded, white spots on hindwing

♂

body tipped with brownish yellow in both sexes

forewing tip of female is fuller than in male

slight scalloping to hindwings

♀ △

AFROTROPICAL

Time of Flight ☼	Habitat 🎋	Wingspan 3¼–4 in (8–10 cm)

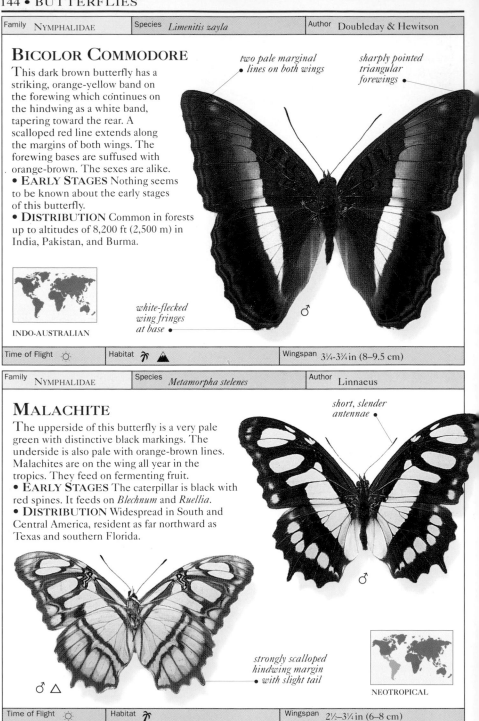

Family NYMPHALIDAE	Species *Limenitis zayla*	Author Doubleday & Hewitson

BICOLOR COMMODORE

This dark brown butterfly has a striking, orange-yellow band on the forewing which continues on the hindwing as a white band, tapering toward the rear. A scalloped red line extends along the margins of both wings. The forewing bases are suffused with orange-brown. The sexes are alike.
• **EARLY STAGES** Nothing seems to be known about the early stages of this butterfly.
• **DISTRIBUTION** Common in forests up to altitudes of 8,200 ft (2,500 m) in India, Pakistan, and Burma.

INDO-AUSTRALIAN

two pale marginal lines on both wings

sharply pointed triangular forewings

white-flecked wing fringes at base

♂

Time of Flight ☀	Habitat 🌴 ⛰	Wingspan 3¼-3¾ in (8–9.5 cm)

Family NYMPHALIDAE	Species *Metamorpha stelenes*	Author Linnaeus

MALACHITE

The upperside of this butterfly is a very pale green with distinctive black markings. The underside is also pale with orange-brown lines. Malachites are on the wing all year in the tropics. They feed on fermenting fruit.
• **EARLY STAGES** The caterpillar is black with red spines. It feeds on *Blechnum* and *Ruellia*.
• **DISTRIBUTION** Widespread in South and Central America, resident as far northward as Texas and southern Florida.

short, slender antennae

♂

strongly scalloped hindwing margin with slight tail

NEOTROPICAL

♂ △

Time of Flight ☀	Habitat 🌴	Wingspan 2½-3¼ in (6–8 cm)

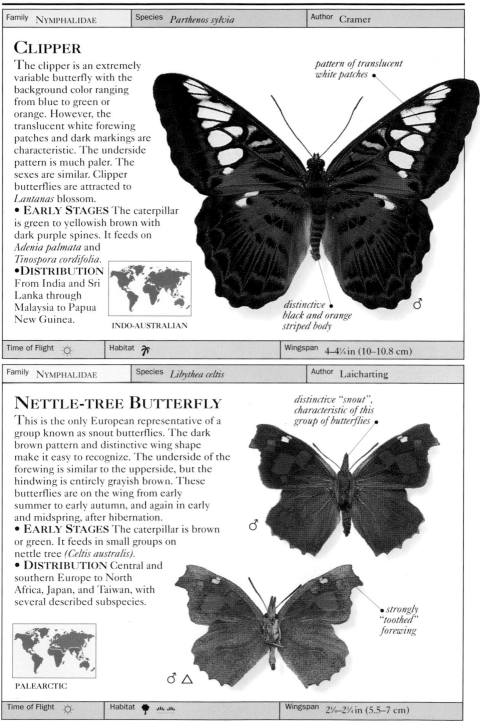

| Family | NYMPHALIDAE | Species | *Parthenos sylvia* | Author | Cramer |

CLIPPER

The clipper is an extremely variable butterfly with the background color ranging from blue to green or orange. However, the translucent white forewing patches and dark markings are characteristic. The underside pattern is much paler. The sexes are similar. Clipper butterflies are attracted to *Lantanas* blossom.
• **EARLY STAGES** The caterpillar is green to yellowish brown with dark purple spines. It feeds on *Adenia palmata* and *Tinospora cordifolia*.
•**DISTRIBUTION** From India and Sri Lanka through Malaysia to Papua New Guinea.

INDO-AUSTRALIAN

pattern of translucent white patches

distinctive black and orange striped body

♂

| Time of Flight ☼ | Habitat 🐦 | Wingspan 4–4¼ in (10–10.8 cm) |

| Family | NYMPHALIDAE | Species | *Libythea celtis* | Author | Laicharting |

NETTLE-TREE BUTTERFLY

This is the only European representative of a group known as snout butterflies. The dark brown pattern and distinctive wing shape make it easy to recognize. The underside of the forewing is similar to the upperside, but the hindwing is entirely grayish brown. These butterflies are on the wing from early summer to early autumn, and again in early and midspring, after hibernation.
• **EARLY STAGES** The caterpillar is brown or green. It feeds in small groups on nettle tree *(Celtis australis)*.
• **DISTRIBUTION** Central and southern Europe to North Africa, Japan, and Taiwan, with several described subspecies.

PALEARCTIC

distinctive "snout", characteristic of this group of butterflies

♂

strongly "toothed" forewing

♂ △

| Time of Flight ☼ | Habitat 🌳 🌿 🌿 | Wingspan 2¼–2¾ in (5.5–7 cm) |

Family NYMPHALIDAE	Species *Libythea geoffroyi*	Author Godart

BEAK BUTTERFLY

Males are black-brown with a purple sheen.
Females are dark brown with an irregular
pattern of white patches. The undersides of
the wings in both sexes are brown and
white with a purple sheen.
• **EARLY STAGES** Nothing is known.
• **DISTRIBUTION** Burma, Thailand,
Philippines, Papua New Guinea, and Australia.

♂

• *notched forewings*

• *scalloped hindwing margin present in both sexes*

♀

INDO-AUSTRALIAN

Time of Flight ☼	Habitat 🌴	Wingspan 2–2¼ in (5–5.5 cm)

Family NYMPHALIDAE	Species *Libytheana carinenta*	Author Cramer

SNOUT BUTTERFLY

The distinctively "notched" and angular
shape of the forewings of this species, and
the more gently scalloped hindwings,
distinguish the snout butterfly from all other
North American butterflies. The undersides
of the forewings are lighter than the
uppersides, while the hindwings are
speckled with grayish brown
markings. The sexes are similar.
Snout butterflies overwinter
as adults.
• **EARLY STAGES** The
caterpillar is dark green
with yellow stripes. It is
known to feed on *Celtis*.
• **DISTRIBUTION** This
butterfly occurs in light
woodland and hilly
scrubland areas, extending
from Paraguay to the
southern USA, and
migrating northward
as far as Nebraska.

long snout •

♂ △

• *characteristic triangle of white spots on wingtips*

♂

NEOTROPICAL
NEARCTIC

Time of Flight ☼	Habitat 🌳 ⸙ ⸙	Wingspan 1½–2 in (4–5 cm)

Family NYMPHALIDAE	Species *Morpho aega*	Author Hübner

BRAZILIAN MORPHO

Male Brazilian morpho butterflies are distinguished by their brilliant metallic-blue wings, which, in the past, were used to make butterfly jewelry. Females are very different from males, displaying a characteristic pattern of pale orange with blackish brown margins. They also have quite different forewing shapes, and altogether stronger patterning on the fore- and hindwings.
• **EARLY STAGES** The caterpillar is yellow, becoming white toward the tail. It is hairy, and has two red and black stripes on the back. This species is known to feed on bamboo *(Chusquea).*
• **DISTRIBUTION** Common in Brazil.

two white marks on forewing tips

darker leading edge to forewing

shiny blue color gives a creased appearance to wings

small, blunt hindwing tails

♂

very heavy body on female

pale borders to hindwings

♀

NEOTROPICAL

Time of Flight ☼	Habitat 🌴	Wingspan 3¼–3½ in (8–9 cm)

Family NYMPHALIDAE	Species *Morpho menelaus*	Author Linnaeus

BLUE MORPHO

Both males and females of this beautiful species are a deep metallic-blue, but females have broad, black margins with white spots. The undersides of both sexes are brown with a row of brown-ringed, orange eyespots outlined with pale, metallic-bronze. Females also have a broken band of metallic-yellow bronze. Blue morphos fly rapidly through dense forest and feed on the juices of fallen fruit. Males are particularly active, chasing each other in bright sunlight. They will even chase a blue cloth waved in the air; this device has been used by collectors to lure these fast-moving butterflies that are otherwise difficult to catch.

• **EARLY STAGES** The hairy caterpillar is reddish brown with brilliant, leaf-shaped patches of lime-green on the back. It feeds at night on *Erythroxylum pulchrum* and various other plants.

• **DISTRIBUTION** Widespread in the South American rain forest from Venezuela to Brazil.

outer edges of forewings are black with two white marks •

dark leading edge • to forewings

wings of female have a more scalloped appearance than • on male

characteristic • elongated hindwings

♂

"toothed" white markings on • wing margins

♀

NEOTROPICAL

Time of Flight ☼	Habitat 🌴	Wingspan 5–5½ in (13–14 cm)

Family NYMPHALIDAE	Species *Morpho peleides*	Author Kollar

COMMON MORPHO

The male of this beautiful species of butterfly has
more blue on the upperside than its female counterpart.
The undersides of the wings have a distinctive, striking
pattern of black- and yellow-ringed eyespots on a brown
background. Common morphos are
attracted to fermenting fruit.
• **EARLY STAGES** The
caterpillar has fine brown, red,
and black lines, and has two
yellow patches on the back
with red lines running
through them. The body is
covered with reddish brown
and white hairs, which form
tufts on the back. It feeds on
the foliage of *Machaerium
seemannii, Lonchocarpus*, and
other plants of the pea family. If
threatened, it releases a strong-
smelling scent from a gland
situated between the forelegs,
which is intended to deter
predators.
• **DISTRIBUTION** Common
and widespread in Central and
South America as well as the
islands of the West Indies.

thick, dark fore- and
• hindwing margin

solid, black
inner margin
• to forewings

black- and
yellow-ringed
• eyespots

small, white •
fringe to wings

• minute white
markings on
black wing
margins

♂

♂ △

NEOTROPICAL

Time of Flight ☼	Habitat 🌴	Wingspan 3¾–4¾ in (9.5–12 cm)

Family NYMPHALIDAE	Species *Morpho rhetenor*	Author Cramer

CRAMER'S BLUE MORPHO

Males are a spectacular metallic-blue color. By contrast, the more robust females are orange-brown and black with a pale orange-yellow triangle on the forewing undersides. The undersides of both sexes are silvery grayish brown with dark spots near the wing bases.

• **EARLY STAGES** The pale, yellowish brown caterpillar has purplish brown markings and two pale, diamond-shaped patches on the back. It feeds on *Macrolobium bifolium*.

• **DISTRIBUTION** Found in the jungles of Colombia, Venezuela, Ecuador, French Guiana, Surinam, and Guyana.

NEOTROPICAL

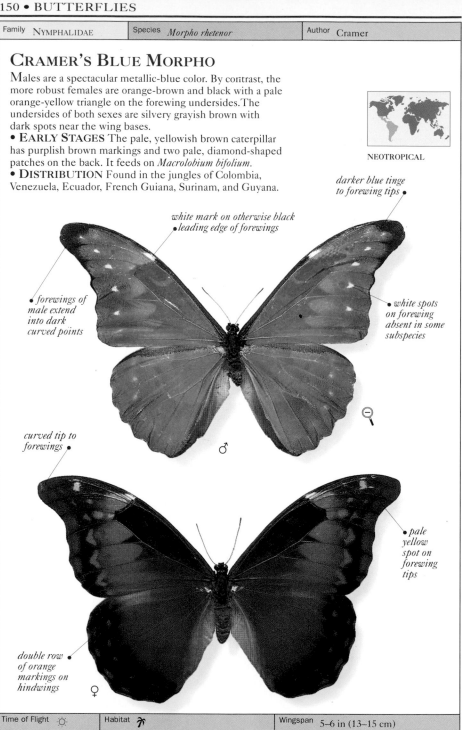

darker blue tinge to forewing tips

white mark on otherwise black leading edge of forewings

forewings of male extend into dark curved points

white spots on forewing absent in some subspecies

curved tip to forewings

♂

pale yellow spot on forewing tips

double row of orange markings on hindwings

♀

Time of Flight ☼	Habitat 🌴	Wingspan 5–6 in (13–15 cm)

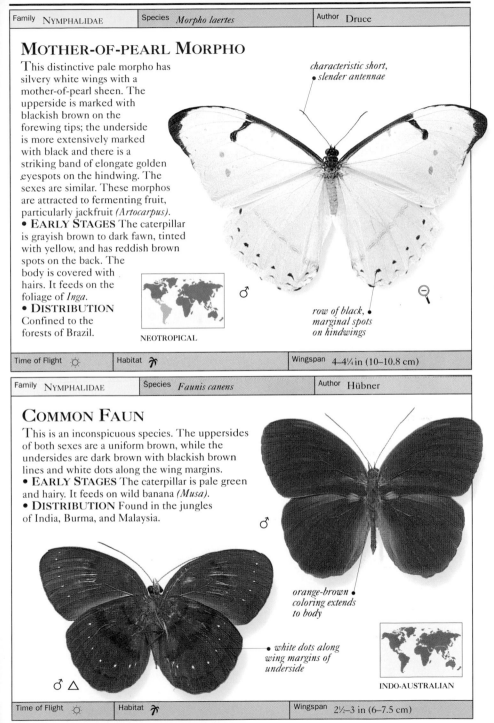

Family NYMPHALIDAE	Species *Morpho laertes*	Author Druce

MOTHER-OF-PEARL MORPHO

This distinctive pale morpho has silvery white wings with a mother-of-pearl sheen. The upperside is marked with blackish brown on the forewing tips; the underside is more extensively marked with black and there is a striking band of elongate golden eyespots on the hindwing. The sexes are similar. These morphos are attracted to fermenting fruit, particularly jackfruit *(Artocarpus)*.
• **EARLY STAGES** The caterpillar is grayish brown to dark fawn, tinted with yellow, and has reddish brown spots on the back. The body is covered with hairs. It feeds on the foliage of *Inga*.
• **DISTRIBUTION** Confined to the forests of Brazil.

characteristic short, slender antennae

♂

row of black, marginal spots on hindwings

NEOTROPICAL

Time of Flight ☼	Habitat 🌴	Wingspan 4–4¼ in (10–10.8 cm)

Family NYMPHALIDAE	Species *Faunis canens*	Author Hübner

COMMON FAUN

This is an inconspicuous species. The uppersides of both sexes are a uniform brown, while the undersides are dark brown with blackish brown lines and white dots along the wing margins.
• **EARLY STAGES** The caterpillar is pale green and hairy. It feeds on wild banana *(Musa)*.
• **DISTRIBUTION** Found in the jungles of India, Burma, and Malaysia.

♂

orange-brown coloring extends to body

white dots along wing margins of underside

♂ △

INDO-AUSTRALIAN

Time of Flight ☼	Habitat 🌴	Wingspan 2½–3 in (6–7.5 cm)

Family NYMPHALIDAE	Species *Amathuxidia amythaon*	Author Doubleday

KOH-I-NOOR BUTTERFLY

Males of this handsome and distinctive butterfly are
blackish brown with a broad, diagonal band of pale blue
on the forewings. Females, on the other hand, have a band
of dark yellow. The underside ranges in color from brown to
pinkish blue with black lines, and there are two eyespots on
each hindwing. These butterflies are reluctant to fly unless
disturbed, but seem to be most active toward dusk – even
then, however, they do not fly very far. They tend to be
attracted to fermenting fruit. Males are reputed to give off a
sweet odor that persists even after they are dead.
• **EARLY STAGES** Nothing seems to be known about the
early stages of this butterfly.
• **DISTRIBUTION** This species occurs from India and
Pakistan to Malaysia, Indonesia, and the Philippines. There
are several described subspecies.

INDO-AUSTRALIAN

*squarish shape
to forewings*

*dark, triangular
tip to forewings*

*long, slender
antennae*

♂

*hindwings are
very plain in
contrast to
forewings*

*hindwings narrow
to taillike lobe*

*scent scales
on hindwings*

Time of Flight ◗	Habitat 🌴		Wingspan 4½–4¾ in (11–12 cm)

Family NYMPHALIDAE	Species *Stichophthalma camadeva*	Author Westwood

NORTHERN JUNGLE QUEEN

This species is very distinctive with its bluish white forewings spotted with black along the margin, and blackish brown hindwings with pale blue and white marginal bands. The undersides are pale yellowish brown patterned with black and brown lines, white bands, and a row of black-ringed, orange eyespots. The sexes are alike. These butterflies do not visit flowers, but are attracted to rotting fruit, fermenting sap, and cattle dung. They are powerful fliers, usually keeping close to the ground. Males are more active than females. There are generally two broods a year, with butterflies on the wing during the summer months.

• **EARLY STAGES** The caterpillar is apparently undescribed, but it is most likely that it feeds on palms (Palmae) or bamboos *(Chusquea)*.

• **DISTRIBUTION** Occurs in dense jungle from northern India and Pakistan to northern Burma.

diamond-shaped black markings on forewings

single brown spot on forewings

blackish brown color of hindwings continues on to body

♂

characteristic white hindwing margins

striking eyespots on underside divert attackers from delicate body

♂ △

INDO-AUSTRALIAN

Time of Flight ☼	Habitat 🌴	Wingspan 4¼–5 in (12–13 cm)

Family NYMPHALIDAE	Species *Thauria aliris*	Author Westwood

TUFTED JUNGLE QUEEN

This large butterfly has square forewings that are mainly black with a diagonal, white band. Males have a large patch of hairlike, specialized scales on their black and orange hindwings, but these are absent in the larger, but otherwise similar, females. The underside is strikingly patterned with orange, brown, and white. Tufted jungle queens fly just before sunset. They are attracted to fermenting fruit. They belong to the subfamily Amathusiinae, part of a small group confined to Southeast Asia.

• **EARLY STAGES**
Little is known of the early stages of this butterfly, but it has been suggested that the foodplant may be bamboo *(Chusquea)*.

• **DISTRIBUTION**
Widespread from Burma to Thailand, Malaysia, and Borneo. There are several similar species in India.

INDO-AUSTRALIAN

white spot has a faded appearance

scale patches on hindwings

featherlike brown patterning on forewing

♂

orange marking at hindwing base

⊖

large eyespots on hindwings to divert predators

♂ △

Time of Flight ◑	Habitat 🌱	Wingspan 4½–5 in (11–13 cm)

Family NYMPHALIDAE	Species *Zeuxidia amethystus*	Author Butler

SATURN BUTTERFLY

Males of this attractive species have sharply pointed forewings and a violet-blue patch on the hindwings. Females are larger than males. They are brown with yellowish brown markings and a diagonal, cream band on the forewing. The species is well camouflaged, as the undersides of both sexes are brown and patterned to resemble leaves.
• **EARLY STAGES** Little is known of the early stages, but caterpillars of other *Zeuxidia* species are known to be hairy with horns on both head and tail.
• **DISTRIBUTION** Found in forests in Thailand, Malaysia, and Sumatra.

INDO-AUSTRALIAN

pointed forewing tips

scale patches on hindwings only present in males

♂

Time of Flight ☼	Habitat 🌴	Wingspan 2¾–4 in (7–10 cm)

Family NYMPHALIDAE	Species *Dynastor napoleon*	Author Westwood

BRAZILIAN DYNASTOR

This orange and brown butterfly is a rare species. The wings are dark brown and the undersides of the forewings are lighter than the uppersides. The undersides of the hindwings have dark brown wing veins that give a leaf-like impression. Females are larger than males and their forewings are more rounded.
• **EARLY STAGES** Little is known of the early stages, but related species are green or brown with ringlike markings on the back. They feed on plants of the pineapple family Bromeliaceae.
• **DISTRIBUTION** Found in high-altitude rain forests in Brazil.

NEOTROPICAL

small, orange markings on wingtips

band of white patches on forewings

broad, orange band on hindwings

♂

Time of Flight ◑	Habitat 🌴	Wingspan 4¾–6¼ in (12–16 cm)

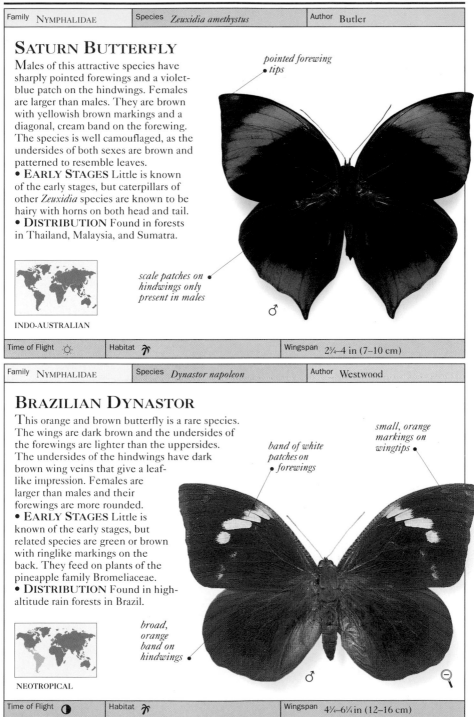

Family NYMPHALIDAE	Species *Caligo idomeneus*	Author Linnaeus

OWL BUTTERFLY

This striking species belongs to a genus of large butterflies characterized by enormous owllike eyespots on the undersides of the hindwings. In both sexes, the uppersides of the forewings are dark brown with a bluish suffusion and a white line running through. The hindwings are black with a dull blue base. The undersides of the wings have an intricate brown and white, featherlike pattern. Owl butterflies fly early in the morning and toward dusk.
• **EARLY STAGES** The large caterpillar is pale grayish brown, shaded with dark brown toward the head and the forked tail. It feeds on the foliage of banana *(Musa)*, and can often be a pest in plantations.
• **DISTRIBUTION** Widespread throughout South America, from Argentina up to Surinam.

white, longitudinal line
• on forewing upperside

♂

prominent veining on
• forewings

• brown and white underside patterning

large owllike eyespots on the hindwing
• undersides

♂ △

NEOTROPICAL

Time of Flight ☼ ◑	Habitat 🌿 🌴	Wingspan 4¾–6 in (12–15 cm)

Family NYMPHALIDAE	Species *Caligo teucer*	Author Linnaeus

COCOA MORT BLEU

The male of the cocoa mort bleu butterfly is blackish brown with a yellowish band and pale base to the forewing, while the base of the hindwing is shot with iridescent violet-blue. The female is larger than the male and has a darker forewing base. The undersides of both sexes are more ornate than the uppersides. They are intricately patterned with brown and have large, owllike eyespots on the hindwings. These butterflies avoid bright sunlight and are on the wing in the afternoon and at dusk. They are attracted to fermenting fruit.

• **EARLY STAGES** The large caterpillar is pale brown with approximately five slender, dark bristles along the back and a pale, central oval, ringed with black. The tail is forked, and the head has a number of curved spines. It feeds on the foliage of various species of banana *(Musa)*.

• **DISTRIBUTION** Occurs from Costa Rica to Guiana, Surinam, Guyana, and Ecuador.

veins are quite prominent on forewings

yellow-colored band on forewings of male

♂

narrow, yellow wing margins on upperside

characteristic owllike eyespots on hindwings

hindwings more scalloped than forewings

♂ △

NEOTROPICAL

Time of Flight ☼ ◑	Habitat 🦋	Wingspan 3¾–4½ in (9.5–11 cm)

| Family | NYMPHALIDAE | Species | *Eryphanis polyxena* | Author | Meerburg |

PURPLE MORT BLEU

This beautiful butterfly has iridescent, deep purple wings with black borders. Females are larger and lack the brilliant purple color of the male, although they often have a purplish blue sheen. The undersides of both sexes, in contrast, are various shades of brown, with large eyespots on the hindwings. These butterflies have a rapid, dipping flight and frequent forest clearings in the late afternoon and at dusk.

• **EARLY STAGES** The caterpillar is pale brown with a series of five black bristles along the back. The long forked tail is covered with hair, and the head has six short, curved spines. It feeds on bamboo *(Chusquea)*.

• **DISTRIBUTION** Widely distributed in Central and South America, including the West Indies.

• *curved forewing tips*

♂

• *patch of yellowish scent scales on inner hindwing margins of male*

brown, leaf-like pattern on undersides
• *of wings*

♂ △

NEOTROPICAL

| Time of Flight ☼ ◑ | Habitat 🎋 | Wingspan 3¼–4 in. (8.25–10 cm) |

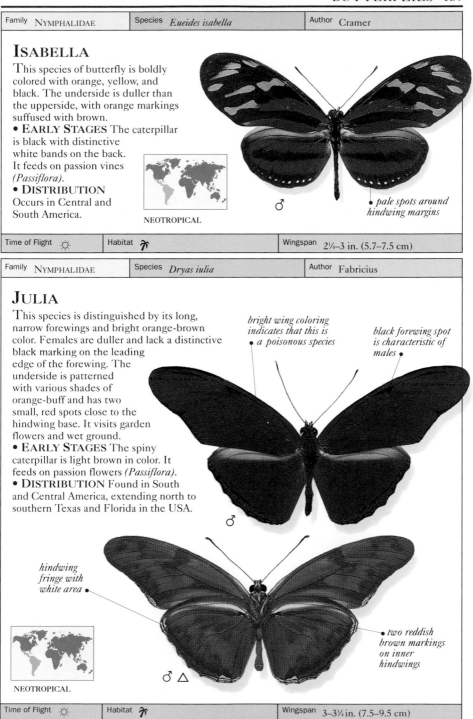

| Family NYMPHALIDAE | Species *Eueides isabella* | Author Cramer |

ISABELLA

This species of butterfly is boldly colored with orange, yellow, and black. The underside is duller than the upperside, with orange markings suffused with brown.
• **EARLY STAGES** The caterpillar is black with distinctive white bands on the back. It feeds on passion vines *(Passiflora).*
• **DISTRIBUTION** Occurs in Central and South America.

NEOTROPICAL

♂

• *pale spots around hindwing margins*

| Time of Flight ☼ | Habitat 🌴 | Wingspan 2¼–3 in. (5.7–7.5 cm) |

| Family NYMPHALIDAE | Species *Dryas iulia* | Author Fabricius |

JULIA

This species is distinguished by its long, narrow forewings and bright orange-brown color. Females are duller and lack a distinctive black marking on the leading edge of the forewing. The underside is patterned with various shades of orange-buff and has two small, red spots close to the hindwing base. It visits garden flowers and wet ground.
• **EARLY STAGES** The spiny caterpillar is light brown in color. It feeds on passion flowers *(Passiflora).*
• **DISTRIBUTION** Found in South and Central America, extending north to southern Texas and Florida in the USA.

bright wing coloring indicates that this is • *a poisonous species*

black forewing spot is characteristic of males •

♂

hindwing fringe with white area •

♂ △

NEOTROPICAL

• *two reddish brown markings on inner hindwings*

| Time of Flight ☼ | Habitat 🌴 | Wingspan 3–3¾ in. (7.5–9.5 cm) |

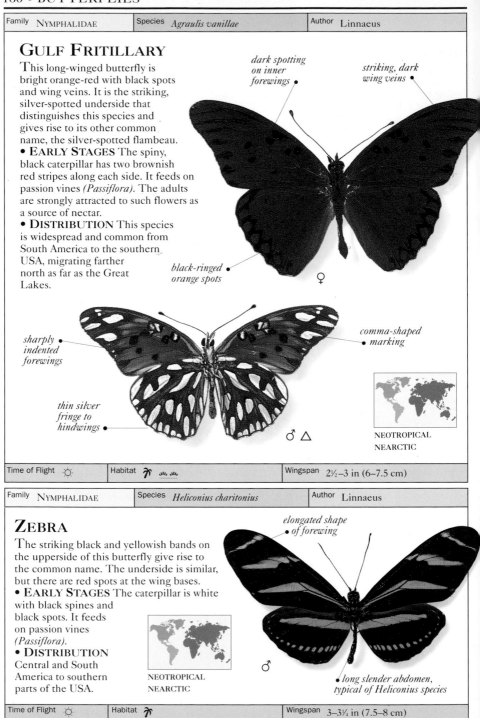

Family	NYMPHALIDAE	Species	Agraulis vanillae	Author	Linnaeus

GULF FRITILLARY

This long-winged butterfly is bright orange-red with black spots and wing veins. It is the striking, silver-spotted underside that distinguishes this species and gives rise to its other common name, the silver-spotted flambeau.
• EARLY STAGES The spiny, black caterpillar has two brownish red stripes along each side. It feeds on passion vines *(Passiflora)*. The adults are strongly attracted to such flowers as a source of nectar.
• DISTRIBUTION This species is widespread and common from South America to the southern USA, migrating farther north as far as the Great Lakes.

dark spotting on inner forewings •

striking, dark wing veins •

black-ringed • orange spots

♀

sharply • indented forewings

comma-shaped • marking

thin silver fringe to hindwings •

♂ △

NEOTROPICAL
NEARCTIC

Time of Flight ☼	Habitat	Wingspan	2½–3 in (6–7.5 cm)

Family	NYMPHALIDAE	Species	Heliconius charitonius	Author	Linnaeus

ZEBRA

The striking black and yellowish bands on the upperside of this butterfly give rise to the common name. The underside is similar, but there are red spots at the wing bases.
• EARLY STAGES The caterpillar is white with black spines and black spots. It feeds on passion vines *(Passiflora)*.
• DISTRIBUTION Central and South America to southern parts of the USA.

elongated shape • of forewing

NEOTROPICAL
NEARCTIC

♂

• long slender abdomen, typical of Heliconius species

Time of Flight ☼	Habitat	Wingspan	3–3¼ in (7.5–8 cm)

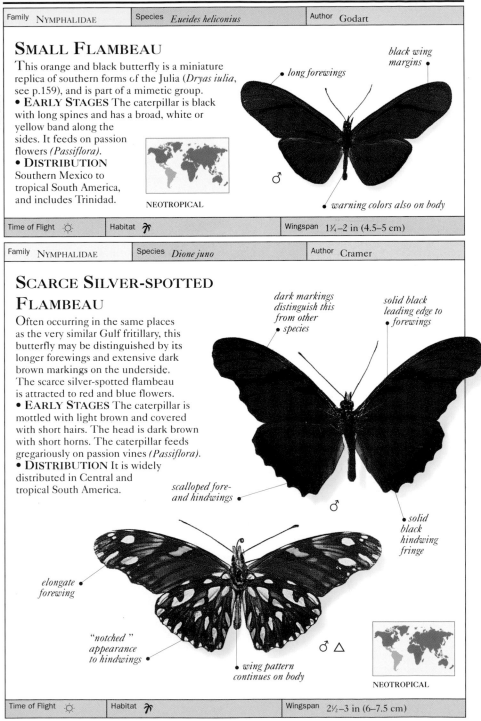

| Family NYMPHALIDAE | Species *Eueides heliconius* | Author Godart |

SMALL FLAMBEAU

This orange and black butterfly is a miniature replica of southern forms of the Julia (*Dryas iulia*, see p.159), and is part of a mimetic group.
• **EARLY STAGES** The caterpillar is black with long spines and has a broad, white or yellow band along the sides. It feeds on passion flowers *(Passiflora)*.
• **DISTRIBUTION** Southern Mexico to tropical South America, and includes Trinidad.

black wing margins •

• long forewings

NEOTROPICAL

♂

• warning colors also on body

| Time of Flight ☼ | Habitat 🦋 | Wingspan 1¾–2 in (4.5–5 cm) |

| Family NYMPHALIDAE | Species *Dione juno* | Author Cramer |

SCARCE SILVER-SPOTTED FLAMBEAU

Often occurring in the same places as the very similar Gulf fritillary, this butterfly may be distinguished by its longer forewings and extensive dark brown markings on the underside. The scarce silver-spotted flambeau is attracted to red and blue flowers.
• **EARLY STAGES** The caterpillar is mottled with light brown and covered with short hairs. The head is dark brown with short horns. The caterpillar feeds gregariously on passion vines *(Passiflora)*.
• **DISTRIBUTION** It is widely distributed in Central and tropical South America.

dark markings distinguish this from other • species

solid black leading edge to • forewings

scalloped fore-and hindwings •

♂

• solid black hindwing fringe

elongate • forewing

"notched" appearance to hindwings •

♂ △

• wing pattern continues on body

NEOTROPICAL

| Time of Flight ☼ | Habitat 🦋 | Wingspan 2½–3 in (6–7.5 cm) |

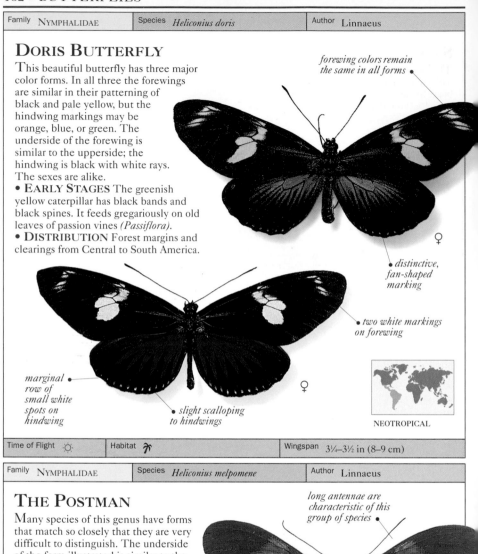

| Family NYMPHALIDAE | Species *Heliconius doris* | Author Linnaeus |

DORIS BUTTERFLY

This beautiful butterfly has three major color forms. In all three the forewings are similar in their patterning of black and pale yellow, but the hindwing markings may be orange, blue, or green. The underside of the forewing is similar to the upperside; the hindwing is black with white rays. The sexes are alike.

• **EARLY STAGES** The greenish yellow caterpillar has black bands and black spines. It feeds gregariously on old leaves of passion vines *(Passiflora)*.

• **DISTRIBUTION** Forest margins and clearings from Central to South America.

forewing colors remain the same in all forms •

♀

• *distinctive, fan-shaped marking*

• *two white markings on forewing*

marginal • *row of small white spots on hindwing*

♀

• *slight scalloping to hindwings*

NEOTROPICAL

| Time of Flight ☼ | Habitat 🦋 | Wingspan 3¼–3½ in (8–9 cm) |

| Family NYMPHALIDAE | Species *Heliconius melpomene* | Author Linnaeus |

THE POSTMAN

Many species of this genus have forms that match so closely that they are very difficult to distinguish. The underside of the form illustrated is similar to the upperside, but is lighter and has red spots at the base of the hindwing. These butterflies fly with the small postman *(Heliconius erato*, see p.163), but tend to avoid direct sunlight.

• **EARLY STAGES** The caterpillar feeds on passion vines *(Passiflora)*.

• **DISTRIBUTION** From Central America to southern Brazil.

long antennae are characteristic of this group of species •

NEOTROPICAL

♂

this color variety is just one of the many forms in this species •

| Time of Flight ☼ | Habitat 🦋 | Wingspan 2½–3¼ in (6–8 cm) |

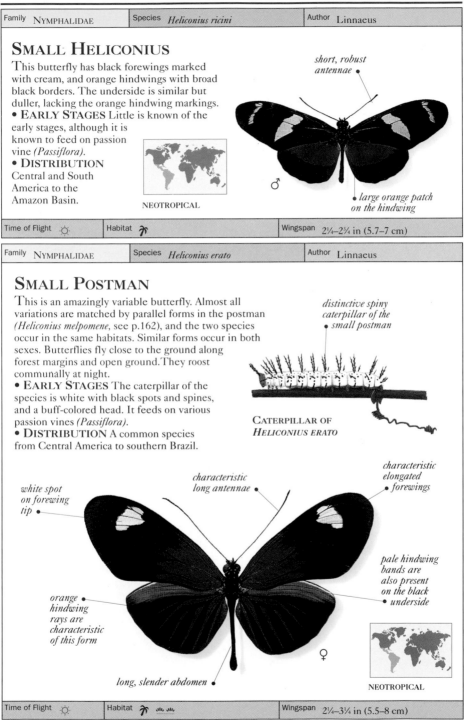

Family NYMPHALIDAE	Species *Heliconius ricini*	Author Linnaeus

SMALL HELICONIUS

This butterfly has black forewings marked with cream, and orange hindwings with broad black borders. The underside is similar but duller, lacking the orange hindwing markings.
• **EARLY STAGES** Little is known of the early stages, although it is known to feed on passion vine *(Passiflora)*.
• **DISTRIBUTION** Central and South America to the Amazon Basin.

short, robust antennae

♂

large orange patch on the hindwing

NEOTROPICAL

Time of Flight ☼	Habitat 🜨	Wingspan 2¼–2¾ in (5.7–7 cm)

Family NYMPHALIDAE	Species *Heliconius erato*	Author Linnaeus

SMALL POSTMAN

This is an amazingly variable butterfly. Almost all variations are matched by parallel forms in the postman *(Heliconius melpomene*, see p.162), and the two species occur in the same habitats. Similar forms occur in both sexes. Butterflies fly close to the ground along forest margins and open ground. They roost communally at night.
• **EARLY STAGES** The caterpillar of the species is white with black spots and spines, and a buff-colored head. It feeds on various passion vines *(Passiflora)*.
• **DISTRIBUTION** A common species from Central America to southern Brazil.

distinctive spiny caterpillar of the small postman

**CATERPILLAR OF
*HELICONIUS ERATO***

characteristic long antennae

characteristic elongated forewings

white spot on forewing tip

pale hindwing bands are also present on the black underside

orange hindwing rays are characteristic of this form

♀

long, slender abdomen

NEOTROPICAL

Time of Flight ☼	Habitat 🜨 🌿 🌿	Wingspan 2¼–3¼ in (5.5–8 cm)

| Family NYMPHALIDAE | Species *Philaethria dido* | Author Linnaeus |

SCARCE BAMBOO PAGE

Belonging to a complex of almost identical species, this butterfly is characterized by its beautiful, bluish green color, and blackish brown markings. The underside is paler and has reddish brown and grayish brown markings. The sexes are similar. These butterflies feed on the nectar of *Lantana* and other flowers, preferring white, blue, and yellow varieties. They generally fly high in the tree canopy, but at times descend to drink and take in salts from damp ground.
• **EARLY STAGES** The caterpillar is pale green with blackish red markings and black-tipped red spines. It feeds on passion vines *(Passiflora)*.
• **DISTRIBUTION** This complex of species occurs from Mexico to Argentina.

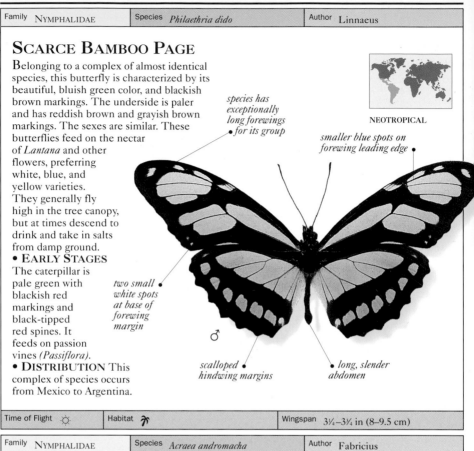

NEOTROPICAL

species has exceptionally long forewings for its group

smaller blue spots on forewing leading edge

two small white spots at base of forewing margin

♂

scalloped hindwing margins

long, slender abdomen

| Time of Flight ☼ | Habitat 🌿 | Wingspan 3¼–3¾ in (8–9.5 cm) |

| Family NYMPHALIDAE | Species *Acraea andromacha* | Author Fabricius |

GLASSWING

This appropriately-named butterfly has transparent forewings, and white hindwings with black borders. The underside is similar, but the hindwing has larger white spots in the black marginal band. The sexes are similar, but females are larger.
• **EARLY STAGES** The caterpillar of this species is a glossy yellowish brown, with long, black, branched spines arising from raised bluish black spots. It feeds on passion vines *(Passiflora)*.
• **DISTRIBUTION** Found from Indonesia to Papua New Guinea, Fiji, and Australia. The glasswing has a number of described subspecies.

spotting from underside shows through on pale forewing

INDO-AUSTRALIAN

♀

band of marginal white spots less developed than on underside

| Time of Flight ☼ | Habitat 🌿 | Wingspan 2–2½ in (5–6 cm) |

Family NYMPHALIDAE	Species *Acraea acerata*	Author Hewitson

SWEET POTATO ACRAEA

This common little African butterfly varies from pale yellow to orange-brown. The underside is paler and has distinctive elongate orange spots in the dark marginal band.
• **EARLY STAGES** The caterpillar is pale green with yellow and black spines. It feeds on sweet potatoes *(Ipomoea)* and can be destructive.
• **DISTRIBUTION** Tropical Africa from Ghana to eastern Africa.

short, robust antennae typical of this butterfly group •

AFROTROPICAL

♂

• warning colors indicate butterfly is distasteful

Time of Flight ☼	Habitat 🌿 🐦	Wingspan 1¼–1½ in (3–4 cm)

Family NYMPHALIDAE	Species *Acraea vesta*	Author Fabricius

YELLOW COSTER

This orange and dark brown butterfly is variable, and some specimens are almost entirely black. The underside is similar to the upperside, but is paler and lacks the dark marginal bands. Females are generally larger and more heavily marked.
• **EARLY STAGES** The spiny black caterpillars have red heads. They live gregariously, which increases their unpleasant warning smell. They feed on *Boehmenia, Debregeasia,* and *Buddleia.* Butterflies are most often found near the caterpillar's foodplant.
• **DISTRIBUTION** Open scrub country from northern India to Pakistan, Burma, and southern China.

dark brown leading edge • to forewing

distinctive • red spots

♂

forewings much darker • than hindwings

• black, U-shaped markings surrounding pale, marginal spots

reddish brown tinge to hindwing margin •

♀

INDO-AUSTRALIAN

Time of Flight ☼	Habitat ⛰ 🌾 🌾	Wingspan 1¾–3¼ in (4.5–8 cm)

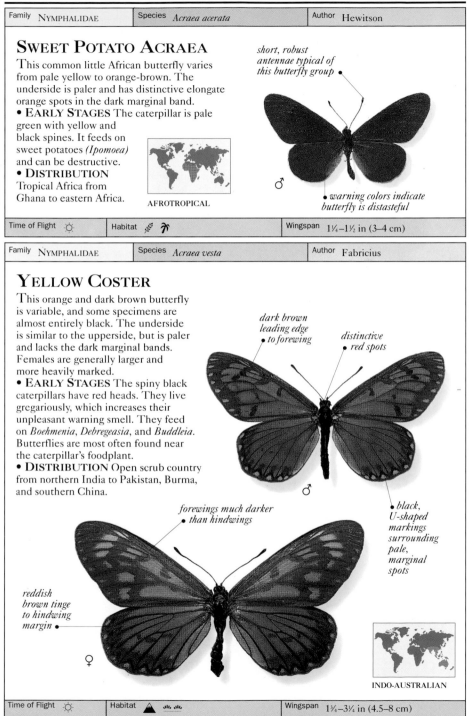

| Family NYMPHALIDAE | Species *Acraea zetes* | Author Linnaeus |

LARGE SPOTTED ACRAEA

This orange and brown butterfly is very variable and several subspecies have been described, some of which are virtually completely suffused with black. The females are larger than the males. They have a greasy appearance and a paler underside.
• **EARLY STAGES** The caterpillar is ochreous yellow with black bands and spines. The head lacks spines. It feeds on passion flowers *(Passiflora)*, *Adenia*, and other plants.
• **DISTRIBUTION** Widespread and common in Africa, south of the Sahara.

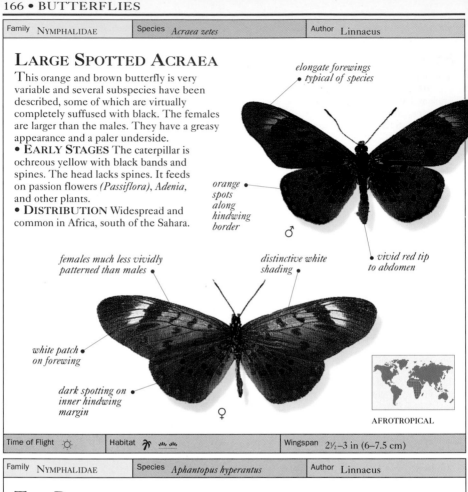

elongate forewings typical of species

orange spots along hindwing border ♂

females much less vividly patterned than males

distinctive white shading

vivid red tip to abdomen

white patch on forewing

dark spotting on inner hindwing margin ♀

AFROTROPICAL

| Time of Flight ☼ | Habitat | Wingspan 2½–3 in (6–7.5 cm) |

| Family NYMPHALIDAE | Species *Aphantopus hyperantus* | Author Linnaeus |

THE RINGLET

Males are blackish on the upperside, with a variable number of indistinct eyespots, while females are larger and paler. The distinctive, yellow-ringed, underside eyespots give rise to the very appropriate common name.
• **EARLY STAGES**
The caterpillar is a pale yellowish brown with light and dark stripes. It feeds on various grasses. There is one generation each year.
• **DISTRIBUTION** It is widespread and common in Europe extending into temperate Asia.

eyespots variable in size and number, and may even be absent

pale wing fringes

♂ △

♂

PALEARCTIC

| Time of Flight ☼ | Habitat | Wingspan 1½–1¾ in (4–4.5 cm) |

| Family NYMPHALIDAE | Species *Actinote pellenea* | Author Hübner |

SMALL LACE-WING

This butterfly is closely related to the *Acraea* butterflies of Africa. The combination of black and orange markings indicates that it is distasteful to birds.
• **EARLY STAGES** The life cycle is unknown, but caterpillars of related species have spiny bodies and smooth heads.
• **DISTRIBUTION** South America from Argentina to Venezuela, and the West Indies.

NEOTROPICAL

unusual, flattened clubs on antennae

elongate, rounded forewings

♂

| Time of Flight ☀ | Habitat 🌿 | Wingspan 1¾–2 in (4.5–5 cm) |

| Family NYMPHALIDAE | Species *Bematistes aganice* | Author Hewitson |

THE WANDERER

Males are black and orange while the larger females are black and white and have more rounded forewings. The undersides are similar, but have distinctive reddish brown, black-spotted hindwing bases. The butterflies have a relatively slow flight, and are attracted to flowers. This is a poisonous species that is mimicked by a number of more palatable African butterflies such as *Pseudacraea eurytus*.
• **EARLY STAGES** The caterpillar is white with purplish red spots and stripes, and yellow spines. It feeds on *Adenia gummifera* and passion flowers *(Passiflora)*.
• **DISTRIBUTION** This species occurs from Ethiopia and Sudan down to South Africa.

AFROTROPICAL

short, robust antennae

forewing tip paler than inner margin

male forewing has distinctive, indented margin

♂

wing veins clearly visible

♀

black spotting on inner hindwing

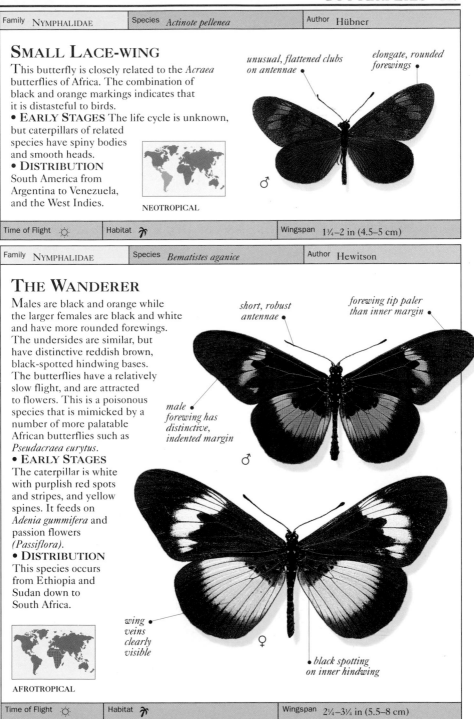

| Time of Flight ☀ | Habitat 🌿 | Wingspan 2¼–3¼ in (5.5–8 cm) |

| Family NYMPHALIDAE | Species *Cepheuptychia cephus* | Author Fabricius |

BLUE NIGHT BUTTERFLY

The iridescent blue of males of this species is most unusual in a group of predominantly brown butterflies. The underside is even more striking with its distinctive black banding. By contrast, females are brown, with a narrow, blue, marginal line on the upperside and blue below, with dark bands and eyespots.
• EARLY STAGES Nothing is known of the early stages of this species.
• DISTRIBUTION Found from Surinam and Colombia to southern Brazil and the West Indies.

heavy, black veining on forewings

♂

the narrow, blue, marginal band occurs in both sexes

two very small eyespots on the hindwing

♂ △

NEOTROPICAL

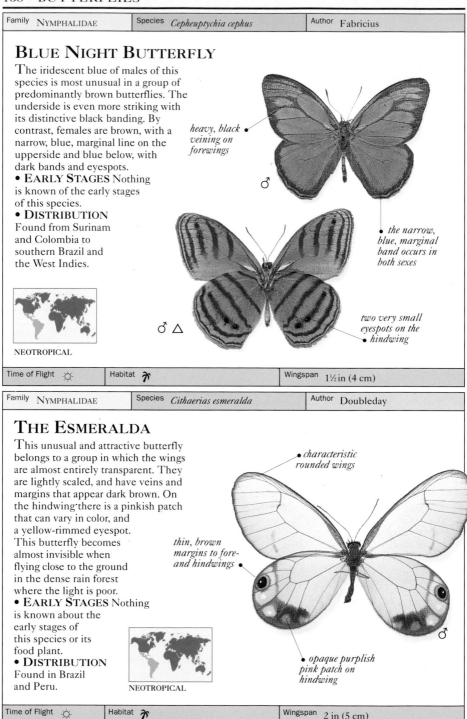

| Time of Flight ☼ | Habitat 🌴 | Wingspan 1½ in (4 cm) |

| Family NYMPHALIDAE | Species *Cithaerias esmeralda* | Author Doubleday |

THE ESMERALDA

This unusual and attractive butterfly belongs to a group in which the wings are almost entirely transparent. They are lightly scaled, and have veins and margins that appear dark brown. On the hindwing there is a pinkish patch that can vary in color, and a yellow-rimmed eyespot. This butterfly becomes almost invisible when flying close to the ground in the dense rain forest where the light is poor.
• EARLY STAGES Nothing is known about the early stages of this species or its food plant.
• DISTRIBUTION Found in Brazil and Peru.

characteristic rounded wings

thin, brown margins to fore- and hindwings

♂

opaque purplish pink patch on hindwing

NEOTROPICAL

| Time of Flight ☼ | Habitat 🌴 | Wingspan 2 in (5 cm) |

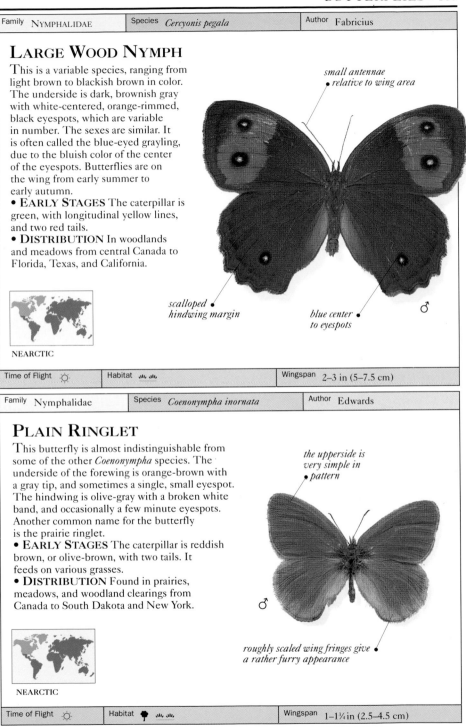

Family NYMPHALIDAE	Species *Cercyonis pegala*	Author Fabricius

LARGE WOOD NYMPH

This is a variable species, ranging from
light brown to blackish brown in color.
The underside is dark, brownish gray
with white-centered, orange-rimmed,
black eyespots, which are variable
in number. The sexes are similar. It
is often called the blue-eyed grayling,
due to the bluish color of the center
of the eyespots. Butterflies are on
the wing from early summer to
early autumn.
• **EARLY STAGES** The caterpillar is
green, with longitudinal yellow lines,
and two red tails.
• **DISTRIBUTION** In woodlands
and meadows from central Canada to
Florida, Texas, and California.

small antennae
• *relative to wing area*

scalloped •
hindwing margin

blue center •
to eyespots

♂

NEARCTIC

Time of Flight ☼	Habitat ⏐⏐ ⏐⏐	Wingspan 2–3 in (5–7.5 cm)

Family Nymphalidae	Species *Coenonympha inornata*	Author Edwards

PLAIN RINGLET

This butterfly is almost indistinguishable from
some of the other *Coenonympha* species. The
underside of the forewing is orange-brown with
a gray tip, and sometimes a single, small eyespot.
The hindwing is olive-gray with a broken white
band, and occasionally a few minute eyespots.
Another common name for the butterfly
is the prairie ringlet.
• **EARLY STAGES** The caterpillar is reddish
brown, or olive-brown, with two tails. It
feeds on various grasses.
• **DISTRIBUTION** Found in prairies,
meadows, and woodland clearings from
Canada to South Dakota and New York.

the upperside is
very simple in
• *pattern*

♂

roughly scaled wing fringes give •
a rather furry appearance

NEARCTIC

Time of Flight ☼	Habitat 🌳 ⏐⏐ ⏐⏐	Wingspan 1–1¾ in (2.5–4.5 cm)

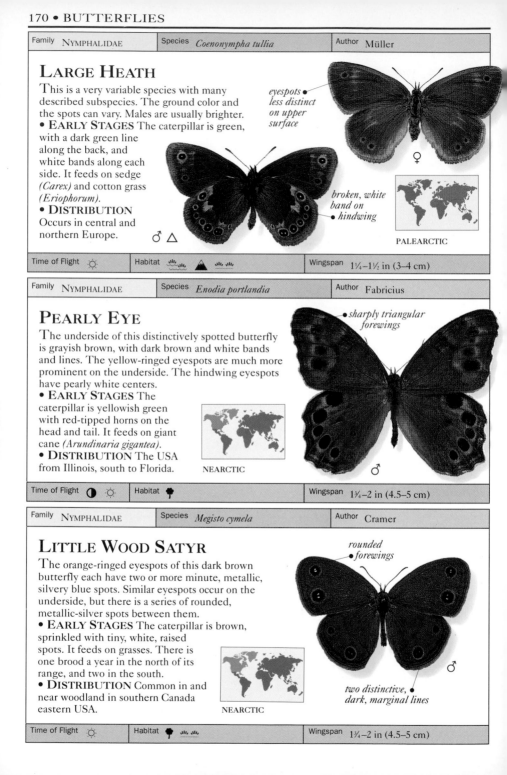

| Family | NYMPHALIDAE | Species | *Coenonympha tullia* | Author | Müller |

LARGE HEATH

This is a very variable species with many described subspecies. The ground color and the spots can vary. Males are usually brighter.
• **EARLY STAGES** The caterpillar is green, with a dark green line along the back, and white bands along each side. It feeds on sedge *(Carex)* and cotton grass *(Eriophorum)*.
• **DISTRIBUTION** Occurs in central and northern Europe.

eyespots less distinct on upper surface

♀

broken, white band on hindwing

♂ △

PALEARCTIC

| Time of Flight ☼ | Habitat | Wingspan 1¼–1½ in (3–4 cm) |

| Family | NYMPHALIDAE | Species | *Enodia portlandia* | Author | Fabricius |

PEARLY EYE

The underside of this distinctively spotted butterfly is grayish brown, with dark brown and white bands and lines. The yellow-ringed eyespots are much more prominent on the underside. The hindwing eyespots have pearly white centers.
• **EARLY STAGES** The caterpillar is yellowish green with red-tipped horns on the head and tail. It feeds on giant cane *(Arundinaria gigantea)*.
• **DISTRIBUTION** The USA from Illinois, south to Florida.

sharply triangular forewings

♂

NEARCTIC

| Time of Flight ◐ ☼ | Habitat | Wingspan 1¾–2 in (4.5–5 cm) |

| Family | NYMPHALIDAE | Species | *Megisto cymela* | Author | Cramer |

LITTLE WOOD SATYR

The orange-ringed eyespots of this dark brown butterfly each have two or more minute, metallic, silvery blue spots. Similar eyespots occur on the underside, but there is a series of rounded, metallic-silver spots between them.
• **EARLY STAGES** The caterpillar is brown, sprinkled with tiny, white, raised spots. It feeds on grasses. There is one brood a year in the north of its range, and two in the south.
• **DISTRIBUTION** Common in and near woodland in southern Canada eastern USA.

rounded forewings

♂

two distinctive, dark, marginal lines

NEARCTIC

| Time of Flight ☼ | Habitat | Wingspan 1¾–2 in (4.5–5 cm) |

Family NYMPHALIDAE	Species *Elymnias agondas*	Author Boisduval

PALMFLY

The male's pale blue-tinged wing margins are more strongly developed in some forms. The underside has an orange patch, enclosing two eyespots, on each hindwing. The females have the same striking, black and white pattern on each surface.
• **EARLY STAGES** The caterpillar is not described, but it is known to feed on palms (Palmae).
• **DISTRIBUTION** From Papua New Guinea to northern Australia.

INDO-AUSTRALIAN

striking, plain black forewings •

long, slender antennae •

blue tinge to wing margins •

brown leading edge to forewings •

♂

• scalloped wing margins

thin, white wing • margins

hindwing eyespots are much smaller than those on • underside

♀

Time of Flight ☼	Habitat 🌴	Wingspan 2¾–3½ in (7–9 cm)

Family NYMPHALIDAE	Species *Heteronympha merope*	Author Fabricius

COMMON BROWN

The sexes of this butterfly are very different. The male underside is similar to the upper surface, but has fewer dark markings and smaller eyespots. The underside of the female forewing is similar to the upperside, but the hindwing is mottled with reddish brown and grayish brown, and has a few eyespots.

• **EARLY STAGES** The caterpillar is very variable in color, ranging from green to gray, or light brown, with darker mottling and two short tails. It feeds on grasses. There are one or two generations a year depending on locality.

• **DISTRIBUTION** Found in southwestern and southeastern Australia, including Tasmania.

female forewing is much broader, and less pointed at the tip

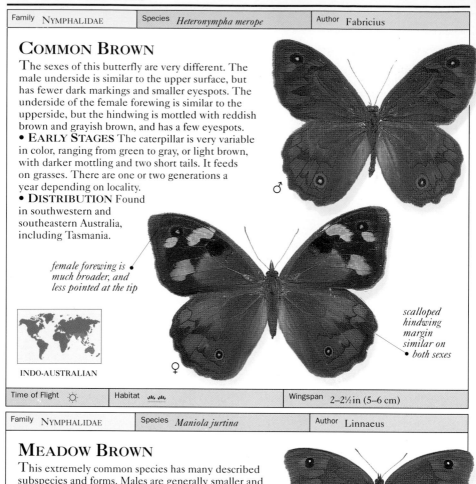

INDO-AUSTRALIAN

♂

♀

scalloped hindwing margin similar on both sexes

Time of Flight ☼	Habitat 〜 〜	Wingspan 2–2½ in (5–6 cm)

Family NYMPHALIDAE	Species *Maniola jurtina*	Author Linnaeus

MEADOW BROWN

This extremely common species has many described subspecies and forms. Males are generally smaller and darker. The undersides of both sexes are similar, with orange forewings and brown hindwings, but females have more clearly defined light and dark regions.

• **EARLY STAGES** The caterpillar is green with long white hairs and yellow lines along the sides. It feeds on grasses, particularly *Poa* and *Agrostis*.

• **DISTRIBUTION** Europe to North Africa, across to Iran.

eyespot diverts birds from the delicate body

irregular dividing line of colors on the hindwing underside

PALEARCTIC

♀

scalloped hindwing margins

♀ △

Time of Flight ☼	Habitat 🌳 〜 〜	Wingspan 1½–2¼ in (4–4.5 cm)

Family NYMPHALIDAE	Species *Hypocysta adiante*	Author Hübner

ORANGE RINGLET

This butterfly has golden-brown fore- and hindwings. The underside of the forewing is similar to the upperside but paler, and the hindwing eyespots are encircled by pale, grayish brown outer rings.

• **EARLY STAGES** The caterpillar is pinkish brown, with darker lines. The head is hairy, with a pair of pointed horns. It feeds on grasses.

• **DISTRIBUTION** Can be found in northern and eastern Australia with two described subspecies.

brown forewing border

brown spot in hindwing corner

♂

hindwing eyespots

INDO-AUSTRALIAN

Time of Flight ☼	Habitat ⬚ ⬚	Wingspan 1¼–1½ in (3–4 cm)

Family NYMPHALIDAE	Species *Hipparchia fagi*	Author Scopoli

WOODLAND GRAYLING

Males tend to have the forewing band suffused with grayish brown and the eyespots are usually less well developed than those of the female. The undersides of the sexes are similar. Butterflies are on the wing in the summer.

• **EARLY STAGES** The caterpillar is pale, grayish brown to yellowish brown, with darker lines and stripes. It feeds chiefly on soft grasses *(Holeus)*. There is one generation a year.

• **DISTRIBUTION** It is widespread in open woodland in central and southern Europe.

♀

jagged white band to forewing

underside hindwing pattern provides good camouflage when species is at rest

scalloped hindwings

♀ △

PALEARCTIC

Time of Flight ☼	Habitat ♣	Wingspan 2¾–3 in (7–7.5 cm)

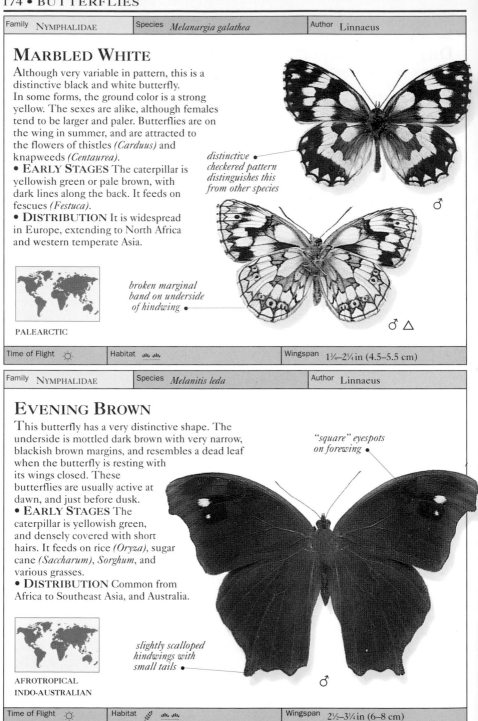

| Family NYMPHALIDAE | Species *Melanargia galathea* | Author Linnaeus |

MARBLED WHITE

Although very variable in pattern, this is a
distinctive black and white butterfly.
In some forms, the ground color is a strong
yellow. The sexes are alike, although females
tend to be larger and paler. Butterflies are on
the wing in summer, and are attracted to
the flowers of thistles *(Carduus)* and
knapweeds *(Centaurea)*.
• **EARLY STAGES** The caterpillar is
yellowish green or pale brown, with
dark lines along the back. It feeds on
fescues *(Festuca)*.
• **DISTRIBUTION** It is widespread
in Europe, extending to North Africa
and western temperate Asia.

distinctive •
checkered pattern
distinguishes this
from other species

♂

broken marginal
band on underside
of hindwing •

♂ △

PALEARCTIC

| Time of Flight ☼ | Habitat | Wingspan 1¾–2¼ in (4.5–5.5 cm) |

| Family NYMPHALIDAE | Species *Melanitis leda* | Author Linnaeus |

EVENING BROWN

This butterfly has a very distinctive shape. The
underside is mottled dark brown with very narrow,
blackish brown margins, and resembles a dead leaf
when the butterfly is resting with
its wings closed. These
butterflies are usually active at
dawn, and just before dusk.
• **EARLY STAGES** The
caterpillar is yellowish green,
and densely covered with short
hairs. It feeds on rice *(Oryza)*, sugar
cane *(Saccharum)*, *Sorghum*, and
various grasses.
• **DISTRIBUTION** Common from
Africa to Southeast Asia, and Australia.

*"square" eyespots
on forewing* •

slightly scalloped
hindwings with
small tails •

♂

AFROTROPICAL
INDO-AUSTRALIAN

| Time of Flight ☼ | Habitat | Wingspan 2½–3¼ in (6–8 cm) |

Family NYMPHALIDAE	Species *Minois dryas*	Author Scopoli

DRYAD BUTTERFLY

Males of this distinctive butterfly are smaller and darker than females, and tend to have smaller eyespots. The underside is paler, and there are sometimes gray bands on the hindwing. The butterflies are on the wing from early summer to early autumn.
• **EARLY STAGES** The caterpillar is dirty white with dark markings and two blackish brown stripes extending to the forked tail. It feeds on various grasses, especially purple moor grass *(Molinia)*.
• **DISTRIBUTION** Can be found in open woodland and on grassy slopes in central and southern Europe, extending across temperate Asia to Japan.

blue centers to eyespots distinguish this from • similar species

scalloped hindwing margins are most noticeable in females

♀

PALEARCTIC

Time of Flight ☼	Habitat ♣ ⅏ ⅏	Wingspan 2–2¾ in (5–7 cm)

Family NYMPHALIDAE	Species *Pararge aegeria*	Author Linnaeus

SPECKLED WOOD

The sexes of this dappled woodland butterfly are very similar. Females have more rounded forewings. The eyespots on the upperside are much more developed than on the underside. The spots vary from creamy white to deep orange. Speckled wood butterflies often feed from the blossoms of bramble *(Rubus)*.
• **EARLY STAGES** The caterpillar is yellowish green with a dark green stripe down the back, and light and dark lines along the sides. It feeds on couch *(Agropyron)* and other grasses.
• **DISTRIBUTION** Widespread in Europe, extending through to central Asia.

pale scalloping • to wing edges

♂

• scalloped hindwing margins

weakly developed eyespots •

♂ △

PALEARCTIC

Time of Flight ☼	Habitat ♣	Wingspan 1½–1¾ in (4–4.5 cm)

Family NYMPHALIDAE	Species *Pararge schakra*	Author Kollar

COMMON WALL BUTTERFLY

Although the upperside of this butterfly is not particularly distinctive, with its black and white eyespots set in orange patches on a brown background, the underside is more easily recognized, with its attractive hindwing row of multi-ringed eyespots, and its "scorched" forewings. These butterflies are active fliers, usually keeping close to the ground. They occur at most times of the year, on sunny hillsides above 6,560 ft (2,000 m).
• **EARLY STAGES** Although little seems to be known about the early stages, it is almost certain that the caterpillar feeds on grasses.
• **DISTRIBUTION** Occurs from Iran throughout northern India to western China.

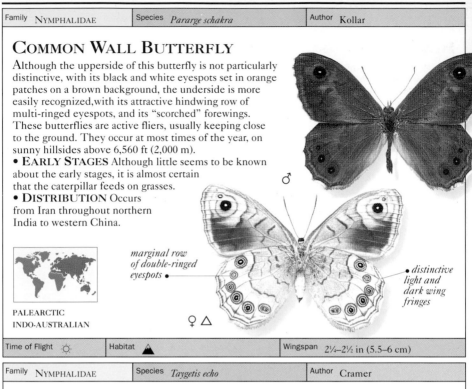

♂

marginal row
of double-ringed
eyespots •

• distinctive
light and
dark wing
fringes

PALEARCTIC
INDO-AUSTRALIAN

♀ △

Time of Flight ☼	Habitat ▲	Wingspan 2¼–2½ in (5.5–6 cm)

Family NYMPHALIDAE	Species *Taygetis echo*	Author Cramer

NIGHT BUTTERFLY

This brown butterfly has a velvety black center to the forewing. The underside is similar in coloration to the upperside, and has a marginal band of minute, yellowish white spots on the forewing, becoming larger on the hindwing. The sexes are similar.
• **EARLY STAGES** Little is known of the early stages, although other members of the genus have smooth caterpillars that feed on grasses, and bamboos *(Chusquea)*.
• **DISTRIBUTION** Found in tropical South America, from Surinam to Brazil. Also occurs in Trinidad.

forewing tip is suffused
• with golden brown

♂

irregular scalloping of •
the hindwing margin

dark color makes •
this butterfly difficult to
see when it flies at night

NEOTROPICAL

Time of Flight ◑ ☼	Habitat 🌴	Wingspan 2¼–2½ in (5.7–6 cm)

Family NYMPHALIDAE	Species *Pierella hyceta*	Author Hewitson

HEWITSON'S PIERELLA

This distinctive angular-shaped butterfly, with its orange-tipped hindwings, belongs to a South American genus of about 50 species. The underside lacks the bright hindwing patch, and thus is better camouflaged when the butterfly closes its wings. The vertical lines crossing the wing veins are very noticeable. The sexes are similar.
• **EARLY STAGES** Little is known of the early stages, although related species have dull brown caterpillars with short, double tails, and feed on the foliage of various Heliconiaceae and Marantaceae.
• **DISTRIBUTION** Widespread in South America from Brazil to Guyana.

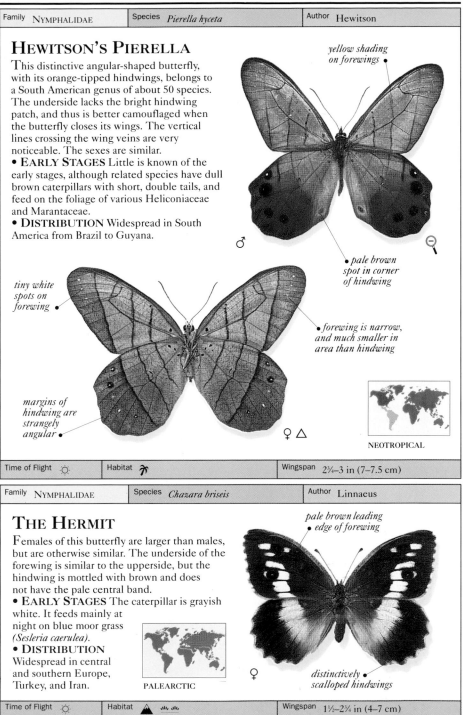

yellow shading on forewings

♂

⊖

pale brown spot in corner of hindwing

forewing is narrow, and much smaller in area than hindwing

tiny white spots on forewing

margins of hindwing are strangely angular

♀ △

NEOTROPICAL

Time of Flight ☼	Habitat 🦅	Wingspan 2¾–3 in (7–7.5 cm)

Family NYMPHALIDAE	Species *Chazara briseis*	Author Linnaeus

THE HERMIT

Females of this butterfly are larger than males, but are otherwise similar. The underside of the forewing is similar to the upperside, but the hindwing is mottled with brown and does not have the pale central band.
• **EARLY STAGES** The caterpillar is grayish white. It feeds mainly at night on blue moor grass *(Sesleria caerulea)*.
• **DISTRIBUTION** Widespread in central and southern Europe, Turkey, and Iran.

pale brown leading edge of forewing

PALEARCTIC

♀

distinctively scalloped hindwings

Time of Flight ☼	Habitat ▲ 🌾 🌾	Wingspan 1½–2¾ in (4–7 cm)

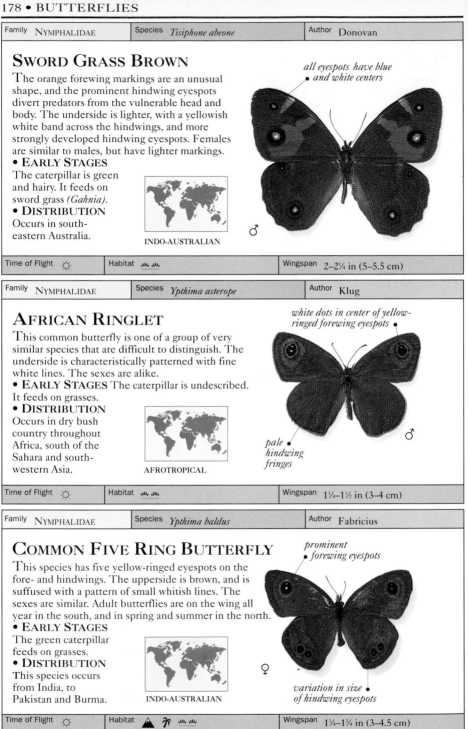

Family NYMPHALIDAE	Species *Tisiphone abeone*	Author Donovan

SWORD GRASS BROWN

The orange forewing markings are an unusual shape, and the prominent hindwing eyespots divert predators from the vulnerable head and body. The underside is lighter, with a yellowish white band across the hindwings, and more strongly developed hindwing eyespots. Females are similar to males, but have lighter markings.
• **EARLY STAGES**
The caterpillar is green and hairy. It feeds on sword grass *(Gahnia)*.
• **DISTRIBUTION**
Occurs in south-eastern Australia.

INDO-AUSTRALIAN

all eyespots have blue and white centers

♂

Time of Flight ☼	Habitat	Wingspan 2–2¼ in (5–5.5 cm)

Family NYMPHALIDAE	Species *Ypthima asterope*	Author Klug

AFRICAN RINGLET

This common butterfly is one of a group of very similar species that are difficult to distinguish. The underside is characteristically patterned with fine white lines. The sexes are alike.
• **EARLY STAGES** The caterpillar is undescribed. It feeds on grasses.
• **DISTRIBUTION**
Occurs in dry bush country throughout Africa, south of the Sahara and south-western Asia.

AFROTROPICAL

white dots in center of yellow-ringed forewing eyespots

pale hindwing fringes

♂

Time of Flight ☼	Habitat	Wingspan 1¼–1½ in (3–4 cm)

Family NYMPHALIDAE	Species *Ypthima baldus*	Author Fabricius

COMMON FIVE RING BUTTERFLY

This species has five yellow-ringed eyespots on the fore- and hindwings. The upperside is brown, and is suffused with a pattern of small whitish lines. The sexes are similar. Adult butterflies are on the wing all year in the south, and in spring and summer in the north.
• **EARLY STAGES**
The green caterpillar feeds on grasses.
• **DISTRIBUTION**
This species occurs from India, to Pakistan and Burma.

INDO-AUSTRALIAN

prominent forewing eyespots

♀

variation in size of hindwing eyespots

Time of Flight ☼	Habitat	Wingspan 1¼–1¾ in (3–4.5 cm)

Family NYMPHALIDAE	Species *Zipaetis scylax*	Author Hewitson

DARK CATSEYE BUTTERFLY

This is one of only three known species in the genus occurring in the region extending from India to China. The brown upperside of both sexes is virtually unmarked, but the underside bears the distinctive yellow-ringed eyespots, which give the species its common name. Butterflies have a weak flight, and mostly stay in areas of dense bush.

• **EARLY STAGES** Nothing seems to be known of the early stages of this species, although the caterpillar probably feeds on grasses.

• **DISTRIBUTION** It is common in the hill ranges of northern India, Pakistan, and Burma.

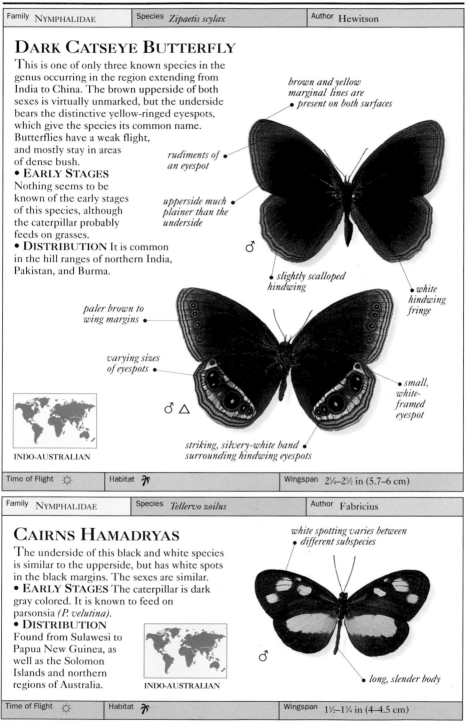

brown and yellow marginal lines are
• present on both surfaces

rudiments of • an eyespot

upperside much • plainer than the underside

♂

• slightly scalloped hindwing

•white hindwing fringe

paler brown to wing margins •

varying sizes of eyespots •

♂ △

• small, white-framed eyespot

striking, silvery-white band • surrounding hindwing eyespots

INDO-AUSTRALIAN

Time of Flight ☼	Habitat 🌿	Wingspan 2¼–2½ in (5.7–6 cm)

Family NYMPHALIDAE	Species *Tellervo zoilus*	Author Fabricius

CAIRNS HAMADRYAS

white spotting varies between
• different subspecies

The underside of this black and white species is similar to the upperside, but has white spots in the black margins. The sexes are similar.

• **EARLY STAGES** The caterpillar is dark gray colored. It is known to feed on parsonsia *(P. velutina)*.

• **DISTRIBUTION** Found from Sulawesi to Papua New Guinea, as well as the Solomon Islands and northern regions of Australia.

INDO-AUSTRALIAN

♂

• long, slender body

Time of Flight ☼	Habitat 🌿	Wingspan 1½–1¾ in (4–4.5 cm)

Family NYMPHALIDAE	Species *Mechanitis isthmia*	Author Bates

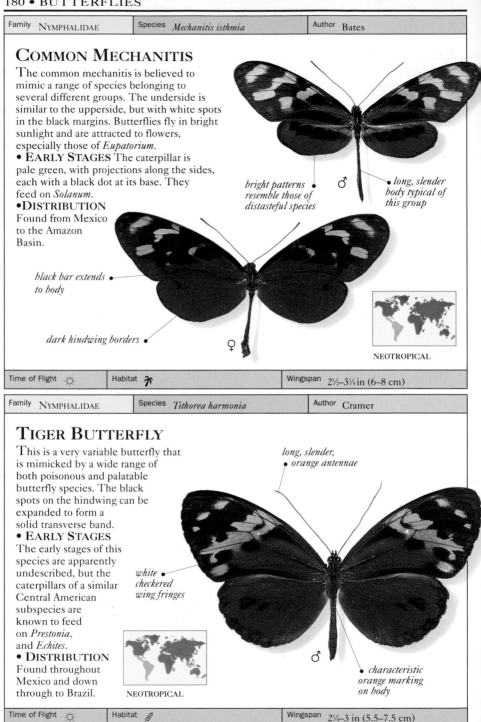

COMMON MECHANITIS

The common mechanitis is believed to mimic a range of species belonging to several different groups. The underside is similar to the upperside, but with white spots in the black margins. Butterflies fly in bright sunlight and are attracted to flowers, especially those of *Eupatorium*.

• **EARLY STAGES** The caterpillar is pale green, with projections along the sides, each with a black dot at its base. They feed on *Solanum*.

•**DISTRIBUTION** Found from Mexico to the Amazon Basin.

bright patterns resemble those of distasteful species

♂

long, slender body typical of this group

black bar extends to body

dark hindwing borders

♀

NEOTROPICAL

Time of Flight ☼	Habitat 🦗	Wingspan 2½–3¼ in (6–8 cm)

Family NYMPHALIDAE	Species *Tithorea harmonia*	Author Cramer

TIGER BUTTERFLY

This is a very variable butterfly that is mimicked by a wide range of both poisonous and palatable butterfly species. The black spots on the hindwing can be expanded to form a solid transverse band.

• **EARLY STAGES** The early stages of this species are apparently undescribed, but the caterpillars of a similar Central American subspecies are known to feed on *Prestonia*, and *Echites*.

• **DISTRIBUTION** Found throughout Mexico and down through to Brazil.

long, slender, orange antennae

white checkered wing fringes

NEOTROPICAL

♂

characteristic orange marking on body

Time of Flight ☼	Habitat	Wingspan 2¼–3 in (5.5–7.5 cm)

Family NYMPHALIDAE	Species *Thyridia themisto*	Author Hübner

SMALL THYRIDIA

Belonging to a group of about seven described
species from South America, this impressive
butterfly has transparent wings, and strong
black veins, bands, and margins. They are
mimicked by several other species
of butterflies and moths,
including the day-flying
Castniid moth, *Gazera linus.*
• **EARLY STAGES** The
caterpillar is black with bright
yellow rings, indicating that
the species is almost certainly
poisonous. It feeds on manaca
(Brunfelsia) shrubs.
• **DISTRIBUTION** Found widely
in Argentina and
Brazil, where it
is often seen
in urban areas.

*long, slender
antennae with
• white clubs*

NEOTROPICAL

*transparent patches where •
wingscales are modified
to form slender hairs*

♀

*forewings of •
this species have
a distinctive
bulbous outline*

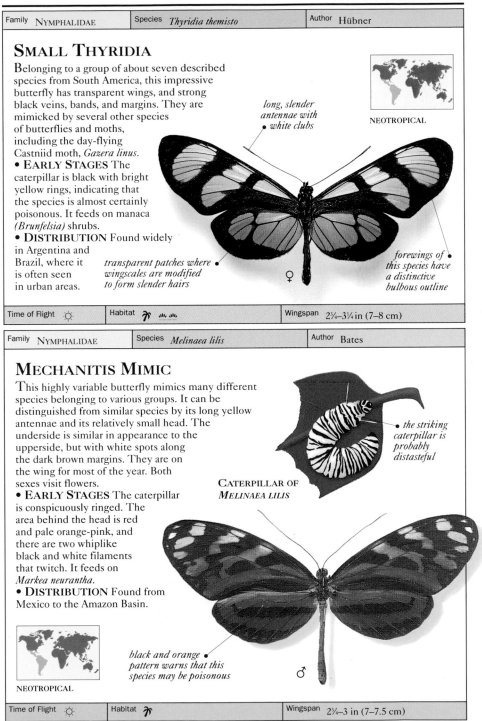

Time of Flight ☼	Habitat 🦋 ⸯ ⸯ	Wingspan 2¼–3¼ in (7–8 cm)

Family NYMPHALIDAE	Species *Melinaea lilis*	Author Bates

MECHANITIS MIMIC

This highly variable butterfly mimics many different
species belonging to various groups. It can be
distinguished from similar species by its long yellow
antennae and its relatively small head. The
underside is similar in appearance to the
upperside, but with white spots along
the dark brown margins. They are on
the wing for most of the year. Both
sexes visit flowers.
• **EARLY STAGES** The caterpillar
is conspicuously ringed. The
area behind the head is red
and pale orange-pink, and
there are two whiplike
black and white filaments
that twitch. It feeds on
Markea neurantha.
• **DISTRIBUTION** Found from
Mexico to the Amazon Basin.

*• the striking
caterpillar is
probably
distasteful*

**CATERPILLAR OF
*MELINAEA LILIS***

NEOTROPICAL

*black and orange •
pattern warns that this
species may be poisonous*

♂

Time of Flight ☼	Habitat 🦋	Wingspan 2¼–3 in (7–7.5 cm)

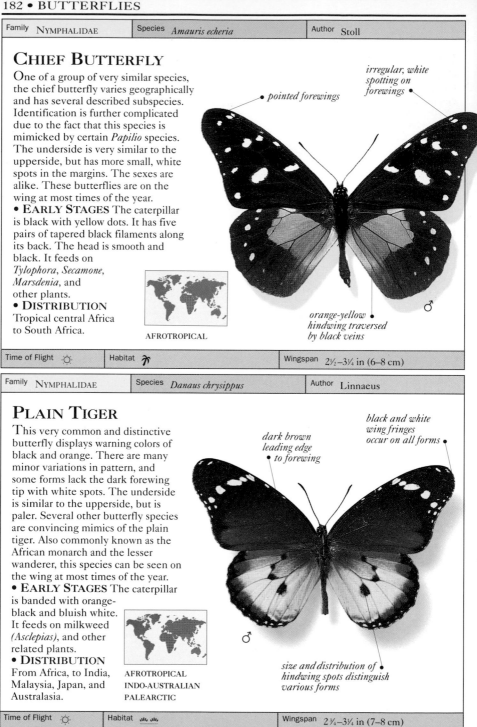

| Family NYMPHALIDAE | Species *Amauris echeria* | Author Stoll |

CHIEF BUTTERFLY

One of a group of very similar species, the chief butterfly varies geographically and has several described subspecies. Identification is further complicated due to the fact that this species is mimicked by certain *Papilio* species. The underside is very similar to the upperside, but has more small, white spots in the margins. The sexes are alike. These butterflies are on the wing at most times of the year.
• **EARLY STAGES** The caterpillar is black with yellow dots. It has five pairs of tapered black filaments along its back. The head is smooth and black. It feeds on *Tylophora, Secamone, Marsdenia*, and other plants.
• **DISTRIBUTION** Tropical central Africa to South Africa.

AFROTROPICAL

pointed forewings

irregular, white spotting on forewings

orange-yellow hindwing traversed by black veins

♂

| Time of Flight ☼ | Habitat 🌿 | Wingspan 2½–3¼ in (6–8 cm) |

| Family NYMPHALIDAE | Species *Danaus chrysippus* | Author Linnaeus |

PLAIN TIGER

This very common and distinctive butterfly displays warning colors of black and orange. There are many minor variations in pattern, and some forms lack the dark forewing tip with white spots. The underside is similar to the upperside, but is paler. Several other butterfly species are convincing mimics of the plain tiger. Also commonly known as the African monarch and the lesser wanderer, this species can be seen on the wing at most times of the year.
• **EARLY STAGES** The caterpillar is banded with orange-black and bluish white. It feeds on milkweed *(Asclepias)*, and other related plants.
• **DISTRIBUTION** From Africa, to India, Malaysia, Japan, and Australasia.

AFROTROPICAL
INDO-AUSTRALIAN
PALEARCTIC

dark brown leading edge to forewing

black and white wing fringes occur on all forms

♂

size and distribution of hindwing spots distinguish various forms

| Time of Flight ☼ | Habitat ⚘ ⚘ | Wingspan 2¾–3¼ in (7–8 cm) |

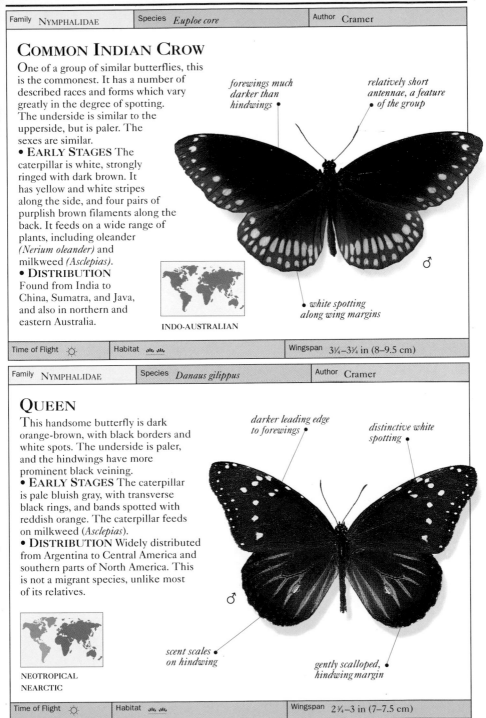

Family NYMPHALIDAE	Species *Euploe core*	Author Cramer

COMMON INDIAN CROW

One of a group of similar butterflies, this
is the commonest. It has a number of
described races and forms which vary
greatly in the degree of spotting.
The underside is similar to the
upperside, but is paler. The
sexes are similar.
• **EARLY STAGES** The
caterpillar is white, strongly
ringed with dark brown. It
has yellow and white stripes
along the side, and four pairs of
purplish brown filaments along the
back. It feeds on a wide range of
plants, including oleander
(Nerium oleander) and
milkweed *(Asclepias)*.
• **DISTRIBUTION**
Found from India to
China, Sumatra, and Java,
and also in northern and
eastern Australia.

*forewings much
darker than
hindwings*

*relatively short
antennae, a feature
of the group*

*white spotting
along wing margins*

INDO-AUSTRALIAN

Time of Flight ☼	Habitat 〰 〰	Wingspan 3¼–3¾ in (8–9.5 cm)

Family NYMPHALIDAE	Species *Danaus gilippus*	Author Cramer

QUEEN

This handsome butterfly is dark
orange-brown, with black borders and
white spots. The underside is paler,
and the hindwings have more
prominent black veining.
• **EARLY STAGES** The caterpillar
is pale bluish gray, with transverse
black rings, and bands spotted with
reddish orange. The caterpillar feeds
on milkweed *(Asclepias)*.
• **DISTRIBUTION** Widely distributed
from Argentina to Central America and
southern parts of North America. This
is not a migrant species, unlike most
of its relatives.

*darker leading edge
to forewings*

*distinctive white
spotting*

*scent scales
on hindwing*

*gently scalloped,
hindwing margin*

NEOTROPICAL
NEARCTIC

Time of Flight ☼	Habitat 〰 〰	Wingspan 2¾–3 in (7–7.5 cm)

| Family NYMPHALIDAE | Species *Danaus plexippus* | Author Linnaeus |

MONARCH

With its bold pattern of black and orange, and wing veins enhanced by dark borders, this is one of the best-known butterflies. The sexes are similar.
• **EARLY STAGES** The caterpillar is banded with black, yellow, and cream, and has tentacles behind the head. It feeds on milkweeds *(Asclepias)* and related plants.
• **DISTRIBUTION** This butterfly is a well-known migrant. It has spread from its home in the Americas to Hawaii, Indonesia, Australasia, and the Canary Islands, recently establishing colonies in Mediterranean countries.

WORLDWIDE

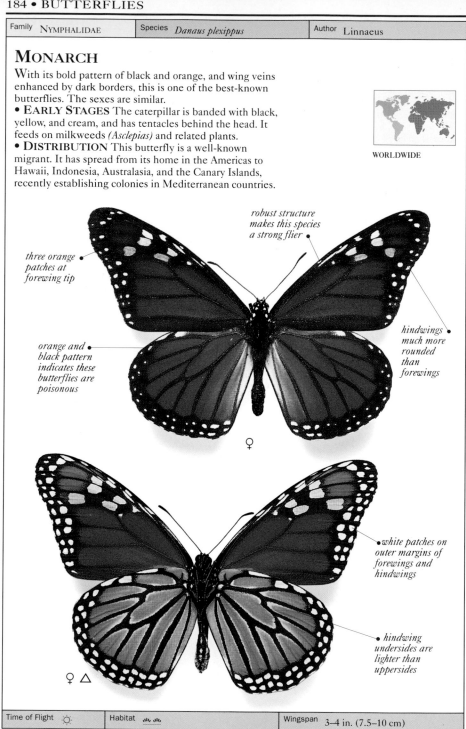

three orange patches at forewing tip

robust structure makes this species a strong flier

orange and black pattern indicates these butterflies are poisonous

hindwings much more rounded than forewings

♀

white patches on outer margins of forewings and hindwings

hindwing undersides are lighter than uppersides

♀ △

| Time of Flight ☼ | Habitat | Wingspan 3–4 in. (7.5–10 cm) |

Family NYMPHALIDAE	Species *Euploea mulciber*	Author Cramer

STRIPED BLUE CROW

The uppersides on the forewings of both sexes of this large butterfly are shot with iridescent purple, although it is most evident in the darker male. The female has brown hindwings shot with white lines. The undersides are similar, but lack the iridescence. This species belongs to a large Indo-Australian genus known as crow butterflies because of their iridescent dark colors. Both caterpillars and adults are poisonous.

• EARLY STAGES The caterpillar is yellowish brown, with paler and darker bands, and four pairs of black-tipped, red filaments. It feeds on oleander *(Nerium)*, fig *(Ficus)*, and various pipevines *(Aristolochia)*.

• DISTRIBUTION India to southern China, Malaysia, and the Philippines.

INDO-AUSTRALIAN

white spots ringed with paler blue

darker brown to forewing base

some spots lack the white center

white-spotted fringes to hindwings

paler triangle at base of hindwings

♂

purple color less distinct than in male

female hindwings rayed with white

♀

Time of Flight ☼	Habitat	Wingspan 3½–4 in.(9–10 cm)

| Family | NYMPHALIDAE | Species | *Idea leuconoe* | Author | Erichson |

LARGE TREE NYMPH

The large wings of this delicate butterfly are translucent grayish white, with distinctive black markings. The wings are often suffused with yellow toward the base. Large tree nymphs have a slow, gliding flight, and prefer to remain just below the forest canopy.
• **EARLY STAGES** The caterpillar is velvety black, with narrow, pale yellow rings, and red spots. There are four pairs of black filaments running along its back. It feeds on *Parsonsia*, *Cynanchum*, and *Tylophora*.
• **DISTRIBUTION** From Thailand to Malaysia, the Philippines, and Taiwan. In Malaysia it is largely coastal, in mangrove swamps.

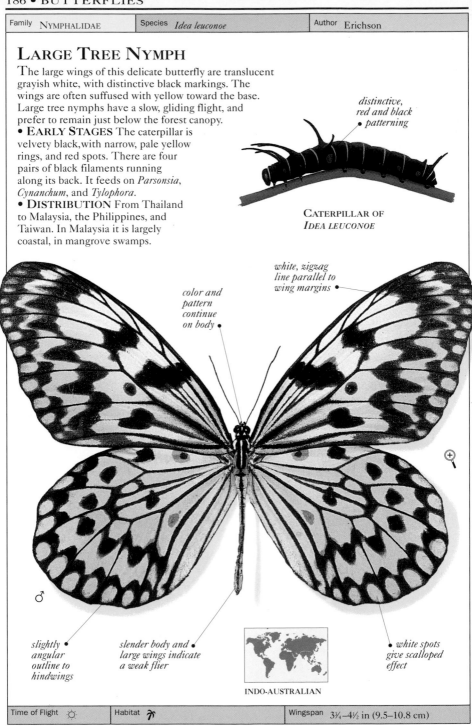

distinctive, red and black patterning

CATERPILLAR OF
IDEA LEUCONOE

white, zigzag line parallel to wing margins •

color and pattern continue on body •

♂

slightly • angular outline to hindwings

slender body and • large wings indicate a weak flier

• white spots give scalloped effect

INDO-AUSTRALIAN

| Time of Flight ☼ | Habitat 🌳 | Wingspan 3¾–4½ in (9.5–10.8 cm) |

Family NYMPHALIDAE	Species *Ideopsis vitrea*	Author Blanchard

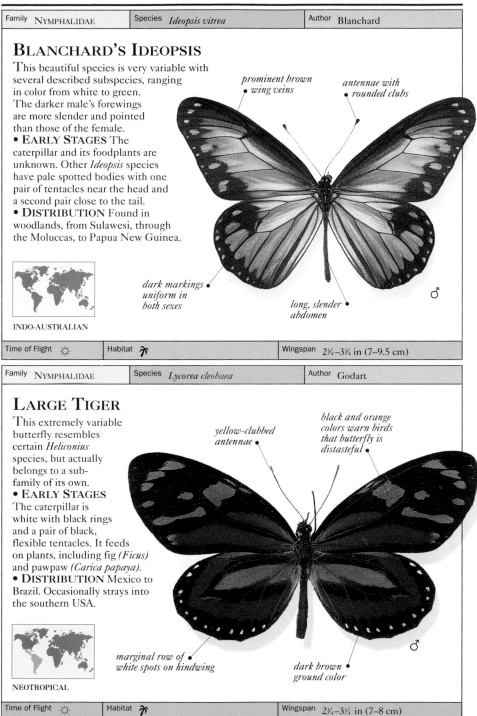

BLANCHARD'S IDEOPSIS

This beautiful species is very variable with
several described subspecies, ranging
in color from white to green.
The darker male's forewings
are more slender and pointed
than those of the female.
• **EARLY STAGES** The
caterpillar and its foodplants are
unknown. Other *Ideopsis* species
have pale spotted bodies with one
pair of tentacles near the head and
a second pair close to the tail.
• **DISTRIBUTION** Found in
woodlands, from Sulawesi, through
the Moluccas, to Papua New Guinea.

*prominent brown
• wing veins*

*antennae with
• rounded clubs*

*dark markings
uniform in
both sexes*

*long, slender •
abdomen*

♂

INDO-AUSTRALIAN

Time of Flight ☼	Habitat 🌱	Wingspan 2¾–3¾ in (7–9.5 cm)

Family NYMPHALIDAE	Species *Lycorea cleobaea*	Author Godart

LARGE TIGER

This extremely variable
butterfly resembles
certain *Heliconius*
species, but actually
belongs to a sub-
family of its own.
• **EARLY STAGES**
The caterpillar is
white with black rings
and a pair of black,
flexible tentacles. It feeds
on plants, including fig *(Ficus)*
and pawpaw *(Carica papaya)*.
• **DISTRIBUTION** Mexico to
Brazil. Occasionally strays into
the southern USA.

*yellow-clubbed
antennae •*

*black and orange
colors warn birds
that butterfly is
distasteful •*

*marginal row of •
white spots on hindwing*

*dark brown •
ground color*

♂

NEOTROPICAL

Time of Flight ☼	Habitat 🌱	Wingspan 2¾–3¼ in (7–8 cm)

MOTHS

THYATIRIDAE

T HE MOTHS BELONGING to this fairly small family, containing about 100 species, occur in many parts of the world. They are, however absent from the Afrotropical and Indo-Australian regions. Sometimes referred to collectively as the lutestrings, these medium-sized moths are generally fairly dull in color. Nevertheless, there are some exceptions that are distinctively and attractively marked with pink spots or pale lines.

———— • ————

The smooth caterpillars either live openly on foliage or else conceal themselves between leaves woven together with silk, where the pupae are formed in their silken cocoons.

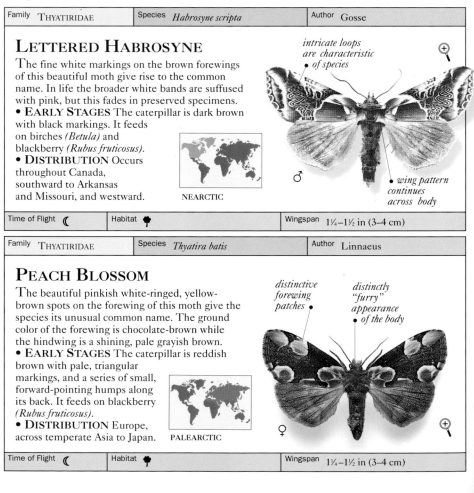

Family THYATIRIDAE	Species *Habrosyne scripta*	Author Gosse

LETTERED HABROSYNE

The fine white markings on the brown forewings of this beautiful moth give rise to the common name. In life the broader white bands are suffused with pink, but this fades in preserved specimens.
• **EARLY STAGES** The caterpillar is dark brown with black markings. It feeds on birches *(Betula)* and blackberry *(Rubus fruticosus).*
• **DISTRIBUTION** Occurs throughout Canada, southward to Arkansas and Missouri, and westward.

NEARCTIC

intricate loops are characteristic of species

♂

wing pattern continues across body

Time of Flight ☾	Habitat ⚇	Wingspan 1¼–1½ in (3–4 cm)

Family THYATIRIDAE	Species *Thyatira batis*	Author Linnaeus

PEACH BLOSSOM

The beautiful pinkish white-ringed, yellow-brown spots on the forewing of this moth give the species its unusual common name. The ground color of the forewing is chocolate-brown while the hindwing is a shining, pale grayish brown.
• **EARLY STAGES** The caterpillar is reddish brown with pale, triangular markings, and a series of small, forward-pointing humps along its back. It feeds on blackberry *(Rubus fruticosus).*
• **DISTRIBUTION** Europe, across temperate Asia to Japan.

PALEARCTIC

distinctive forewing patches

distinctly "furry" appearance of the body

♀

Time of Flight ☾	Habitat ⚇	Wingspan 1¼–1½ in (3–4 cm)

DREPANIDAE

T HIS GROUP OF about 800 species occurs throughout the world, with the exception of Central and South America. The most distinctive characteristic of the Drepanidae is the strongly curved forewing tip that is present in many species. This gives rise to the name hook tips, which is popularly applied to this group. Moths have very poorly formed tongues or no tongue at all, and so are unable to feed in this stage. The caterpillars of this group are distinctive, as they lack the pair of claspers at the end of the body that are common in other families. In many species the body tapers to a distinctive pointed tail instead.

Caterpillars usually feed on the foliage of broad-leaved trees and shrubs. The pupae are sometimes covered with an unusual bluish, waxy coating.

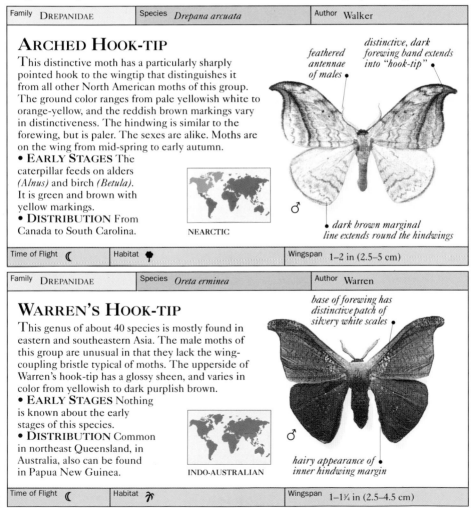

Family DREPANIDAE	Species *Drepana arcuata*	Author Walker

ARCHED HOOK-TIP

This distinctive moth has a particularly sharply pointed hook to the wingtip that distinguishes it from all other North American moths of this group. The ground color ranges from pale yellowish white to orange-yellow, and the reddish brown markings vary in distinctiveness. The hindwing is similar to the forewing, but is paler. The sexes are alike. Moths are on the wing from mid-spring to early autumn.
• EARLY STAGES The caterpillar feeds on alders *(Alnus)* and birch *(Betula)*. It is green and brown with yellow markings.
• DISTRIBUTION From Canada to South Carolina.

NEARCTIC

feathered antennae of males

distinctive, dark forewing band extends into "hook-tip"

dark brown marginal line extends round the hindwings

♂

Time of Flight ☾	Habitat 🌱	Wingspan 1–2 in (2.5–5 cm)

Family DREPANIDAE	Species *Oreta erminea*	Author Warren

WARREN'S HOOK-TIP

This genus of about 40 species is mostly found in eastern and southeastern Asia. The male moths of this group are unusual in that they lack the wing-coupling bristle typical of moths. The upperside of Warren's hook-tip has a glossy sheen, and varies in color from yellowish to dark purplish brown.
• EARLY STAGES Nothing is known about the early stages of this species.
• DISTRIBUTION Common in northeast Queensland, in Australia, also can be found in Papua New Guinea.

INDO-AUSTRALIAN

base of forewing has distinctive patch of silvery white scales

hairy appearance of inner hindwing margin

♂

Time of Flight ☾	Habitat 🌿	Wingspan 1–1¾ in (2.5–4.5 cm)

URANIIDAE

LTHOUGH THIS is a fairly small family of moths, it contains some of the most striking species to be found in the world, including the stunning Madagascan sunset moth (see opposite). They are found in the tropics of America, Africa, and Indo-Australia. The day-flying species are more vivid and beautifully colored than the night fliers; many have iridescent scaling and very well-developed tails to their wings, so that they are often mistaken for butterflies. Those species that fly at night are mostly very flimsy insects that have white or pale-colored wings with darker stripes. Uraniidae are similar to the Geometer moths (Geometridae), to which they are related, but they differ in the arrangement of their wing veins.

Family URANIIDAE	Species *Alcides zodiaca*	Author Butler

ZODIAC MOTH

This is the only member of this genus of eleven day-flying species to occur in Australia. The wings are black with coppery green tones and purplish pink iridescent bands. The hindwing margins are strongly scalloped and have short but distinct, pale bluish green tails. The underside is a pale, iridescent bluish green with black bands. The moths commonly visit flowers by day, and in the evening fly high in the forest canopy.

• **EARLY STAGES**
The caterpillar is black with white bands and an area of bright red on the back, behind the head. It feeds on the foliage of a large vine, *Omphalea queenslandiae*, and also on *Endospermum*.

• **DISTRIBUTION** Papua New Guinea and northeastern Australia.

striped leading edge
of forewing •

long, slender
• antennae

black and white checkered •
forewing edge

♀

silvery fringe to •
hindwing edge

• iridescent color
of wings is matched
on body

INDO-AUSTRALIAN

Time of Flight ☼	Habitat 🌿	Wingspan 3¼–4 in (8–10 cm)

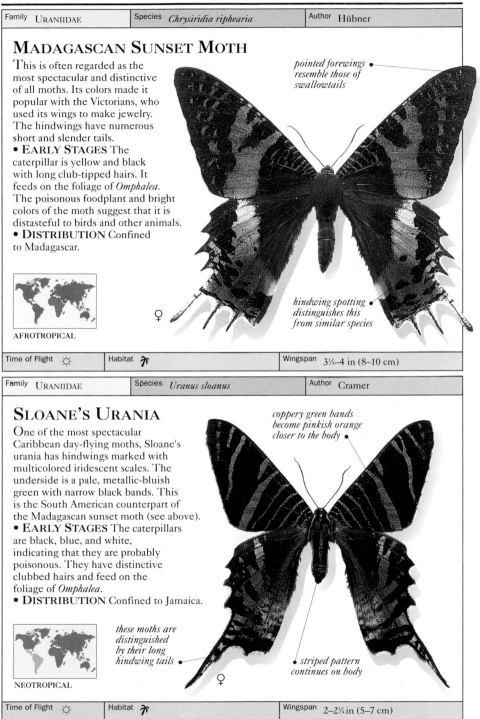

| Family URANIIDAE | Species *Chrysiridia riphearia* | Author Hübner |

MADAGASCAN SUNSET MOTH

This is often regarded as the most spectacular and distinctive of all moths. Its colors made it popular with the Victorians, who used its wings to make jewelry. The hindwings have numerous short and slender tails.
• **EARLY STAGES** The caterpillar is yellow and black with long club-tipped hairs. It feeds on the foliage of *Omphalea*. The poisonous foodplant and bright colors of the moth suggest that it is distasteful to birds and other animals.
• **DISTRIBUTION** Confined to Madagascar.

pointed forewings resemble those of swallowtails

hindwing spotting distinguishes this from similar species

♀

AFROTROPICAL

| Time of Flight ☼ | Habitat 🌿 | Wingspan 3¼–4 in (8–10 cm) |

| Family URANIIDAE | Species *Uranus sloanus* | Author Cramer |

SLOANE'S URANIA

One of the most spectacular Caribbean day-flying moths, Sloane's urania has hindwings marked with multicolored iridescent scales. The underside is a pale, metallic-bluish green with narrow black bands. This is the South American counterpart of the Madagascan sunset moth (see above).
• **EARLY STAGES** The caterpillars are black, blue, and white, indicating that they are probably poisonous. They have distinctive clubbed hairs and feed on the foliage of *Omphalea*.
• **DISTRIBUTION** Confined to Jamaica.

coppery green bands become pinkish orange closer to the body

these moths are distinguished by their long hindwing tails

striped pattern continues on body

♀

NEOTROPICAL

| Time of Flight ☼ | Habitat 🌿 | Wingspan 2–2¼ in (5–7 cm) |

GEOMETRIDAE

THIS IS the second largest family of moths, containing approximately 15,000 described species. Geometridae or "Geometers" typically have fairly large, rounded wings and slender bodies, and their flight is weak and fluttering. In such a large group, however, there are many deviants. In a number of species, the wings of the females are reduced to tiny vestiges so that they are unable to fly. Although most species are rather dull in color and will frequently display camouflage patterns, there are a few tropical groups that are actually very brightly colored. The name Geometridae refers to the looper caterpillars of this family, which are so-called because of their wholly characteristic, ungainly walk. They are also known in the USA as inchworms.

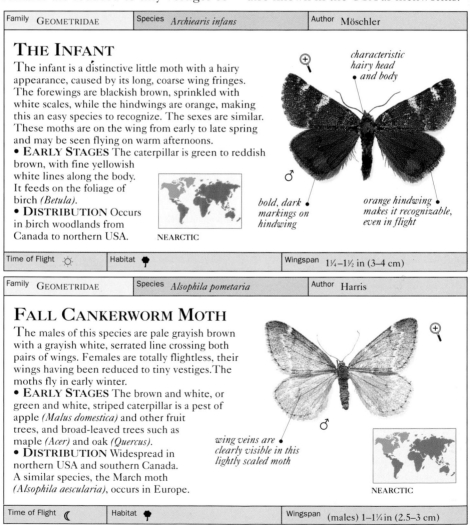

Family GEOMETRIDAE	Species *Archiearis infans*	Author Möschler

THE INFANT

The infant is a distinctive little moth with a hairy appearance, caused by its long, coarse wing fringes. The forewings are blackish brown, sprinkled with white scales, while the hindwings are orange, making this an easy species to recognize. The sexes are similar. These moths are on the wing from early to late spring and may be seen flying on warm afternoons.
• **EARLY STAGES** The caterpillar is green to reddish brown, with fine yellowish white lines along the body. It feeds on the foliage of birch *(Betula)*.
• **DISTRIBUTION** Occurs in birch woodlands from Canada to northern USA.

NEARCTIC

characteristic hairy head and body

♂

bold, dark markings on hindwing

orange hindwing makes it recognizable, even in flight

Time of Flight ☼	Habitat ♠	Wingspan 1¼–1½ in (3–4 cm)

Family GEOMETRIDAE	Species *Alsophila pometaria*	Author Harris

FALL CANKERWORM MOTH

The males of this species are pale grayish brown with a grayish white, serrated line crossing both pairs of wings. Females are totally flightless, their wings having been reduced to tiny vestiges. The moths fly in early winter.
• **EARLY STAGES** The brown and white, or green and white, striped caterpillar is a pest of apple *(Malus domestica)* and other fruit trees, and broad-leaved trees such as maple *(Acer)* and oak *(Quercus)*.
• **DISTRIBUTION** Widespread in northern USA and southern Canada. A similar species, the March moth *(Alsophila aescularia)*, occurs in Europe.

wing veins are clearly visible in this lightly scaled moth

♂

NEARCTIC

Time of Flight ☾	Habitat ♠	Wingspan (males) 1–1¼in (2.5–3 cm)

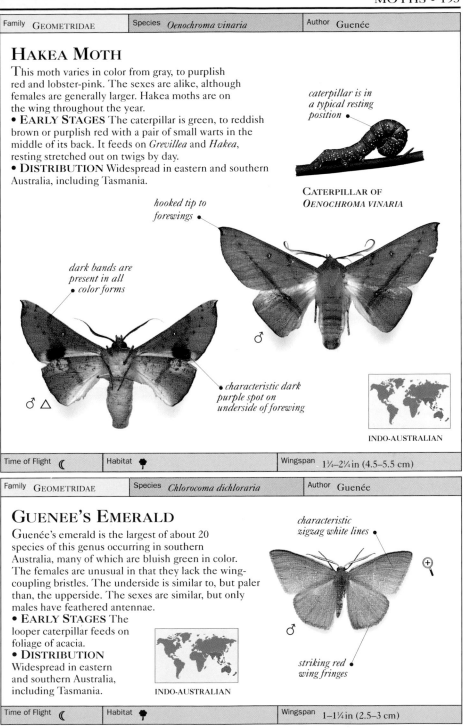

| Family GEOMETRIDAE | Species *Oenochroma vinaria* | Author Guenée |

HAKEA MOTH

This moth varies in color from gray, to purplish red and lobster-pink. The sexes are alike, although females are generally larger. Hakea moths are on the wing throughout the year.
• **EARLY STAGES** The caterpillar is green, to reddish brown or purplish red with a pair of small warts in the middle of its back. It feeds on *Grevillea* and *Hakea*, resting stretched out on twigs by day.
• **DISTRIBUTION** Widespread in eastern and southern Australia, including Tasmania.

caterpillar is in a typical resting position •

CATERPILLAR OF
OENOCHROMA VINARIA

hooked tip to forewings •

dark bands are present in all • color forms

♂

• characteristic dark purple spot on underside of forewing

♂ △

INDO-AUSTRALIAN

| Time of Flight ☾ | Habitat ☘ | Wingspan 1¾–2¼ in (4.5–5.5 cm) |

| Family GEOMETRIDAE | Species *Chlorocoma dichloraria* | Author Guenée |

GUENEE'S EMERALD

Guenée's emerald is the largest of about 20 species of this genus occurring in southern Australia, many of which are bluish green in color. The females are unusual in that they lack the wing-coupling bristles. The underside is similar to, but paler than, the upperside. The sexes are similar, but only males have feathered antennae.
• **EARLY STAGES** The looper caterpillar feeds on foliage of acacia.
• **DISTRIBUTION** Widespread in eastern and southern Australia, including Tasmania.

characteristic zigzag white lines •

♂

striking red • wing fringes

INDO-AUSTRALIAN

| Time of Flight ☾ | Habitat ☘ | Wingspan 1–1¼ in (2.5–3 cm) |

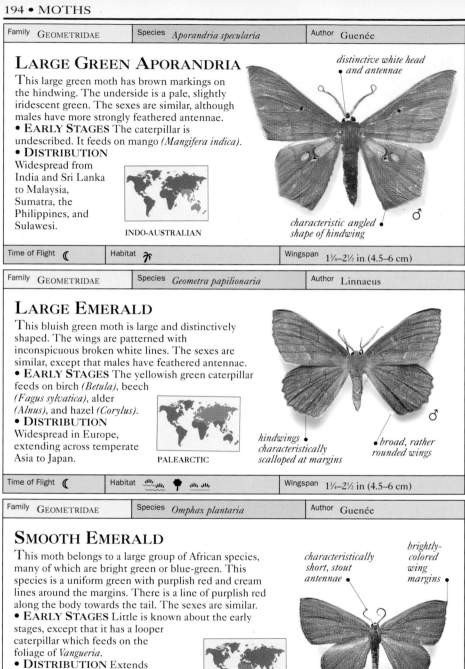

Family GEOMETRIDAE	Species *Aporandria specularia*	Author Guenée

LARGE GREEN APORANDRIA

This large green moth has brown markings on the hindwing. The underside is a pale, slightly iridescent green. The sexes are similar, although males have more strongly feathered antennae.
• **EARLY STAGES** The caterpillar is undescribed. It feeds on mango *(Mangifera indica)*.
• **DISTRIBUTION** Widespread from India and Sri Lanka to Malaysia, Sumatra, the Philippines, and Sulawesi.

INDO-AUSTRALIAN

distinctive white head and antennae

characteristic angled shape of hindwing

♂

Time of Flight ☾	Habitat 🦅	Wingspan 1¾–2½ in (4.5–6 cm)

Family GEOMETRIDAE	Species *Geometra papilionaria*	Author Linnaeus

LARGE EMERALD

This bluish green moth is large and distinctively shaped. The wings are patterned with inconspicuous broken white lines. The sexes are similar, except that males have feathered antennae.
• **EARLY STAGES** The yellowish green caterpillar feeds on birch *(Betula)*, beech *(Fagus sylvatica)*, alder *(Alnus)*, and hazel *(Corylus)*.
• **DISTRIBUTION** Widespread in Europe, extending across temperate Asia to Japan.

PALEARCTIC

hindwings characteristically scalloped at margins

broad, rather rounded wings

♂

Time of Flight ☾	Habitat 🌳	Wingspan 1¾–2½ in (4.5–6 cm)

Family GEOMETRIDAE	Species *Omphax plantaria*	Author Guenée

SMOOTH EMERALD

This moth belongs to a large group of African species, many of which are bright green or blue-green. This species is a uniform green with purplish red and cream lines around the margins. There is a line of purplish red along the body towards the tail. The sexes are similar.
• **EARLY STAGES** Little is known about the early stages, except that it has a looper caterpillar which feeds on the foliage of *Vangueria*.
• **DISTRIBUTION** Extends through southern Africa from Zimbabwe and Mozambique to Transvaal and Natal.

AFROTROPICAL

characteristically short, stout antennae

brightly-colored wing margins

♂

Time of Flight ☾	Habitat 🦅	Wingspan 1¼–1½ in (3–4 cm)

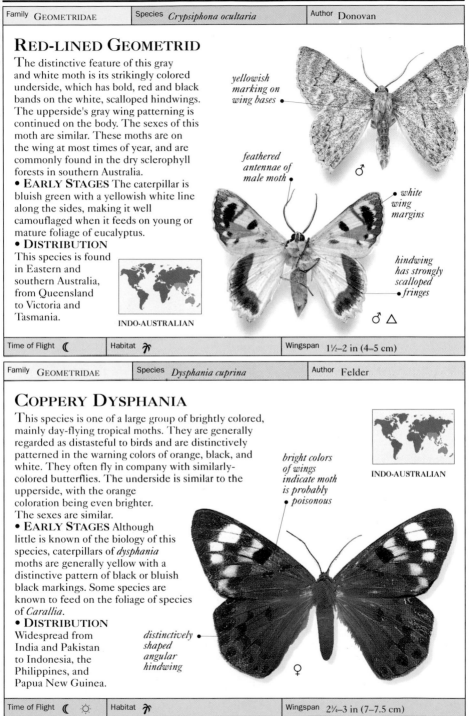

Family GEOMETRIDAE	Species *Crypsiphona ocultaria*	Author Donovan

RED-LINED GEOMETRID

The distinctive feature of this gray and white moth is its strikingly colored underside, which has bold, red and black bands on the white, scalloped hindwings. The upperside's gray wing patterning is continued on the body. The sexes of this moth are similar. These moths are on the wing at most times of year, and are commonly found in the dry sclerophyll forests in southern Australia.
• **EARLY STAGES** The caterpillar is bluish green with a yellowish white line along the sides, making it well camouflaged when it feeds on young or mature foliage of eucalyptus.
• **DISTRIBUTION** This species is found in Eastern and southern Australia, from Queensland to Victoria and Tasmania.

yellowish marking on wing bases

feathered antennae of male moth

♂

white wing margins

hindwing has strongly scalloped fringes

♂ △

INDO-AUSTRALIAN

Time of Flight ☾	Habitat 🌱	Wingspan 1½–2 in (4–5 cm)

Family GEOMETRIDAE	Species *Dysphania cuprina*	Author Felder

COPPERY DYSPHANIA

This species is one of a large group of brightly colored, mainly day-flying tropical moths. They are generally regarded as distasteful to birds and are distinctively patterned in the warning colors of orange, black, and white. They often fly in company with similarly-colored butterflies. The underside is similar to the upperside, with the orange coloration being even brighter. The sexes are similar.
• **EARLY STAGES** Although little is known of the biology of this species, caterpillars of *dysphania* moths are generally yellow with a distinctive pattern of black or bluish black markings. Some species are known to feed on the foliage of species of *Carallia*.
• **DISTRIBUTION** Widespread from India and Pakistan to Indonesia, the Philippines, and Papua New Guinea.

bright colors of wings indicate moth is probably poisonous

INDO-AUSTRALIAN

distinctively shaped angular hindwing

♀

Time of Flight ☾ ☼	Habitat 🌱	Wingspan 2¾–3 in (7–7.5 cm)

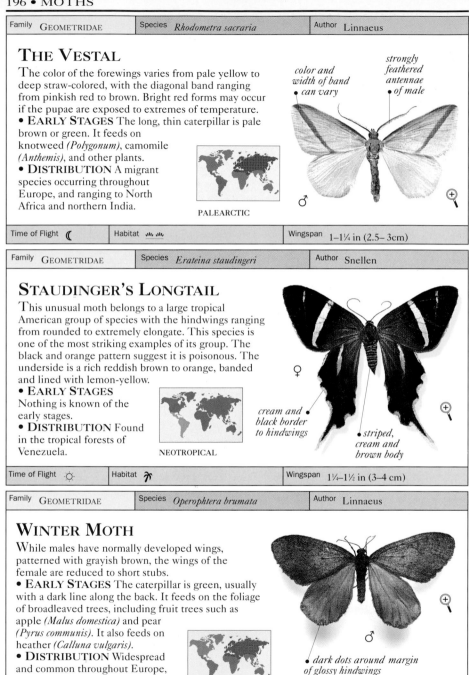

| Family GEOMETRIDAE | Species *Rhodometra sacraria* | Author Linnaeus |

THE VESTAL

The color of the forewings varies from pale yellow to deep straw-colored, with the diagonal band ranging from pinkish red to brown. Bright red forms may occur if the pupae are exposed to extremes of temperature.
• **EARLY STAGES** The long, thin caterpillar is pale brown or green. It feeds on knotweed *(Polygonum)*, camomile *(Anthemis)*, and other plants.
• **DISTRIBUTION** A migrant species occurring throughout Europe, and ranging to North Africa and northern India.

color and width of band can vary

strongly feathered antennae of male

♂

PALEARCTIC

| Time of Flight ☾ | Habitat ⚌ ⚌ | Wingspan 1–1¼ in (2.5–3cm) |

| Family GEOMETRIDAE | Species *Erateina staudingeri* | Author Snellen |

STAUDINGER'S LONGTAIL

This unusual moth belongs to a large tropical American group of species with the hindwings ranging from rounded to extremely elongate. This species is one of the most striking examples of its group. The black and orange pattern suggest it is poisonous. The underside is a rich reddish brown to orange, banded and lined with lemon-yellow.
• **EARLY STAGES** Nothing is known of the early stages.
• **DISTRIBUTION** Found in the tropical forests of Venezuela.

♀

cream and black border to hindwings

striped, cream and brown body

NEOTROPICAL

| Time of Flight ☼ | Habitat 🌴 | Wingspan 1¼–1½ in (3–4 cm) |

| Family GEOMETRIDAE | Species *Operophtera brumata* | Author Linnaeus |

WINTER MOTH

While males have normally developed wings, patterned with grayish brown, the wings of the female are reduced to short stubs.
• **EARLY STAGES** The caterpillar is green, usually with a dark line along the back. It feeds on the foliage of broadleaved trees, including fruit trees such as apple *(Malus domestica)* and pear *(Pyrus communis)*. It also feeds on heather *(Calluna vulgaris)*.
• **DISTRIBUTION** Widespread and common throughout Europe, ranging across temperate Asia to Japan. Also occurs in Canada.

♂

dark dots around margin of glossy hindwings

HOLARCTIC

| Time of Flight ☾ | Habitat ♣ ⚌ ⚌ | Wingspan (male) 1–1¼ in (2.5–3 cm) |

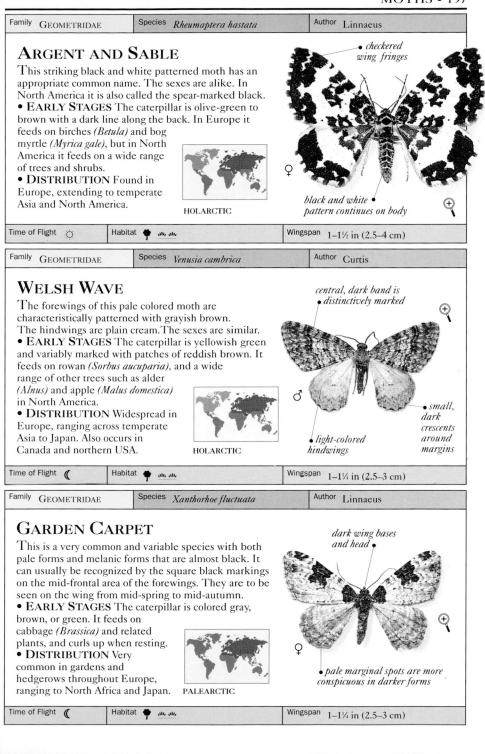

| Family | GEOMETRIDAE | Species | *Rheumaptera hastata* | Author | Linnaeus |

ARGENT AND SABLE

This striking black and white patterned moth has an appropriate common name. The sexes are alike. In North America it is also called the spear-marked black.
• **EARLY STAGES** The caterpillar is olive-green to brown with a dark line along the back. In Europe it feeds on birches *(Betula)* and bog myrtle *(Myrica gale)*, but in North America it feeds on a wide range of trees and shrubs.
• **DISTRIBUTION** Found in Europe, extending to temperate Asia and North America.

• checkered wing fringes

♀

black and white • pattern continues on body

HOLARCTIC

| Time of Flight ☼ | Habitat 🌿 ⚘ ⚘ | Wingspan 1–1½ in (2.5–4 cm) |

| Family | GEOMETRIDAE | Species | *Venusia cambrica* | Author | Curtis |

WELSH WAVE

The forewings of this pale colored moth are characteristically patterned with grayish brown. The hindwings are plain cream. The sexes are similar.
• **EARLY STAGES** The caterpillar is yellowish green and variably marked with patches of reddish brown. It feeds on rowan *(Sorbus aucuparia)*, and a wide range of other trees such as alder *(Alnus)* and apple *(Malus domestica)* in North America.
• **DISTRIBUTION** Widespread in Europe, ranging across temperate Asia to Japan. Also occurs in Canada and northern USA.

central, dark band is • distinctively marked

♂

• small, dark crescents around margins

• light-colored hindwings

HOLARCTIC

| Time of Flight ☾ | Habitat 🌿 ⚘ ⚘ | Wingspan 1–1¼ in (2.5–3 cm) |

| Family | GEOMETRIDAE | Species | *Xanthorhoe fluctuata* | Author | Linnaeus |

GARDEN CARPET

This is a very common and variable species with both pale forms and melanic forms that are almost black. It can usually be recognized by the square black markings on the mid-frontal area of the forewings. They are to be seen on the wing from mid-spring to mid-autumn.
• **EARLY STAGES** The caterpillar is colored gray, brown, or green. It feeds on cabbage *(Brassica)* and related plants, and curls up when resting.
• **DISTRIBUTION** Very common in gardens and hedgerows throughout Europe, ranging to North Africa and Japan.

dark wing bases and head •

♀

• pale marginal spots are more conspicuous in darker forms

PALEARCTIC

| Time of Flight ☾ | Habitat 🌿 ⚘ ⚘ | Wingspan 1–1¼ in (2.5–3 cm) |

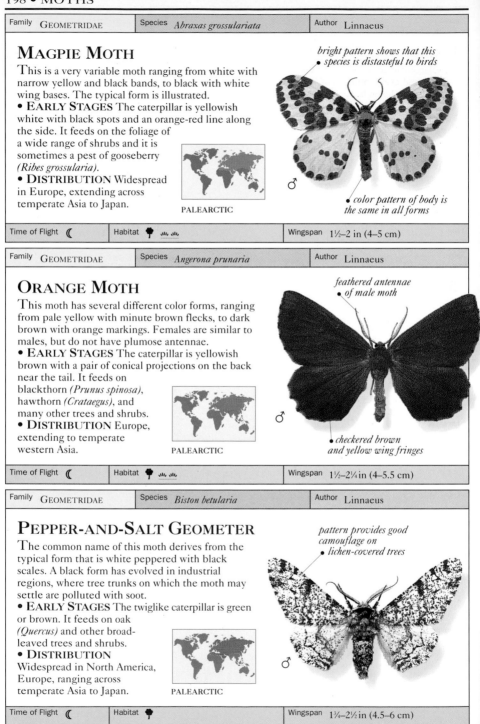

Family GEOMETRIDAE	Species *Abraxas grossulariata*	Author Linnaeus

MAGPIE MOTH

This is a very variable moth ranging from white with narrow yellow and black bands, to black with white wing bases. The typical form is illustrated.
• **EARLY STAGES** The caterpillar is yellowish white with black spots and an orange-red line along the side. It feeds on the foliage of a wide range of shrubs and it is sometimes a pest of gooseberry *(Ribes grossularia)*.
• **DISTRIBUTION** Widespread in Europe, extending across temperate Asia to Japan.

PALEARCTIC

bright pattern shows that this • *species is distasteful to birds*

color pattern of body is the same in all forms

♂

Time of Flight ☾	Habitat	Wingspan 1½–2 in (4–5 cm)

Family GEOMETRIDAE	Species *Angerona prunaria*	Author Linnaeus

ORANGE MOTH

This moth has several different color forms, ranging from pale yellow with minute brown flecks, to dark brown with orange markings. Females are similar to males, but do not have plumose antennae.
• **EARLY STAGES** The caterpillar is yellowish brown with a pair of conical projections on the back near the tail. It feeds on blackthorn *(Prunus spinosa)*, hawthorn *(Crataegus)*, and many other trees and shrubs.
• **DISTRIBUTION** Europe, extending to temperate western Asia.

PALEARCTIC

feathered antennae • *of male moth*

♂

checkered brown and yellow wing fringes

Time of Flight ☾	Habitat	Wingspan 1½–2¼ in (4–5.5 cm)

Family GEOMETRIDAE	Species *Biston betularia*	Author Linnaeus

PEPPER-AND-SALT GEOMETER

The common name of this moth derives from the typical form that is white peppered with black scales. A black form has evolved in industrial regions, where tree trunks on which the moth may settle are polluted with soot.
• **EARLY STAGES** The twiglike caterpillar is green or brown. It feeds on oak *(Quercus)* and other broad-leaved trees and shrubs.
• **DISTRIBUTION** Widespread in North America, Europe, ranging across temperate Asia to Japan.

PALEARCTIC

pattern provides good camouflage on • *lichen-covered trees*

♂

Time of Flight ☾	Habitat	Wingspan 1¾–2½ in (4.5–6 cm)

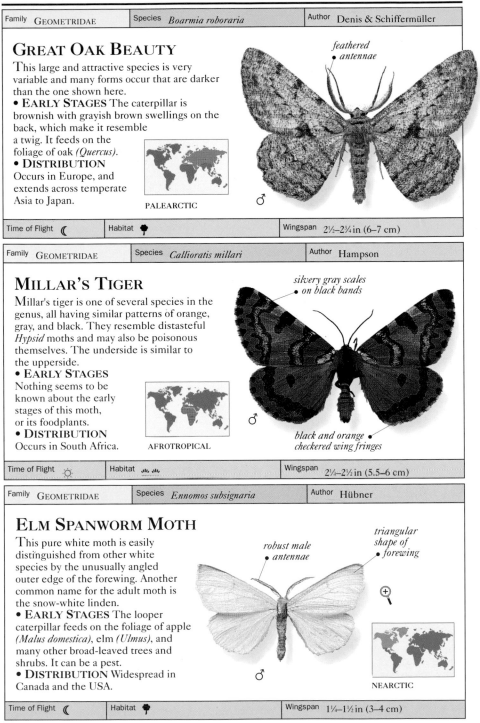

Family GEOMETRIDAE	Species *Boarmia roboraria*	Author Denis & Schiffermüller

GREAT OAK BEAUTY

This large and attractive species is very
variable and many forms occur that are darker
than the one shown here.
• **EARLY STAGES** The caterpillar is
brownish with grayish brown swellings on the
back, which make it resemble
a twig. It feeds on the
foliage of oak *(Quercus)*.
• **DISTRIBUTION**
Occurs in Europe, and
extends across temperate
Asia to Japan.

*feathered
• antennae*

PALEARCTIC

♂

Time of Flight ☾	Habitat ♣	Wingspan 2½–2¾ in (6–7 cm)

Family GEOMETRIDAE	Species *Callioratis millari*	Author Hampson

MILLAR'S TIGER

Millar's tiger is one of several species in the
genus, all having similar patterns of orange,
gray, and black. They resemble distasteful
Hypsid moths and may also be poisonous
themselves. The underside is similar to
the upperside.
• **EARLY STAGES**
Nothing seems to be
known about the early
stages of this moth,
or its foodplants.
• **DISTRIBUTION**
Occurs in South Africa.

*silvery gray scales
• on black bands*

♂

AFROTROPICAL

*black and orange •
checkered wing fringes*

Time of Flight ☼	Habitat ⚲ ⚲	Wingspan 2¼–2½ in (5.5–6 cm)

Family GEOMETRIDAE	Species *Ennomos subsignaria*	Author Hübner

ELM SPANWORM MOTH

This pure white moth is easily
distinguished from other white
species by the unusually angled
outer edge of the forewing. Another
common name for the adult moth is
the snow-white linden.
• **EARLY STAGES** The looper
caterpillar feeds on the foliage of apple
(Malus domestica), elm *(Ulmus)*, and
many other broad-leaved trees and
shrubs. It can be a pest.
• **DISTRIBUTION** Widespread in
Canada and the USA.

*robust male
• antennae*

*triangular
shape of
• forewing*

⊕

♂

NEARCTIC

Time of Flight ☾	Habitat ♣	Wingspan 1¼–1½ in (3–4 cm)

Family GEOMETRIDAE	Species *Epimecis hortaria*	Author Fabricius

TULIP-TREE BEAUTY

A large and beautiful moth, the tulip-tree beauty is very variable, with some forms strongly banded and others almost black. Females are larger than males and have threadlike antennae. These moths can be seen on the wing from spring to autumn.
• **EARLY STAGES** The looper caterpillar feeds on the foliage of poplars *(Populus)*, tulip-tree *(Liriodendron tulipifera)*, and pawpaw *(Asimina)*.
• **DISTRIBUTION** Widespread from southern Canada to Florida.

males have feathered antennae

strongly scalloped edge to hindwings

NEARCTIC

Time of Flight ☾	Habitat 🌱	Wingspan 1¾–2¼ in (4.5–5.5 cm)

Family GEOMETRIDAE	Species *Erannis defoliaria*	Author Clerck

MOTTLED UMBER

Males of this common moth are very variable, ranging from pale straw with brown bands to almost black. The wingless females also have a black form in industrial regions, where they have had to adapt to the surroundings.
• **EARLY STAGES** The caterpillar is brown with patches of yellow and reddish brown along the sides. It feeds on oak *(Quercus)*, birch *(Betula)*, and many other broadleaved trees and shrubs, and can sometimes be a pest.
• **DISTRIBUTION** Widespread in Europe, extending into regions of temperate Asia.

triangular forewing shapes

dark speckling on hindwings

PALEARCTIC

Time of Flight ☾	Habitat 🌱	Wingspan (male) 1¼–1¾ in (3–4.5 cm)

Family GEOMETRIDAE	Species *Lycia hirtaria*	Author Clerck

BRINDLED BEAUTY

The brown and white pattern of this furry-looking moth provides effective camouflage when it rests on tree trunks. A black form has evolved in sooty industrial regions. They are on the wing in spring.
• **EARLY STAGES** The caterpillar is brown to greenish gray, speckled with black, and spotted with yellow. It feeds on the foliage of most broad-leaved trees.
• **DISTRIBUTION** Widespread throughout Europe.

leading edge of forewings paler in females

wings of female suffused with pale yellowish brown

PALEARCTIC

Time of Flight ☾	Habitat 🌱	Wingspan 1½–2 in (4–5 cm)

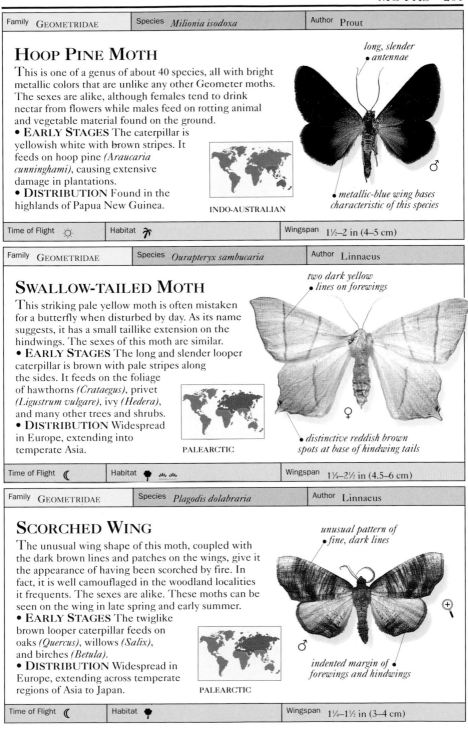

Family GEOMETRIDAE	Species *Milionia isodoxa*	Author Prout

HOOP PINE MOTH

long, slender antennae

This is one of a genus of about 40 species, all with bright metallic colors that are unlike any other Geometer moths. The sexes are alike, although females tend to drink nectar from flowers while males feed on rotting animal and vegetable material found on the ground.
• **EARLY STAGES** The caterpillar is yellowish white with brown stripes. It feeds on hoop pine *(Araucaria cunninghami)*, causing extensive damage in plantations.
• **DISTRIBUTION** Found in the highlands of Papua New Guinea.

INDO-AUSTRALIAN

♂

metallic-blue wing bases characteristic of this species

Time of Flight ☼	Habitat 🦋	Wingspan 1½–2 in (4–5 cm)

Family GEOMETRIDAE	Species *Ourapteryx sambucaria*	Author Linnaeus

SWALLOW-TAILED MOTH

two dark yellow lines on forewings

This striking pale yellow moth is often mistaken for a butterfly when disturbed by day. As its name suggests, it has a small taillike extension on the hindwings. The sexes of this moth are similar.
• **EARLY STAGES** The long and slender looper caterpillar is brown with pale stripes along the sides. It feeds on the foliage of hawthorns *(Crataegus)*, privet *(Ligustrum vulgare)*, ivy *(Hedera)*, and many other trees and shrubs.
• **DISTRIBUTION** Widespread in Europe, extending into temperate Asia.

PALEARCTIC

♀

distinctive reddish brown spots at base of hindwing tails

Time of Flight ☾	Habitat 🌳 🌿 🌿	Wingspan 1¾–2½ in (4.5–6 cm)

Family GEOMETRIDAE	Species *Plagodis dolabraria*	Author Linnaeus

SCORCHED WING

unusual pattern of fine, dark lines

The unusual wing shape of this moth, coupled with the dark brown lines and patches on the wings, give it the appearance of having been scorched by fire. In fact, it is well camouflaged in the woodland localities it frequents. The sexes are alike. These moths can be seen on the wing in late spring and early summer.
• **EARLY STAGES** The twiglike brown looper caterpillar feeds on oaks *(Quercus)*, willows *(Salix)*, and birches *(Betula)*.
• **DISTRIBUTION** Widespread in Europe, extending across temperate regions of Asia to Japan.

PALEARCTIC

♂

⊕

indented margin of forewings and hindwings

Time of Flight ☾	Habitat 🌳	Wingspan 1¼–1½ in (3–4 cm)

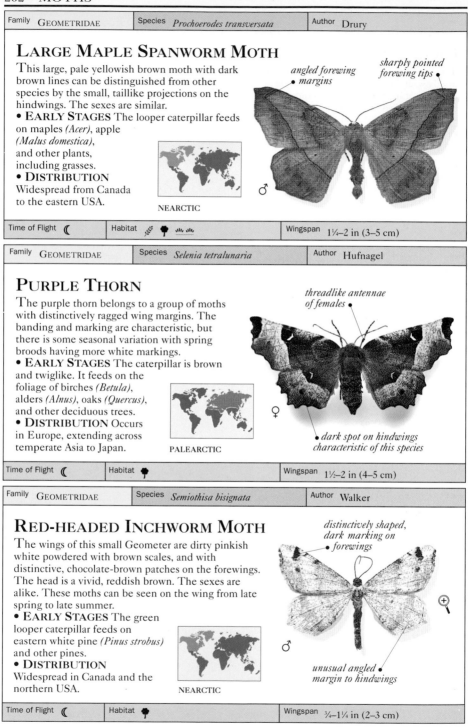

Family GEOMETRIDAE	Species *Prochoerodes transversata*	Author Drury

LARGE MAPLE SPANWORM MOTH

This large, pale yellowish brown moth with dark brown lines can be distinguished from other species by the small, taillike projections on the hindwings. The sexes are similar.
• **EARLY STAGES** The looper caterpillar feeds on maples *(Acer)*, apple *(Malus domestica)*, and other plants, including grasses.
• **DISTRIBUTION** Widespread from Canada to the eastern USA.

angled forewing margins

sharply pointed forewing tips

♂

NEARCTIC

Time of Flight ☾	Habitat 🌿 🌱	Wingspan 1¼–2 in (3–5 cm)

Family GEOMETRIDAE	Species *Selenia tetralunaria*	Author Hufnagel

PURPLE THORN

The purple thorn belongs to a group of moths with distinctively ragged wing margins. The banding and marking are characteristic, but there is some seasonal variation with spring broods having more white markings.
• **EARLY STAGES** The caterpillar is brown and twiglike. It feeds on the foliage of birches *(Betula)*, alders *(Alnus)*, oaks *(Quercus)*, and other deciduous trees.
• **DISTRIBUTION** Occurs in Europe, extending across temperate Asia to Japan.

threadlike antennae of females

♀

PALEARCTIC

dark spot on hindwings characteristic of this species

Time of Flight ☾	Habitat 🌳	Wingspan 1½–2 in (4–5 cm)

Family GEOMETRIDAE	Species *Semiothisa bisignata*	Author Walker

RED-HEADED INCHWORM MOTH

The wings of this small Geometer are dirty pinkish white powdered with brown scales, and with distinctive, chocolate-brown patches on the forewings. The head is a vivid, reddish brown. The sexes are alike. These moths can be seen on the wing from late spring to late summer.
• **EARLY STAGES** The green looper caterpillar feeds on eastern white pine *(Pinus strobus)* and other pines.
• **DISTRIBUTION** Widespread in Canada and the northern USA.

distinctively shaped, dark marking on forewings

♂

unusual angled margin to hindwings

NEARCTIC

Time of Flight ☾	Habitat 🌳	Wingspan ¾–1¼ in (2–3 cm)

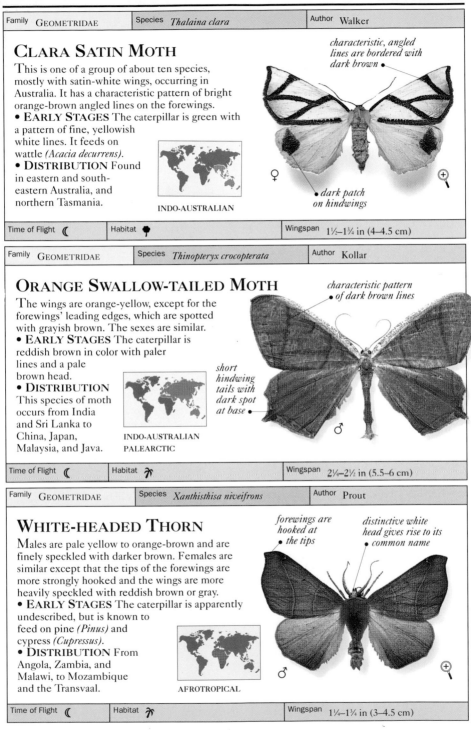

Family GEOMETRIDAE	Species *Thalaina clara*	Author Walker

CLARA SATIN MOTH

This is one of a group of about ten species, mostly with satin-white wings, occurring in Australia. It has a characteristic pattern of bright orange-brown angled lines on the forewings.
• **EARLY STAGES** The caterpillar is green with a pattern of fine, yellowish white lines. It feeds on wattle *(Acacia decurrens)*.
• **DISTRIBUTION** Found in eastern and south-eastern Australia, and northern Tasmania.

INDO-AUSTRALIAN

characteristic, angled lines are bordered with dark brown

♀

dark patch on hindwings

Time of Flight ☾	Habitat ⚘	Wingspan 1½–1¾ in (4–4.5 cm)

Family GEOMETRIDAE	Species *Thinopteryx crocopterata*	Author Kollar

ORANGE SWALLOW-TAILED MOTH

The wings are orange-yellow, except for the forewings' leading edges, which are spotted with grayish brown. The sexes are similar.
• **EARLY STAGES** The caterpillar is reddish brown in color with paler lines and a pale brown head.
• **DISTRIBUTION** This species of moth occurs from India and Sri Lanka to China, Japan, Malaysia, and Java.

INDO-AUSTRALIAN
PALEARCTIC

characteristic pattern of dark brown lines

short hindwing tails with dark spot at base

♂

Time of Flight ☾	Habitat 🌳	Wingspan 2¼–2½ in (5.5–6 cm)

Family GEOMETRIDAE	Species *Xanthisthisa niveifrons*	Author Prout

WHITE-HEADED THORN

Males are pale yellow to orange-brown and are finely speckled with darker brown. Females are similar except that the tips of the forewings are more strongly hooked and the wings are more heavily speckled with reddish brown or gray.
• **EARLY STAGES** The caterpillar is apparently undescribed, but is known to feed on pine *(Pinus)* and cypress *(Cupressus)*.
• **DISTRIBUTION** From Angola, Zambia, and Malawi, to Mozambique and the Transvaal.

AFROTROPICAL

forewings are hooked at the tips

distinctive white head gives rise to its common name

♂

Time of Flight ☾	Habitat 🌳	Wingspan 1¼–1¾ in (3–4.5 cm)

LASIOCAMPIDAE

T HIS IS A FAMILY of about 1,500 species of medium- to large-sized moths occurring around the world. They are generally dull in color, and mostly banded with various shades of brown. Lasiocampidae have two unusual characteristics: they lack the typical wing-coupling device of most moths, and the tongue is reduced and nonfunctional. Caterpillars of this group are particularly hairy; some have long-haired lobes or lappets along their sides, giving rise to their common name of lappet moth.

Pupae are formed in robust cocoons. The egg-like shape of these cocoons provides the origin of the name "eggar," which is applied to many moths in this family.

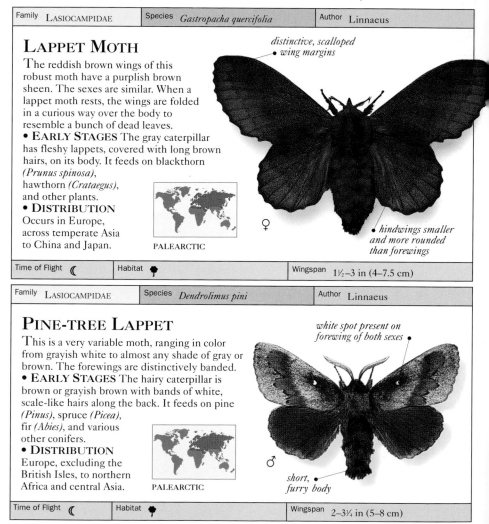

Family LASIOCAMPIDAE	Species *Gastropacha quercifolia*	Author Linnaeus

LAPPET MOTH

The reddish brown wings of this robust moth have a purplish brown sheen. The sexes are similar. When a lappet moth rests, the wings are folded in a curious way over the body to resemble a bunch of dead leaves.
• **EARLY STAGES** The gray caterpillar has fleshy lappets, covered with long brown hairs, on its body. It feeds on blackthorn *(Prunus spinosa)*, hawthorn *(Crataegus)*, and other plants.
• **DISTRIBUTION** Occurs in Europe, across temperate Asia to China and Japan.

distinctive, scalloped wing margins

♀

hindwings smaller and more rounded than forewings

PALEARCTIC

Time of Flight ☾	Habitat ⚘	Wingspan 1½–3 in (4–7.5 cm)

Family LASIOCAMPIDAE	Species *Dendrolimus pini*	Author Linnaeus

PINE-TREE LAPPET

This is a very variable moth, ranging in color from grayish white to almost any shade of gray or brown. The forewings are distinctively banded.
• **EARLY STAGES** The hairy caterpillar is brown or grayish brown with bands of white, scale-like hairs along the back. It feeds on pine *(Pinus)*, spruce *(Picea)*, fir *(Abies)*, and various other conifers.
• **DISTRIBUTION** Europe, excluding the British Isles, to northern Africa and central Asia.

white spot present on forewing of both sexes

♂

short, furry body

PALEARCTIC

Time of Flight ☾	Habitat ⚘	Wingspan 2–3¼ in (5–8 cm)

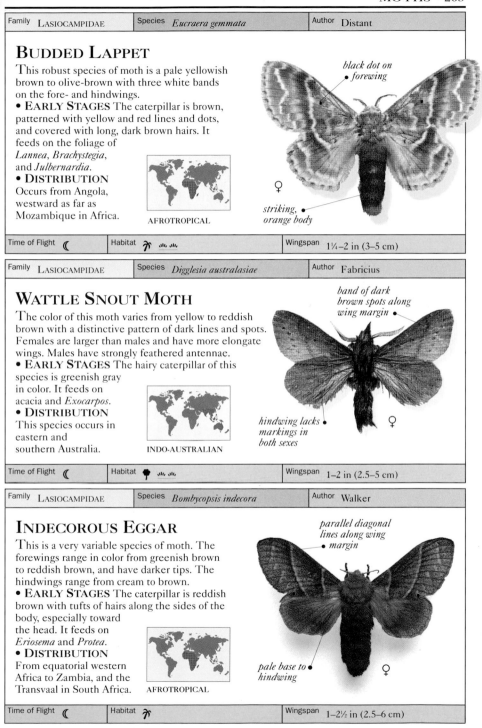

Family	LASIOCAMPIDAE	Species	*Eucraera gemmata*	Author	Distant

BUDDED LAPPET

This robust species of moth is a pale yellowish brown to olive-brown with three white bands on the fore- and hindwings.
• **EARLY STAGES** The caterpillar is brown, patterned with yellow and red lines and dots, and covered with long, dark brown hairs. It feeds on the foliage of *Lannea*, *Brachystegia*, and *Julbernardia*.
• **DISTRIBUTION** Occurs from Angola, westward as far as Mozambique in Africa.

AFROTROPICAL

black dot on
• forewing

♀

striking, •
orange body

Time of Flight	☾	Habitat	🌿 ⸗ ⸗	Wingspan	1¼–2 in (3–5 cm)

Family	LASIOCAMPIDAE	Species	*Digglesia australasiae*	Author	Fabricius

WATTLE SNOUT MOTH

The color of this moth varies from yellow to reddish brown with a distinctive pattern of dark lines and spots. Females are larger than males and have more elongate wings. Males have strongly feathered antennae.
• **EARLY STAGES** The hairy caterpillar of this species is greenish gray in color. It feeds on acacia and *Exocarpos*.
• **DISTRIBUTION** This species occurs in eastern and southern Australia.

INDO-AUSTRALIAN

band of dark
brown spots along
wing margin •

hindwing lacks •
markings in
both sexes

♀

Time of Flight	☾	Habitat	🌿 ⸗ ⸗	Wingspan	1–2 in (2.5–5 cm)

Family	LASIOCAMPIDAE	Species	*Bombycopsis indecora*	Author	Walker

INDECOROUS EGGAR

This is a very variable species of moth. The forewings range in color from greenish brown to reddish brown, and have darker tips. The hindwings range from cream to brown.
• **EARLY STAGES** The caterpillar is reddish brown with tufts of hairs along the sides of the body, especially toward the head. It feeds on *Eriosema* and *Protea*.
• **DISTRIBUTION** From equatorial western Africa to Zambia, and the Transvaal in South Africa.

AFROTROPICAL

parallel diagonal
lines along wing
• margin

pale base to •
hindwing

♀

Time of Flight	☾	Habitat	🌿	Wingspan	1–2½ in (2.5–6 cm)

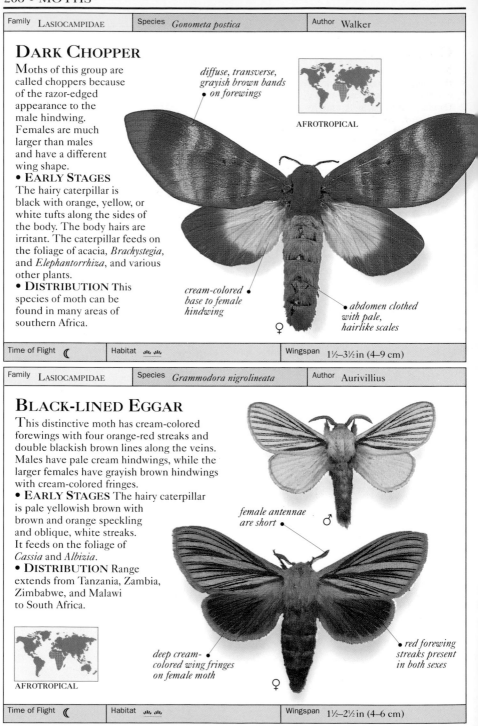

| Family | LASIOCAMPIDAE | Species | *Gonometa postica* | Author | Walker |

DARK CHOPPER

Moths of this group are called choppers because of the razor-edged appearance to the male hindwing. Females are much larger than males and have a different wing shape.

• **EARLY STAGES**
The hairy caterpillar is black with orange, yellow, or white tufts along the sides of the body. The body hairs are irritant. The caterpillar feeds on the foliage of acacia, *Brachystegia*, and *Elephantorrhiza*, and various other plants.

• **DISTRIBUTION** This species of moth can be found in many areas of southern Africa.

diffuse, transverse, grayish brown bands on forewings

AFROTROPICAL

cream-colored base to female hindwing

abdomen clothed with pale, hairlike scales

♀

| Time of Flight ☾ | Habitat | Wingspan 1½–3½ in (4–9 cm) |

| Family | LASIOCAMPIDAE | Species | *Grammodora nigrolineata* | Author | Aurivillius |

BLACK-LINED EGGAR

This distinctive moth has cream-colored forewings with four orange-red streaks and double blackish brown lines along the veins. Males have pale cream hindwings, while the larger females have grayish brown hindwings with cream-colored fringes.

• **EARLY STAGES** The hairy caterpillar is pale yellowish brown with brown and orange speckling and oblique, white streaks. It feeds on the foliage of *Cassia* and *Albizia*.

• **DISTRIBUTION** Range extends from Tanzania, Zambia, Zimbabwe, and Malawi to South Africa.

female antennae are short

♂

AFROTROPICAL

deep cream-colored wing fringes on female moth

red forewing streaks present in both sexes

♀

| Time of Flight ☾ | Habitat | Wingspan 1½–2½ in (4–6 cm) |

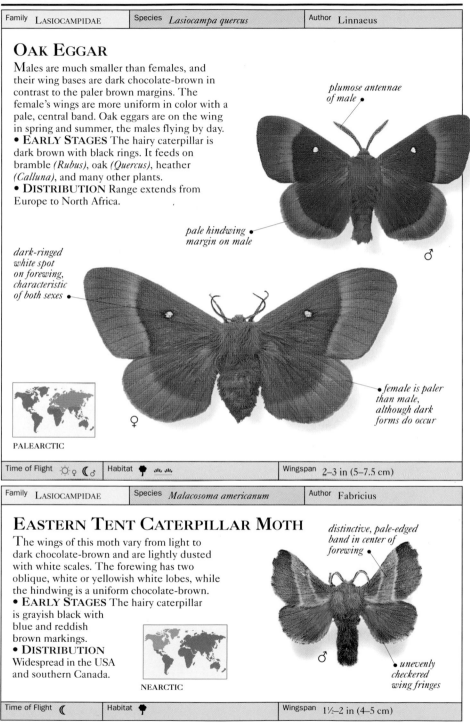

| Family | LASIOCAMPIDAE | Species | *Lasiocampa quercus* | Author | Linnaeus |

OAK EGGAR

Males are much smaller than females, and their wing bases are dark chocolate-brown in contrast to the paler brown margins. The female's wings are more uniform in color with a pale, central band. Oak eggars are on the wing in spring and summer, the males flying by day.
• **EARLY STAGES** The hairy caterpillar is dark brown with black rings. It feeds on bramble *(Rubus)*, oak *(Quercus)*, heather *(Calluna)*, and many other plants.
• **DISTRIBUTION** Range extends from Europe to North Africa.

plumose antennae of male

pale hindwing margin on male

♂

dark-ringed white spot on forewing, characteristic of both sexes

female is paler than male, although dark forms do occur

♀

PALEARCTIC

| Time of Flight | ☼♀ ☾♂ | Habitat | 🌿 ⸎ ⸎ | Wingspan | 2–3 in (5–7.5 cm) |

| Family | LASIOCAMPIDAE | Species | *Malacosoma americanum* | Author | Fabricius |

EASTERN TENT CATERPILLAR MOTH

The wings of this moth vary from light to dark chocolate-brown and are lightly dusted with white scales. The forewing has two oblique, white or yellowish white lobes, while the hindwing is a uniform chocolate-brown.
• **EARLY STAGES** The hairy caterpillar is grayish black with blue and reddish brown markings.
• **DISTRIBUTION** Widespread in the USA and southern Canada.

distinctive, pale-edged band in center of forewing

♂

unevenly checkered wing fringes

NEARCTIC

| Time of Flight | ☾ | Habitat | 🌿 | Wingspan | 1½–2 in (4–5 cm) |

Family Lasiocampidae	Species *Trabala viridana*	Author Joicey & Talbot

MOSS-GREEN LAPPET

This beautiful moth belongs to a large complex of similar species, many occurring in Southeast Asia. The female is much larger than the male and has strongly triangular forewings with large, pale brown patches towards the base. In museum specimens the beautiful, green color of these moths will often fade quite badly.

• EARLY STAGES Little is known of the lifecycle but caterpillars of related species are hairy and have two forward-pointing tufts of bristles situated just behind head. They are known to feed on *Barringtonia*, *Eugenia*, *Rubus*, and *Shorea robusta*.

• DISTRIBUTION Range extends from Malaysia to Sumatra, Java, and Borneo.

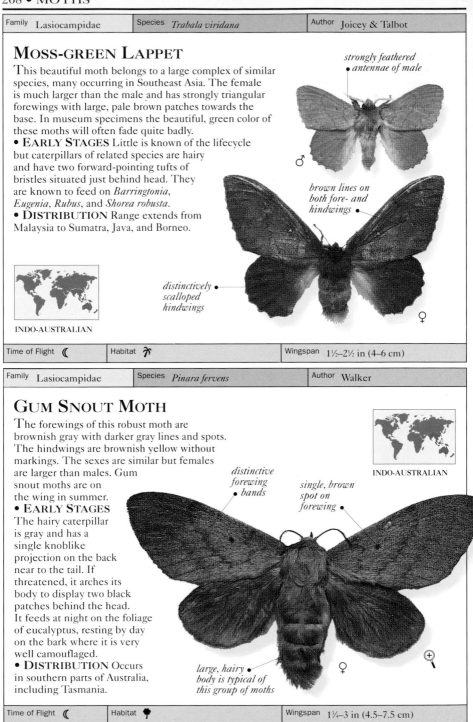

strongly feathered antennae of male

♂

brown lines on both fore- and hindwings

distinctively scalloped hindwings

♀

INDO-AUSTRALIAN

Time of Flight ☾	Habitat 🐦	Wingspan 1½–2½ in (4–6 cm)

Family Lasiocampidae	Species *Pinara fervens*	Author Walker

GUM SNOUT MOTH

The forewings of this robust moth are brownish gray with darker gray lines and spots. The hindwings are brownish yellow without markings. The sexes are similar but females are larger than males. Gum snout moths are on the wing in summer.

• EARLY STAGES The hairy caterpillar is gray and has a single knoblike projection on the back near to the tail. If threatened, it arches its body to display two black patches behind the head. It feeds at night on the foliage of eucalyptus, resting by day on the bark where it is very well camouflaged.

• DISTRIBUTION Occurs in southern parts of Australia, including Tasmania.

INDO-AUSTRALIAN

distinctive forewing bands

single, brown spot on forewing

♀

large, hairy body is typical of this group of moths

⊕

Time of Flight ☾	Habitat 🌱	Wingspan 1¾–3 in (4.5–7.5 cm)

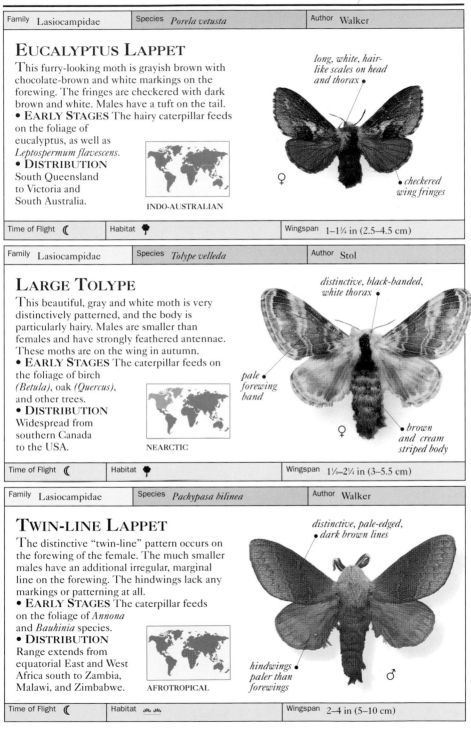

Family Lasiocampidae	Species *Porela vetusta*	Author Walker

EUCALYPTUS LAPPET

This furry-looking moth is grayish brown with chocolate-brown and white markings on the forewing. The fringes are checkered with dark brown and white. Males have a tuft on the tail.
• **EARLY STAGES** The hairy caterpillar feeds on the foliage of eucalyptus, as well as *Leptospermum flavescens*.
• **DISTRIBUTION** South Queensland to Victoria and South Australia.

INDO-AUSTRALIAN

long, white, hair-like scales on head and thorax

♀

checkered wing fringes

Time of Flight ☾	Habitat ⚘	Wingspan 1–1¾ in (2.5–4.5 cm)

Family Lasiocampidae	Species *Tolype velleda*	Author Stol

LARGE TOLYPE

This beautiful, gray and white moth is very distinctively patterned, and the body is particularly hairy. Males are smaller than females and have strongly feathered antennae. These moths are on the wing in autumn.
• **EARLY STAGES** The caterpillar feeds on the foliage of birch *(Betula)*, oak *(Quercus)*, and other trees.
• **DISTRIBUTION** Widespread from southern Canada to the USA.

NEARCTIC

distinctive, black-banded, white thorax

pale forewing band

♀

brown and cream striped body

Time of Flight ☾	Habitat ⚘	Wingspan 1¼–2¼ in (3–5.5 cm)

Family Lasiocampidae	Species *Pachypasa bilinea*	Author Walker

TWIN-LINE LAPPET

The distinctive "twin-line" pattern occurs on the forewing of the female. The much smaller males have an additional irregular, marginal line on the forewing. The hindwings lack any markings or patterning at all.
• **EARLY STAGES** The caterpillar feeds on the foliage of *Annona* and *Bauhinia* species.
• **DISTRIBUTION** Range extends from equatorial East and West Africa south to Zambia, Malawi, and Zimbabwe.

AFROTROPICAL

distinctive, pale-edged, dark brown lines

hindwings paler than forewings

♂

Time of Flight ☾	Habitat ⁓⁓	Wingspan 2–4 in (5–10 cm)

EUPTEROTIDAE

A SMALL FAMILY of just over 300 species of medium-sized to large moths, the Eupterotidae are related to the emperor moths (Saturniidae). They are found in the tropical parts of Africa and Indo-Australia. They are mostly dull-colored with shades of brown and gray predominating. Because of their hairy appearance, they are often known as "monkeys."

The caterpillars are covered in long hairs, which are often highly irritant and cause rashes.

——— • ———

Many of the caterpillars belonging to this family are gregarious and live in communal webs. Some species are known to be pests of certain trees, including the eucalyptus, and cause serious damage to them.

Family EUPTEROTIDAE	Species *Tagora pallida*	Author Walker

PALLID MONKEY MOTH

This large brownish white moth is delicately patterned and lined with darker brown. Females are larger than males and have darker markings and a translucent, white spot in the middle of the forewing.
• **EARLY STAGES** The caterpillar is covered with long, dark, woolly hair which conceals poisonous stinging bristles. It feeds on a wide range of different plants.
• **DISTRIBUTION** Widespread from India to Malaysia, Sumatra, and Borneo.

INDO-AUSTRALIAN

distinctively curved wingtips

single pale spot on forewing

darker brown line diagonally crosses fore- and hindwings

wing bases covered with pale silky hairs

♀

Time of Flight ☾	Habitat	Wingspan 4¼–4½ in (10.8–11 cm)

Family EUPTEROTIDAE	Species *Janomima westwoodi*	Author Aurivillius

INQUISITIVE MONKEY

This large and handsome moth has a distinctly furry appearance. It varies in color from pale fawn to brownish yellow with a pattern of dark brown lines on both the fore- and hindwing. The hindwing has a black spot at the base.
• **EARLY STAGES** The large caterpillar is densely covered with long, back-swept black and white hairs which have irritant properties. It feeds on *Bauhinia*.
• **DISTRIBUTION** Range extends from Zimbabwe to Zambia and Zaire.

AFROTROPICAL

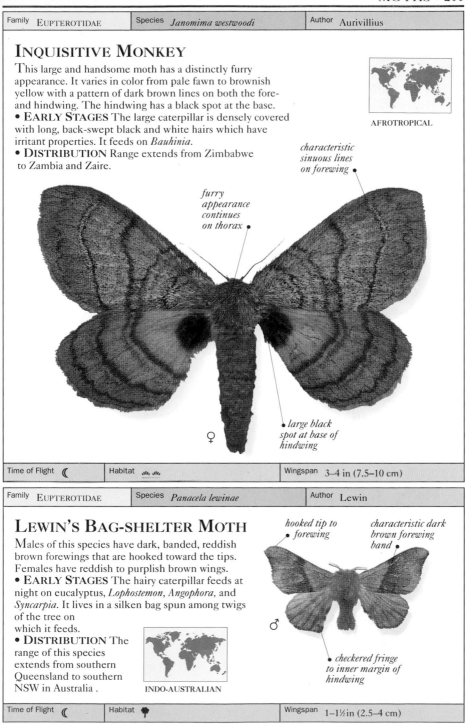

characteristic sinuous lines on forewing

furry appearance continues on thorax

large black spot at base of hindwing

Time of Flight ☾	Habitat ⸜⸜	Wingspan 3–4 in (7.5–10 cm)

Family EUPTEROTIDAE	Species *Panacela lewinae*	Author Lewin

LEWIN'S BAG-SHELTER MOTH

Males of this species have dark, banded, reddish brown forewings that are hooked toward the tips. Females have reddish to purplish brown wings.
• **EARLY STAGES** The hairy caterpillar feeds at night on eucalyptus, *Lophostemon*, *Angophora*, and *Syncarpia*. It lives in a silken bag spun among twigs of the tree on which it feeds.
• **DISTRIBUTION** The range of this species extends from southern Queensland to southern NSW in Australia .

hooked tip to forewing *characteristic dark brown forewing band*

checkered fringe to inner margin of hindwing

INDO-AUSTRALIAN

Time of Flight ☾	Habitat ♣	Wingspan 1–1½in (2.5–4 cm)

ANTHELIDAE

T HIS SMALL FAMILY of less than 100 species of moth is confined to Australia and Papua New Guinea, and is closely related to the families Eupterotidae and Lasiocampidae. Many of the species are distinctively patterned with lines and bands of brown, yellow, and red. The greatly reduced tongues of these moths mean that they are unable to feed in the adult stage. The caterpillars of most species are covered with tufts of hair, which are sometimes irritant. Many feed on eucalyptus or acacia species.

Family ANTHELIDAE	Species *Chelepteryx collesi*	Author Gray

GIANT ANTHELID

The large, batlike female of this species can attain a wingspan of 6¼ in (16 cm). The blackish brown forewings of both sexes are banded and heavily dusted with white and brownish yellow scales. The dark hindwings have a straight inner line of white and a scalloped outer line of orange-yellow. If alarmed, the male rears up to reveal its white underside and dark forelegs, and resembles a large spider.
• **EARLY STAGES** The caterpillar is grayish white with black, transverse bands across the back, and tufts of stout, irritant hairs. It feeds on eucalyptus species.
• **DISTRIBUTION** Range extends from southern Queensland to NSW and Victoria in Australia.

vivid, black stripes along • body

INDO-AUSTRALIAN

CATERPILLAR OF
CHELEPTERYX COLLESI

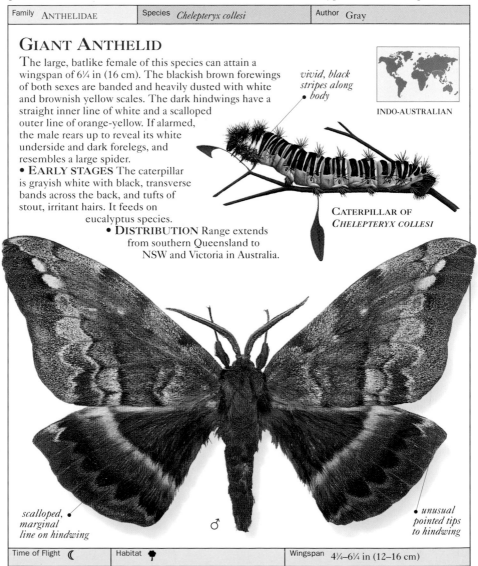

scalloped, • marginal line on hindwing

♂

• unusual pointed tips to hindwing

Time of Flight ☾	Habitat 🌳	Wingspan 4¾–6¼ in (12–16 cm)

Family ANTHELIDAE	Species *Anthela ocellata*	Author Walker

EYESPOT ANTHELID

This brownish white moth has distinctive, dark brown forewing bands and black eyespots which are more strongly developed in females. The pale hindwings have a marginal band of dark spots and a large, inner, black spot. Females are larger than males and have thread-like antennae. Eyespot anthelids are on the wing in the summer. They are mostly inactive and readily feign death if threatened. Moths are on the wing throughout the summer months, and there are thought to be two generations a year.
• **EARLY STAGES** The caterpillar is undescribed, but is known to feed on various native and introduced grasses. When fully grown, it forms its pupa within a double-walled gray cocoon incorporating caterpillar hairs.
• **DISTRIBUTION** Widely distributed throughout eastern and southern Australia, including Tasmania.

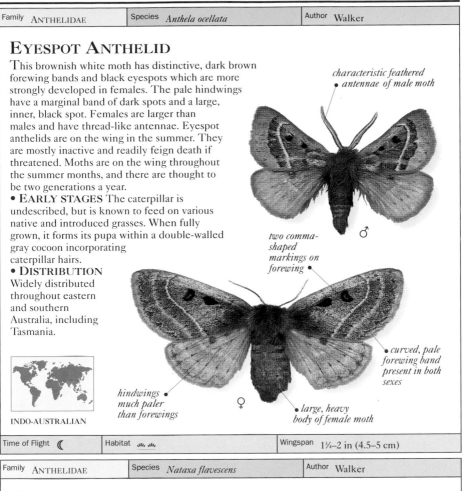

characteristic feathered antennae of male moth

two comma-shaped markings on forewing

♂

curved, pale forewing band present in both sexes

hindwings much paler than forewings

♀

large, heavy body of female moth

INDO-AUSTRALIAN

Time of Flight ☾	Habitat ⸜⸜ ⸜⸜	Wingspan 1¾–2 in (4.5–5 cm)

Family ANTHELIDAE	Species *Nataxa flavescens*	Author Walker

YELLOW-HEADED ANTHELID

Males of this species are brownish red in color with pale yellow bands on both the fore- and hindwings. The larger females are grayish brown in color with a large white patch on the forewing, in the middle of which is a black spot. In contrast with the male, the female body is long and heavy, with a whitish band near the end.
• **EARLY STAGES** The pale-colored, hairy caterpillar has two dark patches on the back behind the head, and a small, black hump towards the tail. It is known to feed on the foliage of acacia.
• **DISTRIBUTION** Range extends from southern Queensland to Victoria and Tasmania in Australia.

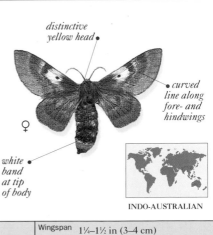

distinctive yellow head

♀

curved line along fore- and hindwings

white band at tip of body

INDO-AUSTRALIAN

Time of Flight ☾	Habitat ♠	Wingspan 1¼–1½ in (3–4 cm)

BOMBYCIDAE

ALTHOUGH THIS IS a relatively small family of some 300 species, mostly confined to the oriental region, it contains some of the most famous of all moths – the silkmoths.

Moths of this family have rounded, furry bodies. Many species have slightly hooked forewing tips. Their mouthparts are not developed, so they are unable to feed as adults. The caterpillars are usually swollen at the front and have a single fleshy horn at the tail. Although they often appear smooth, the caterpillars are, in fact, covered with numerous minute hairs. Many species of this family feed on the foliage of plants of the nettle family (Urticaceae). They form their pupae within silken cocoons.

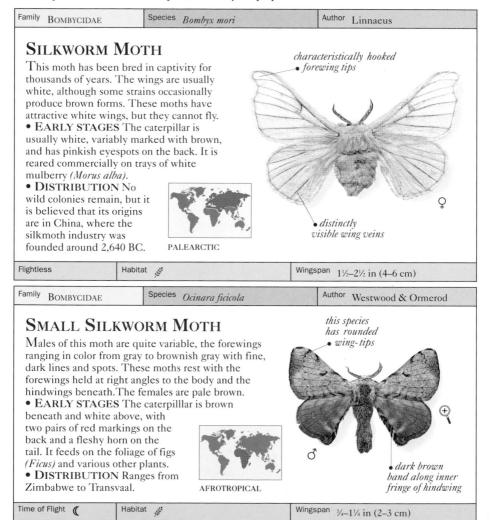

Family BOMBYCIDAE	Species *Bombyx mori*	Author Linnaeus

SILKWORM MOTH

This moth has been bred in captivity for thousands of years. The wings are usually white, although some strains occasionally produce brown forms. These moths have attractive white wings, but they cannot fly.
• **EARLY STAGES** The caterpillar is usually white, variably marked with brown, and has pinkish eyespots on the back. It is reared commercially on trays of white mulberry *(Morus alba)*.
• **DISTRIBUTION** No wild colonies remain, but it is believed that its origins are in China, where the silkmoth industry was founded around 2,640 BC.

characteristically hooked forewing tips

♀

distinctly visible wing veins

PALEARCTIC

Flightless	Habitat	Wingspan 1½–2½ in (4–6 cm)

Family BOMBYCIDAE	Species *Ocinara ficicola*	Author Westwood & Ormerod

SMALL SILKWORM MOTH

Males of this moth are quite variable, the forewings ranging in color from gray to brownish gray with fine, dark lines and spots. These moths rest with the forewings held at right angles to the body and the hindwings beneath. The females are pale brown.
• **EARLY STAGES** The caterpilllar is brown beneath and white above, with two pairs of red markings on the back and a fleshy horn on the tail. It feeds on the foliage of figs *(Ficus)* and various other plants.
• **DISTRIBUTION** Ranges from Zimbabwe to Transvaal.

this species has rounded wing-tips

♂

dark brown band along inner fringe of hindwing

AFROTROPICAL

Time of Flight	Habitat	Wingspan ¾–1¼ in (2–3 cm)

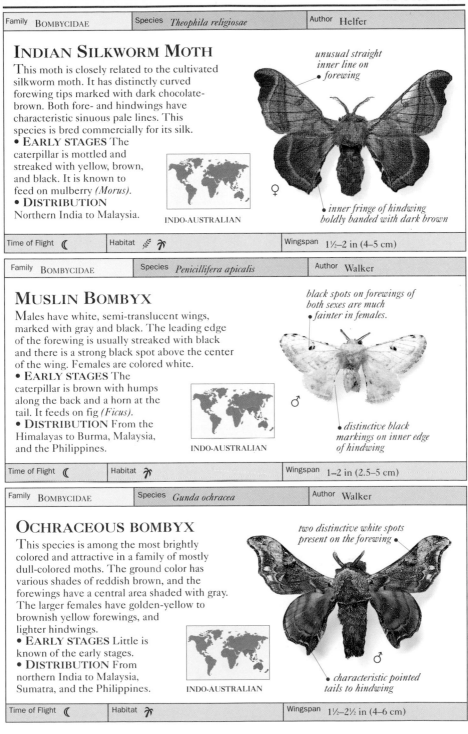

| Family BOMBYCIDAE | Species *Theophila religiosae* | Author Helfer |

INDIAN SILKWORM MOTH

This moth is closely related to the cultivated silkworm moth. It has distinctly curved forewing tips marked with dark chocolate-brown. Both fore- and hindwings have characteristic sinuous pale lines. This species is bred commercially for its silk.
• **EARLY STAGES** The caterpillar is mottled and streaked with yellow, brown, and black. It is known to feed on mulberry *(Morus)*.
• **DISTRIBUTION** Northern India to Malaysia.

unusual straight inner line on • forewing

♀

• inner fringe of hindwing boldly banded with dark brown

INDO-AUSTRALIAN

| Time of Flight ☾ | Habitat 🌱 🌴 | Wingspan 1½–2 in (4–5 cm) |

| Family BOMBYCIDAE | Species *Penicillifera apicalis* | Author Walker |

MUSLIN BOMBYX

Males have white, semi-translucent wings, marked with gray and black. The leading edge of the forewing is usually streaked with black and there is a strong black spot above the center of the wing. Females are colored white.
• **EARLY STAGES** The caterpillar is brown with humps along the back and a horn at the tail. It feeds on fig *(Ficus)*.
• **DISTRIBUTION** From the Himalayas to Burma, Malaysia, and the Philippines.

black spots on forewings of both sexes are much • fainter in females.

♂

• distinctive black markings on inner edge of hindwing

INDO-AUSTRALIAN

| Time of Flight ☾ | Habitat 🌴 | Wingspan 1–2 in (2.5–5 cm) |

| Family BOMBYCIDAE | Species *Gunda ochracea* | Author Walker |

OCHRACEOUS BOMBYX

This species is among the most brightly colored and attractive in a family of mostly dull-colored moths. The ground color has various shades of reddish brown, and the forewings have a central area shaded with gray. The larger females have golden-yellow to brownish yellow forewings, and lighter hindwings.
• **EARLY STAGES** Little is known of the early stages.
• **DISTRIBUTION** From northern India to Malaysia, Sumatra, and the Philippines.

two distinctive white spots present on the forewing •

♂

• characteristic pointed tails to hindwing

INDO-AUSTRALIAN

| Time of Flight ☾ | Habitat 🌴 | Wingspan 1½–2½ in (4–6 cm) |

BRAHMAEIDAE

T HIS is a very small family of only 20 or so described species of moth, confined to Africa, Asia, and Europe. These are medium- to large-sized, and are rather like emperor moths (Saturniidae, p.218) in appearance, but have such a distinctive pattern of their own that they are always easy to recognize. The Brahmaeid moths have well-developed

eyespots, earning for some species the common name of owl moth, although this is a term generally reserved for the family Noctuidae (see p.252). Unlike moths of many related families, adults of this group have well-developed tongues, so they can feed. The caterpillars have long projections on the body in the early stages but these are lost in the final stage.

Family Brahmaeidae	Species *Brahmaea wallichii*	Author Gray

OWL MOTH

One of the largest and most handsome species in the Brahmaeidae family, the owl moth has very well-developed eyespots at the base of the forewings and a characteristic pattern of blackish brown lines. The robust body is colored blackish brown with a distinctive pattern of orange-brown stripes. The males of this species are smaller than females. Although owl moths are active in the evening, they tend to remain resting on tree trunks or on the ground with wings outspread by day. If this moth is disturbed, it rocks back and forth rather than flying off.
• EARLY STAGES In captivity the caterpillar will eat privet *(Ligustrum)*, lilac *(Syringa)*, and elder *(Sambucus)*.
• DISTRIBUTION Occurs from northern India to Nepal, Burma, China, Taiwan, and Japan.

PALEARCTIC
INDO-AUSTRALIAN

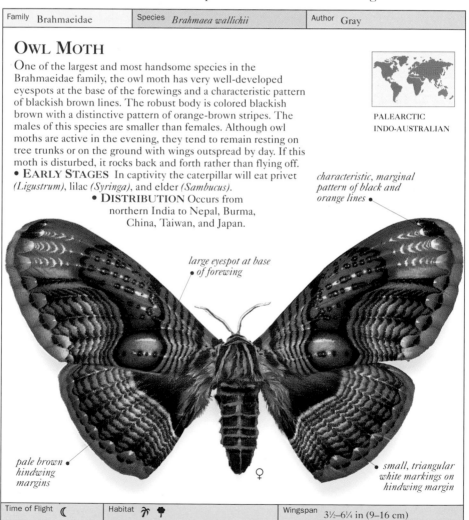

characteristic, marginal pattern of black and orange lines

large eyespot at base of forewing

pale brown hindwing margins

♀

small, triangular white markings on hindwing margin

Time of Flight ☾	Habitat 禾 ❧	Wingspan 3½–6¼ in (9–16 cm)

Family	Brahmaeidae	Species	*Acanthobrahmaea europaea*	Author	Hartig

HARTIG'S BRAHMAEA

This distinctive European moth was discovered less than 30 years ago.
• **EARLY STAGES** The caterpillar is shiny black with white lines and spots on the back and sides, except for the front segments which are patterned with yellow. It feeds on the foliage of ash *(Fraxinus excelsior)*.
• **DISTRIBUTION** In woodlands, on the shores of a volcanic lake in Lucania, Italy. It is now protected by law.

PALEARCTIC

• characteristic dark spot at the wingtip

• wing veins visible through the translucent scales

♂

Time of Flight ☾	Habitat ♣	Wingspan 2–2¼ in (5–7 cm)

Family	Brahmaeidae	Species	*Dactylocerus swanzii*	Author	Butler

BUTLER'S BRAHMIN

This particular moth is distinguishable from other Brahmaeid moths by its more elongate, curved forewings. The forewing eyespot is poorly developed in this species, being represented by a tear-shaped, dark brown spot. The marginal band along the fore-and hindwings is lined with black and orange-brown.
• **EARLY STAGES** Surprisingly, very little seems to be known about the biology of this large and attractive African moth. The caterpillar is said to have paired, conical, hairy spines on each body segment, and it is believed to feed on the foliage of plants of the family Oleaceae.
• **DISTRIBUTION** Occurs in tropical forests of Africa.

AFROTROPICAL

distinctively curved forewing edge •

characteristically • short antennae

brown, • crescent-shaped markings along wing margins

• pale brown line runs down fore- and hindwings

♂

Time of Flight ☾	Habitat 🌿	Wingspan 4¾–6¼ in (12–16 cm)

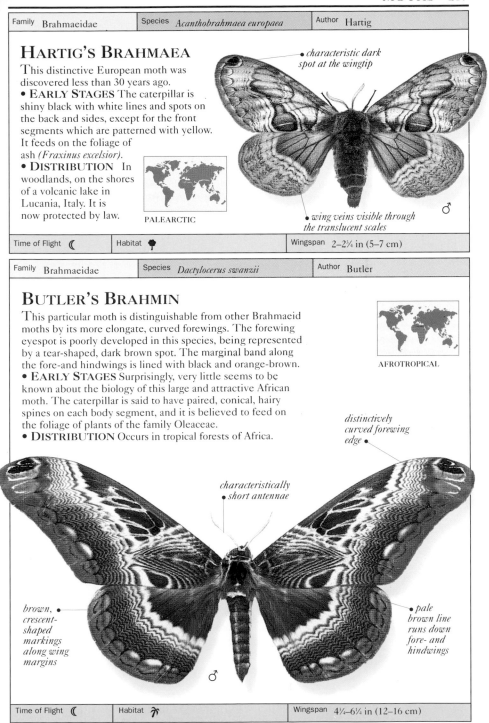

SATURNIIDAE

T HIS VAST, worldwide family of over 1,000 species includes many of the world's largest and most spectacular moths. Because of their size and handsome colors, Saturniid moths are often referred to as emperor moths. Many species have well-developed eyespots or transparent patches on both the fore- and hindwings. A number of species have long tails on the hindwings. Male and female wing patterns can often be totally different. In adult Saturniid moths the tongue is reduced, or absent so that they are unable to feed.

•

When fully grown, the caterpillars spin large cocoons to protect their pupae. These cocoons are sometimes used in the manufacture of coarse silks.

Family SATURNIIDAE	Species *Citheronia regalis*	Author Fabricius

REGAL MOTH

The forewings of this moth are gray with deep orange veins and pale yellow oval spots. The hindwings are orange-brown. The sexes are similar, although females are larger than males. Another common name for the adult moth is the royal walnut moth.
• **EARLY STAGES** The striking caterpillar is green with a group of large branched horns behind the head. It feeds on a wide range of trees, including walnut *(Juglans)* and hickory *(Carya)*, and is known as the hickory horned devil.
• **DISTRIBUTION** Range extends throughout southeastern USA.

NEARCTIC

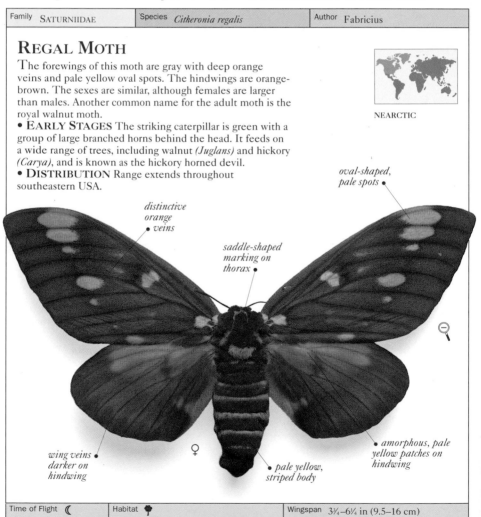

oval-shaped, pale spots

distinctive orange veins

saddle-shaped marking on thorax

wing veins darker on hindwing

♀

pale yellow, striped body

amorphous, pale yellow patches on hindwing

Time of Flight ☾	Habitat 🌳	Wingspan 3¾–6¼ in (9.5–16 cm)

Family SATURNIIDAE	Species *Eacles imperialis*	Author Drury

THE IMPERIAL MOTH

This moth is easily distinguished by its large size and yellow wings, which are variably spotted, banded, and speckled with pinkish to purplish brown.
• **EARLY STAGES** The hairy caterpillar is green or brown with short, fleshy yellow or reddish brown filaments on the back. It feeds on the foliage of a wide variety of trees.
• **DISTRIBUTION** Found in the USA and into southern Canada, with several subspecies.

NEARCTIC

small brown eyespots

wavy, brownish band dissects yellow hindwing

♂

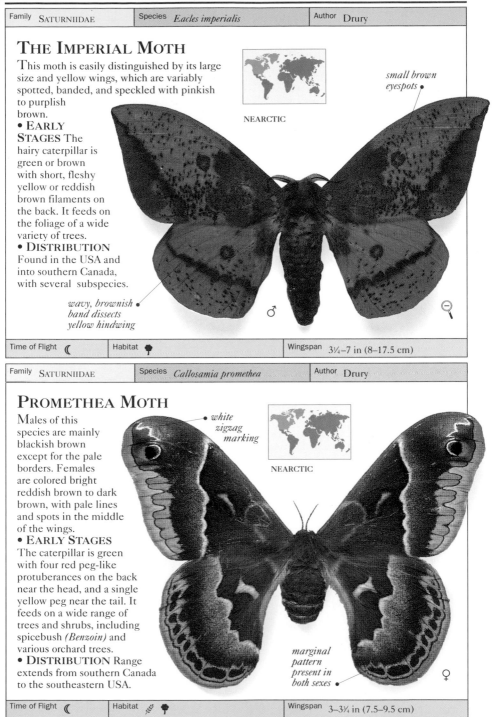

Time of Flight ☾	Habitat 🌳	Wingspan 3¼–7 in (8–17.5 cm)

Family SATURNIIDAE	Species *Callosamia promethea*	Author Drury

PROMETHEA MOTH

Males of this species are mainly blackish brown except for the pale borders. Females are colored bright reddish brown to dark brown, with pale lines and spots in the middle of the wings.
• **EARLY STAGES** The caterpillar is green with four red peg-like protuberances on the back near the head, and a single yellow peg near the tail. It feeds on a wide range of trees and shrubs, including spicebush *(Benzoin)* and various orchard trees.
• **DISTRIBUTION** Range extends from southern Canada to the southeastern USA.

white zigzag marking

NEARCTIC

marginal pattern present in both sexes

♀

Time of Flight ☾	Habitat 🌿 🌳	Wingspan 3–3¾ in (7.5–9.5 cm)

Family SATURNIIDAE	Species *Automeris io*	Author Fabricius

Io Moth

Males of this species have yellow forewings, while those of the females are reddish to purplish brown. The females are larger than the males. The markings are variable in both sexes, and there are many named races.

• **EARLY STAGES** The caterpillar is pale green, with branched, stinging spines along the back, and red and white lines along the sides. It is known to feed on a wide range of plant species, which include birch *(Betula)*, maize *(Zea mays)*, and clover *(Trifolium)*.

• **DISTRIBUTION** Range extends from southern Canada, through to the USA, and south to Mexico.

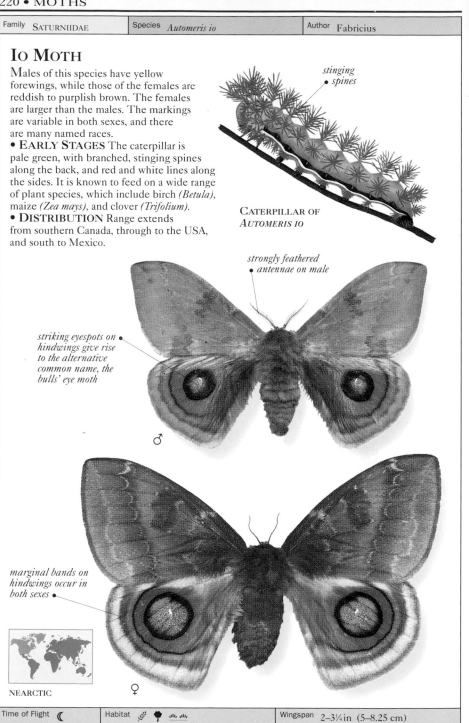

stinging spines

CATERPILLAR OF
AUTOMERIS IO

strongly feathered antennae on male

striking eyespots on hindwings give rise to the alternative common name, the bulls' eye moth

♂

marginal bands on hindwings occur in both sexes

NEARCTIC

♀

Time of Flight ☾	Habitat	Wingspan 2–3¼ in (5–8.25 cm)

| Family SATURNIIDAE | Species *Attacus atlas* | Author Linnaeus |

ATLAS MOTH

This is the world's largest moth in overall size, although the owlet moth (*Thysania agrippina*, see p.265) has a greater wingspan. Distinctively shaped, its wings are richly patterned in various shades of brown. The sexes are similar.
• **EARLY STAGES** The caterpillar is pale yellowish green with long, fleshy spines, which are heavily powdered with a white, waxy substance. It can grow up to 4 in (10 cm) long. It feeds on a wide range of plants, and in captivity will eat willow *(Salix)*, poplar *(Populus)*, and privet *(Ligustrum)*.
• **DISTRIBUTION** Occurs from India and Sri Lanka to China, Malaysia, and Indonesia.

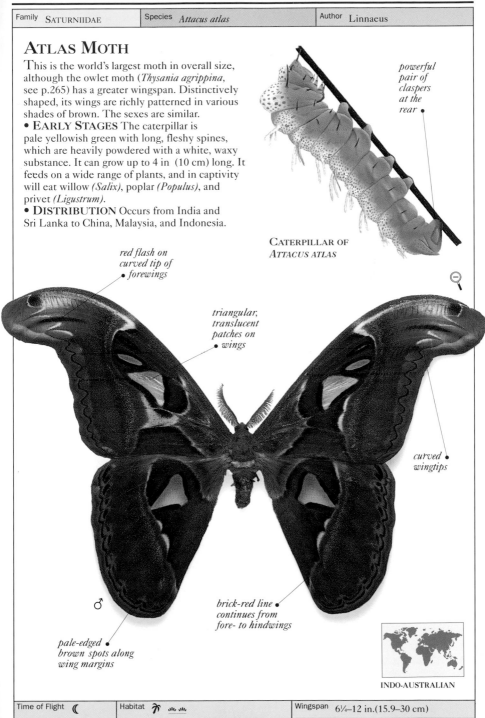

powerful pair of claspers at the rear

CATERPILLAR OF
ATTACUS ATLAS

red flash on curved tip of forewings

triangular, translucent patches on wings

curved wingtips

♂

brick-red line continues from fore- to hindwings

pale-edged brown spots along wing margins

INDO-AUSTRALIAN

| Time of Flight ☾ | Habitat 🌳 🌿 🌿 | Wingspan 6¼–12 in.(15.9–30 cm) |

Family SATURNIIDAE	Species *Actias luna*	Author Linnaeus

LUNA MOTH

This beautiful and distinctive species with long hindwing tails varies in color from yellowish green to pale bluish green, depending on location and season. The sexes are similar, but males have more strongly feathered antennae.

• **EARLY STAGES** The plump, green caterpillar has dark pinkish red raised spots. It feeds on the foliage of many broad-leaved trees, including birch *(Betula)* and alder *(Alnus)*.

• **DISTRIBUTION** Widespread from the USA south to Mexico. This species occurs, but is scarce, in southern Canada.

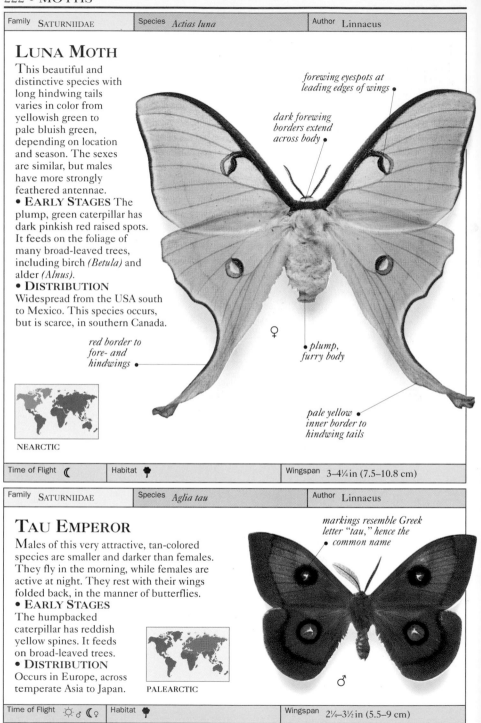

forewing eyespots at leading edges of wings

dark forewing borders extend across body

♀

red border to fore- and hindwings

plump, furry body

pale yellow inner border to hindwing tails

NEARCTIC

Time of Flight ☾	Habitat 🌳	Wingspan 3–4¼ in (7.5–10.8 cm)

Family SATURNIIDAE	Species *Aglia tau*	Author Linnaeus

TAU EMPEROR

Males of this very attractive, tan-colored species are smaller and darker than females. They fly in the morning, while females are active at night. They rest with their wings folded back, in the manner of butterflies.

• **EARLY STAGES** The humpbacked caterpillar has reddish yellow spines. It feeds on broad-leaved trees.

• **DISTRIBUTION** Occurs in Europe, across temperate Asia to Japan.

markings resemble Greek letter "tau," hence the common name

♂

PALEARCTIC

Time of Flight ☼ ♂ ☾♀	Habitat 🌳	Wingspan 2¼–3½ in (5.5–9 cm)

Family SATURNIIDAE	Species *Actias selene*	Author Hübner

INDIAN MOON MOTH

This great favorite of moth breeders is colored a beautiful, pale bluish green, while its long hindwing tails are suffused with yellow and pink. The sexes are similar, but males have more strongly feathered antennae. There are numerous described races.

INDO-AUSTRALIAN

• **EARLY STAGES** The plump caterpillar is bright yellowish green with dark yellow or orange raised warts. It feeds on a wide range of broad-leaved trees and shrubs.
• **DISTRIBUTION** Occurs from India and Sri Lanka, to China, Malaysia, and Indonesia.

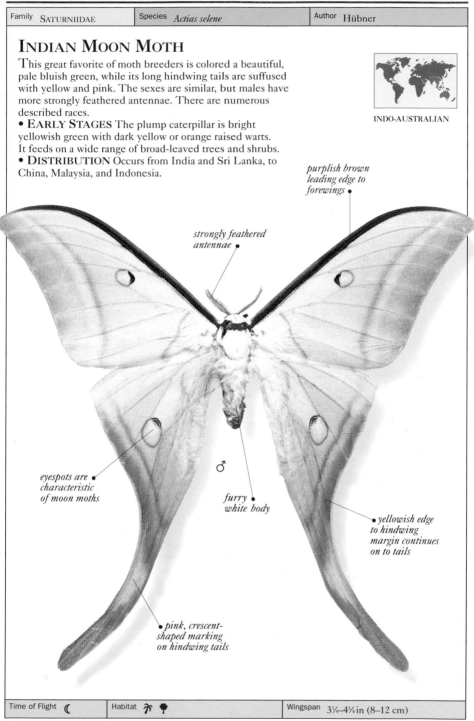

purplish brown leading edge to forewings

strongly feathered antennae

eyespots are characteristic of moon moths

♂

furry white body

yellowish edge to hindwing margin continues on to tails

pink, crescent-shaped marking on hindwing tails

Time of Flight ☾	Habitat 🌿 🌱	Wingspan 3¼–4¾ in (8–12 cm)

Family SATURNIIDAE	Species *Argema mimosae*	Author Boisduval

AFRICAN MOON MOTH

This moth is very similar to the Indian moon moth (*Actias selene*, see p.223), although it belongs to a different genus. Its beautiful color tends to fade in museum specimens. Females can be recognized by their more curved tails.
• **EARLY STAGES** The caterpillar is green with green or yellow warts on the back, which bear short black and yellow bristles. It feeds on the leaves of maroda plum *(Sclerocarya caffra)*, but in captivity will eat walnut *(Juglans)*.
• **DISTRIBUTION** Ranges from Kenya and Zaire to subtropical South Africa.

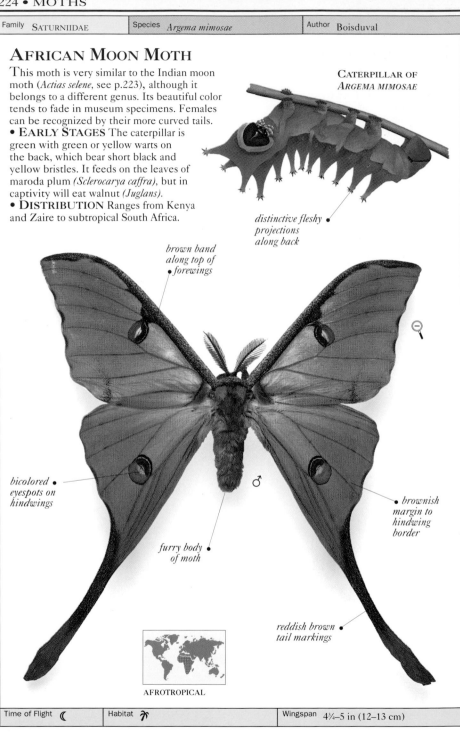

CATERPILLAR OF
ARGEMA MIMOSAE

distinctive fleshy •
projections
along back

brown band
along top of
• forewings

bicolored •
eyespots on
hindwings

♂

• brownish
margin to
hindwing
border

furry body •
of moth

• reddish brown
tail markings

AFROTROPICAL

Time of Flight ☾	Habitat 🎋	Wingspan 4¾–5 in (12–13 cm)

Family	SATURNIIDAE	Species	*Antheraea polyphemus*	Author	Cramer

POLYPHEMUS MOTH

The ground color of this moth's wings varies from yellow to reddish brown, but the distinctive pattern of bands and eyespots makes it an easy species to recognize. The sexes are similar. There are one or two broods a year, with moths on the wing in summer.
• **EARLY STAGES** The plump, bright yellow-green caterpillar is humped along the back and has raised, red spots. It feeds on the foliage of many broad-leaved trees and shrubs, especially that of apple *(Malus domestica)*.
• **DISTRIBUTION** Common in the USA, southern Canada, and northern Mexico.

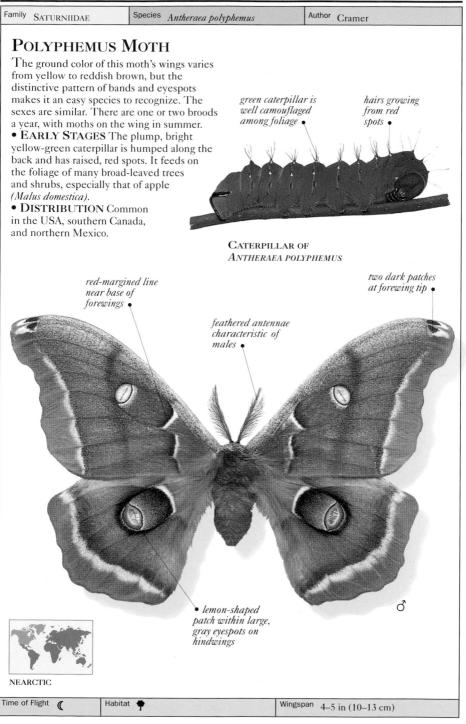

green caterpillar is well camouflaged among foliage •

hairs growing from red spots •

CATERPILLAR OF ANTHERAEA POLYPHEMUS

red-margined line near base of forewings •

feathered antennae characteristic of males •

two dark patches at forewing tip •

• lemon-shaped patch within large, gray eyespots on hindwings

♂

NEARCTIC

Time of Flight ☾	Habitat ♇		Wingspan 4–5 in (10–13 cm)

| Family SATURNIIDAE | Species *Eupackardia calleta* | Author Westwood |

CALLETA SILKMOTH

The blackish brown wings of this moth are banded with white, and each wing has a white V-shaped mark at its center. Females are larger than males, and their wings are more rounded.

• **EARLY STAGES** The caterpillar is green with blue and black, spiny warts on red bases. It feeds on *Leucophyllum, Fouquieria, Prosopis,* and acacia, and in captivity will eat the foliage of ash *(Fraxinus)*, privet *(Ligustrum)*, and other trees.

• **DISTRIBUTION** Range extends from southern Texas to central Mexico.

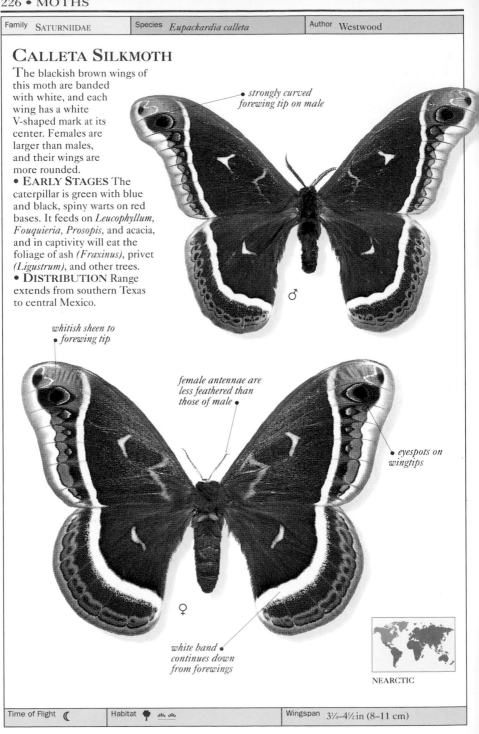

strongly curved
forewing tip on male

♂

whitish sheen to
forewing tip

female antennae are
less feathered than
those of male

eyespots on
wingtips

♀

white band
continues down
from forewings

NEARCTIC

| Time of Flight ☾ | Habitat 🌳 ⚘ ⚘ | Wingspan 3¼–4½ in (8–11 cm) |

Family SATURNIIDAE	Species *Hyalophora cecropia*	Author Linnaeus

CECROPIA MOTH

This easily recognized species has a red body, distinctively banded with white. The dark brown wings are banded with white and pinkish red. The sexes are similar, but males have smaller, featherlike bodies. Another common name is the robin moth.
• **EARLY STAGES** The caterpillar is green with bright yellow, club-shaped protuberances along the back and blue protuberances below. It feeds on a wide range of broad-leaved trees and shrubs.
• **DISTRIBUTION** Widely distributed in forests, arable land, and gardens, from southern Canada through the USA to Mexico.

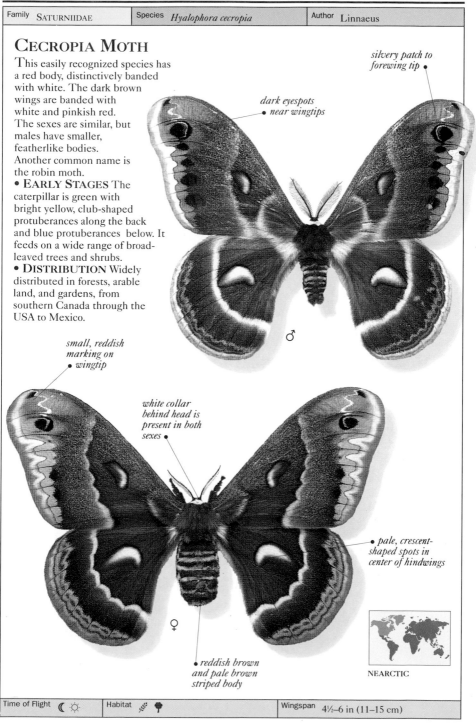

silvery patch to forewing tip

dark eyespots near wingtips

♂

small, reddish marking on wingtip

white collar behind head is present in both sexes

pale, crescent-shaped spots in center of hindwings

♀

reddish brown and pale brown striped body

NEARCTIC

Time of Flight ☾ ☼	Habitat 🌿 🌳	Wingspan 4½–6 in (11–15 cm)

Family SATURNIIDAE	Species *Coscinocera hercules*	Author Miskin

HERCULES MOTH

The common name of this moth refers to its size. Males have distinctive, long tails, while the paler females have broad hindwings with a double lobe in place of a tail.

• **EARLY STAGES** The caterpillar is pale bluish green with yellow spikes on the back, and can grow up to 6¾ in (17 cm) long. It feeds on the foliage of bleeding heart tree *(Homalanthus populifolia)*, *Dysoxylum*, and *Panax*.

• **DISTRIBUTION** Range extends from Papua New Guinea to northern Australia.

INDO-AUSTRALIAN

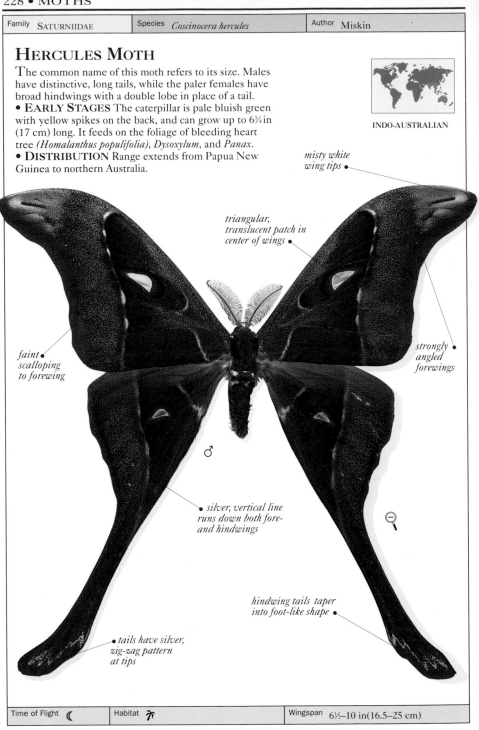

misty white wing tips •

triangular, translucent patch in center of wings •

faint • scalloping to forewing

strongly • angled forewings

♂

• silver, vertical line runs down both fore- and hindwings

hindwing tails taper into foot-like shape •

• tails have silver, zig-zag pattern at tips

Time of Flight ☾	Habitat 🌿	Wingspan 6½–10 in(16.5–25 cm)

Family SATURNIIDAE	Species *Graellsia isabellae*	Author Graëlls

SPANISH MOON MOTH

The Spanish moon moth is considered by many to be the most beautiful of all European moths. The veins on the wings are strongly marked with reddish brown, and outlined with dark brown. Each wing bears a white-centered eyespot, half of which is yellow, and half of which is purplish blue with a reddish brown bar. Males have long, curved hindwing tails; those of females are shorter and broader.

• **EARLY STAGES** The caterpillar is yellowish green, finely spotted with white and banded with chestnut-brown and white. It is covered with long, fine, brown hairs. It feeds on pines, particularly *Pinus sylvestris* and *Pinus laricio*.

• **DISTRIBUTION** Forests in the mountainous regions of central Spain and the Pyrenees.

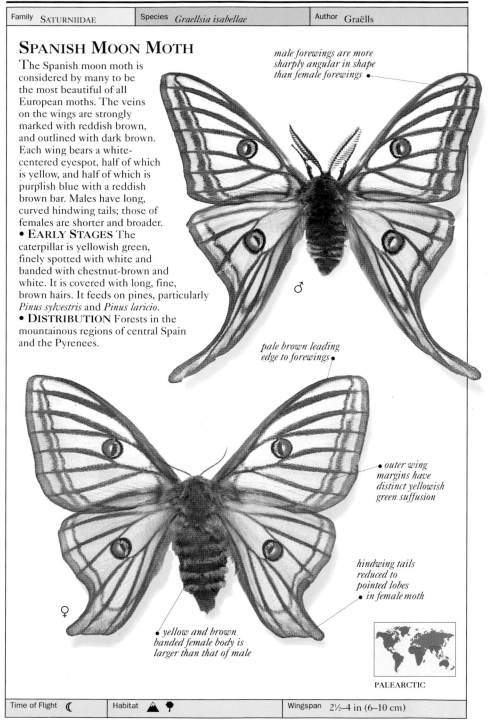

male forewings are more sharply angular in shape than female forewings

♂

pale brown leading edge to forewings

outer wing margins have distinct yellowish green suffusion

hindwing tails reduced to pointed lobes in female moth

♀

yellow and brown banded female body is larger than that of male

PALEARCTIC

Time of Flight ☾	Habitat 🔺 🌳	Wingspan 2½–4 in (6–10 cm)

Family SATURNIIDAE	Species *Loepa katinka*	Author Westwood

GOLDEN EMPEROR

This attractive yellow moth has a streak of dark brown along the leading edge of the forewings. Each wing has a reddish brown ringed eyespot at its center. The wings are also patterned with fine wavy lines of reddish brown. The sexes are alike.

• **EARLY STAGES** Caterpillar is dark brown marbled with light brown and black, and has metallic blue warts. Along the sides are triangular yellow patches. The caterpillar feeds on vines (*Vitis* and *Parthenocisssus*).

• **DISTRIBUTION** Widespread from Northern India to China.

CATERPILLAR OF
LOEPA KATINKA

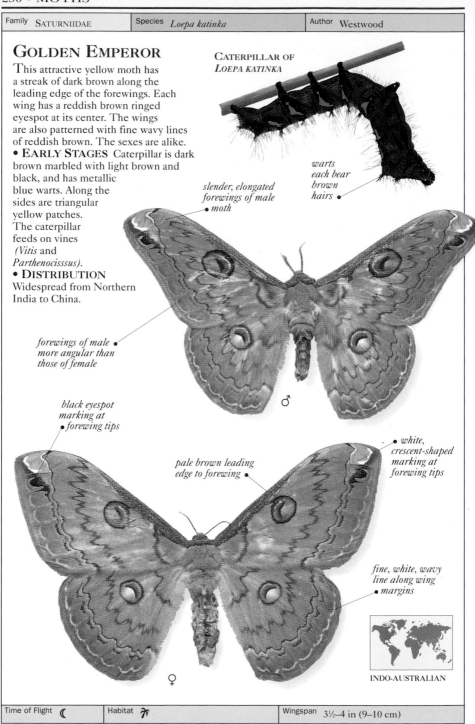

warts each bear brown hairs

slender, elongated forewings of male moth

forewings of male more angular than those of female

black eyespot marking at forewing tips

pale brown leading edge to forewing

white, crescent-shaped marking at forewing tips

fine, white, wavy line along wing margins

INDO-AUSTRALIAN

Time of Flight ☾	Habitat 🌴	Wingspan 3½–4 in (9–10 cm)

Family SATURNIIDAE	Species *Bunaea alcinoe*	Author Stoll

COMMON EMPEROR

The common emperor varies in color from reddish brown to dark purplish brown, with striking pale bands on the fore- and hindwings.
• **EARLY STAGES** The dull black caterpillar has long black spines behind the head, and yellowish white colored protuberances along the rest of the body. It feeds on many types of plant, including *Celtis* and *Terminalia*.
• **DISTRIBUTION** Widespread throughout Africa, south of the Sahara, and also in Madagascar.

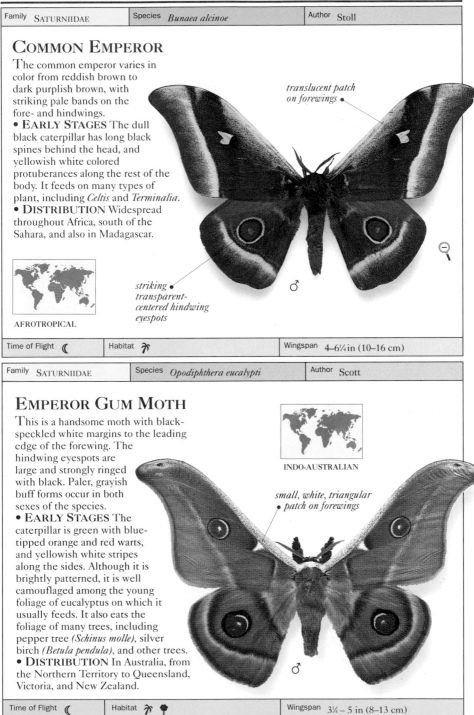

translucent patch on forewings •

♂

striking • transparent-centered hindwing eyespots

AFROTROPICAL

Time of Flight ☾	Habitat 🌿	Wingspan 4–6¼ in (10–16 cm)

Family SATURNIIDAE	Species *Opodiphthera eucalypti*	Author Scott

EMPEROR GUM MOTH

This is a handsome moth with black-speckled white margins to the leading edge of the forewing. The hindwing eyespots are large and strongly ringed with black. Paler, grayish buff forms occur in both sexes of the species.
• **EARLY STAGES** The caterpillar is green with blue-tipped orange and red warts, and yellowish white stripes along the sides. Although it is brightly patterned, it is well camouflaged among the young foliage of eucalyptus on which it usually feeds. It also eats the foliage of many trees, including pepper tree *(Schinus molle)*, silver birch *(Betula pendula)*, and other trees.
• **DISTRIBUTION** In Australia, from the Northern Territory to Queensland, Victoria, and New Zealand.

INDO-AUSTRALIAN

small, white, triangular • patch on forewings

♂

Time of Flight ☾	Habitat 🌿 🌱	Wingspan 3¼ – 5 in (8–13 cm)

| Family | SATURNIIDAE | Species | *Nudaurelia cytherea* | Author | Fabricius |

PINE EMPEROR

This moth is banded and shaded with reddish, yellowish, and purplish brown. The forewing eyespots are ringed with black and orange, and have translucent, oval centers. The hindwing eyespots are broadly ringed with black and orange, and have minute, rounded, transparent centers.

• **EARLY STAGES** The caterpillar is strikingly beautiful with its black body speckled with green, yellow, and silver. There are also striking broad bands of brownish red across the back. This species is a particularly notorious pest of pine trees *(Pinus)*, but also feeds on the foliage of cypress *(Cupressus)* and acacia, apple *(Malus domestica)*, guava *(Psidium guajava)*, and other wild and cultivated trees and shrubs.

• **DISTRIBUTION** Widespread and common in South Africa.

AFROTROPICAL

unmistakable speckled
• patterning

CATERPILLAR OF
NUDAURELIA CYTHEREA

long, hairlike scales at wing
• bases

♂

markings •
distinctively
outlined with
purplish gray

| Time of Flight | ☾ | Habitat | 🌾 🌳 | | Wingspan | 3½–5 in (9–13 cm) |

Family SATURNIIDAE	Species *Rothschildia orizaba*	Author Westwood

ORIZABA SILKMOTH

A handsome and distinctive moth, this silkmoth
belongs to a largely South American genus
which is characterized by the presence of large,
translucent, windowlike patches on both fore-
and hindwings. The reddish brown wings are
lined and patterned with white, black, and
various shades of brown. Females have more
rounded hindwings.
• **EARLY STAGES** The caterpillar is
yellowish green above and bluish green
below. The foodplants of this moth are
apparently unknown. It has been
successfully reared in captivity on
the foliage of privet *(Ligustrum).*
• **DISTRIBUTION** Central and
tropical South America, and can
occur in south Texas, USA.

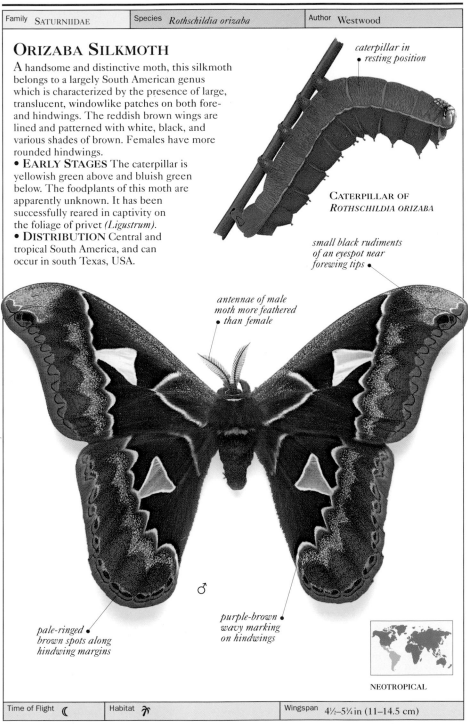

caterpillar in
• *resting position*

CATERPILLAR OF
ROTHSCHILDIA ORIZABA

*small black rudiments
of an eyespot near
forewing tips* •

*antennae of male
moth more feathered
• than female*

♂

pale-ringed •
*brown spots along
hindwing margins*

purple-brown •
*wavy marking
on hindwings*

NEOTROPICAL

Time of Flight ☾	Habitat 🦋	Wingspan 4½–5¾ in (11–14.5 cm)

Family	SATURNIIDAE	Species	*Samia cynthia*	Author	Drury

AILANTHUS SILKMOTH

The ground color of this large moth varies from khaki-brown to an olive-green or orange-brown. The broad, pale band that traverses both fore- and hindwings is characteristic, as are the narrow, crescent-shaped, translucent patches in the center of each wing. Males have more elongate forewings than the females, and their antennae are more strongly feathered.

• **EARLY STAGES** The fleshy, spined caterpillar is bluish green, overlaid with a white, waxy powder. As its common name suggests, it feeds on the foliage of Chinese tree of heaven *(Ailanthus altissima)*, although in captivity it eats privet *(Ligustrum)* or lilac *(Syringa)*. The caterpillars are reared for the silk of their cocoons.

• **DISTRIBUTION** Originating from Asia, this species of silkmoth has been introduced into North America and is now established in parts of Europe.

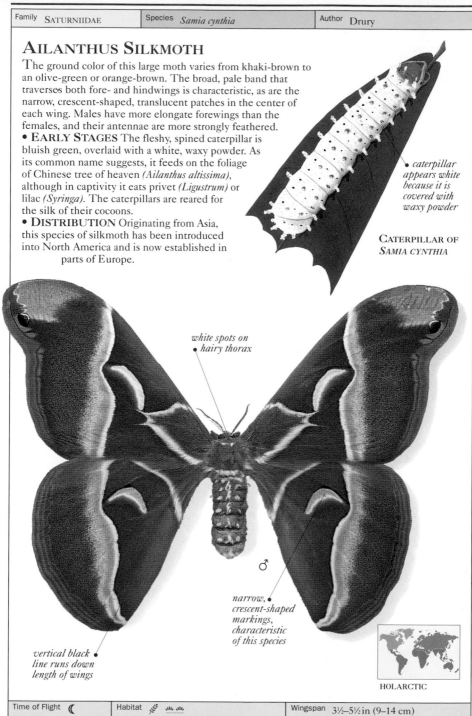

• *caterpillar appears white because it is covered with waxy powder*

CATERPILLAR OF
SAMIA CYNTHIA

white spots on • hairy thorax

♂

narrow, • crescent-shaped markings, characteristic of this species

vertical black line runs down length of wings

HOLARCTIC

Time of Flight	☾	Habitat		Wingspan	3½–5½ in (9–14 cm)

Family	SATURNIIDAE	Species	*Saturnia pyri*	Authors	Denis & Schiffermüller

GREAT PEACOCK MOTH

The great peacock moth is Europe's largest
native moth, and as such is easy to recognize.
It has red, black, and brown ringed eyespots
on all wings. The wings are brown with light
and dark bands, and the leading edge of
the forewing is extensively suffused with
silvery white. The sexes are similar. Other
common names for the adult moth are the
giant emperor and the Viennese emperor.

• **EARLY STAGES** The caterpillar is bright
yellowish green with raised blue warts bearing
tufts of black hairs. It feeds on the foliage of apple
(Malus domestica), pear *(Pyrus communis),*
and other broad-leaved trees, and it is
occasionally a minor orchard pest.

• **DISTRIBUTION** Widespread
in central and southern Europe,
extending to North Africa and
western Asia.

CATERPILLAR OF
SATURNIA PYRI

caterpillar is yellowish
green with white
line along its side

small, dark
marking on
forewing tip

featherlike
antennae

♂

body pattern
echoes wing pattern

pale, outer
marginal band
on both fore-
and hindwings

PALEARCTIC

Time of Flight ☾	Habitat	Wingspan 4–6 in (10–15 cm)

SPHINGIDAE

T HIS IS a worldwide family of about 1,000 medium-sized to large moths. Their very distinctive streamlined wing shapes and robust bodies set them apart from other moths, making them one of the easiest groups to recognize. Because of their structure, they are extremely powerful fliers, some even reaching speeds of up to 50 km (30 miles) per hour. It is probably owing to their speed in flight that they have earned their common name of hawkmoths.

•

Moths from this family usually have well-developed tongues enabling them to take nectar from even the most deep-throated, tubular flowers. Some species are day-fliers, and may be seen hovering over flower beds in gardens.

Family SPHINGIDAE	Species *Acherontia atropos*	Author Linnaeus

DEATH'S HEAD HAWKMOTH

Many superstitions were once based around this distinctive moth, and it was generally considered to be a portent of death or grave misfortune. The moths have a very strong tongue, which they use to pierce the wax cells of beehives so that they can feed on the honey inside.
• **EARLY STAGES** The caterpillar ranges from yellow to green or brown. It feeds on the foliage of potato *(Solanum)*, deadly nightshade *(Atropa)*, and related plants.
• **DISTRIBUTION** Mediterranean, North Africa. It migrates northward into Europe.

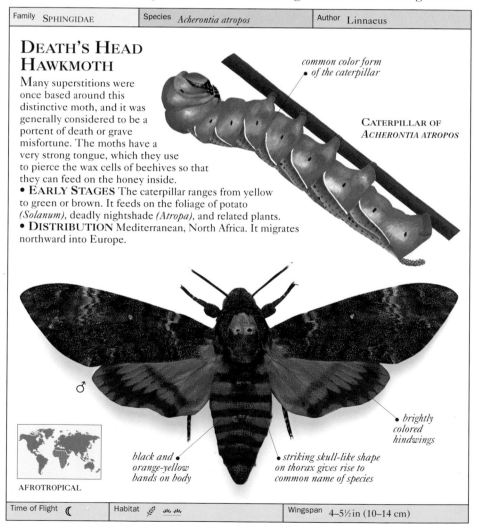

common color form of the caterpillar

CATERPILLAR OF
ACHERONTIA ATROPOS

♂

AFROTROPICAL

black and orange-yellow bands on body

striking skull-like shape on thorax gives rise to common name of species

brightly colored hindwings

Time of Flight ☾	Habitat	Wingspan 4–5½ in (10–14 cm)

| Family SPHINGIDAE | Species *Agrius cingulata* | Author Fabricius |

PINK-SPOTTED HAWKMOTH

This streamlined moth has well
camouflaged forewings,
with an intricate
pattern of gray and
grayish brown. The
hindwings are also gray
with black bands, but
are strongly flushed with
pink toward the base. The
most distinctive feature of the
pink-spotted hawkmoth is a
pattern of pink crossbars
which are evident on the body.
• **EARLY STAGES** The caterpillar is
variable, ranging in color from green to olive-
brown or blackish brown. All forms have paler,
diagonal stripes along the sides. This species is a
well-known pest of sweet potato *(Ipomoea)*, and is
also known as the sweet potato hornworm.
• **DISTRIBUTION** Range extends from South
and Central America to southern parts of the USA,
Hawaii, and sometimes southern Canada.

distinctive antennae

characteristically pointed forewing tips

NEOTROPICAL
NEARCTIC

| Time of Flight ☾ | Habitat | Wingspan 3¼–4¾ in (8–12 cm) |

| Family SPHINGIDAE | Species *Sphinx ligustri* | Author Linnaeus |

PRIVET HAWKMOTH

The forewings
of this very
distinctive
species are dark
brown, shaded
with pale grayish
brown, and finely
streaked with black.
The hindwings are pale,
dusky pink with black
bands. The body is deep
pink with black bands and a
central, pale brown, longitudinal
stripe. The sexes are alike.
• **EARLY STAGES** The plump caterpillar
is bright yellowish green with a series of striking,
oblique, purple stripes along the sides, and a
sharply pointed, shiny, black tailhorn. It mostly
feeds on the foliage of common privet *(Ligustrum
vulgare)* and lilac *(Syringa vulgaris)*.
• **DISTRIBUTION** Widespread and common
in Europe, extending across temperate
Asia to China.

white antennae

whitish border to outer sides of thorax

pale margin present on forewings

PALEARCTIC

| Time of Flight ☾ | Habitat | Wingspan 3¼–4½ in (8–11 cm) |

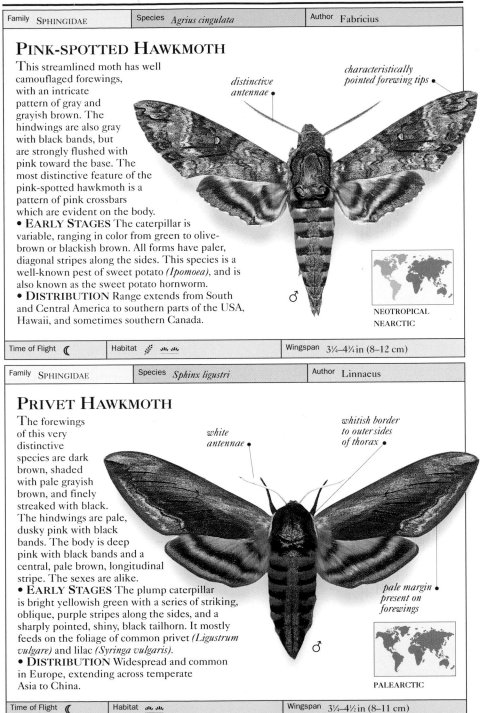

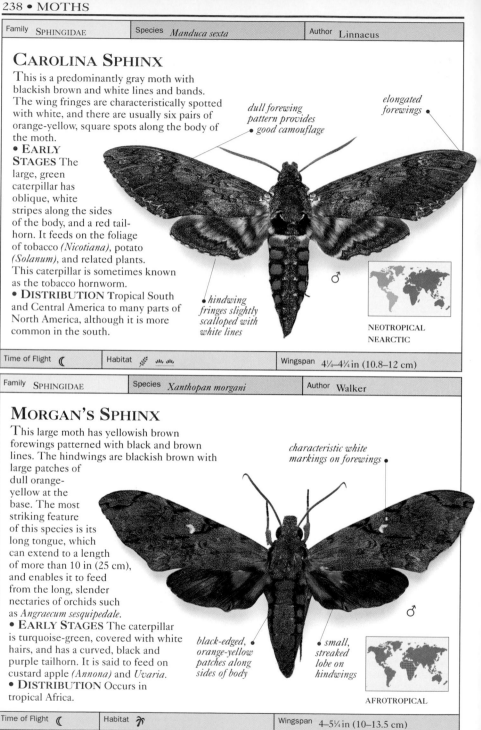

Family SPHINGIDAE	Species *Manduca sexta*	Author Linnaeus

CAROLINA SPHINX

This is a predominantly gray moth with blackish brown and white lines and bands. The wing fringes are characteristically spotted with white, and there are usually six pairs of orange-yellow, square spots along the body of the moth.
- **EARLY STAGES** The large, green caterpillar has oblique, white stripes along the sides of the body, and a red tailhorn. It feeds on the foliage of tobacco *(Nicotiana)*, potato *(Solanum)*, and related plants. This caterpillar is sometimes known as the tobacco hornworm.
- **DISTRIBUTION** Tropical South and Central America to many parts of North America, although it is more common in the south.

dull forewing pattern provides good camouflage

elongated forewings

♂

hindwing fringes slightly scalloped with white lines

NEOTROPICAL
NEARCTIC

Time of Flight ☾	Habitat	Wingspan 4¼–4¾ in (10.8–12 cm)

Family SPHINGIDAE	Species *Xanthopan morgani*	Author Walker

MORGAN'S SPHINX

This large moth has yellowish brown forewings patterned with black and brown lines. The hindwings are blackish brown with large patches of dull orange-yellow at the base. The most striking feature of this species is its long tongue, which can extend to a length of more than 10 in (25 cm), and enables it to feed from the long, slender nectaries of orchids such as *Angraecum sesquipedale*.
- **EARLY STAGES** The caterpillar is turquoise-green, covered with white hairs, and has a curved, black and purple tailhorn. It is said to feed on custard apple *(Annona)* and *Uvaria*.
- **DISTRIBUTION** Occurs in tropical Africa.

characteristic white markings on forewings

♂

black-edged, orange-yellow patches along sides of body

small, streaked lobe on hindwings

AFROTROPICAL

Time of Flight ☾	Habitat	Wingspan 4–5¼ in (10–13.5 cm)

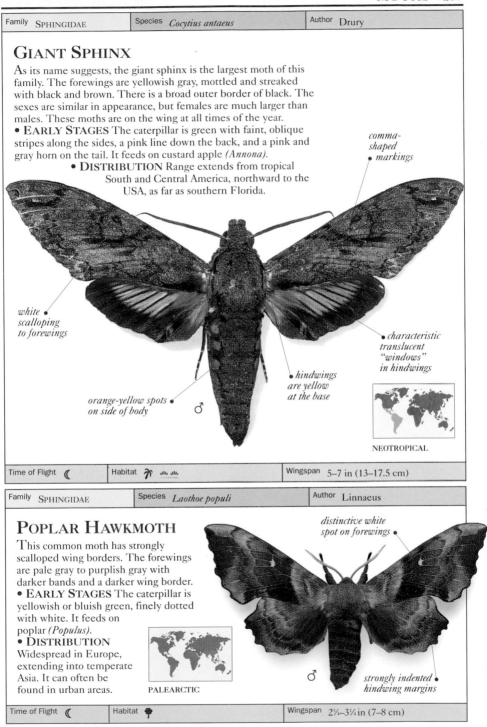

Family SPHINGIDAE	Species *Cocytius antaeus*	Author Drury

GIANT SPHINX

As its name suggests, the giant sphinx is the largest moth of this family. The forewings are yellowish gray, mottled and streaked with black and brown. There is a broad outer border of black. The sexes are similar in appearance, but females are much larger than males. These moths are on the wing at all times of the year.

• **EARLY STAGES** The caterpillar is green with faint, oblique stripes along the sides, a pink line down the back, and a pink and gray horn on the tail. It feeds on custard apple *(Annona)*.

• **DISTRIBUTION** Range extends from tropical South and Central America, northward to the USA, as far as southern Florida.

comma-shaped • markings

white • scalloping to forewings

• characteristic translucent "windows" in hindwings

orange-yellow spots • on side of body   ♂

• hindwings are yellow at the base

NEOTROPICAL

Time of Flight ☾	Habitat 🌳 ⚘ ⚘	Wingspan 5–7 in (13–17.5 cm)

Family SPHINGIDAE	Species *Laothoe populi*	Author Linnaeus

POPLAR HAWKMOTH

This common moth has strongly scalloped wing borders. The forewings are pale gray to purplish gray with darker bands and a darker wing border.

• **EARLY STAGES** The caterpillar is yellowish or bluish green, finely dotted with white. It feeds on poplar *(Populus)*.

• **DISTRIBUTION** Widespread in Europe, extending into temperate Asia. It can often be found in urban areas.

distinctive white spot on forewings •

PALEARCTIC

♂

strongly indented • hindwing margins

Time of Flight ☾	Habitat ⚘	Wingspan 2¾–3¼ in (7–8 cm)

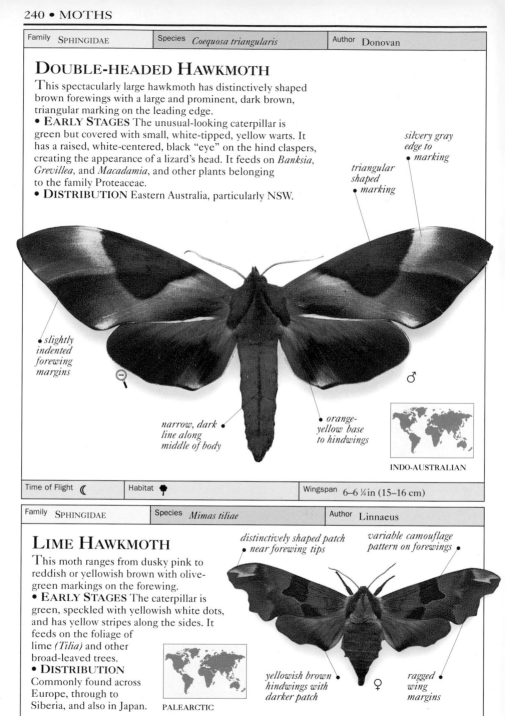

| Family SPHINGIDAE | Species *Coequosa triangularis* | Author Donovan |

DOUBLE-HEADED HAWKMOTH

This spectacularly large hawkmoth has distinctively shaped
brown forewings with a large and prominent, dark brown,
triangular marking on the leading edge.
• **EARLY STAGES** The unusual-looking caterpillar is
green but covered with small, white-tipped, yellow warts. It
has a raised, white-centered, black "eye" on the hind claspers,
creating the appearance of a lizard's head. It feeds on *Banksia*,
Grevillea, and *Macadamia*, and other plants belonging
to the family Proteaceae.
• **DISTRIBUTION** Eastern Australia, particularly NSW.

*silvery gray
edge to
• marking*

*triangular
shaped
• marking*

*• slightly
indented
forewing
margins*

♂

*narrow, dark
line along
middle of body*

*• orange-
yellow base
to hindwings*

INDO-AUSTRALIAN

| Time of Flight ☾ | Habitat ♣ | Wingspan 6–6 ¼ in (15–16 cm) |

| Family SPHINGIDAE | Species *Mimas tiliae* | Author Linnaeus |

LIME HAWKMOTH

This moth ranges from dusky pink to
reddish or yellowish brown with olive-
green markings on the forewing.
• **EARLY STAGES** The caterpillar is
green, speckled with yellowish white dots,
and has yellow stripes along the sides. It
feeds on the foliage of
lime *(Tilia)* and other
broad-leaved trees.
• **DISTRIBUTION**
Commonly found across
Europe, through to
Siberia, and also in Japan.

*distinctively shaped patch
• near forewing tips*

*variable camouflage
pattern on forewings •*

*yellowish brown
hindwings with
darker patch*

♀

*ragged •
wing
margins*

PALEARCTIC

| Time of Flight ☾ | Habitat ♣ | Wingspan 2½–3 in (6–7.5 cm) |

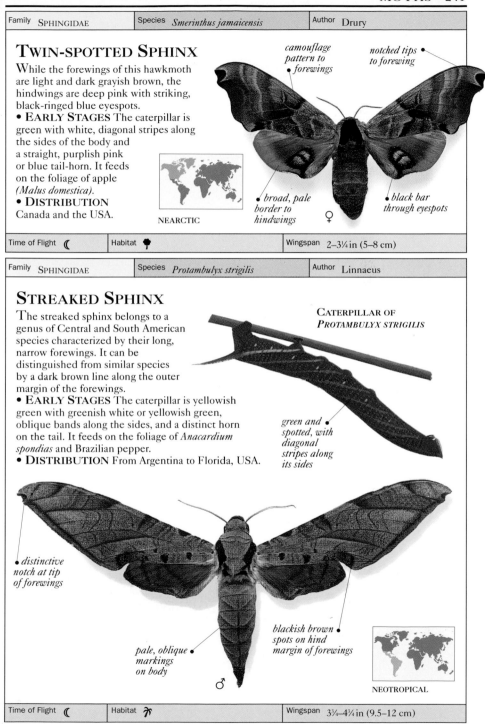

| Family SPHINGIDAE | Species *Smerinthus jamaicensis* | Author Drury |

TWIN-SPOTTED SPHINX

While the forewings of this hawkmoth are light and dark grayish brown, the hindwings are deep pink with striking, black-ringed blue eyespots.
• **EARLY STAGES** The caterpillar is green with white, diagonal stripes along the sides of the body and a straight, purplish pink or blue tail-horn. It feeds on the foliage of apple (*Malus domestica*).
• **DISTRIBUTION** Canada and the USA.

camouflage pattern to forewings

notched tips to forewing

NEARCTIC

broad, pale border to hindwings

black bar through eyespots

♀

| Time of Flight ☾ | Habitat 🌳 | Wingspan 2–3¼ in (5–8 cm) |

| Family SPHINGIDAE | Species *Protambulyx strigilis* | Author Linnaeus |

STREAKED SPHINX

The streaked sphinx belongs to a genus of Central and South American species characterized by their long, narrow forewings. It can be distinguished from similar species by a dark brown line along the outer margin of the forewings.
• **EARLY STAGES** The caterpillar is yellowish green with greenish white or yellowish green, oblique bands along the sides, and a distinct horn on the tail. It feeds on the foliage of *Anacardium spondias* and Brazilian pepper.
• **DISTRIBUTION** From Argentina to Florida, USA.

CATERPILLAR OF PROTAMBULYX STRIGILIS

green and spotted, with diagonal stripes along its sides

distinctive notch at tip of forewings

pale, oblique markings on body

blackish brown spots on hind margin of forewings

♂

NEOTROPICAL

| Time of Flight ☾ | Habitat 🌴 | Wingspan 3¾–4¾ in (9.5–12 cm) |

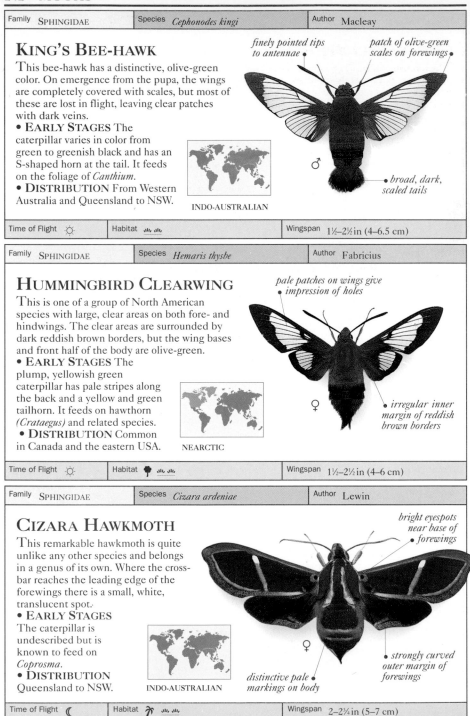

| Family SPHINGIDAE | Species *Cephonodes kingi* | Author Macleay |

KING'S BEE-HAWK

This bee-hawk has a distinctive, olive-green color. On emergence from the pupa, the wings are completely covered with scales, but most of these are lost in flight, leaving clear patches with dark veins.
• **EARLY STAGES** The caterpillar varies in color from green to greenish black and has an S-shaped horn at the tail. It feeds on the foliage of *Canthium*.
• **DISTRIBUTION** From Western Australia and Queensland to NSW.

finely pointed tips to antennae

patch of olive-green scales on forewings

♂

broad, dark, scaled tails

INDO-AUSTRALIAN

| Time of Flight ☼ | Habitat ⬟⬟ | Wingspan 1½–2½ in (4–6.5 cm) |

| Family SPHINGIDAE | Species *Hemaris thysbe* | Author Fabricius |

HUMMINGBIRD CLEARWING

This is one of a group of North American species with large, clear areas on both fore- and hindwings. The clear areas are surrounded by dark reddish brown borders, but the wing bases and front half of the body are olive-green.
• **EARLY STAGES** The plump, yellowish green caterpillar has pale stripes along the back and a yellow and green tailhorn. It feeds on hawthorn (*Crataegus*) and related species.
 • **DISTRIBUTION** Common in Canada and the eastern USA.

pale patches on wings give impression of holes

♀

irregular inner margin of reddish brown borders

NEARCTIC

| Time of Flight ☼ | Habitat 🌳 ⬟⬟ | Wingspan 1½–2½ in (4–6 cm) |

| Family SPHINGIDAE | Species *Cizara ardeniae* | Author Lewin |

CIZARA HAWKMOTH

This remarkable hawkmoth is quite unlike any other species and belongs in a genus of its own. Where the cross-bar reaches the leading edge of the forewings there is a small, white, translucent spot.
• **EARLY STAGES** The caterpillar is undescribed but is known to feed on *Coprosma*.
• **DISTRIBUTION** Queensland to NSW.

bright eyespots near base of forewings

♀

distinctive pale markings on body

strongly curved outer margin of forewings

INDO-AUSTRALIAN

| Time of Flight ☾ | Habitat 🌴 ⬟⬟ | Wingspan 2–2¾ in (5–7 cm) |

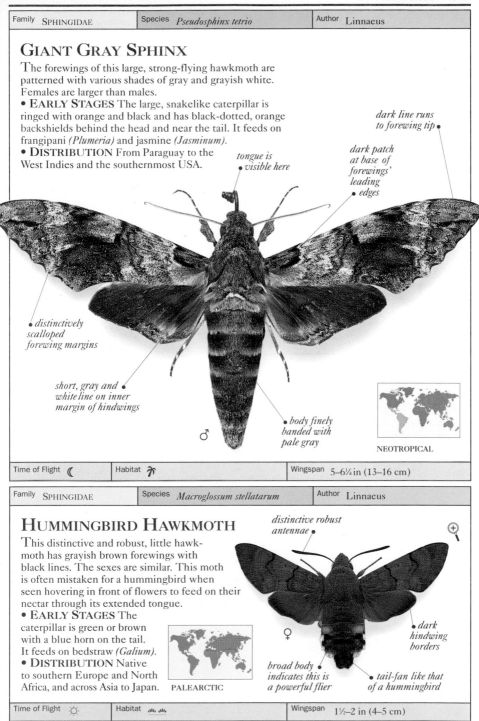

| Family SPHINGIDAE | Species *Pseudosphinx tetrio* | Author Linnaeus |

GIANT GRAY SPHINX

The forewings of this large, strong-flying hawkmoth are patterned with various shades of gray and grayish white. Females are larger than males.
• **EARLY STAGES** The large, snakelike caterpillar is ringed with orange and black and has black-dotted, orange backshields behind the head and near the tail. It feeds on frangipani *(Plumeria)* and jasmine *(Jasminum).*
• **DISTRIBUTION** From Paraguay to the West Indies and the southernmost USA.

dark line runs to forewing tip

dark patch at base of forewings' leading edges

tongue is visible here

distinctively scalloped forewing margins

short, gray and white line on inner margin of hindwings

body finely banded with pale gray

♂

NEOTROPICAL

| Time of Flight ☾ | Habitat | Wingspan 5–6¼ in (13–16 cm) |

| Family SPHINGIDAE | Species *Macroglossum stellatarum* | Author Linnaeus |

HUMMINGBIRD HAWKMOTH

This distinctive and robust, little hawk-moth has grayish brown forewings with black lines. The sexes are similar. This moth is often mistaken for a hummingbird when seen hovering in front of flowers to feed on their nectar through its extended tongue.
• **EARLY STAGES** The caterpillar is green or brown with a blue horn on the tail. It feeds on bedstraw *(Galium).*
• **DISTRIBUTION** Native to southern Europe and North Africa, and across Asia to Japan.

distinctive robust antennae

♀

dark hindwing borders

broad body indicates this is a powerful flier

tail-fan like that of a hummingbird

PALEARCTIC

| Time of Flight ☼ | Habitat | Wingspan 1½–2 in (4–5 cm) |

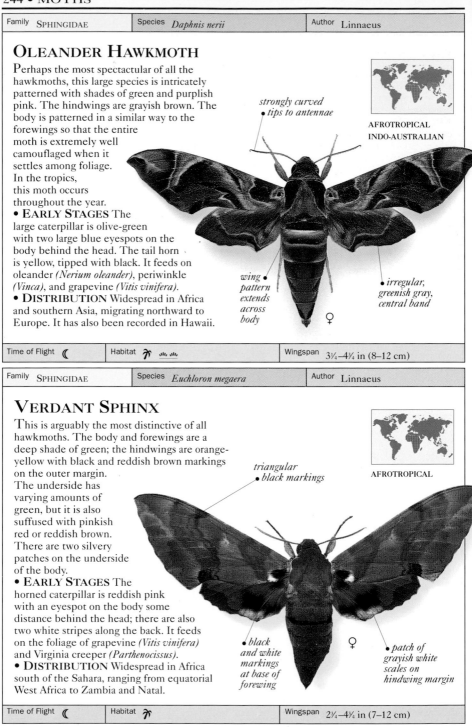

| Family SPHINGIDAE | Species *Daphnis nerii* | Author Linnaeus |

OLEANDER HAWKMOTH

Perhaps the most spectacular of all the hawkmoths, this large species is intricately patterned with shades of green and purplish pink. The hindwings are grayish brown. The body is patterned in a similar way to the forewings so that the entire moth is extremely well camouflaged when it settles among foliage. In the tropics, this moth occurs throughout the year.

• **EARLY STAGES** The large caterpillar is olive-green with two large blue eyespots on the body behind the head. The tail horn is yellow, tipped with black. It feeds on oleander *(Nerium oleander)*, periwinkle *(Vinca)*, and grapevine *(Vitis vinifera)*.

• **DISTRIBUTION** Widespread in Africa and southern Asia, migrating northward to Europe. It has also been recorded in Hawaii.

strongly curved tips to antennae

AFROTROPICAL
INDO-AUSTRALIAN

wing pattern extends across body

irregular, greenish gray, central band

♀

| Time of Flight ☾ | Habitat 🌴 ⚘ ⚘ | Wingspan 3¼–4¾ in (8–12 cm) |

| Family SPHINGIDAE | Species *Euchloron megaera* | Author Linnaeus |

VERDANT SPHINX

This is arguably the most distinctive of all hawkmoths. The body and forewings are a deep shade of green; the hindwings are orange-yellow with black and reddish brown markings on the outer margin. The underside has varying amounts of green, but it is also suffused with pinkish red or reddish brown. There are two silvery patches on the underside of the body.

• **EARLY STAGES** The horned caterpillar is reddish pink with an eyespot on the body some distance behind the head; there are also two white stripes along the back. It feeds on the foliage of grapevine *(Vitis vinifera)* and Virginia creeper *(Parthenocissus)*.

• **DISTRIBUTION** Widespread in Africa south of the Sahara, ranging from equatorial West Africa to Zambia and Natal.

triangular black markings

AFROTROPICAL

black and white markings at base of forewing

♀

patch of grayish white scales on hindwing margin

| Time of Flight ☾ | Habitat 🌴 | Wingspan 2¾–4¾ in (7–12 cm) |

Family SPHINGIDAE	Species *Hippotion celerio*	Author Linnaeus

SILVER-STRIPED HAWKMOTH

The brown forewings strongly striped with silvery white give this moth its common name. The hindwings are bright pink at the base, becoming paler towards the margin.
• **EARLY STAGES** The caterpillar is very variable with a ground color of dark brown, light brown, or green. Caterpillars feed on bedstraw *(Galium)* and Virginia creeper *(Parthenocissus)*.
• **DISTRIBUTION** Africa to Australia, and southern Europe.

AFROTROPICAL
INDO-AUSTRALIAN
PALEARCTIC

small lobe on hindwing

forewing pointed at rear margin

♀

Time of Flight ☾	Habitat	Wingspan 2¾–3¼ in (7–8 cm)

Family SPHINGIDAE	Species *Hyles lineata*	Author Fabricius

WHITE-LINED SPHINX

This worldwide species has dark olive-brown forewings, banded and streaked with pinkish white; the pink hindwings are margined with black. It visits flowers such as honeysuckle *(Lonicera)* and valerian *(Valeriana)*.
• **EARLY STAGES** The caterpillar of this species is dark green or black, with yellow dots. It feeds on many plants, including bedstraw *(Galium)*.
• **DISTRIBUTION** North and South America, Europe, Africa, Asia, and Australia.

WORLDWIDE

pinkish white streaks along distinctively patterned body

pale grayish brown margins to fore- and hindwings

♂

Time of Flight ☾ ☼	Habitat	Wingspan 2¾–3¼ in (7–8 cm)

Family SPHINGIDAE	Species *Deilephila elpenor*	Author Linnaeus

ELEPHANT HAWKMOTH

The forewings of this moth are olive-brown, banded with dusky pink, while the hindwings are deep pink. The underside is predominantly bright pink.
• **EARLY STAGES** The large caterpillar is green or grayish brown with prominent false eyespots on the body behind the head. It feeds on willowherb *(Epilobium)* and bedstraw *(Galium)*.
• **DISTRIBUTION** Widespread in Europe and across temperate Asia to Japan.

forewing tip tapers abruptly to a point

PALEARCTIC

white hindwing fringes

pink and olive-brown stripes on body

♂

Time of Flight ☾	Habitat	Wingspan 2¼–2½ in (5.5–6 cm)

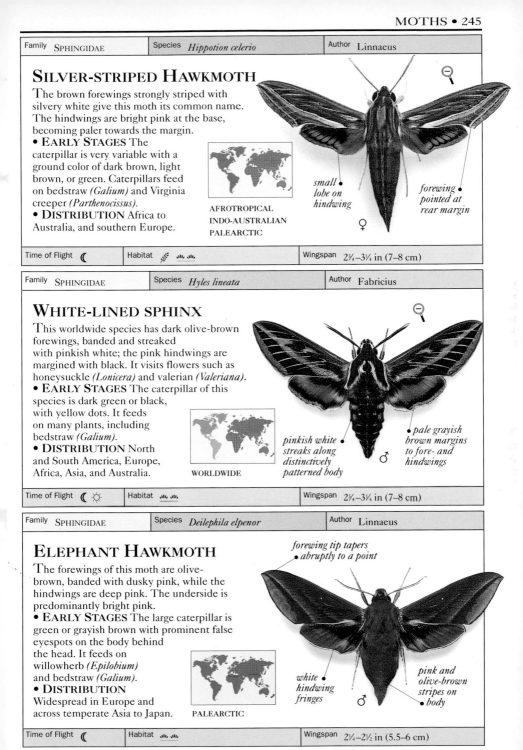

NOTODONTIDAE

T HIS IS a large family of more than 2,500 small- to medium-sized species with a worldwide distribution. The moths generally have long forewings and a longish body. The predominant wing colors are brown, gray, and green, but some species are more brightly colored. One of the characteristic features of many of the members in this group is a tuft of scales projecting from the middle of the hind edge of the forewing. When the wings are folded, these tufts project conspicuously, giving rise to the common name "prominents."

The caterpillars of this family display a great variety of forms, ranging from hairy species that live in communal nests – the "processionary" caterpillars – to smooth species with humps on their backs, or with whiplike tails.

Family NOTODONTIDAE	Species *Cerura vinula*	Author Linnaeus

PUSS MOTH

The white forewings of this distinctive species are patterned with grayish black zigzag lines. The hindwings lack markings but are heavily suffused with gray and have dark veins. The sexes are alike. These moths are on the wing in spring and summer.
• **EARLY STAGES** The striking caterpillar is bright green with a purple, saddle-shaped marking in the middle of the back and two long tails at the rear end. When the caterpillar is disturbed, these tails are thrust forward over the head and emit slender, whiplike, pink filaments. The caterpillar can also squirt formic acid from a gland in the throat. It feeds on willow *(Salix)*, and poplar *(Populus)*.
• **DISTRIBUTION** Widespread in Europe, ranging to North Africa, and across temperate Asia to Japan.

caterpillar in "threat" posture

CATERPILLAR OF
CERURA VINULA

short, white, robust antennae

dark band near base of forewing

slightly angled forewing margin

♀

distinctive pattern on furry body

long, white scales are present on wing bases

PALEARCTIC

Time of Flight ☾	Habitat ⚘	Wingspan 2½–3¼ in (6–8 cm)

Family NOTODONTIDAE	Species *Chliara cresus*	Author Cramer

CROESUS PROMINENT

The family Notodontidae is richly represented in South America, but very little is known about the individual species. This beautiful moth belongs to a genus of about ten described species, most of them with metallic markings on the forewing. The forewings of the Croesus prominent are patterned with a network of dark brown lines and suffused with a scattering of golden brown scales – hence the common name, which refers to the wealthy King Croesus of antiquity. The striking, silver spots are grouped in the center of the wing and at the base.
• **EARLY STAGES** The caterpillar of this species has not been described and its foodplants are unknown.
• **DISTRIBUTION** Occurs throughout tropical South and Central America.

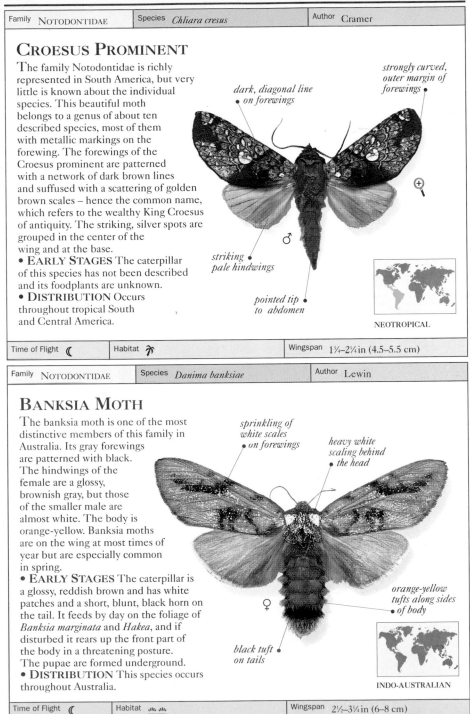

dark, diagonal line on forewings

strongly curved, outer margin of forewings

♂

striking pale hindwings

pointed tip to abdomen

NEOTROPICAL

Time of Flight ☾	Habitat 🜨	Wingspan 1¾–2¼ in (4.5–5.5 cm)

Family NOTODONTIDAE	Species *Danima banksiae*	Author Lewin

BANKSIA MOTH

The banksia moth is one of the most distinctive members of this family in Australia. Its gray forewings are patterned with black. The hindwings of the female are a glossy, brownish gray, but those of the smaller male are almost white. The body is orange-yellow. Banksia moths are on the wing at most times of year but are especially common in spring.
• **EARLY STAGES** The caterpillar is a glossy, reddish brown and has white patches and a short, blunt, black horn on the tail. It feeds by day on the foliage of *Banksia marginata* and *Hakea*, and if disturbed it rears up the front part of the body in a threatening posture. The pupae are formed underground.
• **DISTRIBUTION** This species occurs throughout Australia.

sprinkling of white scales on forewings

heavy white scaling behind the head

♀

orange-yellow tufts along sides of body

black tuft on tails

INDO-AUSTRALIAN

Time of Flight ☾	Habitat	Wingspan 2½–3¼ in (6–8 cm)

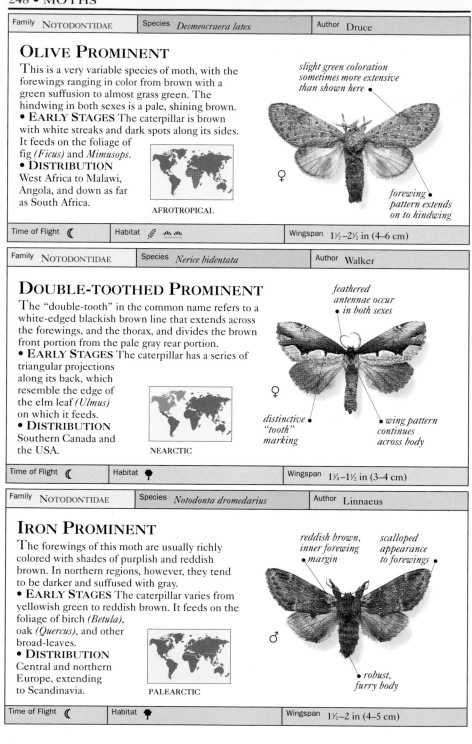

Family NOTODONTIDAE	Species *Desmeocraera latex*	Author Druce

OLIVE PROMINENT

This is a very variable species of moth, with the forewings ranging in color from brown with a green suffusion to almost grass green. The hindwing in both sexes is a pale, shining brown.
• **EARLY STAGES** The caterpillar is brown with white streaks and dark spots along its sides. It feeds on the foliage of fig *(Ficus)* and *Mimusops*.
• **DISTRIBUTION** West Africa to Malawi, Angola, and down as far as South Africa.

AFROTROPICAL

slight green coloration sometimes more extensive than shown here

♀

forewing pattern extends on to hindwing

Time of Flight ☾	Habitat	Wingspan 1½–2½ in (4–6 cm)

Family NOTODONTIDAE	Species *Nerice bidentata*	Author Walker

DOUBLE-TOOTHED PROMINENT

The "double-tooth" in the common name refers to a white-edged blackish brown line that extends across the forewings, and the thorax, and divides the brown front portion from the pale gray rear portion.
• **EARLY STAGES** The caterpillar has a series of triangular projections along its back, which resemble the edge of the elm leaf *(Ulmus)* on which it feeds.
• **DISTRIBUTION** Southern Canada and the USA.

NEARCTIC

feathered antennae occur in both sexes

♀

distinctive "tooth" marking

wing pattern continues across body

Time of Flight ☾	Habitat	Wingspan 1¼–1½ in (3–4 cm)

Family NOTODONTIDAE	Species *Notodonta dromedarius*	Author Linnaeus

IRON PROMINENT

The forewings of this moth are usually richly colored with shades of purplish and reddish brown. In northern regions, however, they tend to be darker and suffused with gray.
• **EARLY STAGES** The caterpillar varies from yellowish green to reddish brown. It feeds on the foliage of birch *(Betula)*, oak *(Quercus)*, and other broad-leaves.
• **DISTRIBUTION** Central and northern Europe, extending to Scandinavia.

PALEARCTIC

reddish brown, inner forewing margin

scalloped appearance to forewings

♂

robust, furry body

Time of Flight ☾	Habitat	Wingspan 1½–2 in (4–5 cm)

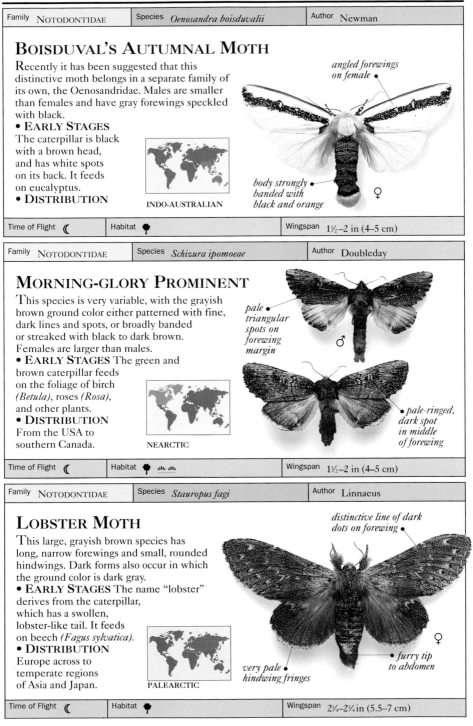

Family NOTODONTIDAE	Species *Oenosandra boisduvalii*	Author Newman

BOISDUVAL'S AUTUMNAL MOTH

Recently it has been suggested that this distinctive moth belongs in a separate family of its own, the Oenosandridae. Males are smaller than females and have gray forewings speckled with black.
• **EARLY STAGES**
The caterpillar is black with a brown head, and has white spots on its back. It feeds on eucalyptus.
• **DISTRIBUTION**

INDO-AUSTRALIAN

angled forewings on female

body strongly banded with black and orange

♀

Time of Flight ☾	Habitat ⬥	Wingspan 1½–2 in (4–5 cm)

Family NOTODONTIDAE	Species *Schizura ipomoeae*	Author Doubleday

MORNING-GLORY PROMINENT

This species is very variable, with the grayish brown ground color either patterned with fine, dark lines and spots, or broadly banded or streaked with black to dark brown. Females are larger than males.
• **EARLY STAGES** The green and brown caterpillar feeds on the foliage of birch *(Betula)*, roses *(Rosa)*, and other plants.
• **DISTRIBUTION**
From the USA to southern Canada.

NEARCTIC

pale triangular spots on forewing margin

♂

pale-ringed, dark spot in middle of forewing

Time of Flight ☾	Habitat ⬥ ⬖ ⬖	Wingspan 1½–2 in (4–5 cm)

Family NOTODONTIDAE	Species *Stauropus fagi*	Author Linnaeus

LOBSTER MOTH

This large, grayish brown species has long, narrow forewings and small, rounded hindwings. Dark forms also occur in which the ground color is dark gray.
• **EARLY STAGES** The name "lobster" derives from the caterpillar, which has a swollen, lobster-like tail. It feeds on beech *(Fagus sylvatica)*.
• **DISTRIBUTION**
Europe across to temperate regions of Asia and Japan.

PALEARCTIC

distinctive line of dark dots on forewing

♀

very pale hindwing fringes

furry tip to abdomen

Time of Flight ☾	Habitat ⬥	Wingspan 2¼–2¾ in (5.5–7 cm)

| Family NOTODONTIDAE | Species *Clostera albosigma* | Author Fitch |

SIGMOID PROMINENT

The pale brown forewings of this moth are patterned with light and dark lines and tipped with dark chocolate-brown. The common name derives from the white, sigma-shaped marking on the forewing.
• **EARLY STAGES** The caterpillar is black, covered with fine white hairs, and has four orange-yellow lines along the back. It feeds on poplar *(Populus).*
• **DISTRIBUTION** Found in southern Canada and the USA.

NEARCTIC

distinctively shaped, dark tip to forewings

slightly concave leading edge to forewings

♂

pale hindwings with no patterning

| Time of Flight ☾ | Habitat 🌳 ⚘ ⚘ | Wingspan 1¼–1½ in (3–4 cm) |

| Family NOTODONTIDAE | Species *Datana ministra* | Author Drury |

YELLOW-NECKED CATERPILLAR MOTH

This fairly large prominent belongs to a group of similar species called handmaid moths. It can be distinguished from other similar species by the distinctively scalloped outer margin, shaded with black, that gives it an almost scorched appearance.
• **EARLY STAGES** The caterpillar is striped black and yellow. It feeds on the foliage of many broad-leaved trees, including apple *(Malus domestica).*
• **DISTRIBUTION** Common in southern Canada and USA.

NEARCTIC

slightly darker central band to forewings

♀

darker tip to body

distinctive scalloped forewing margins

| Time of Flight ☾ | Habitat 🌱 🌳 | Wingspan 1½–2 in (4–5 cm) |

| Family NOTODONTIDAE | Species *Phalera bucephala* | Author Linnaeus |

BUFF-TIP

The buff-tip is a very distinctive species with its purplish gray forewings suffused with light silvery gray and lined with black and brown. The common name derives from the forewing that camouflages the moth when it rests.
• **EARLY STAGES** The caterpillar is orange-yellow with black bands. It feeds on the foliage of various broad-leaved trees and shrubs.
• **DISTRIBUTION** Widespread in Europe, and eastward to Siberia.

PALEARCTIC

buff patch resembles end of a twig

♀

pale hindwings are concealed when moth is at rest

scalloped pattern along forewing margins

| Time of Flight ☾ | Habitat 🌳 | Wingspan 2¼–2¾ in (5.5–7 cm) |

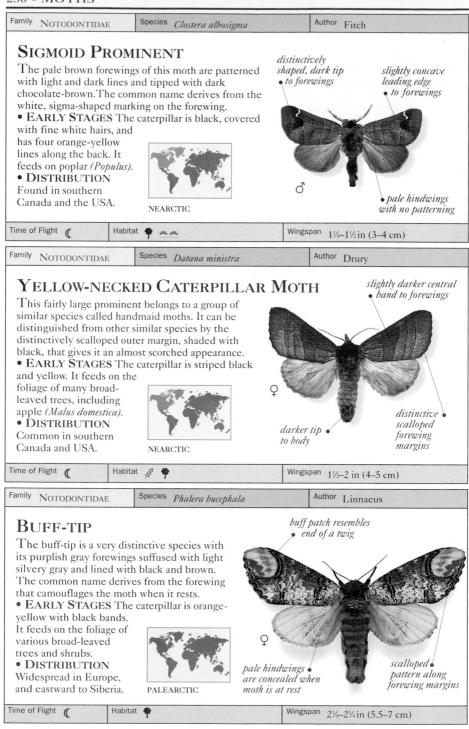

Family NOTODONTIDAE	Species *Anaphe panda*	Author Boisduval

BANDED BAGNEST

The white forewings of this striking moth are strongly patterned with dark chocolate-brown; the white hindwings lack markings. The sexes are similar.
• **EARLY STAGES** The hairy caterpillar is an off-white color. It feeds on the foliage of *Diplorhynchus* and *Bridelia*.
• **DISTRIBUTION** West Africa through to Kenya, Mozambique, and South Africa.

AFROTROPICAL

black, feathered antennae

♀

tuft carries irritant hairs

Time of Flight ☾	Habitat	Wingspan 1½–2¼ in (4–5.5 cm)

Family NOTODONTIDAE	Species *Epicoma melanosticta*	Author Donovan

COMMON EPICOMA MOTH

This beautiful species has white forewings speckled with black scaling and margined with a checkered pattern of black and yellow. The hindwings are blackish and richly margined with a golden, yellow, toothed pattern.
• **EARLY STAGES** The caterpillar is dark brown in color and has tufts of short, brown hairs. It tends to feed on the foliage of eucalyptus.
• **DISTRIBUTION** Widespread in eastern and southern Australia.

INDO-AUSTRALIAN

very hairy thorax is characteristic of this species

yellow hindwing margins

♂

bright yellow tail-fans

Time of Flight ☾	Habitat	Wingspan 1½–2 in (4–5 cm)

Family NOTODONTIDAE	Species *Thaumetopoea pityocampa*	Author Denis & Schiffermüller

PINE PROCESSIONARY MOTH

This is a rather drab species with grayish white forewings banded with dark, grayish brown.
• **EARLY STAGES** The grayish black caterpillar is covered with fine, white hairs along the sides, and has reddish brown warts. Caterpillars move in a head-to-tail procession in search of pine needles on which they feed. They can cause damage to forest plantations.
• **DISTRIBUTION** Found in Mediterranean countries, including those of North Africa.

PALEARCTIC

darker brown leading edge to forewings

black spot on hindwings is present in both sexes

♀

broken, dark line along margin of forewings

Time of Flight ☾	Habitat	Wingspan 1½–2 in (4–5 cm)

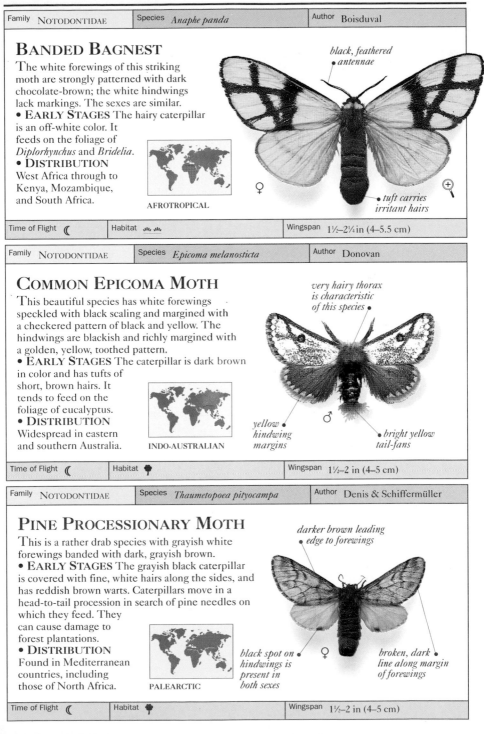

NOCTUIDAE

T HIS IS THE LARGEST and most important moth family, with more than 25,000 species occurring worldwide. Noctuid moths are quite robust, and range in size from extremely small to very large. Most are nocturnal and for this reason are often known as owlet moths. The majority of the species are drab in color, ranging from brown to gray, but others are quite bright and may even mimic butterflies. This family contains two important groups of caterpillars that are notorious pests: cutworms that bite through plant stems at ground level; and armyworms that swarm in bands and can devastate entire crops. The pupae of many species of Noctuid moths are formed in the soil at the base of the foodplant.

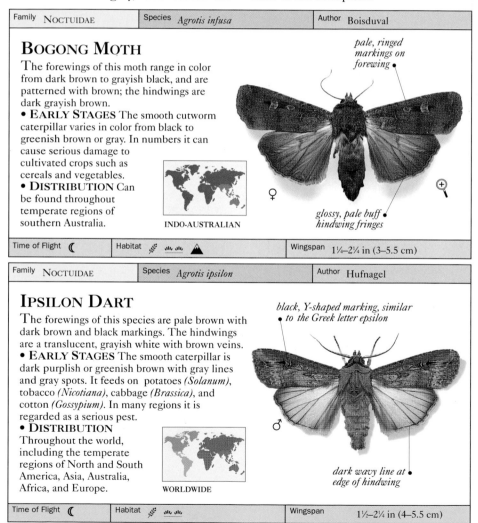

Family NOCTUIDAE	Species *Agrotis infusa*	Author Boisduval

BOGONG MOTH

The forewings of this moth range in color from dark brown to grayish black, and are patterned with brown; the hindwings are dark grayish brown.
• **EARLY STAGES** The smooth cutworm caterpillar varies in color from black to greenish brown or gray. In numbers it can cause serious damage to cultivated crops such as cereals and vegetables.
• **DISTRIBUTION** Can be found throughout temperate regions of southern Australia.

INDO-AUSTRALIAN

pale, ringed markings on forewing

♀

glossy, pale buff hindwing fringes

Time of Flight ☾	Habitat	Wingspan 1¼–2¼ in (3–5.5 cm)

Family NOCTUIDAE	Species *Agrotis ipsilon*	Author Hufnagel

IPSILON DART

The forewings of this species are pale brown with dark brown and black markings. The hindwings are a translucent, grayish white with brown veins.
• **EARLY STAGES** The smooth caterpillar is dark purplish or greenish brown with gray lines and gray spots. It feeds on potatoes *(Solanum)*, tobacco *(Nicotiana)*, cabbage *(Brassica)*, and cotton *(Gossypium)*. In many regions it is regarded as a serious pest.
• **DISTRIBUTION** Throughout the world, including the temperate regions of North and South America, Asia, Australia, Africa, and Europe.

WORLDWIDE

black, Y-shaped marking, similar to the Greek letter epsilon

♂

dark wavy line at edge of hindwing

Time of Flight ☾	Habitat	Wingspan 1½–2¼ in (4–5.5 cm)

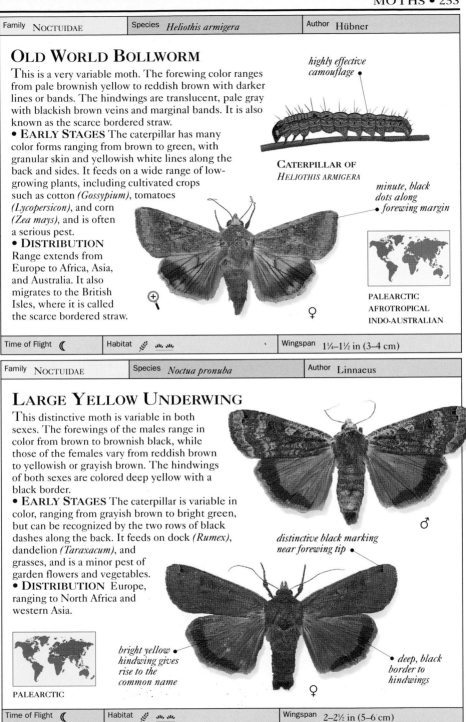

| Family | NOCTUIDAE | Species | *Heliothis armigera* | Author | Hübner |

OLD WORLD BOLLWORM

This is a very variable moth. The forewing color ranges from pale brownish yellow to reddish brown with darker lines or bands. The hindwings are translucent, pale gray with blackish brown veins and marginal bands. It is also known as the scarce bordered straw.

• **EARLY STAGES** The caterpillar has many color forms ranging from brown to green, with granular skin and yellowish white lines along the back and sides. It feeds on a wide range of low-growing plants, including cultivated crops such as cotton *(Gossypium)*, tomatoes *(Lycopersicon)*, and corn *(Zea mays)*, and is often a serious pest.

• **DISTRIBUTION** Range extends from Europe to Africa, Asia, and Australia. It also migrates to the British Isles, where it is called the scarce bordered straw.

highly effective camouflage

CATERPILLAR OF
HELIOTHIS ARMIGERA

minute, black dots along forewing margin

PALEARCTIC
AFROTROPICAL
INDO-AUSTRALIAN

| Time of Flight | ☾ | Habitat | | | Wingspan | 1¼–1½ in (3–4 cm) |

| Family | NOCTUIDAE | Species | *Noctua pronuba* | Author | Linnaeus |

LARGE YELLOW UNDERWING

This distinctive moth is variable in both sexes. The forewings of the males range in color from brown to brownish black, while those of the females vary from reddish brown to yellowish or grayish brown. The hindwings of both sexes are colored deep yellow with a black border.

• **EARLY STAGES** The caterpillar is variable in color, ranging from grayish brown to bright green, but can be recognized by the two rows of black dashes along the back. It feeds on dock *(Rumex)*, dandelion *(Taraxacum)*, and grasses, and is a minor pest of garden flowers and vegetables.

• **DISTRIBUTION** Europe, ranging to North Africa and western Asia.

distinctive black marking near forewing tip

bright yellow hindwing gives rise to the common name

deep, black border to hindwings

PALEARCTIC

| Time of Flight | ☾ | Habitat | | | Wingspan | 2–2½ in (5–6 cm) |

Family NOCTUIDAE	Species *Peridroma saucia*	Author Hübner

VARIEGATED CUTWORM MOTH

This notorious pest has reddish brown or grayish
brown forewings, variably patterned with blackish
brown. The hindwings are pearly gray, with brown
veins and a dark brown suffusion toward the margins.
• **EARLY STAGES** The plump caterpillar is
colored grayish brown
tinged with purplish red
on its back.
• **DISTRIBUTION** Europe
to Turkey, India, North
Africa, and the Canary
Islands, and North America.

HOLARCTIC

slightly scalloped forewing margin

dark, kidney-shaped mark on forewing

pale hindwing fringes

♂

Time of Flight ☾	Habitat	Wingspan 1½–2¼ in (4–5.5 cm)

Family NOCTUIDAE	Species *Cerapteryx graminis*	Author Linnaeus

ANTLER MOTH

This distinctive species gets its name from the antler-
shaped yellowish white markings on the brown
forewings. These markings are variable and are
often interspersed with dark brown streaks. It is
attracted to thistles *(Cirsium)* and other flowers.
• **EARLY STAGES** The caterpillar is bronze,
with three pale brown
stripes and a wrinkled,
glossy skin. It feeds on
various grasses.
• **DISTRIBUTION** Europe
across temperate Asia to
Siberia, and North America.

PALEARCTIC

blackish brown streaks along forewing margin

♂

pale fringes to hindwings

Time of Flight ☾ ☼	Habitat	Wingspan 1–1¼ in (2.5–3 cm)

Family NOCTUIDAE	Species *Mamestra brassicae*	Author Linnaeus

CABBAGE MOTH

The forewing of this dark brown mottled moth
is distinctively marked with shining white spots
and lines. The hindwing is dark grayish brown,
becoming paler toward the base.
• **EARLY STAGES** The caterpillar is green when
young, but in the final stage it is brown with a broad
orange band along each side.
As its name suggests, this
species feeds on cabbage
(Brassica), as well as
various other plants.
• **DISTRIBUTION** Europe
and Asia, from India to Japan.

PALEARCTIC

white, marginal line

kidney-shaped mark on forewing

pale line around hindwing margin

♀

Time of Flight ☾	Habitat	Wingspan 1¼–2 in (3–5 cm)

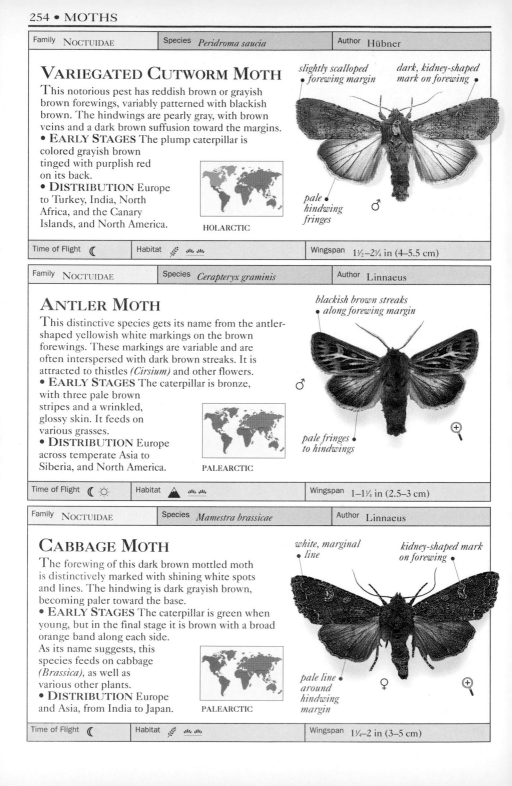

Family NOCTUIDAE	Species *Mythimna unipuncta*	Author Haworth

WHITESPECK

This distinctive cinnamon brown moth has a small, white spot in the middle of the forewings, which are often speckled with black and sometimes tinged with orange. The brown-veined hindwings are a glossy translucent gray suffused with dark brown.
• **EARLY STAGES** The caterpillar is grayish brown and has an orange band along the sides. It feeds on grasses.
• **DISTRIBUTION** North and South America, Mediterranean Europe, and parts of Africa.

HOLARCTIC

short, dark, diagonal streak at wingtip

silvery white fringes on hindwing

Time of Flight ☾	Habitat	Wingspan 1¼–1½ in (3–4 cm)

Family NOCTUIDAE	Species *Xanthopastis timais*	Author Cramer

SPANISH MOTH

With its pink forewings marked with black and orange, this species is unmistakable. Despite its bright colors, however this moth is well camouflaged when it rests on tree trunks with folded wings.
• **EARLY STAGES** The caterpillar is grayish black spotted with white. It feeds on the foliage of fig *(Ficus)* and narcissi *(Narcissus)*.
• **DISTRIBUTION** Tropical South and Central America, into the USA.

NEOTROPICAL
NEARCTIC

black double "boomerang" markings on forewing

furry black body

black forewing fringes

Time of Flight ☾	Habitat	Wingspan 1½–1¾ in (4–4.5 cm)

Family NOCTUIDAE	Species *Cucullia convexipennis*	Author Grote & Robinson

BROWN HOODED OWLET

This moth belongs to a large and distinctive group known collectively as the sharks, presumably because of the streamlined appearance of their folded wings when they are at rest.
• **EARLY STAGES** The caterpillar is striped with red and black. It feeds on the flowers of aster, goldenrod *(Solidago virgaurea)*, and various other low-growing plants.
• **DISTRIBUTION** Widespread in the USA, extending northward into southern Canada.

NEARCTIC

dark streak on forewing

raised tufts along back of body

pale marginal line on both fore- and hindwing

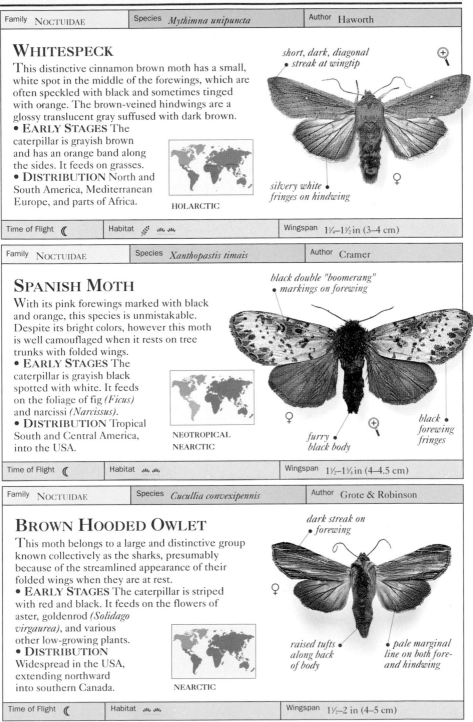

Time of Flight ☾	Habitat	Wingspan 1½–2 in (4–5 cm)

Family NOCTUIDAE	Species *Xanthia togata*	Author Esper

PINK-BARRED SALLOW

The common name of this brightly colored moth is misleading as it is not pink-barred at all. Its forewings are yellow to orange-yellow, with a broad red or purple band. The sexes are alike.
• **EARLY STAGES** The caterpillar is reddish or purplish brown with dark speckling. It feeds on willow catkins *(Salix)* and low plants.
• **DISTRIBUTION** Occurs from Europe to temperate Asia; also in southern Canada and the northern USA.

HOLARCTIC

sharply pointed forewing tips

reddish brown head and front of thorax

♂

pale yellowish hindwings

Time of Flight ☾	Habitat	Wingspan 1¼–1½ in (3–4 cm)

Family NOCTUIDAE	Species *Acronicta psi*	Author Linnaeus

GRAY DAGGER

The forewings of this moth vary in color from grayish white to dark gray, but they all have the distinctive dagger-shaped marking on the margin that gives rise to the common name. The sexes are similar, but females have darker hindwings.
• **EARLY STAGES** The caterpillar is dark bluish gray with a broad band of yellow along the back and red spots along the sides. It feeds on deciduous trees.
• **DISTRIBUTION** Occurs in Europe, through to North Africa, and Central Asia.

PALEARCTIC

fine, black, irregular line on inner margin of forewings

♂

broken, black line along margin of hindwings

Time of Flight ☾	Habitat	Wingspan 1¼–1¾ in (3–4.5 cm)

Family NOCTUIDAE	Species *Amphipyra pyramidoides*	Author Guenée

AMERICAN COPPER UNDERWING

This attractive moth is easily recognized by its coppery brown hindwings. The dark brown forewings are variably patterned with light and dark lines. The sexes are similar.
• **EARLY STAGES** The green caterpillar feeds on a wide range of broadleaved trees and shrubs, including apple *(Malus domestica)* and species of hawthorn *(Crataegus)*.
• **DISTRIBUTION** Widespread from southern Canada through the USA south to Mexico.

NEARCTIC

white rings in center of forewings

♂

finely scalloped, pale, marginal lines on hindwings

Time of Flight ☾	Habitat	Wingspan 1½–2 in (4–5 cm)

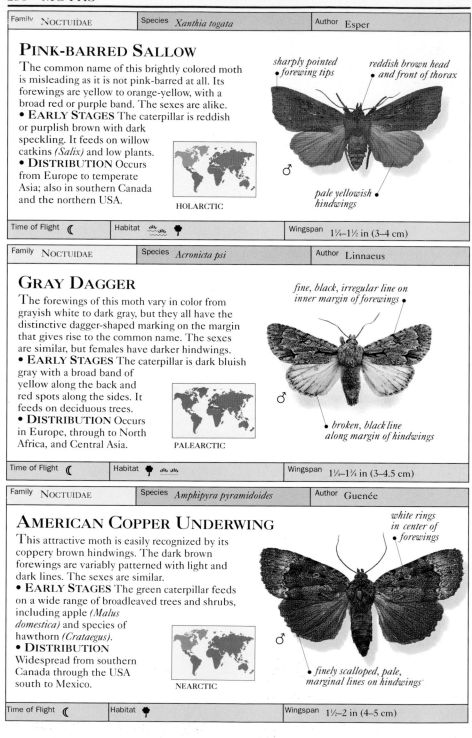

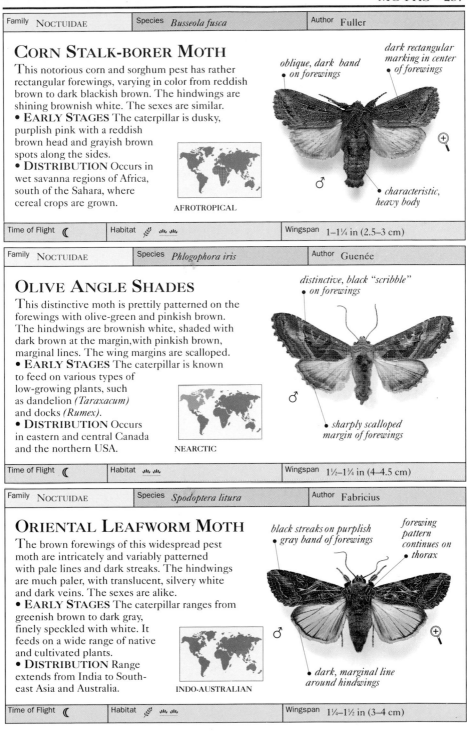

| Family NOCTUIDAE | Species *Busseola fusca* | Author Fuller |

CORN STALK-BORER MOTH

This notorious corn and sorghum pest has rather rectangular forewings, varying in color from reddish brown to dark blackish brown. The hindwings are shining brownish white. The sexes are similar.
• **EARLY STAGES** The caterpillar is dusky, purplish pink with a reddish brown head and grayish brown spots along the sides.
• **DISTRIBUTION** Occurs in wet savanna regions of Africa, south of the Sahara, where cereal crops are grown.

oblique, dark band on forewings

dark rectangular marking in center of forewings

♂

characteristic, heavy body

AFROTROPICAL

| Time of Flight ☾ | Habitat | Wingspan 1–1¼ in (2.5–3 cm) |

| Family NOCTUIDAE | Species *Phlogophora iris* | Author Guenée |

OLIVE ANGLE SHADES

This distinctive moth is prettily patterned on the forewings with olive-green and pinkish brown. The hindwings are brownish white, shaded with dark brown at the margin, with pinkish brown, marginal lines. The wing margins are scalloped.
• **EARLY STAGES** The caterpillar is known to feed on various types of low-growing plants, such as dandelion *(Taraxacum)* and docks *(Rumex)*.
• **DISTRIBUTION** Occurs in eastern and central Canada and the northern USA.

distinctive, black "scribble" on forewings

♂

sharply scalloped margin of forewings

NEARCTIC

| Time of Flight ☾ | Habitat | Wingspan 1½–1¾ in (4–4.5 cm) |

| Family NOCTUIDAE | Species *Spodoptera litura* | Author Fabricius |

ORIENTAL LEAFWORM MOTH

The brown forewings of this widespread pest moth are intricately and variably patterned with pale lines and dark streaks. The hindwings are much paler, with translucent, silvery white and dark veins. The sexes are alike.
• **EARLY STAGES** The caterpillar ranges from greenish brown to dark gray, finely speckled with white. It feeds on a wide range of native and cultivated plants.
• **DISTRIBUTION** Range extends from India to Southeast Asia and Australia.

black streaks on purplish gray band of forewings

forewing pattern continues on thorax

♂

dark, marginal line around hindwings

INDO-AUSTRALIAN

| Time of Flight ☾ | Habitat | Wingspan 1¼–1½ in (3–4 cm) |

| Family NOCTUIDAE | Species *Spodoptera exigua* | Author Hübner |

SMALL MOTTLED WILLOW MOTH

This grayish brown, mottled moth is a notorious pest species in many parts of the world. It has translucent, pearly white hindwings with dark brown veins.
• **EARLY STAGES** The caterpillar varies in color from green to dark gray, with black markings on the back and a pinkish brown line along the sides. It feeds on crops such as corn *(Zea mays)* and cotton *(Gossypium)*.
• **DISTRIBUTION** Virtually throughout the world, in both tropical and temperate regions.

gray dots along forewing border

♂

dark brown outline to translucent hindwing

WORLDWIDE

| Time of Flight ☾ | Habitat | Wingspan 1–1¼ in (2.5–3 cm) |

| Family NOCTUIDAE | Species *Syntheta nigerrima* | Author Guenée |

BLACK TURNIP MOTH

One of two species in an exclusively Australian genus, this is a very dark moth with black forewings patterned with intense jet black.
• **EARLY STAGES** The green caterpillar has two white spots on the back near the tail. It feeds on a range of wild and cultivated plants, and is sometimes a serious pest of such field crops as turnip *(Brassica)*, sugar beet *(Beta vulgaris)*, and corn *(Zea mays)*.
• **DISTRIBUTION** From southern Queensland to south-western Australia and Tasmania.

front part of body thickly scaled to match black forewings

♀

white base to hindwings

lightly scalloped wing margins

INDO-AUSTRALIAN

| Time of Flight ☾ | Habitat | Wingspan 1½–1¾ in (4–4.5 cm) |

| Family NOCTUIDAE | Species *Earias biplaga* | Author Walker |

SPINY BOLLWORM MOTH

This pretty little moth is one of a group of species that are major pests of cultivated cotton in Africa and Asia. This species is very variable, ranging in forewing color from moss-green to greenish yellow, and is sometimes strongly suffused with purplish red.
• **EARLY STAGES** The small, grayish brown caterpillar is finely banded with white and spotted with red, and has spines along the back and sides. It feeds on cotton *(Gossypium)* and related plants.
• **DISTRIBUTION** Widespread in Africa, south of the Sahara.

distinctive squarish forewings

dark purplish patch on forewings

♀

⊕

characteristic dark fringes on hindwings

AFROTROPICAL

| Time of Flight ☾ | Habitat | Wingspan ¾–1 in (2–2.5 cm) |

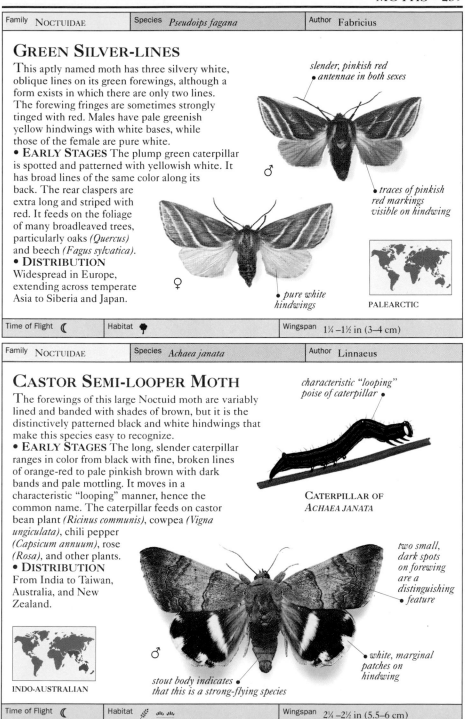

| Family | NOCTUIDAE | Species | *Pseudoips fagana* | Author | Fabricius |

GREEN SILVER-LINES

This aptly named moth has three silvery white, oblique lines on its green forewings, although a form exists in which there are only two lines. The forewing fringes are sometimes strongly tinged with red. Males have pale greenish yellow hindwings with white bases, while those of the female are pure white.
• **EARLY STAGES** The plump green caterpillar is spotted and patterned with yellowish white. It has broad lines of the same color along its back. The rear claspers are extra long and striped with red. It feeds on the foliage of many broadleaved trees, particularly oaks *(Quercus)* and beech *(Fagus sylvatica)*.
• **DISTRIBUTION** Widespread in Europe, extending across temperate Asia to Siberia and Japan.

slender, pinkish red antennae in both sexes

♂

traces of pinkish red markings visible on hindwing

♀

pure white hindwings

PALEARCTIC

| Time of Flight ☾ | Habitat 🌳 | Wingspan 1¼ –1½ in (3–4 cm) |

| Family | NOCTUIDAE | Species | *Achaea janata* | Author | Linnaeus |

CASTOR SEMI-LOOPER MOTH

The forewings of this large Noctuid moth are variably lined and banded with shades of brown, but it is the distinctively patterned black and white hindwings that make this species easy to recognize.
• **EARLY STAGES** The long, slender caterpillar ranges in color from black with fine, broken lines of orange-red to pale pinkish brown with dark bands and pale mottling. It moves in a characteristic "looping" manner, hence the common name. The caterpillar feeds on castor bean plant *(Ricinus communis)*, cowpea *(Vigna ungiculata)*, chili pepper *(Capsicum annuum)*, rose *(Rosa)*, and other plants.
• **DISTRIBUTION** From India to Taiwan, Australia, and New Zealand.

characteristic "looping" poise of caterpillar

CATERPILLAR OF
ACHAEA JANATA

two small, dark spots on forewing are a distinguishing feature

♂

white, marginal patches on hindwing

stout body indicates that this is a strong-flying species

INDO-AUSTRALIAN

| Time of Flight ☾ | Habitat | Wingspan 2¼ –2½ in (5.5–6 cm) |

| Family NOCTUIDAE | Species *Catocala fraxini* | Author Linnaeus |

CLIFDEN NONPAREIL

The forewings of this handsome species have a camouflage pattern of grayish white and dark grayish brown. The hindwings are blackish brown with a distinctive band of dusky blue. The sexes are similar.

• **EARLY STAGES** The long caterpillar is gray, mottled with brown. It is well camouflaged when it rests on a twig. It feeds primarily on ash *(Fraxinus excelsior)*, and aspen *(Populus tremula)*.

• **DISTRIBUTION** Widespread in central and northern Europe. Formerly resident in the British Isles, it now occurs there only as an occasional migrant. Ranges across temperate Asia to Japan.

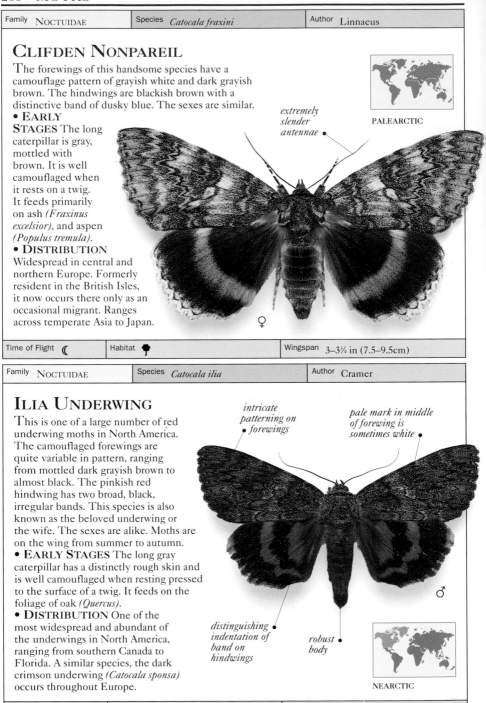

extremely slender antennae

PALEARCTIC

♀

| Time of Flight ☾ | Habitat | Wingspan 3–3¾ in (7.5–9.5cm) |

| Family NOCTUIDAE | Species *Catocala ilia* | Author Cramer |

ILIA UNDERWING

This is one of a large number of red underwing moths in North America. The camouflaged forewings are quite variable in pattern, ranging from mottled dark grayish brown to almost black. The pinkish red hindwing has two broad, black, irregular bands. This species is also known as the beloved underwing or the wife. The sexes are alike. Moths are on the wing from summer to autumn.

• **EARLY STAGES** The long gray caterpillar has a distinctly rough skin and is well camouflaged when resting pressed to the surface of a twig. It feeds on the foliage of oak *(Quercus)*.

• **DISTRIBUTION** One of the most widespread and abundant of the underwings in North America, ranging from southern Canada to Florida. A similar species, the dark crimson underwing *(Catocala sponsa)* occurs throughout Europe.

intricate patterning on forewings

pale mark in middle of forewing is sometimes white

distinguishing indentation of band on hindwings

robust body

♂

NEARCTIC

| Time of Flight ☾ | Habitat | Wingspan 2¾–3¼ in (7–8 cm) |

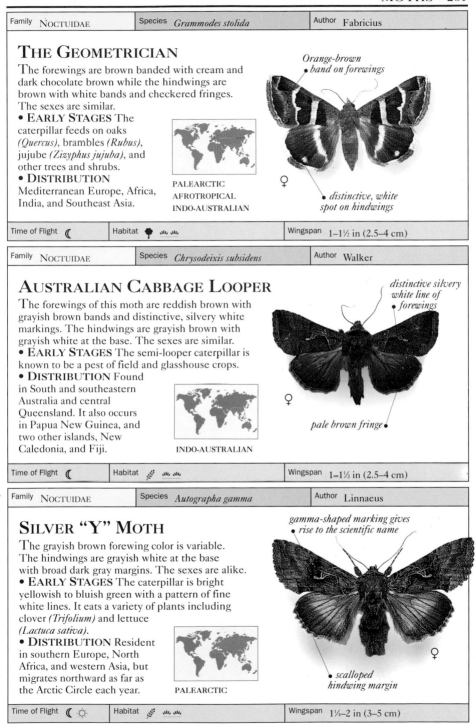

Family NOCTUIDAE	Species *Grammodes stolida*	Author Fabricius

THE GEOMETRICIAN

The forewings are brown banded with cream and
dark chocolate brown while the hindwings are
brown with white bands and checkered fringes.
The sexes are similar.
- **EARLY STAGES** The
caterpillar feeds on oaks
(Quercus), brambles *(Rubus)*,
jujube *(Zizyphus jujuba)*, and
other trees and shrubs.
- **DISTRIBUTION**
Mediterranean Europe, Africa,
India, and Southeast Asia.

PALEARCTIC
AFROTROPICAL
INDO-AUSTRALIAN

Orange-brown
• band on forewings

♀

• distinctive, white
spot on hindwings

Time of Flight (	Habitat	Wingspan 1–1½ in (2.5–4 cm)

Family NOCTUIDAE	Species *Chrysodeixis subsidens*	Author Walker

AUSTRALIAN CABBAGE LOOPER

The forewings of this moth are reddish brown with
grayish brown bands and distinctive, silvery white
markings. The hindwings are grayish brown with
grayish white at the base. The sexes are similar.
- **EARLY STAGES** The semi-looper caterpillar is
known to be a pest of field and glasshouse crops.
- **DISTRIBUTION** Found
in South and southeastern
Australia and central
Queensland. It also occurs
in Papua New Guinea, and
two other islands, New
Caledonia, and Fiji.

INDO-AUSTRALIAN

distinctive silvery
white line of
• forewings

♀

pale brown fringe •

Time of Flight (	Habitat	Wingspan 1–1½ in (2.5–4 cm)

Family NOCTUIDAE	Species *Autographa gamma*	Author Linnaeus

SILVER "Y" MOTH

The grayish brown forewing color is variable.
The hindwings are grayish white at the base
with broad dark gray margins. The sexes are alike.
- **EARLY STAGES** The caterpillar is bright
yellowish to bluish green with a pattern of fine
white lines. It eats a variety of plants including
clover *(Trifolium)* and lettuce
(Lactuca sativa).
- **DISTRIBUTION** Resident
in southern Europe, North
Africa, and western Asia, but
migrates northward as far as
the Arctic Circle each year.

PALEARCTIC

gamma-shaped marking gives
• *rise to the scientific name*

♀

• *scalloped
hindwing margin*

Time of Flight (☼	Habitat	Wingspan 1¼–2 in (3–5 cm)

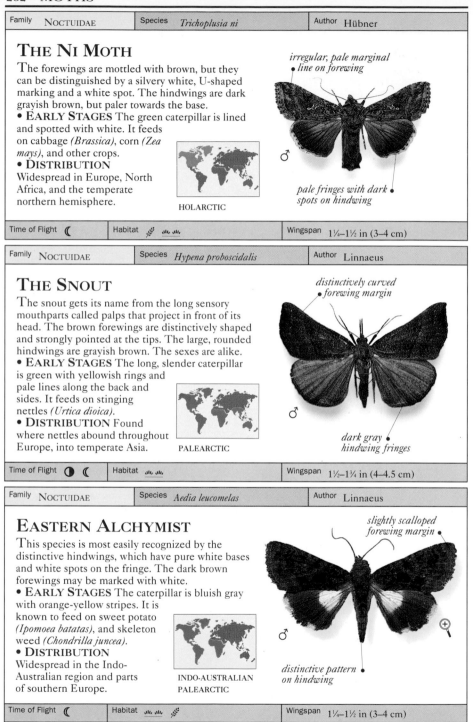

Family NOCTUIDAE	Species *Trichoplusia ni*	Author Hübner

THE NI MOTH

The forewings are mottled with brown, but they can be distinguished by a silvery white, U-shaped marking and a white spot. The hindwings are dark grayish brown, but paler towards the base.
• **EARLY STAGES** The green caterpillar is lined and spotted with white. It feeds on cabbage *(Brassica)*, corn *(Zea mays)*, and other crops.
• **DISTRIBUTION** Widespread in Europe, North Africa, and the temperate northern hemisphere.

irregular, pale marginal line on forewing

pale fringes with dark spots on hindwing

HOLARCTIC

Time of Flight ☾	Habitat	Wingspan 1¼–1½ in (3–4 cm)

Family NOCTUIDAE	Species *Hypena proboscidalis*	Author Linnaeus

THE SNOUT

The snout gets its name from the long sensory mouthparts called palps that project in front of its head. The brown forewings are distinctively shaped and strongly pointed at the tips. The large, rounded hindwings are grayish brown. The sexes are alike.
• **EARLY STAGES** The long, slender caterpillar is green with yellowish rings and pale lines along the back and sides. It feeds on stinging nettles *(Urtica dioica)*.
• **DISTRIBUTION** Found where nettles abound throughout Europe, into temperate Asia.

distinctively curved forewing margin

dark gray hindwing fringes

PALEARCTIC

Time of Flight ◐ ☾	Habitat	Wingspan 1½–1¾ in (4–4.5 cm)

Family NOCTUIDAE	Species *Aedia leucomelas*	Author Linnaeus

EASTERN ALCHYMIST

This species is most easily recognized by the distinctive hindwings, which have pure white bases and white spots on the fringe. The dark brown forewings may be marked with white.
• **EARLY STAGES** The caterpillar is bluish gray with orange-yellow stripes. It is known to feed on sweet potato *(Ipomoea batatas)*, and skeleton weed *(Chondrilla juncea)*.
• **DISTRIBUTION** Widespread in the Indo-Australian region and parts of southern Europe.

slightly scalloped forewing margin

distinctive pattern on hindwing

INDO-AUSTRALIAN PALEARCTIC

Time of Flight ☾	Habitat	Wingspan 1¼–1½ in (3–4 cm)

Family NOCTUIDAE	Species *Alabama argillacea*	Author Hübner

COTTON MOTH

The forewings of this moth vary from pinkish to olive-brown. The adults can pierce the skins of fruit with their tongues, causing damage.
• **EARLY STAGES** The caterpillar is yellowish green, marked with black, with white lines along the back. It feeds on cotton plants *(Gossypium)*, and is a serious pest of cultivated cotton in the USA.
• **DISTRIBUTION** Tropical South and Central America to the temperate USA and Canada.

NEOTROPICAL
NEARCTIC

pale-centered, dark oval marking in center of forewing

♂

ringed appearance to body

Time of Flight ☾	Habitat	Wingspan 1¼–1½ in (3–4 cm)

Family NOCTUIDAE	Species *Ascalapha odorata*	Author Linnaeus

BLACK WITCH

This large, dark brown moth has sharply pointed forewings and square hindwings. The forewings each have a dark, comma-shaped marking, while the hindwings have large and irregular-shaped eyespots. Black witches have hairy bodies. Females have a pale, purplish pink band crossing their fore- and hindwings.
• **EARLY STAGES** The caterpillar is dark brown, becoming lighter towards the tail. It feeds on *Cassia* and related plants.
• **DISTRIBUTION** Occurs in tropical South and Central America, also California and the southern parts of the USA.

NEOTROPICAL
NEARCTIC

distinctive comma-shaped marking bears metallic-blue scales

whitish suffusion to wing margins

wavy, dark line along wing margins

♂

toothed appearance of eyespot

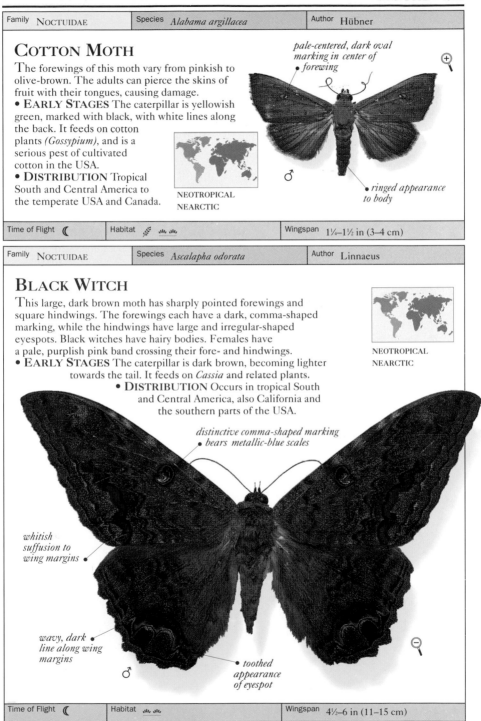

Time of Flight ☾	Habitat	Wingspan 4½–6 in (11–15 cm)

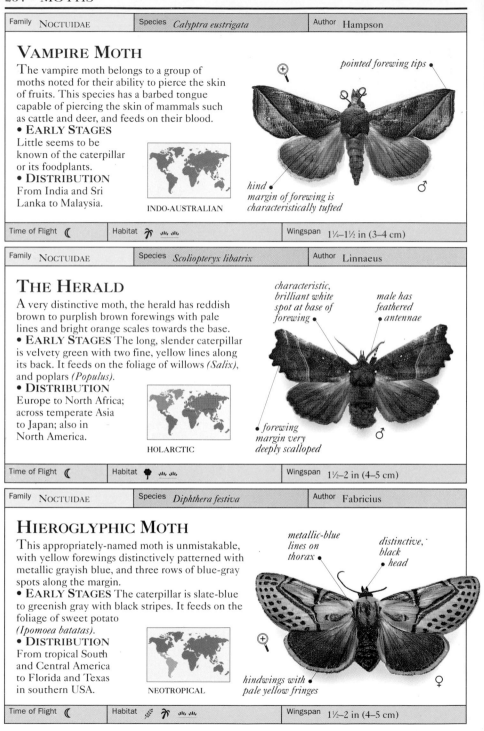

Family NOCTUIDAE	Species *Calyptra eustrigata*	Author Hampson

VAMPIRE MOTH

The vampire moth belongs to a group of moths noted for their ability to pierce the skin of fruits. This species has a barbed tongue capable of piercing the skin of mammals such as cattle and deer, and feeds on their blood.
• **EARLY STAGES** Little seems to be known of the caterpillar or its foodplants.
• **DISTRIBUTION** From India and Sri Lanka to Malaysia.

INDO-AUSTRALIAN

pointed forewing tips

hind margin of forewing is characteristically tufted

Time of Flight ☾	Habitat	Wingspan 1¼–1½ in (3–4 cm)

Family NOCTUIDAE	Species *Scoliopteryx libatrix*	Author Linnaeus

THE HERALD

A very distinctive moth, the herald has reddish brown to purplish brown forewings with pale lines and bright orange scales towards the base.
• **EARLY STAGES** The long, slender caterpillar is velvety green with two fine, yellow lines along its back. It feeds on the foliage of willows *(Salix)*, and poplars *(Populus)*.
• **DISTRIBUTION** Europe to North Africa; across temperate Asia to Japan; also in North America.

HOLARCTIC

characteristic, brilliant white spot at base of forewing

male has feathered antennae

forewing margin very deeply scalloped

Time of Flight ☾	Habitat	Wingspan 1½–2 in (4–5 cm)

Family NOCTUIDAE	Species *Diphthera festiva*	Author Fabricius

HIEROGLYPHIC MOTH

This appropriately-named moth is unmistakable, with yellow forewings distinctively patterned with metallic grayish blue, and three rows of blue-gray spots along the margin.
• **EARLY STAGES** The caterpillar is slate-blue to greenish gray with black stripes. It feeds on the foliage of sweet potato *(Ipomoea batatas)*.
• **DISTRIBUTION** From tropical South and Central America to Florida and Texas in southern USA.

NEOTROPICAL

metallic-blue lines on thorax

distinctive, black head

hindwings with pale yellow fringes

Time of Flight ☾	Habitat	Wingspan 1½–2 in (4–5 cm)

Family NOCTUIDAE	Species *Othreis fullonia*	Author Clerck

TROPICAL FRUIT-PIERCER

This is a very distinctive, large moth with orange or orange-yellow hindwings with black markings.
• **EARLY STAGES** The long caterpillar varies in color from green to black, and has well developed false eyespots on the body.
• **DISTRIBUTION** Tropical Africa, South-east Asia, to Australia.

AFROTROPICAL
INDO-AUSTRALIAN

whitish blue suffusion over forewings

pointed forewing tips

purple-brown forewings

distinctive, curved, black marking on hindwing

♀

tip of body tinged with orange

Time of Flight ☾	Habitat	Wingspan 3¼–4 in (8–10 cm)

Family NOCTUIDAE	Species *Thysania agrippina*	Author Cramer

GIANT AGRIPPA

The giant agrippa has the largest wingspan of any moth in the world. Both fore- and hindwings are grayish white with an intricate pattern of blackish brown lines.
• **EARLY STAGES** The caterpillar is undescribed but feeds on Leguminosae shrubs.
• **DISTRIBUTION** Southern Brazil through Central America.

NEOTROPICAL

zigzag pattern on forewings

very slender antennae

distinctive dark, squarish marking in middle of forewing

brownish double scalloped lines along the hind margin

banded abdomen

strongly scalloped wing margins

♀

Time of Flight ☾	Habitat	Wingspan 9–12 in (23–30 cm)

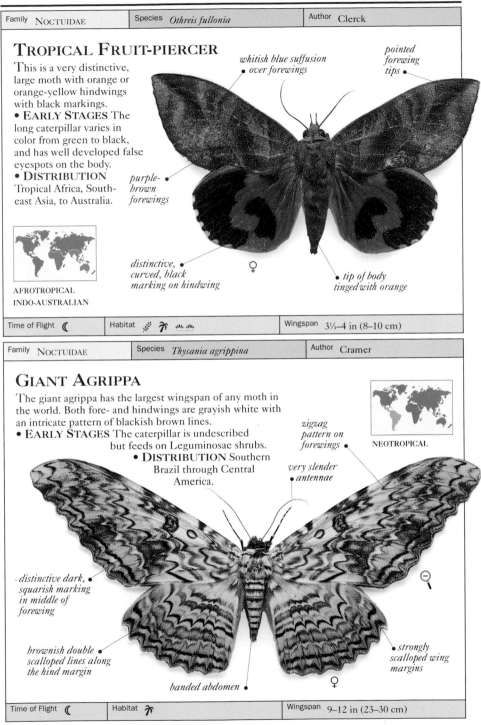

AGARISTIDAE

T HIS RELATIVELY small family of moths is composed of about 300 species occurring throughout the tropical forest regions of the world. They are similar in general appearance to moths of the family Noctuidae, but can usually be distinguished by their distinctive antennae which tend to be thickened towards the tips. Most of the Agaristid moths are day fliers; they have a rapid, powerful flight.

Many species are brightly colored, and their caterpillars also appear to be avoided by predators, suggesting that they are distasteful to birds.

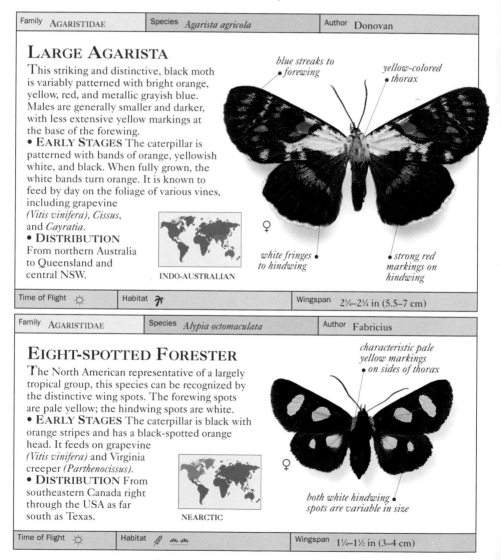

Family AGARISTIDAE	Species *Agarista agricola*	Author Donovan

LARGE AGARISTA

This striking and distinctive, black moth is variably patterned with bright orange, yellow, red, and metallic grayish blue. Males are generally smaller and darker, with less extensive yellow markings at the base of the forewing.
• EARLY STAGES The caterpillar is patterned with bands of orange, yellowish white, and black. When fully grown, the white bands turn orange. It is known to feed by day on the foliage of various vines, including grapevine *(Vitis vinifera)*, *Cissus*, and *Cayratia*.
• DISTRIBUTION From northern Australia to Queensland and central NSW.

INDO-AUSTRALIAN

blue streaks to forewing

yellow-colored thorax

♀

white fringes to hindwing

strong red markings on hindwing

Time of Flight ☀	Habitat 🦗		Wingspan 2¼–2¾ in (5.5–7 cm)

Family AGARISTIDAE	Species *Alypia octomaculata*	Author Fabricius

EIGHT-SPOTTED FORESTER

The North American representative of a largely tropical group, this species can be recognized by the distinctive wing spots. The forewing spots are pale yellow; the hindwing spots are white.
• EARLY STAGES The caterpillar is black with orange stripes and has a black-spotted orange head. It feeds on grapevine *(Vitis vinifera)* and Virginia creeper *(Parthenocissus)*.
• DISTRIBUTION From southeastern Canada right through the USA as far south as Texas.

NEARCTIC

characteristic pale yellow markings on sides of thorax

♀

both white hindwing spots are variable in size

Time of Flight ☀	Habitat 🌾 🌾		Wingspan 1¼–1½ in (3–4 cm)

LYMANTRIIDAE

T HIS LARGE FAMILY of some 2,500 species occurs worldwide, but is most strongly represented in the tropics of Africa. The moths are similar to those of the family Noctuidae, but they are generally rather hairy in appearance. The wings are usually pale or dull in color, although some tropical species are more brightly patterned. Some females have greatly reduced wings, so they are unable to fly. Lymantriid moths like some other moth families lack functional tongues and cannot feed in the adult stage.

———— • ————

The caterpillars are hairy and often brightly colored. Many species have body hairs grouped in distinctive toothbrush-like tufts, giving rise to the common name of tussock moths. The hairs of many of these caterpillars are irritant, and can cause rashes.

Family LYMANTRIIDAE	Species *Lymantria dispar*	Author Linnaeus

GYPSY MOTH

The sexes of this well-known pest moth are very different from each other. Males are pale yellowish brown with dark brown patterning on the forewings and dark brown borders to the hindwings, while the larger females are predominantly white with distinctive, black markings on the forewings. Gypsy moths are on the wing in summer. Males fly by day, but the sluggish females do not fly at all, and seldom move far from their emergence place.

• **EARLY STAGES** The caterpillar is bluish gray with raised, red and blue, tufted spots on the back. Although showing a preference for oaks *(Quercus)*, they will eat the foliage of most trees and shrubs and are often a serious pest, sometimes stripping the foliage from large areas of forest. There is one generation a year.

• **DISTRIBUTION** Originally a native of Europe and temperate Asia, this moth was introduced into North America in the mid-19th century with a view to using it for silk production. However, moths escaped and the species became established as one of the worst insect pests in North America. It is not regarded as such a serious pest in Europe.

HOLARCTIC

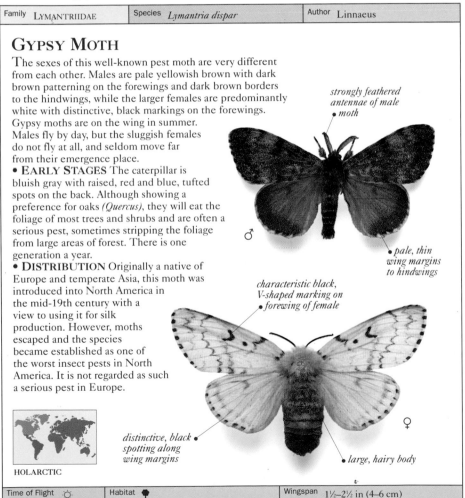

strongly feathered antennae of male • *moth*

♂

• *pale, thin wing margins to hindwings*

characteristic black, V-shaped marking on • *forewing of female*

distinctive, black • *spotting along wing margins*

♀

• *large, hairy body*

Time of Flight ☼	Habitat ♣	Wingspan 1½–2½ in (4–6 cm)

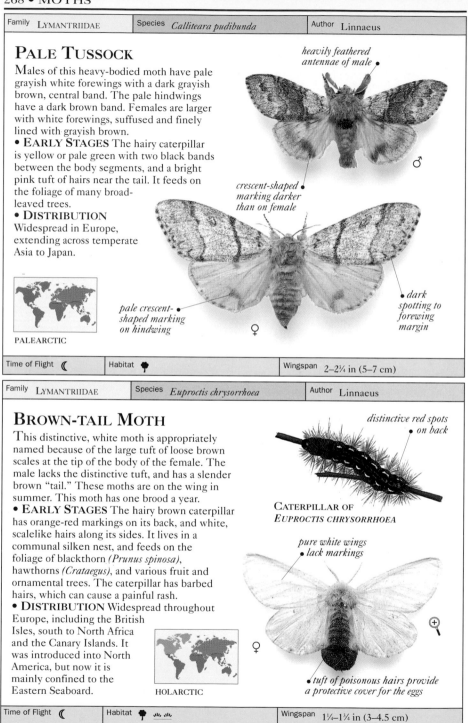

Family LYMANTRIIDAE	Species *Calliteara pudibunda*	Author Linnaeus

PALE TUSSOCK

Males of this heavy-bodied moth have pale grayish white forewings with a dark grayish brown, central band. The pale hindwings have a dark brown band. Females are larger with white forewings, suffused and finely lined with grayish brown.

• **EARLY STAGES** The hairy caterpillar is yellow or pale green with two black bands between the body segments, and a bright pink tuft of hairs near the tail. It feeds on the foliage of many broad-leaved trees.

• **DISTRIBUTION** Widespread in Europe, extending across temperate Asia to Japan.

heavily feathered antennae of male

♂

crescent-shaped marking darker than on female

pale crescent-shaped marking on hindwing

dark spotting to forewing margin

♀

PALEARCTIC

Time of Flight ☾	Habitat 🌳	Wingspan 2–2¾ in (5–7 cm)

Family LYMANTRIIDAE	Species *Euproctis chrysorrhoea*	Author Linnaeus

BROWN-TAIL MOTH

This distinctive, white moth is appropriately named because of the large tuft of loose brown scales at the tip of the body of the female. The male lacks the distinctive tuft, and has a slender brown "tail." These moths are on the wing in summer. This moth has one brood a year.

• **EARLY STAGES** The hairy brown caterpillar has orange-red markings on its back, and white, scalelike hairs along its sides. It lives in a communal silken nest, and feeds on the foliage of blackthorn *(Prunus spinosa)*, hawthorns *(Crataegus)*, and various fruit and ornamental trees. The caterpillar has barbed hairs, which can cause a painful rash.

• **DISTRIBUTION** Widespread throughout Europe, including the British Isles, south to North Africa and the Canary Islands. It was introduced into North America, but now it is mainly confined to the Eastern Seaboard.

distinctive red spots on back

CATERPILLAR OF
EUPROCTIS CHRYSORRHOEA

pure white wings lack markings

♀

⊕

tuft of poisonous hairs provide a protective cover for the eggs

HOLARCTIC

Time of Flight ☾	Habitat 🌳 ⚘ ⚘	Wingspan 1¼–1¾ in (3–4.5 cm)

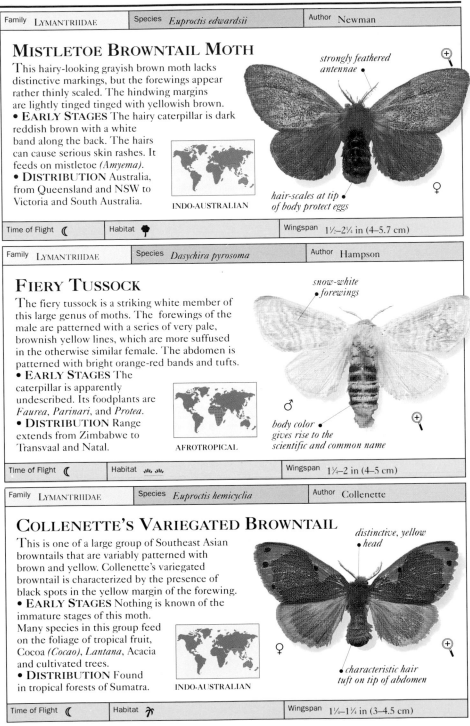

| Family | LYMANTRIIDAE | Species | *Euproctis edwardsii* | Author | Newman |

MISTLETOE BROWNTAIL MOTH

This hairy-looking grayish brown moth lacks distinctive markings, but the forewings appear rather thinly scaled. The hindwing margins are lightly tinged tinged with yellowish brown.
• **EARLY STAGES** The hairy caterpillar is dark reddish brown with a white band along the back. The hairs can cause serious skin rashes. It feeds on mistletoe *(Amyema)*.
• **DISTRIBUTION** Australia, from Queensland and NSW to Victoria and South Australia.

strongly feathered antennae

hair-scales at tip of body protect eggs

♀

INDO-AUSTRALIAN

| Time of Flight ☾ | Habitat 🌳 | Wingspan 1½–2¼ in (4–5.7 cm) |

| Family | LYMANTRIIDAE | Species | *Dasychira pyrosoma* | Author | Hampson |

FIERY TUSSOCK

The fiery tussock is a striking white member of this large genus of moths. The forewings of the male are patterned with a series of very pale, brownish yellow lines, which are more suffused in the otherwise similar female. The abdomen is patterned with bright orange-red bands and tufts.
• **EARLY STAGES** The caterpillar is apparently undescribed. Its foodplants are *Faurea, Parinari,* and *Protea*.
• **DISTRIBUTION** Range extends from Zimbabwe to Transvaal and Natal.

snow-white forewings

♂

body color gives rise to the scientific and common name

AFROTROPICAL

| Time of Flight ☾ | Habitat 🌿, 🌿 | Wingspan 1¾–2 in (4–5 cm) |

| Family | LYMANTRIIDAE | Species | *Euproctis hemicyclia* | Author | Collenette |

COLLENETTE'S VARIEGATED BROWNTAIL

This is one of a large group of Southeast Asian browntails that are variably patterned with brown and yellow. Collenette's variegated browntail is characterized by the presence of black spots in the yellow margin of the forewing.
• **EARLY STAGES** Nothing is known of the immature stages of this moth. Many species in this group feed on the foliage of tropical fruit, Cocoa *(Cocao)*, *Lantana*, Acacia and cultivated trees.
• **DISTRIBUTION** Found in tropical forests of Sumatra.

distinctive, yellow head

♀

characteristic hair tuft on tip of abdomen

INDO-AUSTRALIAN

| Time of Flight ☾ | Habitat 🌴 | Wingspan 1¼–1¾ in (3–4.5 cm) |

Family LYMANTRIIDAE	Species *Orygia leucostigma*	Author Smith

WHITE-MARKED TUSSOCK MOTH

Males of this species have dark brownish gray wings. The forewings are banded with brown. The grayish white females are wingless.
• **EARLY STAGES** The brownish yellow caterpillar has long, plumelike tufts of black and white hairs at the head and tail. It feeds on a wide range of broadleaved and coniferous trees and is sometimes a pest in forest plantations.
• **DISTRIBUTION** Occurs in many parts of the USA, especially in North America.

distinctive black, marginal
• line on forewing

♂

small white patch gives
rise to the common name

NEARCTIC

Time of Flight ☾	Habitat ❦	Wingspan 1–1½ in (2.5–4 cm)

Family LYMANTRIIDAE	Species *Leptocneria reducta*	Author Walker

CEDAR TUSSOCK

This rather dull brown moth is one of two species in a genus which is confined to Australia. The forewing has distinctive dark brown markings and an indistinct, brown, marginal line. The hindwings of the male are a pale translucent brown with darker fringes, and a pale brown marking.
• **EARLY STAGES** The hairy caterpillar feeds on the foliage of white cedar *(Melia azedarach)*, and trees that grow in urban areas.
• **DISTRIBUTION** Northern Queensland to southern NSW.

faint, dark dots along
• forewing margin

♂

• characteristic dark
marking on hindwing

INDO-AUSTRALIAN

Time of Flight ☾	Habitat ❦ ⸜ ⸜	Wingspan 1¼–2¾ in (3–7 cm)

Family LYMANTRIIDAE	Species *Aroa discalis*	Author Walker

BANDED VAPORER

The sexes of this moth are completely different. Males are dark reddish brown, with pale orange markings on the forewings and broad orange bands on the hindwings. Females have orange-yellow wings and their forewings are patterned with brown lines. The body is orange and black.
• **EARLY STAGES** The hairy caterpillar is dark brown. It feeds on various grasses.
• **DISTRIBUTION** Range extends from Kenya and Zaire to Angola, Mozambique, and South Africa.

characteristic line of black spots
• along forewing margin of female

♂

⊕

distinctive orange and •
black banded hindwing

AFROTROPICAL

Time of Flight ☾ ☼	Habitat ⸜ ⸜	Wingspan 1¼–1½ in (3–4 cm)

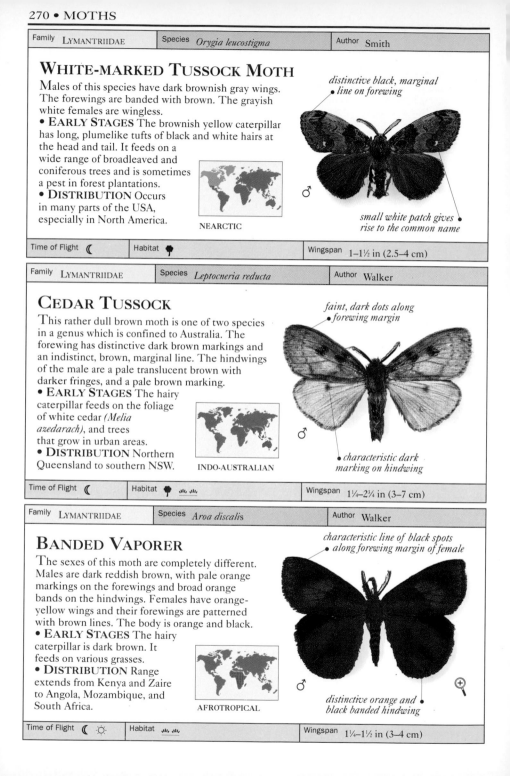

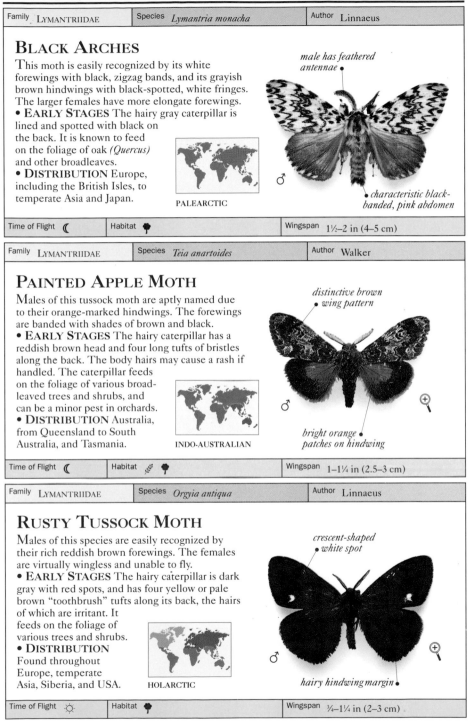

Family LYMANTRIIDAE	Species *Lymantria monacha*	Author Linnaeus

BLACK ARCHES

This moth is easily recognized by its white forewings with black, zigzag bands, and its grayish brown hindwings with black-spotted, white fringes. The larger females have more elongate forewings.
• **EARLY STAGES** The hairy gray caterpillar is lined and spotted with black on the back. It is known to feed on the foliage of oak *(Quercus)* and other broadleaves.
• **DISTRIBUTION** Europe, including the British Isles, to temperate Asia and Japan.

PALEARCTIC

male has feathered antennae

♂

characteristic black-banded, pink abdomen

Time of Flight ☾	Habitat ♠	Wingspan 1½–2 in (4–5 cm)

Family LYMANTRIIDAE	Species *Teia anartoides*	Author Walker

PAINTED APPLE MOTH

Males of this tussock moth are aptly named due to their orange-marked hindwings. The forewings are banded with shades of brown and black.
• **EARLY STAGES** The hairy caterpillar has a reddish brown head and four long tufts of bristles along the back. The body hairs may cause a rash if handled. The caterpillar feeds on the foliage of various broad-leaved trees and shrubs, and can be a minor pest in orchards.
• **DISTRIBUTION** Australia, from Queensland to South Australia, and Tasmania.

INDO-AUSTRALIAN

distinctive brown wing pattern

♂

⊕

bright orange patches on hindwing

Time of Flight ☾	Habitat 🌾 ♠	Wingspan 1–1¼ in (2.5–3 cm)

Family LYMANTRIIDAE	Species *Orgyia antiqua*	Author Linnaeus

RUSTY TUSSOCK MOTH

Males of this species are easily recognized by their rich reddish brown forewings. The females are virtually wingless and unable to fly.
• **EARLY STAGES** The hairy caterpillar is dark gray with red spots, and has four yellow or pale brown "toothbrush" tufts along its back, the hairs of which are irritant. It feeds on the foliage of various trees and shrubs.
• **DISTRIBUTION** Found throughout Europe, temperate Asia, Siberia, and USA.

HOLARCTIC

crescent-shaped white spot

♂

⊕

hairy hindwing margin

Time of Flight ☼	Habitat ♠	Wingspan ¾–1¼ in (2–3 cm)

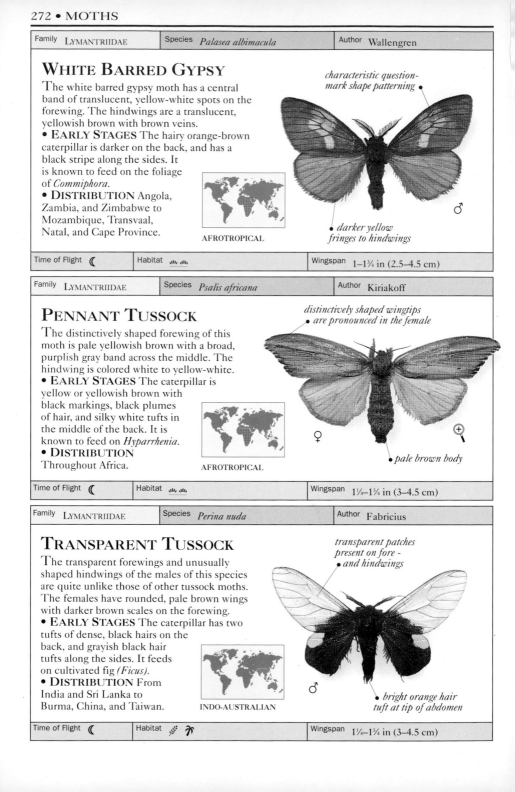

| Family LYMANTRIIDAE | Species *Palasea albimacula* | Author Wallengren |

WHITE BARRED GYPSY

The white barred gypsy moth has a central
band of translucent, yellow-white spots on the
forewing. The hindwings are a translucent,
yellowish brown with brown veins.
• **EARLY STAGES** The hairy orange-brown
caterpillar is darker on the back, and has a
black stripe along the sides. It
is known to feed on the foliage
of *Commiphora*.
• **DISTRIBUTION** Angola,
Zambia, and Zimbabwe to
Mozambique, Transvaal,
Natal, and Cape Province.

characteristic question-
mark shape patterning

♂

• darker yellow
fringes to hindwings

AFROTROPICAL

| Time of Flight ☾ | Habitat | Wingspan 1–1¾ in (2.5–4.5 cm) |

| Family LYMANTRIIDAE | Species *Psalis africana* | Author Kiriakoff |

PENNANT TUSSOCK

The distinctively shaped forewing of this
moth is pale yellowish brown with a broad,
purplish gray band across the middle. The
hindwing is colored white to yellow-white.
• **EARLY STAGES** The caterpillar is
yellow or yellowish brown with
black markings, black plumes
of hair, and silky white tufts in
the middle of the back. It is
known to feed on *Hyparrhenia*.
• **DISTRIBUTION**
Throughout Africa.

distinctively shaped wingtips
• are pronounced in the female

♀

⊕

• pale brown body

AFROTROPICAL

| Time of Flight ☾ | Habitat | Wingspan 1¼–1¾ in (3–4.5 cm) |

| Family LYMANTRIIDAE | Species *Perina nuda* | Author Fabricius |

TRANSPARENT TUSSOCK

The transparent forewings and unusually
shaped hindwings of the males of this species
are quite unlike those of other tussock moths.
The females have rounded, pale brown wings
with darker brown scales on the forewing.
• **EARLY STAGES** The caterpillar has two
tufts of dense, black hairs on the
back, and grayish black hair
tufts along the sides. It feeds
on cultivated fig *(Ficus)*.
• **DISTRIBUTION** From
India and Sri Lanka to
Burma, China, and Taiwan.

transparent patches
present on fore -
• and hindwings

♂

• bright orange hair
tuft at tip of abdomen

INDO-AUSTRALIAN

| Time of Flight ☾ | Habitat | Wingspan 1¼–1¾ in (3–4.5 cm) |

ARCTIIDAE

THIS IS A LARGE family containing some 10,000 species of moths occurring worldwide, with the greatest numbers present in the tropics. Many are brightly patterned with warning colors, either because they are distasteful, or because they mimic less palatable species. The brightly striped patterns of some species have given rise to the common name of tiger moths. Arctiidae moths have robust wings and bodies; moths belonging to the sub-family Lithosiinae tend to be generally smaller, with delicate wings and much more slender bodies.

•

The caterpillars of many Arctiids often feed on poisonous plants, storing the toxins in their bodies where they provide protection from predators.

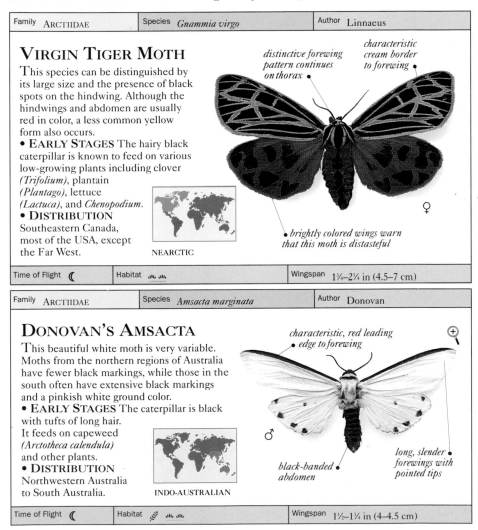

| Family ARCTIIDAE | Species *Gnammia virgo* | Author Linnaeus |

VIRGIN TIGER MOTH

This species can be distinguished by its large size and the presence of black spots on the hindwing. Although the hindwings and abdomen are usually red in color, a less common yellow form also occurs.
• **EARLY STAGES** The hairy black caterpillar is known to feed on various low-growing plants including clover (*Trifolium*), plantain (*Plantago*), lettuce (*Lactuca*), and *Chenopodium*.
• **DISTRIBUTION** Southeastern Canada, most of the USA, except the Far West.

NEARCTIC

distinctive forewing pattern continues on thorax

characteristic cream border to forewing

♀

brightly colored wings warn that this moth is distasteful

| Time of Flight ☾ | Habitat | Wingspan 1¾–2¾ in (4.5–7 cm) |

| Family ARCTIIDAE | Species *Amsacta marginata* | Author Donovan |

DONOVAN'S AMSACTA

This beautiful white moth is very variable. Moths from the northern regions of Australia have fewer black markings, while those in the south often have extensive black markings and a pinkish white ground color.
• **EARLY STAGES** The caterpillar is black with tufts of long hair. It feeds on capeweed (*Arctotheca calendula*) and other plants.
• **DISTRIBUTION** Northwestern Australia to South Australia.

INDO-AUSTRALIAN

characteristic, red leading edge to forewing

⊕

♂

black-banded abdomen

long, slender forewings with pointed tips

| Time of Flight ☾ | Habitat | Wingspan 1½–1¾ in (4–4.5 cm) |

Family ARCTIIDAE	Species *Arctia caja*	Author Linnaeus

GREAT TIGER MOTH

With its distinctive brown and white forewings and bluish, black-spotted, orange hindwings, this handsome moth is unmistakable. The markings on both fore- and hindwings are very variable. Rare yellow forms also occur.

• **EARLY STAGES** The black wooly bear caterpillar has rusty red hairs along the lower parts of the body and around the first body segments. It feeds on the foliage of a wide range of low-growing plants and broad-leaved shrubs.

• **DISTRIBUTION** Europe, across temperate Asia to Japan. Occurs less frequently in Canada and the northern USA.

CATERPILLAR OF *ARCTIA CAJA*

• red-colored body hair

furry brown thorax •

black-ringed grayish markings •

• *pale orange hindwing fringes*

HOLARCTIC

♂

Time of Flight ☾	Habitat 🌿 🌾 🌾	Wingspan 2–3 in (5–7.5 cm)

Family ARCTIIDAE	Species *Estigmene acrea*	Author Drury

SALT MARSH MOTH

This common species can be recognized by the black-spotted forewings, which are tinged with pale yellow in the male. The hindwings each bear three or four black spots. The ground color of the male hindwings is orange-yellow, while that of the female is white.

• **EARLY STAGES** The caterpillar is mottled light and dark brown and covered with long, brown hairs. It feeds on foliage of various low-growing plants and broad-leaved trees, and is often a pest of cabbage *(Brassica oleracea)*, and clover *(Trifolium)*.

• **DISTRIBUTION** Southeastern Canada, eastern USA, into Central USA.

♂

furry white thorax •

♀

distinctive, black-spotted, orange abdomen •

• *faint, broken, black line around hindwing margin*

NEARCTIC

Time of Flight ☾	Habitat 🌿 🌾 🌾	Wingspan 1¾–2¾ in (4.5–7 cm)

Family ARCTIIDAE	Species *Ecpantheria scribonia*	Author Stoll

GIANT LEOPARD MOTH

This striking species can be easily
recognized by the distinctive
pattern of blackish brown
to bluish black, ringlike
markings on the forewing.
• **EARLY STAGES** The hairy
caterpillar is black with crimson
rings between the segments,
which are revealed when it curls up
in a defensive position. It feeds on a
many plants, including cherry *(Prunus)*,
and banana *(Musa)*.
• **DISTRIBUTION** Southeastern
Canada through eastern USA to Mexico.
Common in the southern part of its range.

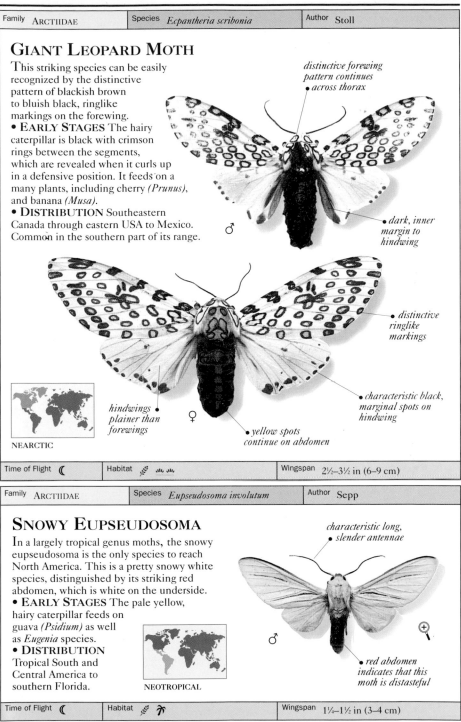

distinctive forewing pattern continues across thorax

dark, inner margin to hindwing

distinctive ringlike markings

characteristic black, marginal spots on hindwing

hindwings plainer than forewings

yellow spots continue on abdomen

NEARCTIC

♂ ♀

Time of Flight ☾	Habitat	Wingspan 2½–3½ in (6–9 cm)

Family ARCTIIDAE	Species *Eupseudosoma involutum*	Author Sepp

SNOWY EUPSEUDOSOMA

In a largely tropical genus moths, the snowy
eupseudosoma is the only species to reach
North America. This is a pretty snowy white
species, distinguished by its striking red
abdomen, which is white on the underside.
• **EARLY STAGES** The pale yellow,
hairy caterpillar feeds on
guava *(Psidium)* as well
as *Eugenia* species.
• **DISTRIBUTION**
Tropical South and
Central America to
southern Florida.

characteristic long, slender antennae

red abdomen indicates that this moth is distasteful

♂

NEOTROPICAL

Time of Flight ☾	Habitat	Wingspan 1¼–1½ in (3–4 cm)

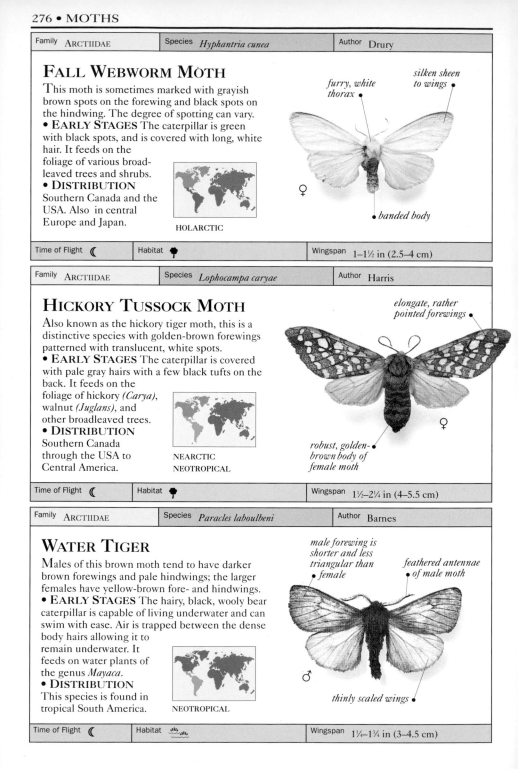

| Family ARCTIIDAE | Species *Hyphantria cunea* | Author Drury |

FALL WEBWORM MOTH

This moth is sometimes marked with grayish
brown spots on the forewing and black spots on
the hindwing. The degree of spotting can vary.
• **EARLY STAGES** The caterpillar is green
with black spots, and is covered with long, white
hair. It feeds on the
foliage of various broad-
leaved trees and shrubs.
• **DISTRIBUTION**
Southern Canada and the
USA. Also in central
Europe and Japan.

HOLARCTIC

furry, white thorax
silken sheen to wings
♀
banded body

| Time of Flight ☾ | Habitat | Wingspan 1–1½ in (2.5–4 cm) |

| Family ARCTIIDAE | Species *Lophocampa caryae* | Author Harris |

HICKORY TUSSOCK MOTH

Also known as the hickory tiger moth, this is a
distinctive species with golden-brown forewings
patterned with translucent, white spots.
• **EARLY STAGES** The caterpillar is covered
with pale gray hairs with a few black tufts on the
back. It feeds on the
foliage of hickory *(Carya)*,
walnut *(Juglans)*, and
other broadleaved trees.
• **DISTRIBUTION**
Southern Canada
through the USA to
Central America.

NEARCTIC
NEOTROPICAL

elongate, rather pointed forewings
♀
robust, golden-brown body of female moth

| Time of Flight ☾ | Habitat | Wingspan 1½–2¼ in (4–5.5 cm) |

| Family ARCTIIDAE | Species *Paracles laboulbeni* | Author Barnes |

WATER TIGER

Males of this brown moth tend to have darker
brown forewings and pale hindwings; the larger
females have yellow-brown fore- and hindwings.
• **EARLY STAGES** The hairy, black, wooly bear
caterpillar is capable of living underwater and can
swim with ease. Air is trapped between the dense
body hairs allowing it to
remain underwater. It
feeds on water plants of
the genus *Mayaca*.
• **DISTRIBUTION**
This species is found in
tropical South America.

NEOTROPICAL

male forewing is shorter and less triangular than female
feathered antennae of male moth
♂
thinly scaled wings

| Time of Flight ☾ | Habitat | Wingspan 1¼–1¾ in (3–4.5 cm) |

Family ARCTIIDAE	Species *Premolis semirufa*	Author Walker

SEMIRUFOUS TIGER

A pretty moth, it has yellow-brown patterned forewings. Its hindwings and body are flushed with pink as a warning that it is distasteful.
• **EARLY STAGES** The hairy caterpillar lives around the rubber tree *(Hevea braziliensis)*. It is notorious among rubber tappers as its body hairs are highly irritant if touched.
• **DISTRIBUTION** Occurs in tropical South America.

NEOTROPICAL

semitransparent area towards wingtip

♂

hindwings plainer than forewings

distinctive concave hindwing

Time of Flight ☾	Habitat 🐾	Wingspan 1½–2½ in (4–6 cm)

Family ARCTIIDAE	Species *Phragmatobia fuliginosa*	Author Linnaeus

RUBY TIGER MOTH

The ruby tiger is recognizable by its translucent, brownish red forewings and pink or red hindwings with large, black, marginal spots. The forewings can be pale reddish or grayish brown.
• **EARLY STAGES** The brown caterpillar is covered with reddish or yellowish brown hairs. It feeds on a wide range of low-growing plants, including dock *(Rumex)*.
• **DISTRIBUTION** Europe to North Africa and Japan; Canada and the northern USA.

HOLARCTIC

furry, brown thorax

characteristic central black spots on forewing

♀

rows of black spots on red abdomen

hindwings more vivid than forewings

Time of Flight ☾	Habitat 🌿 ⚘ ⚘	Wingspan 1¼–1½ in (3–4 cm)

Family ARCTIIDAE	Species *Rhodogastria crokeri*	Author Macleay

CROKER'S FROTHER

These moths have elongate brown forewings with a translucent, pale central region and a yellowish white base. The hindwings are yellowish white.
• **EARLY STAGES** Little is known of this moth. Some related species are known to feed on the native vine *Gymnanthera nitida*, others feed on plants containing heart poisons, so it may be poisonous.
• **DISTRIBUTION** Northwestern Australia to Queensland and northern NSW.

INDO-AUSTRALIAN

distinctive black-spotted thorax

spotting continues onto forewing from thorax

♀

red abdomen suggests that this species is poisonous

Time of Flight ☾	Habitat 🐾 🌳	Wingspan 2¼–2¾ in (5.5–7 cm)

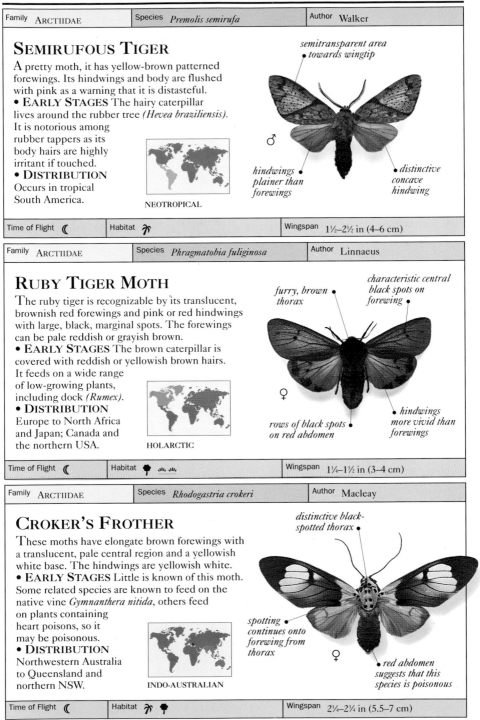

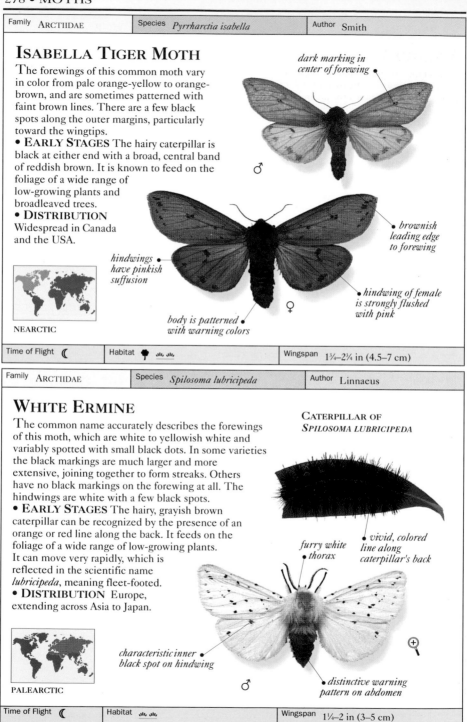

Family ARCTIIDAE	Species *Pyrrharctia isabella*	Author Smith

ISABELLA TIGER MOTH

The forewings of this common moth vary
in color from pale orange-yellow to orange-
brown, and are sometimes patterned with
faint brown lines. There are a few black
spots along the outer margins, particularly
toward the wingtips.
• **EARLY STAGES** The hairy caterpillar is
black at either end with a broad, central band
of reddish brown. It is known to feed on the
foliage of a wide range of
low-growing plants and
broadleaved trees.
• **DISTRIBUTION**
Widespread in Canada
and the USA.

dark marking in
center of forewing

brownish
leading edge
to forewing

hindwings
have pinkish
suffusion

hindwing of female
is strongly flushed
with pink

body is patterned
with warning colors

NEARCTIC

Time of Flight ☾	Habitat 🌳 ⚘ ⚘	Wingspan 1¾–2¾ in (4.5–7 cm)

Family ARCTIIDAE	Species *Spilosoma lubricipeda*	Author Linnaeus

WHITE ERMINE

The common name accurately describes the forewings
of this moth, which are white to yellowish white and
variably spotted with small black dots. In some varieties
the black markings are much larger and more
extensive, joining together to form streaks. Others
have no black markings on the forewing at all. The
hindwings are white with a few black spots.
• **EARLY STAGES** The hairy, grayish brown
caterpillar can be recognized by the presence of an
orange or red line along the back. It feeds on the
foliage of a wide range of low-growing plants.
It can move very rapidly, which is
reflected in the scientific name
lubricipeda, meaning fleet-footed.
• **DISTRIBUTION** Europe,
extending across Asia to Japan.

**CATERPILLAR OF
*SPILOSOMA LUBRICIPEDA***

vivid, colored
line along
caterpillar's back

furry white
thorax

characteristic inner
black spot on hindwing

distinctive warning
pattern on abdomen

PALEARCTIC

Time of Flight ☾	Habitat ⚘ ⚘	Wingspan 1¼–2 in (3–5 cm)

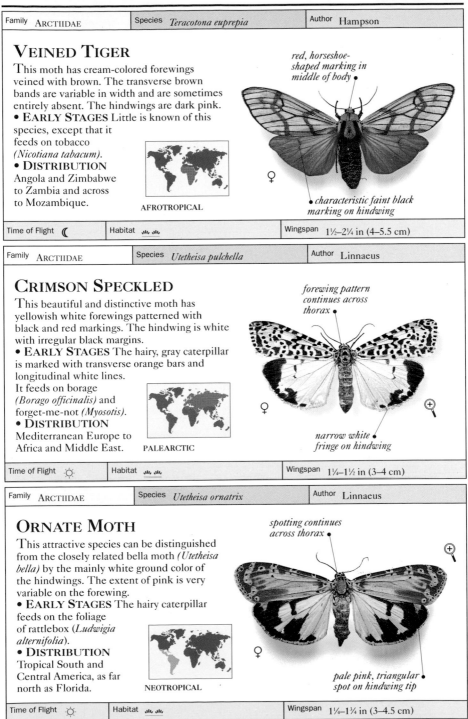

| Family ARCTIIDAE | Species *Teracotona euprepia* | Author Hampson |

VEINED TIGER

This moth has cream-colored forewings
veined with brown. The transverse brown
bands are variable in width and are sometimes
entirely absent. The hindwings are dark pink.
• **EARLY STAGES** Little is known of this
species, except that it
feeds on tobacco
(Nicotiana tabacum).
• **DISTRIBUTION**
Angola and Zimbabwe
to Zambia and across
to Mozambique.

AFROTROPICAL

red, horseshoe-
shaped marking in
middle of body •

♀

• characteristic faint black
marking on hindwing

| Time of Flight ☾ | Habitat | Wingspan 1½–2¼ in (4–5.5 cm) |

| Family ARCTIIDAE | Species *Utetheisa pulchella* | Author Linnaeus |

CRIMSON SPECKLED

This beautiful and distinctive moth has
yellowish white forewings patterned with
black and red markings. The hindwing is white
with irregular black margins.
• **EARLY STAGES** The hairy, gray caterpillar
is marked with transverse orange bars and
longitudinal white lines.
It feeds on borage
(Borago officinalis) and
forget-me-not *(Myosotis).*
• **DISTRIBUTION**
Mediterranean Europe to
Africa and Middle East.

PALEARCTIC

forewing pattern
continues across
thorax •

♀

⊕

narrow white •
fringe on hindwing

| Time of Flight ☼ | Habitat | Wingspan 1¼–1½ in (3–4 cm) |

| Family ARCTIIDAE | Species *Utetheisa ornatrix* | Author Linnaeus |

ORNATE MOTH

This attractive species can be distinguished
from the closely related bella moth *(Utetheisa
bella)* by the mainly white ground color of
the hindwings. The extent of pink is very
variable on the forewing.
• **EARLY STAGES** The hairy caterpillar
feeds on the foliage
of rattlebox *(Ludwigia
alternifolia).*
• **DISTRIBUTION**
Tropical South and
Central America, as far
north as Florida.

NEOTROPICAL

spotting continues
across thorax •

⊕

♀

pale pink, triangular •
spot on hindwing tip

| Time of Flight ☼ | Habitat | Wingspan 1¼–1¾ in (3–4.5 cm) |

Family ARCTIIDAE	Species *Termessa sheperdi*	Author Newman

SHEPERD'S FOOTMAN

This attractively marked moth belongs to a
genus of twelve species peculiar to Australia.
Most species are boldly marked with patterns
of orange and black. The hindwings are a
deeper orange-yellow with distinctive black
markings on the margins.
• **EARLY STAGES**
Little seems to be
known about this moth.
• **DISTRIBUTION**
Occurs in NSW and
Victoria in Australia.

INDO-AUSTRALIAN

*orange-yellow forewings,
banded with black*

*black marking on hindwing
sometimes lacks curved "tail"*

♂

Time of Flight ☾	Habitat 🌳	Wingspan 1¼–1½ in (3–4 cm)

Family ARCTIIDAE	Species *Eilema complana*	Author Linnaeus

SCARCE FOOTMAN

This is one of a group of footman moths with narrow,
shiny, gray forewings with a bold, golden yellow
stripe along the leading edge. Scarce footman moths
visit flowers of thistles, and related plants, at dusk.
• **EARLY STAGES** The hairy gray caterpillar has
rows of alternate orange and white spots along the
back, and a yellow stripe
along the sides. It feeds
on various lichens.
• **DISTRIBUTION**
Europe, across temperate
Asia to Siberia, and
North America.

HOLARCTIC

*orange head
and collar*

*yellow forewing
stripe extends
onto fringe*

♂

*yellow tip
to abdomen*

Time of Flight ☾	Habitat 🌳 ⚘ ⚘	Wingspan 1¼–1½ in (3–4 cm)

Family ARCTIIDAE	Species *Lithosia quadra*	Author Linnaeus

FOUR-SPOTTED FOOTMAN

It is the female of this relatively large footman moth
that earns the name, four-spotted. Each forewing
has two black spots, which vary in size. The
forewing of the male is gray, shading to a darker
orange-yellow at the base, and over the thorax.
• **EARLY STAGES** The caterpillar has a
yellowish band, with red
spots. It feeds on *Peltigera
canina* and other lichens.
• **DISTRIBUTION**
Widespread in Europe,
extending to temperate
Asia and to Japan.

PALEARCTIC

*forewing fringe
suffused with gray*

♂

*distinctively shaped,
broad hindwing*

Time of Flight ☾	Habitat 🌳	Wingspan 1¼–2¼ in (3–5.5 cm)

Family ARCTIIDAE	Species *Amphicallia bellatrix*	Author Dalman

BEAUTIFUL TIGER

The forewings and hindwings of this moth are bright orange with blue-black irregular stripes which are outlined with a thin black outline.
• **EARLY STAGES** The red-headed caterpillar is white with gray hairs and black, transverse bands. It feeds on *Crotalaria* and plants of the pea family (Leguminosae).
• **DISTRIBUTION** Found from Kenya to Zambia, Mozambique, and the Cape Province.

AFROTROPICAL

forewing pattern extends onto thorax

♀

abdomen characteristically spotted

Time of Flight ☾	Habitat ▲ 🌴	Wingspan 2–2¼ in (5–7 cm)

Family ARCTIIDAE	Species *Nyctemera amica*	Author White

AUSTRALIAN MAGPIE MOTH

This is an easily recognized species, having black-brown wings with yellowish white spots. The black and orange ringed abdomen suggests that this moth is distasteful. The sexes are similar, but females tend to be smaller than males.
• **EARLY STAGES** The hairy black caterpillar of this species has red stripes along the back and sides. It feeds on the foliage of *Senecio*.
• **DISTRIBUTION** Widespread throughout most of Australia.

INDO-AUSTRALIAN

strongly feathered antennae

♂

distinctive orange fringes

Time of Flight ☾ ☼	Habitat ◖◗ ◖◗	Wingspan 1½–1¾ in (4–4.5 cm)

Family ARCTIIDAE	Species *Callimorpha dominula*	Author Linnaeus

SCARLET TIGER

This moth has greenish black forewings, spotted with yellowish white, but sometimes these spots are greatly reduced in size.
• **EARLY STAGES** The caterpillar is black with tufts of black and gray hairs, and broken bands of yellowish white along the back and sides. It feeds on comfrey *(Symphytum officinale)*, dock *(Rumex)* and other plants.
• **DISTRIBUTION** Found throughout Europe, and eastward into temperate Asia.

PALEARCTIC

forewing pattern continues across thorax

♂

abdomen is red with black central stripe

Time of Flight ☼	Habitat ≈◖◗ ◖◗ ◖◗	Wingspan 1¾–2¼ in (4.5–5.5 cm)

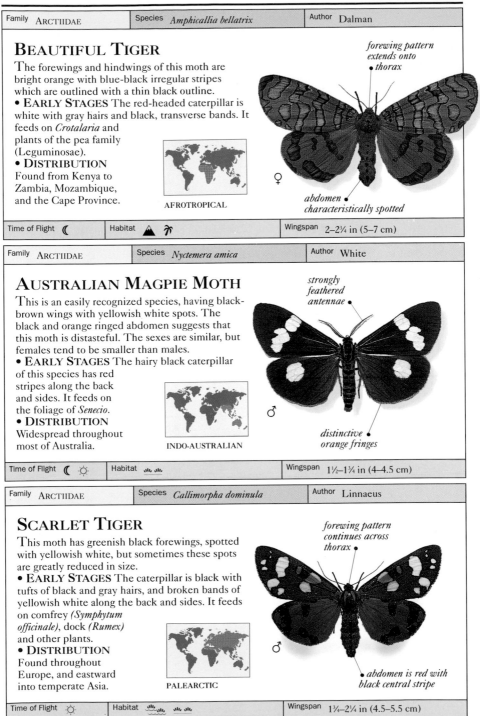

Family ARCTIIDAE	Species *Euplagia quadripunctaria*	Author Poda

JERSEY TIGER

This species has black stripes on yellowish white forewings. The black-spotted hindwings are usually red, but a yellow variety also exists.
• **EARLY STAGES** The caterpillar is dark brown, covered with short yellow-brown hair with yellow bands on its back and sides. It feeds on the foliage of a range of low-growing plants.
• **DISTRIBUTION** Europe, extending across temperate Asia.

PALEARCTIC

unusually angled stripes on forewings

♀

Time of Flight	Habitat	Wingspan 2–2½ in (5–6 cm)

Family ARCTIIDAE	Species *Tyria jacobeae*	Author Linnaeus

CINNABAR MOTH

This day-flying moth is often mistaken for a butterfly. It is easily recognized by its forewings, which are distinctively streaked and spotted with red. The hindwings are red, though yellow forms occur occasionally.
• **EARLY STAGES** The orange-yellow caterpillar is boldly ringed with black and feeds openly on ragwort and groundsel *(Senecio)*.
• **DISTRIBUTION** Europe and the Pacific coast of the USA.

PALEARCTIC

greenish black forewings

♀

glossy black body

black hindwing fringes

Time of Flight	Habitat	Wingspan 1¼–1¾ in (3–4.5 cm)

Family ARCTIIDAE	Species *Antichloris viridis*	Author Druce

BANANA MOTH

This unusual moth has slender pointed forewings that are metallic blue-green or black. In many specimens, two small tufts of red, hairlike scales are visible behind the head, indicating that it is a poisonous species.
• **EARLY STAGES** The caterpillar is covered with pale yellow hairs. It is known to feed on banana foliage *(Musa)* and is regarded as a pest.
• **DISTRIBUTION** Found in South and Central America.

NEOTROPICAL

antennae are strongly feathered at the base, and taper to a slender tip

small, black hindwings

♂

long, slender abdomen

Time of Flight	Habitat	Wingspan 1¼–1½ in (3–4 cm)

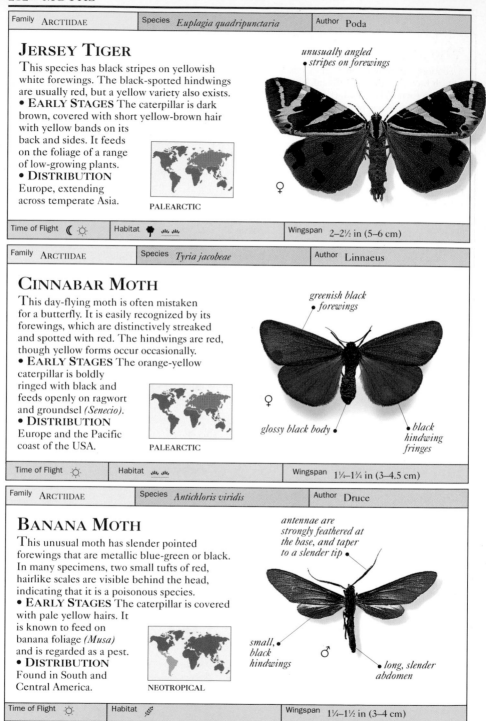

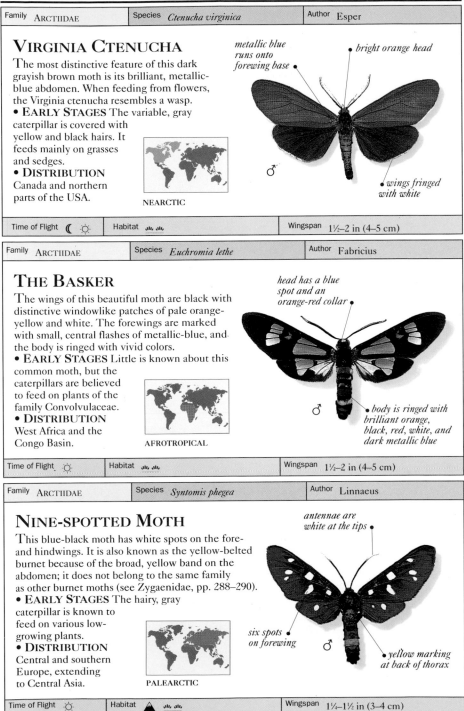

Family ARCTIIDAE	Species *Ctenucha virginica*	Author Esper

VIRGINIA CTENUCHA

The most distinctive feature of this dark grayish brown moth is its brilliant, metallic-blue abdomen. When feeding from flowers, the Virginia ctenucha resembles a wasp.
• **EARLY STAGES** The variable, gray caterpillar is covered with yellow and black hairs. It feeds mainly on grasses and sedges.
• **DISTRIBUTION** Canada and northern parts of the USA.

NEARCTIC

metallic blue runs onto forewing base

bright orange head

♂

wings fringed with white

Time of Flight ☾ ☼	Habitat 🌾 🌾	Wingspan 1½–2 in (4–5 cm)

Family ARCTIIDAE	Species *Euchromia lethe*	Author Fabricius

THE BASKER

The wings of this beautiful moth are black with distinctive windowlike patches of pale orange-yellow and white. The forewings are marked with small, central flashes of metallic-blue, and the body is ringed with vivid colors.
• **EARLY STAGES** Little is known about this common moth, but the caterpillars are believed to feed on plants of the family Convolvulaceae.
• **DISTRIBUTION** West Africa and the Congo Basin.

AFROTROPICAL

head has a blue spot and an orange-red collar

♂

body is ringed with brilliant orange, black, red, white, and dark metallic blue

Time of Flight ☼	Habitat 🌾 🌾	Wingspan 1½–2 in (4–5 cm)

Family ARCTIIDAE	Species *Syntomis phegea*	Author Linnaeus

NINE-SPOTTED MOTH

This blue-black moth has white spots on the fore- and hindwings. It is also known as the yellow-belted burnet because of the broad, yellow band on the abdomen; it does not belong to the same family as other burnet moths (see Zygaenidae, pp. 288–290).
• **EARLY STAGES** The hairy, gray caterpillar is known to feed on various low-growing plants.
• **DISTRIBUTION** Central and southern Europe, extending to Central Asia.

PALEARCTIC

antennae are white at the tips

six spots on forewing

♂

yellow marking at back of thorax

Time of Flight ☼	Habitat ⛰ 🌾 🌾	Wingspan 1¼–1½ in (3–4 cm)

CASTNIIDAE

T HIS IS A RELATIVELY small family of some 200 species of tropical moth occurring mainly in South and Central America. They are generally medium to large, robust, day-flying moths that are often mistaken for butterflies. The forewings are usually dull in color and provide camouflage when the moths are at rest, but the hindwings are sometimes brilliantly colored. These bright colors are revealed quite suddenly, with any wing movement if the moth is disturbed, and can startle potential predators, allowing the moth to make an escape.

•

The caterpillars of Castniid moths are mainly root and stem borers. They feed while they are concealed within the actual plants.

Family CASTNIIDAE	Species *Castnia licus*	Author Fabricius

GIANT SUGARCANE-BORER

This distinctive and very butterflylike moth can be recognized by the yellowish white, diagonal bands on the brownish black forewings, although other forewing markings are variable. The hindwings are banded with white and have a series of square, red spots along the margin.
• **EARLY STAGES** The white, grublike caterpillar bores into stems of sugar cane *(Saccharum oficinarum)*. Discovered to be a sugar cane pest at the turn of the century, it has subsequently also become a pest of cultivated bananas *(Musa)*, and probably feeds on the roots of related native plants in the wild.
• **DISTRIBUTION** Widespread in tropical South and Central America, particularly where sugar cane and bananas are grown.

NEOTROPICAL

distinctive boring caterpillar

antennae are thickened and hooked at the tips

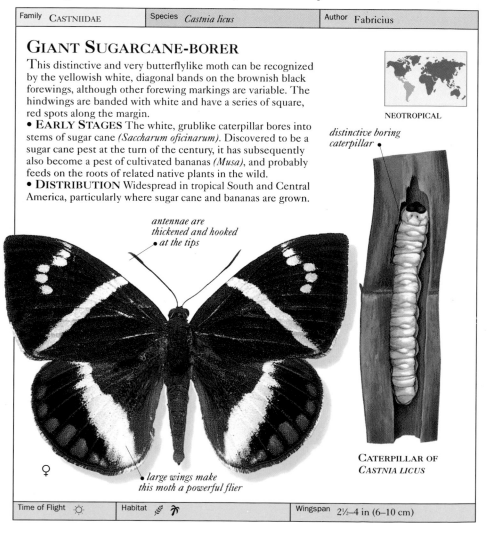

♀

large wings make this moth a powerful flier

CATERPILLAR OF
CASTNIA LICUS

Time of Flight ☼	Habitat 🌾 🎋	Wingspan 2½–4 in (6–10 cm)

Family CASTNIIDAE	Species *Divana diva*	Author Butler

DIVA MOTH

This species is confined to Central and South America and is notable for its brilliantly colored hindwings. The forewings of this moth are well camouflaged with a pattern of dark yellowish brown, with white spots, resembling a dead leaf. The hindwings are an excellent example of flash coloration with deep, metallic violet-blue, bordered with black and orange-red.
• **EARLY STAGES** Nothing appears to be known about the caterpillar or its foodplants.
• **DISTRIBUTION** Widespread in tropical South and Central America.

NEOTROPICAL

characteristic slightly curved wingtips

distinctive white spotting

paler orange color on forewings

black fringes to hindwing

orange-red border to hindwing

metallic-blue bases to hindwings

♀

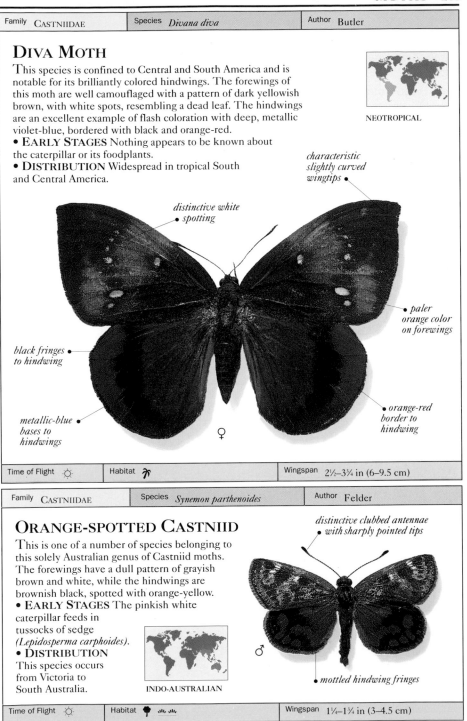

Time of Flight ☼	Habitat 🌿	Wingspan 2½–3¾ in (6–9.5 cm)

Family CASTNIIDAE	Species *Synemon parthenoides*	Author Felder

ORANGE-SPOTTED CASTNIID

This is one of a number of species belonging to this solely Australian genus of Castniid moths. The forewings have a dull pattern of grayish brown and white, while the hindwings are brownish black, spotted with orange-yellow.
• **EARLY STAGES** The pinkish white caterpillar feeds in tussocks of sedge (*Lepidosperma carphoides*).
• **DISTRIBUTION** This species occurs from Victoria to South Australia.

distinctive clubbed antennae with sharply pointed tips

♂

mottled hindwing fringes

INDO-AUSTRALIAN

Time of Flight ☼	Habitat 🌳 ⚘ ⚘	Wingspan 1¼–1¾ in (3–4.5 cm)

SESIIDAE

T HIS worldwide family of over 1,000 species is notable for containing some of the best wasp mimics among all insects. Most of these small- to medium-sized moths have areas of the wings that are lacking in scales, hence the common name clearwings that is applied to the family as a whole. The hind legs are usually clothed with dense, long hairs. These moths are not only superb wasp mimics in appearance, but also in behavior, some even producing a buzzing sound when in flight. They are mostly day-flying species and frequently visit flowers. The caterpillars of clearwing moths mostly tunnel in stems of trees, shrubs and other plants, and a number are regarded as pests.

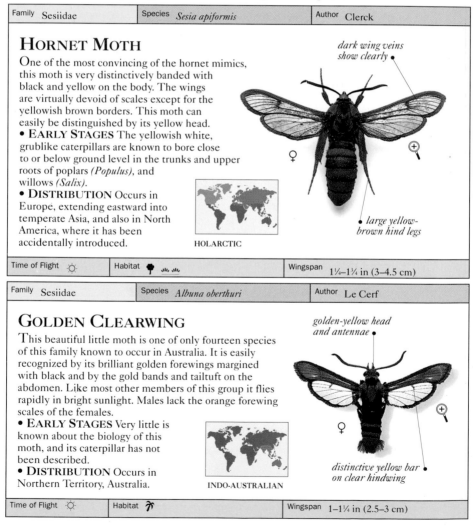

Family Sesiidae	Species *Sesia apiformis*	Author Clerck

HORNET MOTH

One of the most convincing of the hornet mimics, this moth is very distinctively banded with black and yellow on the body. The wings are virtually devoid of scales except for the yellowish brown borders. This moth can easily be distinguished by its yellow head.
• **EARLY STAGES** The yellowish white, grublike caterpillars are known to bore close to or below ground level in the trunks and upper roots of poplars *(Populus)*, and willows *(Salix)*.
• **DISTRIBUTION** Occurs in Europe, extending eastward into temperate Asia, and also in North America, where it has been accidentally introduced.

dark wing veins show clearly •

♀

• large yellow-brown hind legs

HOLARCTIC

Time of Flight ☀	Habitat 🌳 ⚊ ⚊	Wingspan 1¼–1¾ in (3–4.5 cm)

Family Sesiidae	Species *Albuna oberthuri*	Author Le Cerf

GOLDEN CLEARWING

This beautiful little moth is one of only fourteen species of this family known to occur in Australia. It is easily recognized by its brilliant golden forewings margined with black and by the gold bands and tailtuft on the abdomen. Like most other members of this group it flies rapidly in bright sunlight. Males lack the orange forewing scales of the females.
• **EARLY STAGES** Very little is known about the biology of this moth, and its caterpillar has not been described.
• **DISTRIBUTION** Occurs in Northern Territory, Australia.

golden-yellow head and antennae •

♀

INDO-AUSTRALIAN

distinctive yellow bar on clear hindwing •

Time of Flight ☀	Habitat 🌴	Wingspan 1–1¼ in (2.5–3 cm)

LIMACODIDAE

T HIS is a family of about 1,000 species occurring worldwide, but most commonly found in the tropics. They are small- to medium sized and have reduced mouthparts, and rather rounded wings. Some moths are bright green or yellow but most have fairly dull colors and simple patterns. The name Limacodidae, meaning sluglike, derives from the caterpillars of this family. These caterpillars, which look like slugs and move like them, are often very brightly colored, indicating that they are poisonous. Many of the Limacodid caterpillars have stinging hairs that can cause a very painful reaction and so are known as nettle caterpillars. A number of species feed on cultivated crops and are often regarded as pests.

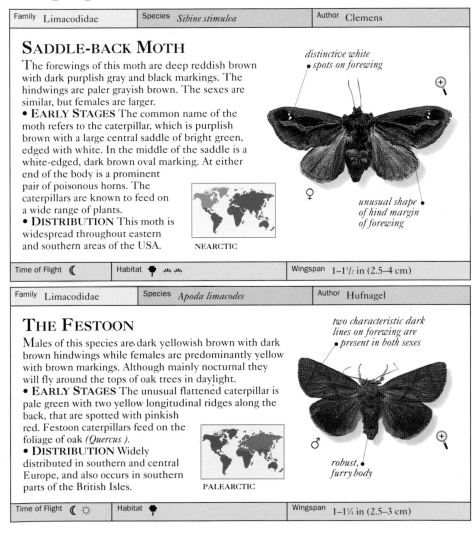

Family Limacodidae	Species *Sibine stimulea*	Author Clemens

SADDLE-BACK MOTH

The forewings of this moth are deep reddish brown with dark purplish gray and black markings. The hindwings are paler grayish brown. The sexes are similar, but females are larger.
• **EARLY STAGES** The common name of the moth refers to the caterpillar, which is purplish brown with a large central saddle of bright green, edged with white. In the middle of the saddle is a white-edged, dark brown oval marking. At either end of the body is a prominent pair of poisonous horns. The caterpillars are known to feed on a wide range of plants.
• **DISTRIBUTION** This moth is widespread throughout eastern and southern areas of the USA.

distinctive white spots on forewing

unusual shape of hind margin of forewing

NEARCTIC

Time of Flight ☽	Habitat ♣ ⚘ ⚘	Wingspan 1–1½ in (2.5–4 cm)

Family Limacodidae	Species *Apoda limacodes*	Author Hufnagel

THE FESTOON

Males of this species are dark yellowish brown with dark brown hindwings while females are predominantly yellow with brown markings. Although mainly nocturnal they will fly around the tops of oak trees in daylight.
• **EARLY STAGES** The unusual flattened caterpillar is pale green with two yellow longitudinal ridges along the back, that are spotted with pinkish red. Festoon caterpillars feed on the foliage of oak *(Quercus)*.
• **DISTRIBUTION** Widely distributed in southern and central Europe, and also occurs in southern parts of the British Isles.

two characteristic dark lines on forewing are present in both sexes

robust, furry body

PALEARCTIC

Time of Flight ☽ ☀	Habitat ♣	Wingspan 1–1¼ in (2.5–3 cm)

ZYGAENIDAE

THIS WORLDWIDE FAMILY of some 800 species of small- to medium-sized moth is one of the most distinctive groups of all. Most are day-flying and many are brightly colored, indicating that they are poisonous.

Several of the predominantly red species of the genus *Zygaena* that occur in Europe are known as burnets, while green species of the genus *Adscita* are known as foresters. Most Zygaenid moths have well-developed tongues, and the antennae are usually thickened towards the tips. While most have normally developed wings, the hindwings of one group, (*Himantopterus* see p. 290), are reduced to slender filaments. The poisonous caterpillars are stout and sluglike.

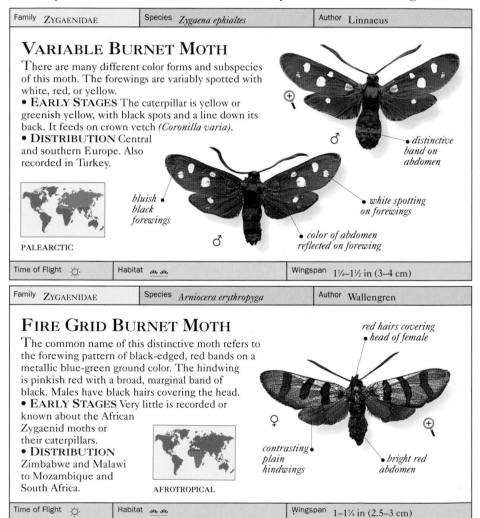

Family ZYGAENIDAE	Species *Zygaena ephialtes*	Author Linnaeus

VARIABLE BURNET MOTH

There are many different color forms and subspecies of this moth. The forewings are variably spotted with white, red, or yellow.

- **EARLY STAGES** The caterpillar is yellow or greenish yellow, with black spots and a line down its back. It feeds on crown vetch *(Coronilla varia)*.
- **DISTRIBUTION** Central and southern Europe. Also recorded in Turkey.

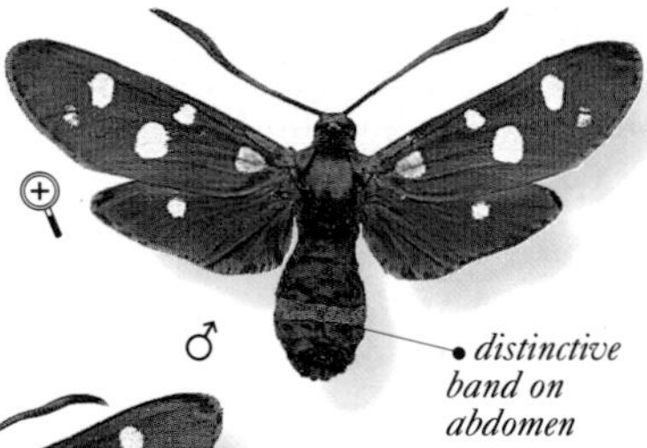
♂
distinctive band on abdomen

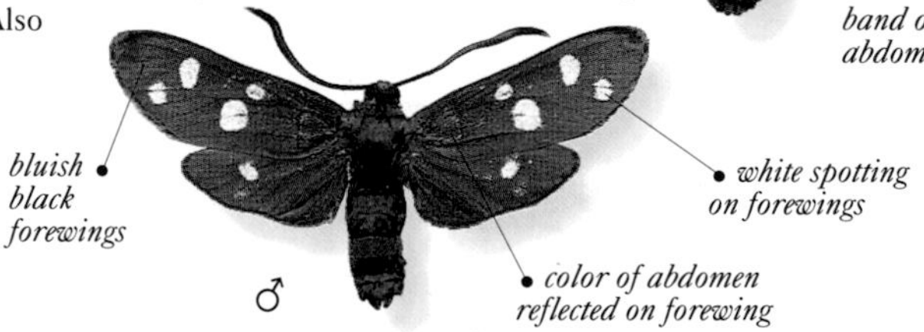
bluish black forewings
white spotting on forewings
color of abdomen reflected on forewing
♂

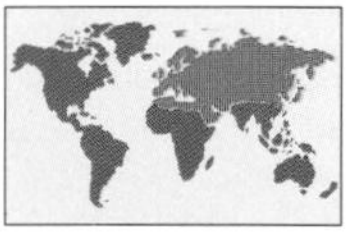

PALEARCTIC

Time of Flight ☼	Habitat	Wingspan 1¼–1½ in (3–4 cm)

Family ZYGAENIDAE	Species *Arniocera erythropyga*	Author Wallengren

FIRE GRID BURNET MOTH

The common name of this distinctive moth refers to the forewing pattern of black-edged, red bands on a metallic blue-green ground color. The hindwing is pinkish red with a broad, marginal band of black. Males have black hairs covering the head.

- **EARLY STAGES** Very little is recorded or known about the African Zygaenid moths or their caterpillars.
- **DISTRIBUTION** Zimbabwe and Malawi to Mozambique and South Africa.

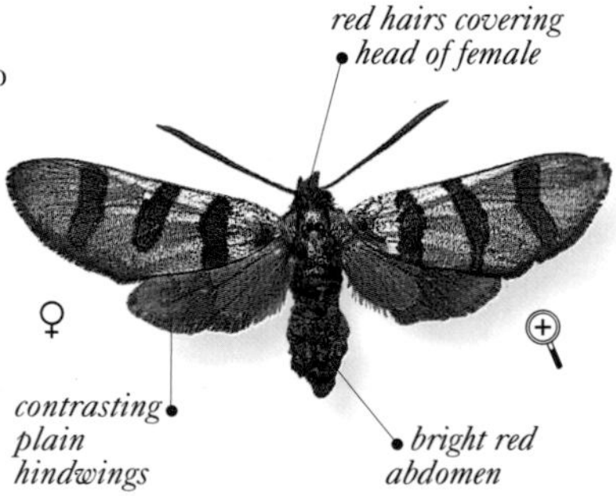
red hairs covering head of female
♀
contrasting plain hindwings
bright red abdomen

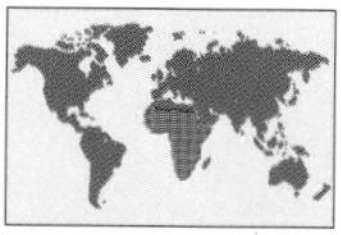

AFROTROPICAL

Time of Flight ☼	Habitat	Wingspan 1–1¼ in (2.5–3 cm)

Family ZYGAENIDAE	Species *Zygaena occitanica*	Author de Villers

PROVENCE BURNET MOTH

The Provence burnet is distinguished by its small size and an all-white, elongate, spot on the outer edge of the forewing. The tip of the abdomen is colored with a broad band of red.
• **EARLY STAGES** The caterpillar is light green, spotted with yellow, and has black dots on its sides. It feeds on plants of the pea family.
• **DISTRIBUTION** Southern France and Spain. Similar species occur in southern and eastern Europe.

characteristic white collar behind head

red hindwings are fringed with black

PALEARCTIC

Time of Flight ☼	Habitat ⸜⸝ ⸜⸝	Wingspan 1¼–1½ in (3–4 cm)

Family ZYGAENIDAE	Species *Zygaena filipendulae*	Author Linnaeus

SIX-SPOT BURNET

As its common name suggests, this species is distinguished by having six large, red spots on each greenish black forewing.
• **EARLY STAGES** The yellowish green caterpillar has yellow and black spots. It feeds on bird's-foot trefoil *(Lotus corniculatus)* and related plants of the pea family (Leguminosae).
• **DISTRIBUTION** Widespread and common throughout Europe.

the head and body are entirely black

bright warning colors indicate that this moth is poisonous

PALEARCTIC

Time of Flight ☼	Habitat ⸜⸝ ⸜⸝	Wingspan 1–1½ in (2.5–4 cm)

Family ZYGAENIDAE	Species *Adscita statices*	Author Linnaeus

THE FORESTER

This is one of a group of species with metallic-green wings. Several other species are similar, but are distinguishable by small differences in the structure of the wings and antennae.
• **EARLY STAGES** The caterpillar is pale yellow or greenish white, suffused with pinkish brown on the sides, and has brown, hairy warts. It feeds on sorrel *(Rumex)*.
• **DISTRIBUTION** Europe, extending into temperate Asia.

strongly feathered antennae of male

blackish hindwings are characteristic of all foresters

PALEARCTIC

Time of Flight ☼	Habitat ⸜⸝ ⸜⸝	Wingspan 1–1¼ in (2.5–3 cm)

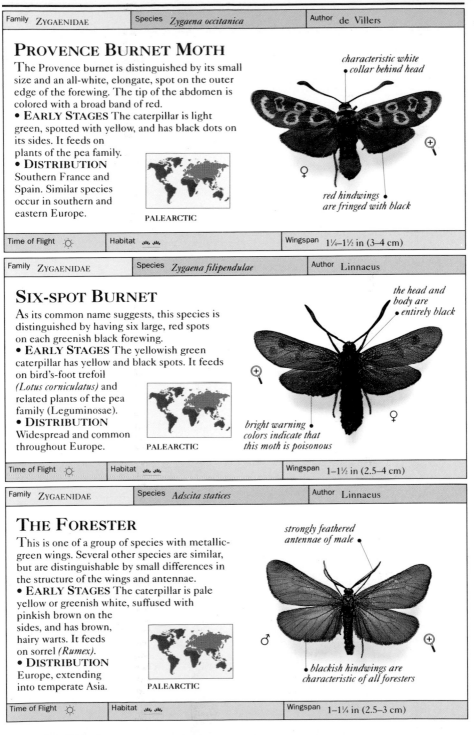

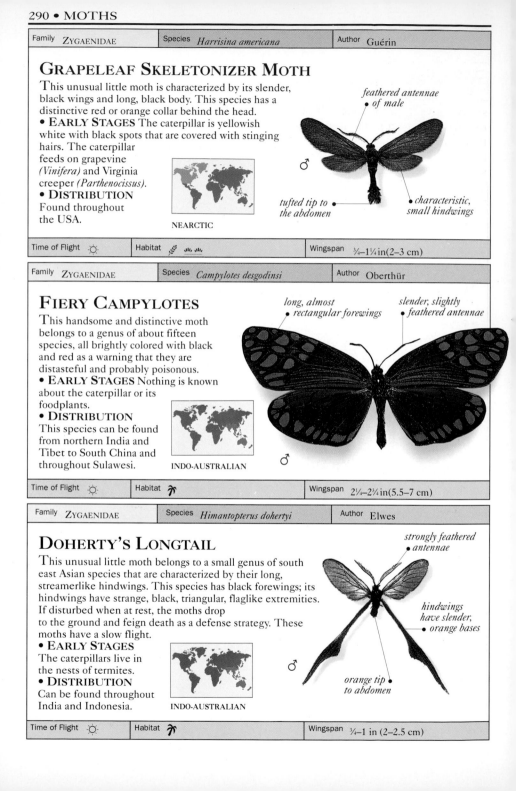

| Family | ZYGAENIDAE | Species | *Harrisina americana* | Author | Guérin |

GRAPELEAF SKELETONIZER MOTH

This unusual little moth is characterized by its slender, black wings and long, black body. This species has a distinctive red or orange collar behind the head.
• **EARLY STAGES** The caterpillar is yellowish white with black spots that are covered with stinging hairs. The caterpillar feeds on grapevine *(Vinifera)* and Virginia creeper *(Parthenocissus)*.
• **DISTRIBUTION** Found throughout the USA.

NEARCTIC

feathered antennae of male

♂

tufted tip to the abdomen

characteristic, small hindwings

| Time of Flight | ☼ | Habitat | | Wingspan | ¾–1¼ in (2–3 cm) |

| Family | ZYGAENIDAE | Species | *Campylotes desgodinsi* | Author | Oberthür |

FIERY CAMPYLOTES

This handsome and distinctive moth belongs to a genus of about fifteen species, all brightly colored with black and red as a warning that they are distasteful and probably poisonous.
• **EARLY STAGES** Nothing is known about the caterpillar or its foodplants.
• **DISTRIBUTION** This species can be found from northern India and Tibet to South China and throughout Sulawesi.

INDO-AUSTRALIAN

long, almost rectangular forewings

slender, slightly feathered antennae

♂

| Time of Flight | ☼ | Habitat | | Wingspan | 2¼–2¾ in (5.5–7 cm) |

| Family | ZYGAENIDAE | Species | *Himantopterus dohertyi* | Author | Elwes |

DOHERTY'S LONGTAIL

This unusual little moth belongs to a small genus of south east Asian species that are characterized by their long, streamerlike hindwings. This species has black forewings; its hindwings have strange, black, triangular, flaglike extremities. If disturbed when at rest, the moths drop to the ground and feign death as a defense strategy. These moths have a slow flight.
• **EARLY STAGES** The caterpillars live in the nests of termites.
• **DISTRIBUTION** Can be found throughout India and Indonesia.

INDO-AUSTRALIAN

strongly feathered antennae

♂

hindwings have slender, orange bases

orange tip to abdomen

| Time of Flight | ☼ | Habitat | | Wingspan | ¾–1 in (2–2.5 cm) |

COSSIDAE

T HIS IS A WORLDWIDE FAMILY of some 500 species of medium-sized to very large moth. They are usually rather dull in color, ranging from gray and brown to white, and are patterned with contrasting streaks or spots. The caterpillars feed mainly on wood by boring holes in the branches and trunks of trees, and are therefore commonly known as carpenterworms.

Because of the low nutritional value of their food, some species take several years to complete their development.

| Family COSSIDAE | Species *Xyleutes strix* | Author Linnaeus |

ASIAN CARPENTER MOTH

This large and robust moth has a very small head with prominent eyes. The finely mottled, grayish brown markings on the wings provide good camouflage, the lighter markings resembling patches of lichen. Females of the Asian carpenter moth have a long egg-laying tube that can extend to ⅜ in (1 cm) and may be mistaken for a sting.

• **EARLY STAGES** Little seems to be known of the biology of this common moth, but a closely related species, *Xyleutes leuconotus*, has a white-colored caterpillar that bores in the wood of *Sesbania grandiflora*.

• **DISTRIBUTION** Northern India to Malaysia and Papua New Guinea.

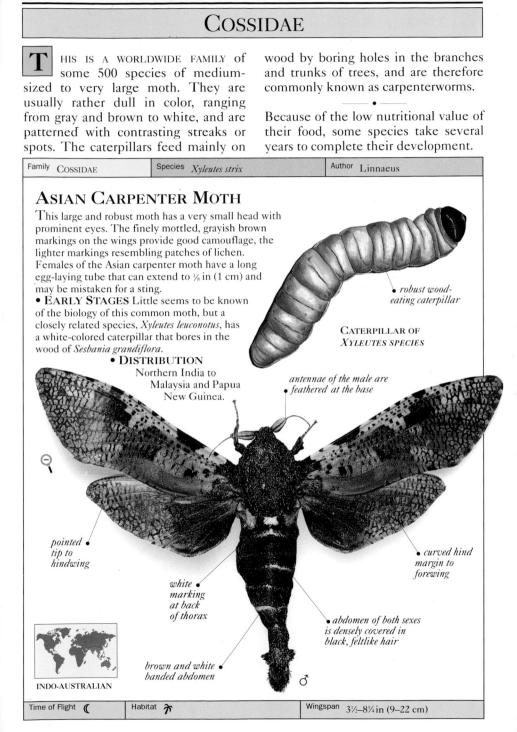

• *robust wood-eating caterpillar*

CATERPILLAR OF XYLEUTES SPECIES

antennae of the male are • feathered at the base

pointed • tip to hindwing

curved hind • margin to forewing

white marking at back of thorax

abdomen of both sexes is densely covered in black, feltlike hair •

brown and white banded abdomen •

INDO-AUSTRALIAN

| Time of Flight ☾ | Habitat | Wingspan 3½–8¾ in (9–22 cm) |

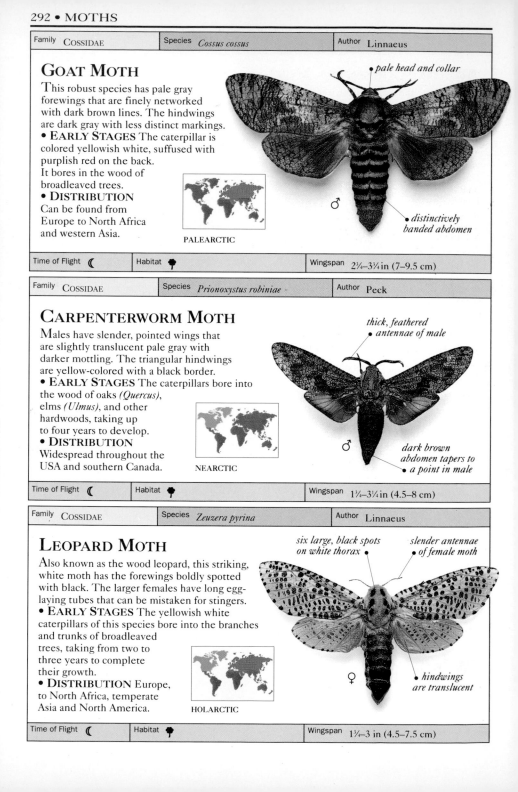

| Family | COSSIDAE | Species | *Cossus cossus* | Author | Linnaeus |

GOAT MOTH

This robust species has pale gray
forewings that are finely networked
with dark brown lines. The hindwings
are dark gray with less distinct markings.
• **EARLY STAGES** The caterpillar is
colored yellowish white, suffused with
purplish red on the back.
It bores in the wood of
broadleaved trees.
• **DISTRIBUTION**
Can be found from
Europe to North Africa
and western Asia.

pale head and collar

♂

distinctively banded abdomen

PALEARCTIC

| Time of Flight ☾ | Habitat 🌳 | Wingspan 2¾–3¾ in (7–9.5 cm) |

| Family | COSSIDAE | Species | *Prionoxystus robiniae* | Author | Peck |

CARPENTERWORM MOTH

Males have slender, pointed wings that
are slightly translucent pale gray with
darker mottling. The triangular hindwings
are yellow-colored with a black border.
• **EARLY STAGES** The caterpillars bore into
the wood of oaks *(Quercus)*,
elms *(Ulmus)*, and other
hardwoods, taking up
to four years to develop.
• **DISTRIBUTION**
Widespread throughout the
USA and southern Canada.

thick, feathered antennae of male

♂

dark brown abdomen tapers to a point in male

NEARCTIC

| Time of Flight ☾ | Habitat 🌳 | Wingspan 1¾–3¼ in (4.5–8 cm) |

| Family | COSSIDAE | Species | *Zeuzera pyrina* | Author | Linnaeus |

LEOPARD MOTH

Also known as the wood leopard, this striking,
white moth has the forewings boldly spotted
with black. The larger females have long egg-
laying tubes that can be mistaken for stingers.
• **EARLY STAGES** The yellowish white
caterpillars of this species bore into the branches
and trunks of broadleaved
trees, taking from two to
three years to complete
their growth.
• **DISTRIBUTION** Europe,
to North Africa, temperate
Asia and North America.

six large, black spots on white thorax

slender antennae of female moth

♀

hindwings are translucent

HOLARCTIC

| Time of Flight ☾ | Habitat 🌳 | Wingspan 1¾–3 in (4.5–7.5 cm) |

Family COSSIDAE	Species *Xyleutes eucalypti*	Author Herrich-Schäffer

ACACIA CARPENTER MOTH

This is one of the most attractive and distinctive Australian carpenter moths. The forewings are gray with a fine network pattern of black and dark brown, while the hindwings are reddish brown with fine, dark brown markings. The body is banded with white.
• **EARLY STAGES** The robust, white caterpillar has a large, brown, shieldlike plate on its back behind the head. It attacks acacia species.
• **DISTRIBUTION** Occurs in NSW and Queensland.

INDO-AUSTRALIAN

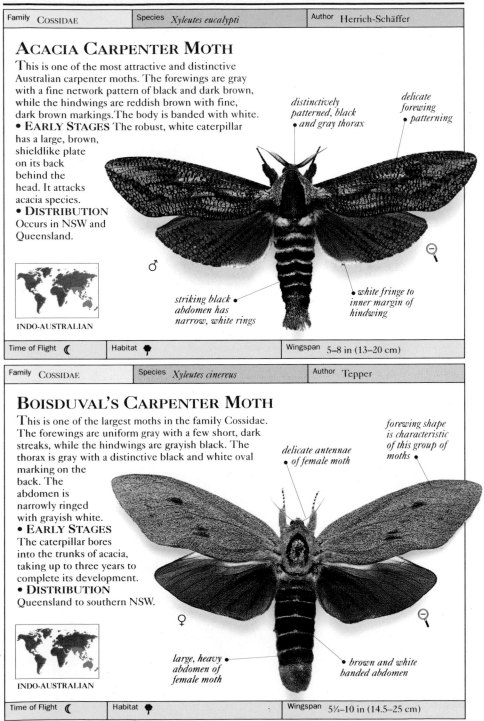

distinctively patterned, black and gray thorax

delicate forewing patterning

♂

striking black abdomen has narrow, white rings

white fringe to inner margin of hindwing

Time of Flight ☾	Habitat ♣	Wingspan 5–8 in (13–20 cm)

Family COSSIDAE	Species *Xyleutes cinereus*	Author Tepper

BOISDUVAL'S CARPENTER MOTH

This is one of the largest moths in the family Cossidae. The forewings are uniform gray with a few short, dark streaks, while the hindwings are grayish black. The thorax is gray with a distinctive black and white oval marking on the back. The abdomen is narrowly ringed with grayish white.
• **EARLY STAGES** The caterpillar bores into the trunks of acacia, taking up to three years to complete its development.
• **DISTRIBUTION** Queensland to southern NSW.

INDO-AUSTRALIAN

forewing shape is characteristic of this group of moths

delicate antennae of female moth

♀

large, heavy abdomen of female moth

brown and white banded abdomen

Time of Flight ☾	Habitat ♣	Wingspan 5¾–10 in (14.5–25 cm)

HEPIALIDAE

T HIS FAMILY OF SOME 300 species of moth displays a number of primitive features that distinguish them from all other large moths. The wings lack the usual bristle-and-catch linking system and instead have a lobe on the forewing that overlaps the hindwing, thus holding them together when in flight. Another more obvious and primitive feature is that the hindwing and forewing are usually very similar in shape and have a similar arrangement of wing veins.

Hepialid moths vary in size from small to very large. They are worldwide in distribution, and are very strongly represented in Australia where some of the largest species occur. They are generally most active at dusk.

Family HEPIALIDAE	Species *Zelotypia stacyi*	Author Scott

BENT-WING GHOST MOTH

The forewings of this large and beautiful moth are intricately patterned with brown and white and have a distinct eyespot at their centers. The hindwings are orange with brown markings at the extreme tip but are otherwise quite plain. The sexes are alike. These moths are on the wing in summer.
• **EARLY STAGES** The caterpillar is yellowish brown with stout, reddish brown plates on the back immediately behind the head. Along the back is a series of yellowish white, oval markings. Caterpillars bore in the stems and branches of Sydney blue gum (*Eucalyptus saligna*) and related trees. They are sometimes pests of young trees used for paper pulp.
• **DISTRIBUTION** Occurs in eastern Australia from Queensland to NSW.

INDO-AUSTRALIAN

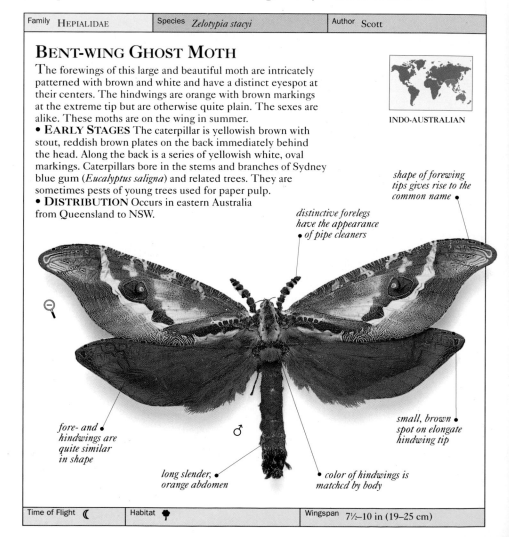

shape of forewing
tips gives rise to the
common name •

distinctive forelegs
have the appearance
• of pipe cleaners

fore- and •
hindwings are
quite similar
in shape

♂

small, brown •
spot on elongate
hindwing tip

long slender, •
orange abdomen

• color of hindwings is
matched by body

Time of Flight ☾	Habitat ♠	Wingspan 7½–10 in (19–25 cm)

| Family | HEPIALIDAE | Species | *Aenetus eximius* | Author | Scott |

COMMON AENETUS

There are fifteen Australian species in this genus, often called splendid ghost moths. They are remarkable not only for their large size, but for the difference between the sexes. The males of the common Aenetus have pale bluish green forewings and white hindwings tinged with green on the hind margin. The much larger females have rich, mottled, moss-green forewings with a diagonal line of brown-ringed white markings. The hindwings are a pinkish red which continues onto the abdomen. The abdomen tip is colored a vivid green.

• **EARLY STAGES** The caterpillar feeds on eucalyptus, *Waterhousea*, *Doryphora*, *Glochidion*, *Nothofagus*, and *Dodonaea* species. They bore into the stem or trunk of the plant, and tunnel down into the main root. Some of the *Aenetus* caterpillars take up to five years to complete their development.

• **DISTRIBUTION** Range extends from Queensland to Victoria and Tasmania in Australia.

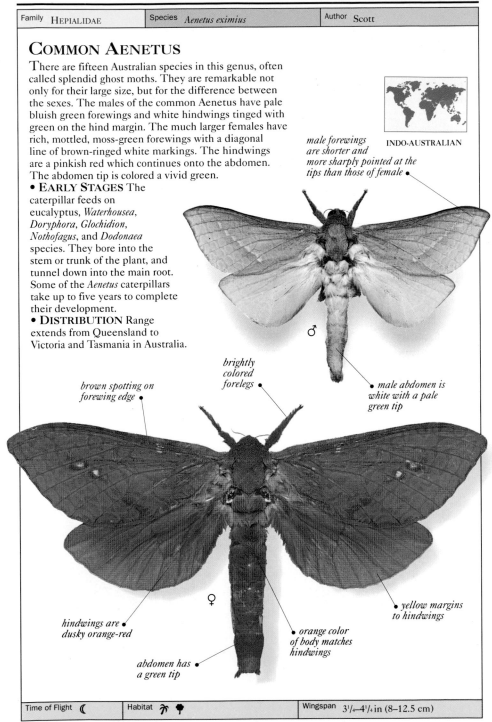

INDO-AUSTRALIAN

male forewings are shorter and more sharply pointed at the tips than those of female •

♂

• *male abdomen is white with a pale green tip*

brightly colored forelegs •

brown spotting on forewing edge •

♀

hindwings are dusky orange-red •

abdomen has a green tip •

• *orange color of body matches hindwings*

• *yellow margins to hindwings*

| Time of Flight ☾ | Habitat 🌲 🌴 | Wingspan 3¼–4¼ in (8–12.5 cm) |

Family HEPIALIDAE	Species *Leto venus*	Author Stoll

VENUS MOTH

As its common name suggests, this is probably the most beautiful of all Hepialid moths, with its rich orange-brown forewings brilliantly patterned with silver spots. The hindwings are a uniform salmon-pink with slightly darker veins. Males have long, orange hairs on the underside of the wings.
• **EARLY STAGES** Little is known of the early stages of this moth and the caterpillar appears to be undescribed. It bores into the trunks of Keurboom trees and it probably feeds between the wood and the bark.
• **DISTRIBUTION** Confined to Cape Province, South Africa.

AFROTROPICAL

distinctive triangular, silver spots along forewing margin

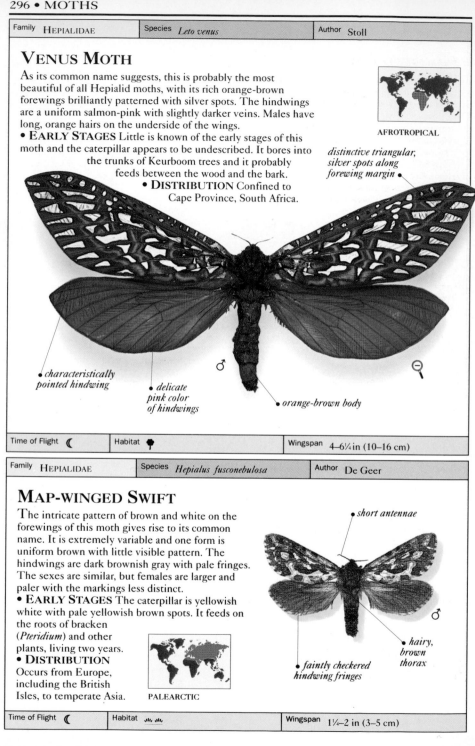

characteristically pointed hindwing

delicate pink color of hindwings

orange-brown body

Time of Flight ☾	Habitat ♣	Wingspan 4–6¼ in (10–16 cm)

Family HEPIALIDAE	Species *Hepialus fusconebulosa*	Author De Geer

MAP-WINGED SWIFT

The intricate pattern of brown and white on the forewings of this moth gives rise to its common name. It is extremely variable and one form is uniform brown with little visible pattern. The hindwings are dark brownish gray with pale fringes. The sexes are similar, but females are larger and paler with the markings less distinct.
• **EARLY STAGES** The caterpillar is yellowish white with pale yellowish brown spots. It feeds on the roots of bracken (*Pteridium*) and other plants, living two years.
• **DISTRIBUTION** Occurs from Europe, including the British Isles, to temperate Asia.

PALEARCTIC

short antennae

hairy, brown thorax

faintly checkered hindwing fringes

Time of Flight ☾	Habitat 〰 〰	Wingspan 1¼–2 in (3–5 cm)

Family HEPIALIDAE	Species *Hepialus humuli*	Author Linnaeus

GHOST MOTH

The silvery white males are appropriately named as they look ghostly when hovering over vegetation at dusk. A northern form exists in which the male wings are patterned with brown. Females are generally larger and have pale yellow forewings patterned with pink or pinkish brown.
• **EARLY STAGES** The yellowish white caterpillar has small, dark brown spots. It feeds on the roots of grasses and other plants and is sometimes an agricultural pest. Presumably because of its burrowing habits, this species is also known as the otter.
• **DISTRIBUTION** Widespread from Europe, including the British Isles to Asia.

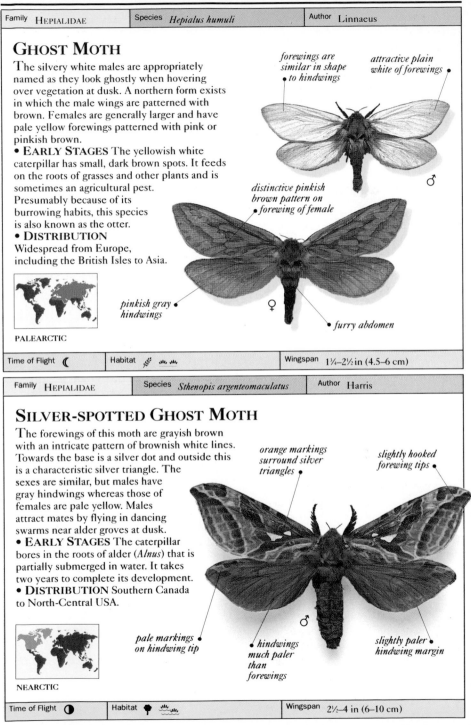

forewings are similar in shape to hindwings

attractive plain white of forewings

♂

distinctive pinkish brown pattern on forewing of female

pinkish gray hindwings

♀

furry abdomen

PALEARCTIC

Time of Flight ☾	Habitat	Wingspan 1¾–2½ in (4.5–6 cm)

Family HEPIALIDAE	Species *Sthenopis argenteomaculatus*	Author Harris

SILVER-SPOTTED GHOST MOTH

The forewings of this moth are grayish brown with an intricate pattern of brownish white lines. Towards the base is a silver dot and outside this is a characteristic silver triangle. The sexes are similar, but males have gray hindwings whereas those of females are pale yellow. Males attract mates by flying in dancing swarms near alder groves at dusk.
• **EARLY STAGES** The caterpillar bores in the roots of alder (*Alnus*) that is partially submerged in water. It takes two years to complete its development.
• **DISTRIBUTION** Southern Canada to North-Central USA.

orange markings surround silver triangles

slightly hooked forewing tips

♂

pale markings on hindwing tip

hindwings much paler than forewings

slightly paler hindwing margin

NEARCTIC

Time of Flight ◑	Habitat	Wingspan 2½–4 in (6–10 cm)

GLOSSARY

TECHNICAL EXPRESSIONS have been avoided wherever possible, but a limited use of them is unavoidable in a book of this nature. The terms listed below, many of them peculiar to butterflies and moths, are defined in a concise manner. Some definitions have been simplified and generalized in order to avoid obscure language, and they are to be regarded as definitive for this book only. Words in bold type are explained elsewhere in the glossary.

- **ABDOMEN**
Rear part of the body behind **thorax**
- **CARDENOLIDE POISON**
A heart poison
- **CLASPERS**
False, suckerlike legs on the **abdomen**
- **COCOON**
Protective enclosure for the pupa, usually made of silk

- **EYESPOT**
Circular color markings found on the wings
- **LUNULE**
Small, moonlike shape
- **MELANIC**
Black or dark form of species, due to increased melanin
- **MIMETIC GROUP**
Species which mimic one another to gain protection

- **PALPS**
Sensory mouthparts used for investigating food
- **SCENT SCALES**
Scales that release an aphrodisiac scent
- **SCLEROPHYLL FOREST**
A forest of hardleaved trees
- **THORAX**
Middle of the body immediately behind the head

USEFUL ADDRESSES

Day Butterfly Center
Callaway Gardens
Pine Mountain, GA 31822
Tel: (404) 663 2281

American Museum of Natural History
Biology of Invertebrates Hall
79th Street and Central Park West
New York, NY 10024
Tel: (212) 769 5000

Butterfly World
Tradewinds Park South
3600 West Sample Road
Coconur Creek, FL 33073
Tel: (305) 977 4400

World of Insects Exhibit
Cincinnati Zoo
3400 Vine Street
Cincinnati, OH 45220
Tel: (513) 281 4701

Young Entomologists' Society
International Hedquarters
1915 Peggy Place
Lansing, MI 48910

Butterfly Exhibit
Marine World Africa-USA
Marine World Parkway
(Junction of I-80 and California 37)
Vallejo, CA 94589
Tel: (707) 643 6722

Insect Zoo
Smithsonian Institution
National Museum of Natural History
Tenth and Constitution Avenues, N.W.
Washington, DC 20560
Tel : (202) 673 4717

SASI Insect Zoo
Sponsored by Sonoran Arthropod Studies, Inc.
2437 North Stone Avenue
Tucson, AZ 85703

INDEX